The criticisms I hear about expository preaching are in reality criticisms about "boring preaching." The greatest preaching in the earth is still captivating, prophetic, invigorating, Christ-honoring exposition. Vines and Shaddix tell you how to do that in a way that will win the lost and revive the saints. If you preach, do not miss this book.

PAIGE PATTERSON, PRESIDENT
SOUTHEASTERN BAPTIST THEOLOGICAL SEMINARY
WAKE FOREST, NORTH CAROLINA

POWER
in the
PULPIT

How to
Prepare
and Deliver
Expository
Sermons

JERRY VINES
AND
JIM SHADDIX

MOODY PRESS
CHICAGO

ISBN: 0-8024-7740-2

7 9 10 8

Printed in the United States of America

CONTENTS

115510

ACKNOWLEDGMENTS

My book, *A Practical Guide to Sermon Preparation* was published by Moody Press in 1985. The companion volume, *A Guide to Effective Sermon Delivery* was also published by Moody Press, in 1986. I am grateful they have been in continuous use since that time. Numerous colleges, seminaries, and preaching institutes have used them. I have been thankful for the many positive responses I have received concerning them.

For a number of years I have felt the need for these two volumes to be updated, revised and expanded. When Dr. Jim Shaddix, Professor of Preaching at my alma mater, New Orleans Baptist Theological Seminary, approached me about doing just that and putting them into one volume, I was delighted and grateful. Moody was very gracious to agree to this revision. The result is this new, expanded *Power in the Pulpit*. Special thanks to Bill Soderberg who has provided marvelous editorial guidance.

Dr. Shaddix has done a tremendous work. Almost all the original material in the previous works has been retained. In addition, he has rendered it new millennium compliant! The result is a volume that should be suitable for the classroom setting and also helpful to the pastor who prepares and delivers many sermons each week. I am deeply grateful to him. We have enjoyed a very congenial and pleasant relationship throughout the project. In the course of this revision, I have gained a new friend!

Again, I want to thank Dr. Paige Patterson, who needled and badgered me until I undertook the project almost fifteen years ago. I want to thank again my secretary, Shirley Cannon, who helps me in my writing projects. I want to express appreciation for the saints of First Baptist Church, Jacksonville, Florida, who listen to me preach and encourage me so much. I want to pay tribute to all my many preacher friends who have taught me so much about preaching through the years. And, again, thanks to my wonderful wife, Janet, who makes it possible for me to spend the necessary time to study and prepare so I might preach with "Power in the Pulpit."

JERRY VINES

PREFACE

Several years ago Stuart Briscoe, the noted preaching pastor at Elmbrook Church in Milwaukee, shared with me a story. He had been invited by a certain seminary to come and teach a course on preaching. Briscoe responded to the invitation by saying, "I don't know how to teach preaching."

"Just come and tell us what you do," encouraged the anxious school officials.

"I don't know what I do," Briscoe said. "I just do it."

The persistent academicians quickly replied, "Well, just come and do it, and we'll figure it out together!"

That scenario is a fairly good description of the development of this book. The weekly pulpit and the daily classroom have worked together in an attempt to provide some relevant, practical help for preachers. The reason for this effort is simple: Works on preaching often are presented from an imbalanced perspective. Many books on the subject are written by academicians who have lost touch with the realities of weekly pastoral preaching. Other works reflect church traditions in which pastors preach one time each week for ten to fifteen minutes. Still other preaching literature is written by practitioners who struggle to communicate the nuts and bolts of the techniques that have worked for them. The need exists for practical preaching help from a pastoral perspective in the tradition where preaching is a paramount and frequent event in the life of the local church.

Dr. Jerry Vines has been expounding the Word of God as a pastor for more than four decades, half of which have been in the pulpit at the First Baptist Church in Jacksonville. He shared some of his experience and knowledge with his fellow preachers in the mid-1980s when he published two books on preaching: *A Practical Guide to Sermon Preparation* and *A Guide to Effective Sermon Delivery.*

I have been listening to Dr. Vines preach in various contexts since I was a boy. When I started to teach preaching several years ago, I knew I wanted two things from a textbook for my basic course. I wanted a book that championed an expository approach to preaching. And I wanted a book that was sensitive to the nuances of pastoral preaching—feeding the flock of God on a weekly basis. Needless to say, I quickly gravitated to Dr. Vines's book on preparation and his sequel on delivery. I have never regretted those choices. Some time later, he and the good people at Moody Press presented me with the opportunity to revise the two books into one volume. Obviously, I jumped at the chance. I do not regret that choice either.

This particular book seeks to capitalize on the twofold dimension of practical experience and classroom training. It has been written from the perspective of a pastor who actually is involved in the week-to-week discipline of sermon preparation. His material has been reorganized and supplemented by another preacher who preaches weekly but who also devotes daily time to training preachers in the context of theological education. Both contributors face the same weekly time pressures that face everyone who reads this work. The information being offered is an effort to close the gap that often exists between classroom theory and what actually works in a pastor's weekly preparation.

The two earlier works by Dr. Vines, from which this revision has been developed, have served pastors and other preachers well for more than a decade. The intent of this new work is not to fix something that was not broken but simply to expand its use in a variety of training contexts. Almost 100 percent of the original material has been preserved in this new format. The information simply has been reorganized, updated, and expanded in order to broaden its application to include preachers in training as well as pastors already serving in the field. Hopefully, the new format will extend the longevity of the impact of Dr. Vines's work.

The awesome privilege I have been given in this project has been supported by many loving people. My family—Debra, Clint, Shane, and Dallys—has sacrificed through two doctorates and now this endeavor. Never have they complained. Always they have encouraged. My Emmaus Road guys, who study expository preaching with me—Blake, Brian, Israel, Michael, and Brian—have offered tremendous insights from the perspective of preachers in training. Several pastors who are effective expositors of the Word have guided me from the standpoint of weekly practitioners. My administrative assistant, Gina Alvaro, has patiently offered much indispensable work. Most of all, Dr. Jerry Vines has entrusted me with his work and afforded me a great opportunity. Thanks to all of you. I trust that the product will make a contribution to the enhancement of expository preaching in the local church and elsewhere.

JIM SHADDIX

INTRODUCTION

Upon meeting a fellow pastor who was studying his sermon notes, a well-meaning preacher declared, "I don't study to preach. I just get in the pulpit, and the Holy Spirit fills me." The preacher who was studying his notes asked, "What if the Holy Spirit doesn't fill you?" The other pastor replied, "I just mess around until He does." A lot of congregations would lament that too much messing around is going on and not enough preaching.

Some preachers, like the one mentioned above, do not prepare, claiming they allow the Holy Spirit to fill them when they preach. They use Mark 13:11 as a proof text: "Do not worry beforehand, or premeditate what you will speak. But whatever is given you in that hour, speak that; for it is not you who speak, but the Holy Spirit." Though this contention sounds very spiritual to some men, it actually is a way for them to avoid as much work as possible. In most cases when they stand to preach, their mouths are indeed filled—with hot air!

The call to preach is exactly that—a call to preach. The call to preach, however, is more than just preaching. The call to preach is also a call to *prepare*. God gives to those He calls the necessary gifts to preach, and He expects them to prepare as much as possible. In one sense, that preparation involves a man's lifetime. Men prepare sermons; God prepares men. The man who would preach, then, has the responsibility of learning to prepare.

This book is about such preparation. Perhaps most of the time in any given week of a pastor's life is devoted to preaching. Most of his hours are spent preparing sermons. Several other hours are spent delivering them. Of course, sermon preparation alone does not make a man a preacher. Only God can make a preacher. A man so called, however, can learn basic principles of effective sermon preparation and delivery. Erasmus once said, "If elephants can be trained to dance, lions to play, and leopards to hunt, surely preachers can be taught to preach."

This book has a specific focus. Its purpose is to give practical help specifically to the man who is faced with the responsibility of preaching weekly. Preaching in the pastoral context is a radically different kind of preaching than the preaching done by those in itinerant ministries. Also, the material in this book specifically addresses the preparation and delivery of *expository* sermons. Thousands of churchgoers throughout America are desperately hungry for good preaching. They are looking for a Bible study, a church, some service where their souls can be fed from the Word of God. Much of the preaching of our day is dry, irrelevant, and deadening. A large part of the solution is to be found in expository preaching.

Part 1, "The Preparation for Exposition," lays the groundwork for expository preaching. The entire process and presentation of the exposition of Scripture are rooted in the very nature of preaching as revealed in the Bible. Engaging in expository preaching, then, demands that the pastor have certain convictions about his call to ministry, his Bible, his worship, and the ongoing work of God in his life.

Part 2, "The Process of Exposition," traces the stages through which the preacher must travel in order to expose a text of Scripture and make ready an expository sermon. Expository sermon preparation can be one of the richest experiences in which the preacher ever engages. We could compare it to mining a beautiful diamond. Everyone admires the beauty of a well-cut diamond. If, however, you were to find the diamond yourself—dig diligently for it, cut it carefully, then polish it to a brilliant shine—your sense of fulfillment would be even greater. Such is something of the richness of expository sermon preparation.

Part 3, "The Presentation of the Exposition," is dedicated to the nuts and bolts of effective sermon delivery. After the preacher has learned to put together an expository sermon, he must then know how to present that sermon in a persuasive manner. Much of the success of an expository sermon lies in its delivery.

Power in the Pulpit aims to help fellow preachers. If it can be used to help you reach your fullest potential in ministry, something will have been accomplished for the kingdom. Sermon preparation and delivery are two of the most fulfilling and frustrating experiences a man can undergo. This book, hopefully, will help reduce the frustration and increase the fulfillment. In addition, maybe it will stimulate others to dig even deeper and to uncover additional insights in the area of exegetical, expository preaching.

But enough said by way of introduction. Let us get about the task of preparing and preaching expository sermons.

PART ONE

THE PREPARATION FOR EXPOSITION

CHAPTER 1: Defining the Task

A Practical Theology of Preaching
A Philosophy of Preaching
A Rationale for Expository Preaching

CHAPTER 2: Laying the Foundation

The Call of God
The Word of God
The Worship of God
The Anointing of God

CHAPTER 3: Developing the Preacher

A Healthy Heart
A Healthy Mind
A Healthy Body
A Healthy Routine

The last half of the twentieth century has witnessed a dearth of good preaching in America and abroad. Many people have lamented this decline. As the curtain rises on a new millennium, a famine of solid Bible preaching continues to paralyze the church. The church's weak condition once again has called attention to the rarity of Bible exposition.

Many pastors have begun to rethink their philosophies of preaching in the wake of powerless churches and a flood of sermonic trends. Interest has arisen in revisiting the timeless, dependable method of biblical exposition. In most churches that evidence solid and substantial growth, a commitment to and practice of biblical preaching exists. As many young preachers turn back to the Bible for the substance and authority of their preaching, the time is right for a fresh look at the subject.

Part 1 of this book is intended to provide this needed glimpse. Reformation in the pulpit will come about only as God-called men return to the basics of the preaching event. Once again we must embrace the nature of preaching as it is informed by the Bible itself and championed by faithful preachers throughout the course of history. This renewed understanding then must be fleshed out in our personal convictions and walks with God. The result will be a new generation of godly men who preach the gospel with character, integrity, and spiritual vitality.

CHAPTER ONE

DEFINING
THE TASK

*There is a continuing crisis in that expository preaching has
lain dormant and without many advocates, practitioners, or
even demands from the pew during this critical century that
could ill afford such a tragic loss.*

WALTER KAISER

Ichabod—the glory has departed!" Sad was the day when the ark, the
representation of God's glory, was taken from His people. Yet a similar
commentary has been offered about much modern preaching, God's primary means of propagating His gospel. Merrill Unger observed, "To an
alarming extent the glory is departing from the pulpit of the twentieth
century."[1] Like the powerless Israelites without the ark, the church without strong preaching will have to welcome the new millennium defense-
less and weak.

Any effort at renewal must start with a clear definition of the task at
hand, beginning with a right understanding of the theology of preaching.
First, the consistent practice of good exposition will take place only when
the preacher has a firm conviction that his approach has biblical support.
Next, the biblical roots give rise to certain key terms that serve as a framework for the development of a right philosophy for preaching. Finally, a
rationale for the expository process underscores its advantages and provides support and encouragement for its continued practice.

A PRACTICAL THEOLOGY OF PREACHING

Edwin Charles Dargan suggested that the development of modern
preaching was largely influenced by three factors: ancient oratory and

---

1. Merrill F. Unger, *Principles of Expository Preaching* (Grand Rapids: Zondervan, 1955),
11.

rhetoric, Hebrew prophecy, and the Christian gospel.[2] Ancient oratory and rhetoric, which will be addressed specifically in chapter 6, heavily influenced the development of sermon form. Hebrew prophecy, however, gave preaching its roots in the divine with regard to both message and motivation. Later, the Christian gospel provided preaching with its specific content and commissioned it as the primary means of propagation. A consideration of certain biblical terms provides some indication of the roots of preaching as revealed in the Bible, specifically related to the latter two influences. These roots serve as the foundation for a practical theology of preaching.

DIVINE REVELATION

First and foremost, preaching is rooted in the divine. God has chosen to reveal Himself to mankind, and He has chosen human vessels to be mediums of that revelation. The Hebrew word *nābî,* one of the most common terms for prophet, conveys the idea of one who pours forth or announces. It includes the implication of being moved by divine impulse to prophesy (see Deut. 13:1; 18:20; Jer. 23:21; Num. 11:25–29). Two other Hebrew words are translated "seer" in the Old Testament. *Hōzeh* suggests to glow or to grow warm (e.g., Amos 7:12). *Rōéh* simply means one who sees (e.g., 1 Chron. 29:29; Isa. 30:10). These terms indicate that the prophet was one whose heart had been warmed by something the Lord allowed him to see.

Some New Testament terms also imply the divine origin of preaching. The word *logos* is used to refer to a word, or saying. Sometimes the communication of God's message to man is referred to as preaching the Word, or *Logos,* to people (e.g., 2 Tim. 4:2). Another word, *rhēma,* emphasizes that which has been uttered by the voice (see Rom. 10:17). When the Word was spoken in the New Testament, God actually was communicating Himself through the act of proclamation. New Testament preaching was in actuality divine instruction by those who communicated the gospel (see Eph. 2:17).

The frequently used *kērussō* means to proclaim after the manner of a herald. This word also implies a message of authority that calls upon the listeners to hear and to obey (see Rom. 10:14–15; 1 Cor. 1:21, 23; 2 Tim. 4:2). Jesus used this word to commission His followers just prior to His ascension, ordaining preaching as the primary method of dispensing the gospel (see Mark 16:15; Luke 24:47). The New Testament preacher was one who proclaimed the message of the King of Kings to men. The preaching event, then, was accompanied by an atmosphere of seriousness, authority, and divine mandate.

---

2. Edwin Charles Dargan, *A History of Preaching,* vol. 2 (New York: George H. Doran, 1905), 14.

CLEAR EXPLANATION

Preaching also has its roots in the clear explanation of God's revelation. God has always provided teachers to help people understand His Word. Nehemiah 8, for example, is an excellent illustration of a preaching event. The ingredients in many modern worship experiences were present—a pulpit, a worship leader, the book of God's Law, a unified and expectant congregation, proclamation, and both verbal and physical response. The Levites taught the people God's Word as "they read distinctly from the book, in the Law of God; and they gave the sense, and helped them to understand the reading" (Neh. 8:8). "Distinctly" is the Hebrew *pārash*, which means to distinguish, or to specify clearly. The word "sense" is *śēkel*, which means to give the meaning, indicating perception, or insight. The word for "helped them to understand" is *bîn*, which means to separate mentally, or to assist in understanding. The idea of clarity to make understanding possible was paramount.

Jewish religious life served to carry on this explanatory emphasis. Hebrew scribes served as conservators of God's truth as they interpreted Scripture, copied Scripture, and preserved the oral law. From their ministries emerged the term "homily," which means a talk based upon Scripture.[3] Synagogue services included Scripture reading and exposition as a part of worship. Regular meetings in the synagogue included a time when rabbis would read a portion of Scripture and then explain it to the people in attendance. This activity constituted the focal point of the meetings and gave synagogues an educational quality.[4] These practices later would influence the development of Christian worship, including the reading and explanation of Scripture.

Jesus Himself was set upon providing clear explanation to His hearers, both in the synagogue worship and in other contexts. He often read and explained the Scriptures as a visiting rabbi (see Luke 4:16–21). To the disciples on the Emmaus road, "beginning at Moses and all the Prophets, He expounded to them in all the Scriptures the things concerning Himself" (Luke 24:27). The word translated "expounded" is the Greek *diermēneuō*, which means to unfold the meaning of what is said, or to explain through. Reflecting upon the teaching of Jesus, those disciples used a similar word: "Did not our heart burn within us while He talked with us on the road, and while He opened the Scriptures to us?" (Luke

---

3. Vernon L. Stanfield, "The History of Homiletics," in *Baker's Dictionary of Practical Theology*, ed. Ralph G. Turnbull (Grand Rapids: Baker, 1967), 50.
4. I. Sonne, "Synagogue," in *The Interpreter's Dictionary of the Bible*, vol. 4, ed. George Arthur Buttrick (Nashville: Abingdon, 1962), 487.

24:32). The word "opened" is *dianoigo,* which means to open thoroughly. The word means to open the sense of the Scriptures, or to explain them. Paul did the same thing in Thessalonica, "explaining and demonstrating that the Christ had to suffer and rise again from the dead" (Acts 17:2–3).

New Testament preaching also included the element of teaching. The word used to describe this element is *didasko.* The apostles "did not cease teaching and preaching Jesus as the Christ" (Acts 5:42). In listing the requirements of the bishop-pastor, Paul said that the man had to be "able to teach" (1 Tim. 3:2). He also charged the young pastor Timothy to

> hold fast the pattern of sound words which you have heard from me, in faith and love which are in Christ Jesus. That good thing which was committed to you, keep by the Holy Spirit who dwells in us. . . . And the things that you have heard from me among many witnesses, commit these to faithful men who will be able to teach others also. (2 Tim. 1:13–14; 2:2)

New Testament preachers prioritized the systematic, intentional teaching of basic doctrine.

Other words also highlight the idea of understanding in New Testament preaching. *Epiluo* literally means to unloose, or to untie. The word conveys the idea of explaining what is obscure and hard to understand (see 2 Pet. 1:20). Thus, the word means to interpret. The word is used to describe the preaching ministry of Jesus and His use of parables (see Mark 4:34). New Testament preaching involved unloosing God's revelation. *Suzeteo* means to seek or to examine together. Paul "spoke boldly in the name of the Lord Jesus and disputed against the Hellenists" (Acts 9:29). New Testament preachers sought to lead their listeners to examine with them the truths of God's Word and to seek understanding of them.

PRACTICAL APPLICATION

Preaching also is informed by the biblical emphasis on the practical application of God's Word to the lives of contemporary listeners. The word translated "demonstrating" is used in reference to Paul's preaching method in Thessalonica (Acts 17:3). The Greek word is *paratithemi,* which means to place alongside. Paul's preaching was an applicable presentation of Scripture. The same word is used with regard to Jesus' use of the parable (see Matt. 13:34). He took parables, laid them alongside the issues of life faced by the people, and made practical application. New Testament preachers made personal, specific application to their hearers.

Sometimes the application came in the form of encouragement. The Greek *parakaleo* means to call to one's side. It carries the idea of comfort, exhortation, and instruction. The ideas of strength and encouragement also are embedded in the word. Paul admonished Timothy to "exhort, with all longsuffering and teaching" (2 Tim. 4:2). New Testament preachers were gifted to bring strength and encouragement to those who listened to them preach.

At other times the application came by way of rebuke or conviction. The word *elegchō* suggests to bring to light or to expose by conviction. Paul said pastors should "be able, by sound doctrine, both to exhort and convict those who contradict" (Titus 1:9). He further commanded Titus to "rebuke with all authority" (Titus 2:15). New Testament preachers often had to deal directly with the sins of the people. By preaching the Word they turned on the light so that their hearers could see themselves as God saw them.

ETERNAL REDEMPTION

Preaching also can be traced back to God's redemptive activity with mankind. The Hebrew word *bāsar* means to be fresh or full or to announce glad tidings (e.g., Isa. 61:1; Ps. 40:9). God's messengers were men who brought good news. A parallel word in the New Testament is *euangelizō*, "to announce glad tidings." Specifically, it refers to the good news of salvation that God gives to men in Christ Jesus. A note of joy and victory characterizes the word. Jesus' own job description on earth was to announce good news (see Luke 4:18). The New Testament preachers went everywhere announcing these glad tidings (e.g., Acts 8:4, 35). This good news, or gospel, provided preaching with its content.

This message of good news was centered in Christ Himself. Early in His ministry, Jesus charged His listeners, "Do not think that I came to destroy the Law or the Prophets. I did not come to destroy but to fulfill" (Matt. 5:17). He told the religious hypocrites, "You search the Scriptures, for in them you think you have eternal life; and these are they which testify of Me" (John 5:39). We noted that after His resurrection Jesus unfolded His fulfillment of the Old Testament to the disciples on the road to Emmaus: "Beginning at Moses and all the Prophets, He expounded to them in all the Scriptures the things concerning Himself" (Luke 24:27). Philip did the same for the Ethiopian eunuch as he "opened his mouth, and beginning at this Scripture, preached Jesus to him" (Acts 8:35).

Paul, too, centered his preaching on Jesus, claiming to the Corinthians that he had "determined not to know anything among you except Jesus Christ and Him crucified" (1 Cor. 2:2). He used *kērugma* to describe the foolish event that God had chosen to save people (see 1 Cor. 1:21). The word is from *kērussō* and refers to the message of the herald rather than to his action. In *The Apostolic Preaching and Its Developments*, C. H. Dodd identified seven facts about the message as preached by Paul: (1) Old Testament prophecies were fulfilled and the new age was inaugurated by the coming of Christ; (2) He was born of the seed of David; (3) He died according to Scripture to deliver mankind out of this present evil age; (4) He was buried; (5) He rose on the third day according to Scripture; (6) He is now exalted at the right hand of God as the Son of God and Lord of the living and the dead; and (7) He will come again as the Judge and Savior of men.[5] The message of Jesus Christ was good news, and New Testament preachers proclaimed it joyfully and victoriously. Their preaching truly was driven by the Christ event.

PUBLIC PROCLAMATION

Preaching also is informed by the idea of public proclamation before a corporate assembly. The Hebrew *qōhelet* means a caller, preacher, or lecturer (e.g., Eccl. 1:1). The root word is *qāhal,* which means to assemble together. The implication is of one who spoke before an assembly of people. Another significant Old Testament word is *qārā',* which means to call out (e.g., Isa. 61:1). The prophet was one who called out to the people, addressing the message of God to them.

New Testament preaching also involved the dynamic of dialogue. At Thessalonica, Paul "reasoned with them from the Scriptures" (Acts 17:2). The word is *dialegomai,* which means to speak through or to ponder or revolve in the mind. It came to mean to converse with or to discuss. New Testament preaching had a conversational nature about it, engaging the listeners in a journey of discovery. A similar thought is found in the verb *homileō,* which means to converse, or talk with (e.g., Acts 20:11). Biblical preachers were not giving a soliloquy. They preached, and the people listened, but the listeners sometimes responded with feedback.

PERSONAL CONFESSION

The personal confession of the preacher was another aspect of the biblical preaching event. Preaching often was viewed as giving a witness before a group of people. The word *martureō* means simply to be a witness, to affirm that one has seen, heard, or experienced something. Paul, in his beautiful and insightful summary of his ministry at Ephesus, defined his preaching content as "testifying . . . repentance toward God, and faith toward our Lord Jesus Christ" (Acts 20:21). New Testament preachers who

---

5. C. H. Dodd, *The Apostolic Preaching and Its Development* (New York: Harper and Row, 1964), 17.

faithfully proclaimed the truth of God did not do so from secondhand experience. They knew from experience the truth of what they preached to others. Like John, they were able to say, "We have seen and testify that the Father has sent the Son as Savior of the world" (1 John 4:14).

Another word used to describe the public nature of New Testament preaching is *homologeō*. This word, made up of two Greek words, means to say the same thing, or to agree with. Preaching in the New Testament sense had the idea of confession, or profession. About young Timothy, Paul said that he had "confessed the good confession in the presence of many witnesses" (1 Tim. 6:12). Rightly understood, Bible preaching was confessional in nature. The preachers said what God said, agreeing with Him about the truth proclaimed.

INTENTIONAL PERSUASION

One of the most important elements in the preaching event was persuasion. The New Testament word *peithō* means to use words to persuade others to believe. In Acts 13:43 we are told that Paul and Barnabas spoke to Christian converts and "persuaded them to continue in the grace of God." In Corinth, Paul "reasoned in the synagogue every Sabbath, and persuaded both Jews and Greeks" (Acts 18:4). Paul brought into focus the whole matter of persuasion as a part of preaching when he said, "Knowing, therefore, the terror of the Lord, we persuade men; but we are well known to God, and I also trust are well known in your consciences" (2 Cor. 5:11). The particular word used in this passage means to persuade, or to induce one by words, to believe. The Bible preachers were persuaders. By use of preaching, they brought men to the point of believing that Jesus was the Christ and deciding to commit themselves to Him.

Scripture indicates that New Testament preaching was apologetic in nature as well. The word *apologia* suggests a verbal defense, or a speech in defense of something. Addressing the Jerusalem mob, Paul said, "Brethren and fathers, hear my defense before you now" (Acts 22:1). Other passages use the same terminology (see Phil. 1:7,17; 2 Tim. 4:16). Bible preachers, in the best sense of the term, gave a defense for the gospel. They presented the message of the Lord Jesus in the most convincing, appealing, and persuasive way possible.

A PHILOSOPHY OF PREACHING

Consideration of these roots reveals two primary forms for preaching in the Bible. First, preachers during the biblical period were involved in *revelatory* preaching. The prophets, Jesus, and then the apostles proclaimed God's first-time revelation as they spoke. In other words, they spoke information from God that man had never heard before. Second, preachers during the biblical period also engaged in *explanatory* preaching. After God's revelation had been given, they provided explanation of that revealed information as people returned to it time and time again.

As the biblical period closed, however, preaching naturally evolved to include the explanatory form only.[6] This uniform quality, which characterized all post-apostolic proclamation, establishes certain parameters for a philosophy of modern preaching.

THE NATURE OF PREACHING

Much activity goes on today in various religious gatherings under the guise of preaching. Consequently, preachers must be held accountable for making sure they are engaging in the real thing. Some standard must be employed for judging the genuineness of the preaching event. Five particular criteria can be elucidated from our consideration of the theological roots of preaching.

The mode: oral communication. Preaching, by and large, is oral communication. V. L. Stanfield once described it as "giving the Bible a voice." Al Fasol defined preaching as "orally communicating truth as found in the Bible."[7] Although there may be selected and limited exceptions, preaching primarily has been an oral event in which a man speaks the words of God before a gathering of people. The visual orientation of modern listeners indeed provides new challenges for contemporary preachers, and some of these will be discussed in more detail in later chapters. Oral speech, however, is an effective, timeless mode of communication.

Centuries ago God chose this mode, knowing it would defy cultural nuances through the years. Oral speech still moves nations, as is evidenced in its continued adoption by political and social leaders as a primary means of influence. Daniel Webster said, "If all my possessions and powers were to be taken from me with one exception, I would choose to keep the power of speech, for by it I could soon recover all the rest."[8]

The message: biblical truth. Preaching has a specific content—the Word of God as revealed in the Bible. The fine expositor G. Campbell Morgan said,

We must enter upon the Christian ministry on the assumption that God has

---

6. James F. Stitzinger, "The History of Expository Preaching," in John MacArthur Jr., *Rediscovering Expository Preaching,* ed. Richard L. Mayhue (Dallas: Word, 1992), 38–42.
7. Al Fasol, *Essentials for Biblical Preaching* (Grand Rapids: Baker, 1989), 16.
8. Quoted in James C. McCroskey, *An Introduction to Rhetorical Communication,* 3d ed. (Englewood Cliffs, N.J.: Prentice-Hall, 1978), 3.

expressed Himself in His Son, and the Bible is the literature of that self-expression. The minute we lose our Bible in that regard, we have lost Christ as the final revelation.[9]

Morgan considered every sermon that failed to have some interpretation of God's holy truth to be a failure.[10]

Along with Stanfield and Fasol, Morgan specified the truth that preachers were to preach as that which was contained in the Bible. Preaching is not communication about just any subject, however good and beneficial that subject may be. Although all truth is God's truth, He never intended for His preachers to speak about every true and right idea under the sun. From Genesis to Revelation, the Bible primarily recounts God's activity of re-creating mankind into His image through a relationship with Jesus Christ. The preacher is responsible for immersing people in that process. He has not been given the responsibility of addressing every good subject known to man, nor is he to become an expert in every field. Instead, he must meet the tension of speaking rightly about the same subject over and over again in fresh and creative ways.

The medium: Holy Spirit/human personality. The message of the Bible is communicated through a twofold medium: the Holy Spirit and a human personality. From outset to conclusion, preaching is the communication of the Holy Spirit. John Knox said, "True preaching from start to finish is the work of the Spirit."[11] He inspired the Word we preach. He illuminates our understanding as to its meaning. He anoints our communication of it. He enlightens the minds of listeners. He convicts their hearts and prompts them to respond. Preaching is the Holy Spirit's event. If He is left out, preaching does not happen.[12]

At the same time, God has chosen to use twice-born individuals as the human instruments through which to communicate His truth. Probably the most famous definition of preaching came from Phillips Brooks during the Yale Lectures in 1877. He defined preaching as "the communication of truth by man to men. It has in it two essential elements, truth and personality. Neither of these can it spare and still be preaching."[13]

True preaching, then, demands that each preacher be true to his

9. G. Campbell Morgan, *Preaching* (New York: Revell, 1937), 18.
10. Ibid., 19.
11. John Knox, *The Integrity of Preaching* (Nashville: Abingdon, 1957), 89.
12. For a fuller discussion of the role of the Holy Spirit in preaching, see J. Daniel Baumann, *An Introduction to Contemporary Preaching* (Grand Rapids: Baker, 1972), 277–91.
13. Phillips Brooks, *Lectures on Preaching* (New York: E. P. Dalton; reprint, Grand Rapids: Baker, 1969), 5 (page citation is to the reprint edition).

unique personality. He is free and responsible to shun the temptation and/or pressure to imitate another preacher. God has chosen the individual, and the moment he tries to be someone else when he preaches, he ceases to preach. Both the Holy Spirit and the human instrument are necessary for genuine preaching. The absence of either—as with the absence of truth—means that preaching cannot take place.

The mark: given audience. Preaching is directed intentionally at a given audience. In his comprehensive definition of preaching, J. I. Packer described it as "the event of God bringing to an audience a Bible-based, Christ-related, life-impacting message of instruction and direction from Himself through the words of a spokesperson."[14]

Preaching was never intended to be a general dispensation of information void of any consideration of the listeners. No two preaching events ever will involve exactly the same audience. Even if this week's congregation is made up of all the same people as last week's, their experiences, attitudes, and emotions are different. The preacher, then, must approach every sermon with a particular audience in mind. This demand means that he study the people and the context every time he prepares a sermon. He is bringing God's message to a particular group of people, and real preaching involves a consideration of that group's character and circumstances.

The motive: positive response. The preaching event is driven by the desire to see people respond positively to God's Word. Daniel J. Baumann said preaching is "the communication of biblical truth by man to men with the explicit purpose of eliciting behavioral change."[15] This definition highlights the implicit call for decision in the preaching event. Biblical truth innately demands a response. It was not given for the purpose of trivial consideration or entertainment. God's Word was intended to be acted upon. Consequently, every sermon must be prepared and delivered with the intent of persuading people to say yes to the message.

The Word is supernatural, and the preacher's responsibility is to present it in a clear and understandable way so that it can take root in people's hearts and do its work. Whether or not the preacher calls for some physical indication of response, true preaching always will involve the call for action. His passion must be for the message to be lived out in the lives of his listeners once they leave the preaching arena.

As the nature of preaching is viewed in light of these criteria, the fol-

---

14. J. I. Packer, "Authority in Preaching," in *The Gospel in the Modern World,* ed. Martyn Eden and David F. Wells (London: InterVarsity, 1991), 199.
15. Baumann, *Contemporary Preaching,* 13.

lowing working definition is suggested in an attempt to capture concisely, yet thoroughly, the essence of preaching:

Def'ə-nish'ən

preaching *n.* The oral communication of biblical truth by the Holy Spirit through a human personality to a given audience with the intent of enabling a positive response.

THE PROCESS OF PREACHING

The very nature of preaching demands that the preacher apply the process of exposition. Viewing this process as a journey can be helpful—a road on which one travels to communicate rightly God's revelation. Several key terms identify the various key parts of the process along the way.

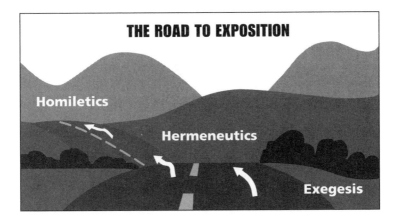

THE ROAD TO EXPOSITION

Homiletics

Hermeneutics

Exegesis

Exegesis

The road to exposition begins with careful exegesis.[16] This can be defined as the procedure one follows for discovering the Holy Spirit's intent in a Bible passage. The idea comes from the Greek *exēgēsis*, which means a narration or explanation. Although the noun form of the Greek word does not occur in the New Testament, the verb—*exēgeomai*—is used in

16. For a thorough discussion of the exegetical process and its relationship to hermeneutics, see Gordon D. Fee and Douglas Stuart, *How to Read the Bible for All Its Worth* (Grand Rapids: Zondervan, 1982) and Fee, *New Testament Exegesis: A Handbook for Students and Pastors* (Philadelphia: Westminster, 1983).

several places (see Luke 24:35; John 1:18; Acts 10:8; 15:12,14; 21:19). This word means to lead out of. The preacher wants adequately to represent what the Scripture itself says by "leading out" the right meaning of a text. John 1:18 reveals that Christ "exegeted" the Father to man—He "led out" the meaning of God to man. Exegesis is the opposite of *eisegesis,* which is reading into the text what the preacher would like it to say.

Hermeneutics

Careful exegesis leads the expositor to good hermeneutics—the science of interpreting what a passage of Scripture means. The Greek word translated hermeneutics is *hermēneuō.* In half of its occurrences, the word means to translate. A related word, *diermēneuō,* means to expound or to interpret. Hermeneutics enables the preacher to determine what a text *means* as opposed to just what it *says.* In addition, right meaning implies application to a particular audience. Thus, hermeneutics enables the preacher to expose the meaning of a text and apply its meaning to a given audience.

Homiletics

Careful exegesis and good hermeneutics enable the preacher to practice "homiletics," which is the art and science of saying the same thing that the text of Scripture says.[17] Technically, it is the study of sermon preparation, thus establishing an unbreakable link between the sermon and a right understanding of the meaning of the text on which it is based. Homiletics is the culmination of applying the principles of hermeneutics and exegesis in an effort to understand a biblical text and communicate it to listeners.

Exposition

When delivery is added to this whole process of exegesis, hermeneutics, and homiletics, the result can be described as exposition. "Expose" means to lay open, or uncover. When the preacher travels this road with integrity, he will be able to lay open the mind of the Holy Spirit in the biblical text. Exposition, then, may be defined as the process of laying open a biblical text in such a way that its original meaning is brought to bear on the lives of contemporary listeners.

Some homileticians have defined exposition by the length of the given text. Andrew Blackwood, for example, described it as being based on "a Bible passage longer than two or three consecutive verses."[18] Exposition, however, is not determined by the length of a passage but by the *manner of treatment* of the passage. G. Campbell Morgan wrote, "Being sure that our text is in the Bible, we proceed to find out its actual mean-

17. Walter C. Kaiser Jr., *Toward an Exegetical Theology* (Grand Rapids: Baker, 1981), 193.
18. Andrew Blackwood, *Preaching from the Bible* (New York: Abingdon, 1941), 38.

ing, and then to elaborate its message. The text has postulates, implicates, deductions, application."[19] Thus, exposition is not a sermon form but a *process* by which the words of God are communicated.

Expository sermon

The sermon is the final product of the expositional process. Blackwood said, "Homiletics is the science of which preaching is the art and the sermon is the finished product."[20] An *expository* sermon, then, can be defined as follows:

Def'ə-nish'ən

expository sermon *n.* A discourse that expounds a passage of Scripture, organizes it around a central theme and main divisions which issue forth from the given text, and then decisively applies its message to the listeners.

TRADITIONAL SERMON MODELS

Traditionally, sermons have been categorized according to various forms based upon certain qualities. Delineations of these forms frequently have included the expository sermon as another sermon model. Each of the following forms, however, could and should be subjected to the expositional process.

Topical. The *topical sermon* is built around some particular subject. The idea for the subject may be taken from the Bible or elsewhere. Usually the preacher gathers what the Bible teaches about one particular topic, organizes those passages into a logical presentation, and then delivers a topical sermon. Doctrinal sermons easily lend themselves to this approach.

Textual. A *textual sermon* is one based on one or two verses from the Bible. The main theme and the major divisions of the sermon come from the text itself. This sermon seeks to expound what the text itself actually says.

Narrative. Traditionally, a *narrative sermon* has been considered simply as one based upon a narrative text. In recent days, however, some

---

19. Farris D. Whitesell, *Power in Expository Preaching* (Old Tappan, N.J.: Revell, 1963), xii.
20. Andrew Blackwood, *The Preparation of Sermons* (Nashville: Abingdon, 1948), 18.

homileticians have defined it by sermonic form instead of literary genre. Thus, contemporary narrative sermons frequently encompass those messages that, from outset to conclusion, bind the entire message to a single plot as theme. Such a sermon may be better described as a *story sermon*.

Biographical. A *biographical sermon* presents a study of the life of a particular Bible character. The facts about that particular character form the basis for a message with contemporary application.

Dramatic monologue. A *dramatic monologue sermon* is a specialized form of a biographical sermon in which the preacher becomes the character he is seeking to present. He acts out the message of the character, often dressing himself in authentic biblical attire.

Theological. The *theological sermon* may be similar to a topical, doctrinal sermon in that it expounds some basic Christian belief in order to convey understanding and foster belief. The difference, however, is that theological sermons usually rely more on references to general theological concepts in Scripture than on specific texts themselves.

Ethical discourse. The *ethical discourse* is based upon a specific Bible motif that teaches the believer an ethical lesson. The purpose is to build Bible morality into the members of the congregation.

In essence, the expository sermon is the package in which the truth is delivered by the preacher to the people, resulting from his own investigation and organization of the biblical text.

An important ingredient of the expository sermon is application. Because the Bible is God's Word to man, a good expository sermon makes plain what the Bible says and gives clear application to the lives of the hearers. The expositor's main concern is to set forth the truth of God's revelation in language that can be understood. The faithful pastor will make a serious and sincere attempt to unfold the actual grammatical, historical, contextual, and theological meaning of a passage. He then will seek to establish the relevancy of that passage to the lives of his listeners. To do this, he will properly organize, adequately illustrate, and forcibly apply its message. Jeff Ray summarized this process well when he said, "In preaching, exposition is the detailed interpretation, logical amplification, and practical application of Scripture."[21]

Expository sermons may or may not stand in contrast to other traditional sermon forms. Because exposition is a *process*, it should never be

---

21. Jefferson D. Ray, *Expository Preaching* (Grand Rapids: Zondervan, 1940), 71.

put in juxtaposition to other sermonic models. All preaching should be expositional in nature. The preacher should utilize only sermon forms that issue forth from good hermeneutics, thorough exegesis, and credible homiletics. The following checklist is suggested as a guide for determining a sermon's expository nature:

EXPOSITORY SERMON CHECKLIST

❏ It must be based upon a passage from the Bible. The actual meaning of the passage must be found.

❏ The meaning must be related to the immediate and general context of the passage.

❏ The eternal, timeless truths in the passage must be elucidated.

❏ The truths must be gathered around a compelling theme.

❏ The main divisions of the sermon must be drawn from the structure of the passage itself.

❏ Every possible method to apply the truths must be utilized.

❏ The hearers must be called to obey those truths and to live them out in daily life.

Expository Preaching

The delivery of expository sermons on a consistent and regular basis is called *expository preaching*. Paige Patterson has described this practice simply as helping people read the Bible better. Expository preaching can be divided into two types.

First, *general exposition* involves preaching expository sermons on selected and distinct Bible texts. Donald Grey Barnhouse said, "Expository preaching is the art of explaining the text of the Word of God, using all the experiences of life and learning to illuminate the exposition."[22] Although general exposition may tie various texts together in a series, the texts are not necessarily consecutive Bible passages or exhaustive treatments of an entire Bible book. Examples of general exposition might include sermons from totally unrelated texts each week or a series on the miracles of Jesus in John's gospel.

Second, *systematic exposition,* is the consecutive and exhaustive treatment of a book of the Bible or extended portions thereof, dividing the text

---

22. Whitesell, *Power in Expository Preaching,* xi.

into paragraphs and consecutively preaching from them. William M. Taylor defined expository preaching as "the consecutive interpretation and practical enforcement of a book of the Bible."[23] F. B. Meyer described it as the consecutive treatment of some book or extended portion of Scripture on which the preacher has concentrated head and heart, brain and brawn, over which he has thought and wept and prayed, until it has yielded up its inner secret, and the spirit has passed into his spirit.[24]

The best preaching you can do is to go through books of the Bible—chapter by chapter and paragraph by paragraph—in a systematic fashion. Such an approach will ensure the keenest interpretation and the best use of context.

A RATIONALE FOR EXPOSITORY PREACHING

These biblical roots and subsequent homiletical concepts inform a rationale for embracing exposition as the intrinsic nature of the preaching event. This rationale includes the many benefits of expository preaching, an awareness of the potential dangers of the approach, and the great heritage of Bible expositors through the years.

THE BENEFITS OF EXPOSITION

Numerous benefits surface when the truth of God's Word is exposed, especially through the systematic preaching of a Bible book. Many of the same benefits, however, apply to the general exposition of various passages.

Biblical Literacy

Today, biblical literacy is at an all-time low in evangelical churches in the United States. This "dumbing of the church," as Joseph Stowell called it, makes the shepherd's task all the more difficult with regard to discipling his congregation.[25]In days gone by, a preacher could announce a text and assume that most people were holding a Bible and could locate the passage. Neither are safe assumptions any longer. Many Americans do not know even the most basic Bible stories. Lamenting this new challenge, George Barna observed, "It seems that no amount of Bible-based preaching, scriptural teaching, or small group meetings moves the congregation to a higher

---

23. Blackwood, *Preaching from the Bible*, 39.
24. F. B. Meyer, *Expository Preaching* (Grand Rapids: Baker, 1974), 32.
25. Joseph M. Stowell, *Shepherding the Church into the 21st Century* (Wheaton, Ill.: Victor, 1994), 21.

plane of Bible knowledge."[26] More tragically, many ministerial students themselves have only a limited, selective knowledge of the Word.

EMBRACING EXPOSITORY PREACHING
A Personal Testimony

This book has been written largely from my own experience. My life and ministry were changed when I decided to devote myself to expository preaching. After a rough start and some failed attempts at exposition, my sermons generally became topical in nature during my first ten years of ministry. The Lord blessed my meager efforts. My churches had some growth. People came to Christ. Then I actually stumbled upon the method of expository preaching. At a Bible conference I had the opportunity to hear Dr. Warren Wiersbe teach the Word. Although I was a seminary graduate and had been preaching for several years, I had never heard anyone take the Bible and expound it as did Dr. Wiersbe.

My approach to preaching completely changed. I determined to begin using the expository method. All I had to go by was Dr. Wiersbe's example. I had never studied the expository method. I was aware of no books on the subject, and I had heard very little preaching of that kind. I just had the conviction in my heart that exposition was the kind of preaching the Lord wanted me to do. So I started.

My efforts at the beginning were poor and tentative. As I went along, however, I began to notice a change in my ministry. The people started bringing their Bibles; they showed more interest. I saw growth in the spiritual lives of my people. That convinced me of the value of expository preaching. The value to my own life is beyond my ability to place on the printed page. Only eternity will reveal what the expository method of preaching has done for me. The value in the lives of the people who have heard me preach will await the evaluation of the judgment seat of Christ. But there is little doubt in my mind that the people themselves have been blessed through the preaching of expository sermons.

Jerry Vines

This scenario leaves the preacher with two options: either resign to the generation by minimizing the role of the Bible in his preaching or determine to change the generation by systematically teaching the Scriptures. Systematic exposition, especially, enhances knowledge of the Bible. By care-

26. George Barna, *Today's Pastor* (Ventura, Calif.: Regal, 1993), 48.

ful, exegetical study through books of the Bible you will become a master of the Scriptures, and your listeners will become knowledgeable students.

One reason for increasing biblical illiteracy in the church is the "hop, skip, and jump" approach to Bible study. The preacher who jumps from book to book and text to text in his preaching will greatly impoverish his own understanding of the Word as well as that of his people. Such an approach is similar to the "lucky dip" method, which many Christians employ in their daily Bible reading. They close their eyes (figuratively if not literally), let their Bibles fall open, and read at that particular point. Although some important truths certainly can be learned with that method, more profit will be realized by a systematic, book-by-book approach. People whose eating habits are planned are likely to be healthier than those who eat randomly and on the spur of the moment.

Accountability

Exposing the truth of a given text holds the preacher accountable in a number of areas.

First, it holds him accountable for preaching what God says and not what the preacher wants to say. In recent days, much discussion has taken place regarding the authority of the pastor—whether it comes by virtue of his position or is earned through tenure and track record. Imbalance and exclusiveness make much of this discussion vain. Actually, the pastor's authority comes by means of the One whose words he speaks.

When you stand to preach an expository sermon, you know you have given yourself to serious and sincere study of the Word. You can stand with a sense that you speak from the authority of the Bible, not your own. You are merely the mouth and lips through which the living Word of God is conveyed to the congregation. Both you and your people can be confident that you are not speaking your own thoughts or opinions. You are speaking "Thus saith the Lord." That confidence gives immense force to your ministry.

Second, exposition in general makes the preacher work. A lazy preacher is inexcusable. You should never work less than your people. When they come to hear you preach on Sunday, they will have worked hard all week long. They should expect no less from you.

Most ministries provide flexibility for the pastor to set his own schedule. This privilege can be bittersweet if you are not given to discipline and hard work. You cannot be lazy and do the necessary preparation to develop and deliver good expository sermons. You should be up early and study long. The degree of additional demands in your ministry will determine the necessary adjustments and sacrifices you have to make. Preaching will not be effective unless it comes through suffering on the part of the preacher.

To stand in the pulpit unprepared—with little forethought—and deliver a message off the top of your head is not worthy of the Savior you represent.

Third, systematic exposition forces preachers to deal with passages that might otherwise be overlooked or even intentionally avoided. The temptation exists to dodge certain delicate subjects in the Bible such as the roles of husbands and wives, church discipline, leadership in the church, and the like. When you meet them in an expository series, however, you must deal with them at that point. Systematic exposition enables you to do so without creating the impression you are singling out some member of the church. For instance, if you come to the subject of divorce in the course of an expository series, people will not be curious to know why you chose that particular text. They would be if you selected it out of the clear blue sky.

Protection

Systematic exposition protects the preacher from a number of preaching pitfalls. For example, it keeps him out of a rut. Preachers have a tendency to develop a one-subject mentality. Every pastor has his special areas of interests, such as the Second Coming, spiritual gifts, certain ethical issues, or abundant life passages. The Bible is like a magnificent fruit grove with all kinds of trees. Some people like apples best, but there are also pears and cherries and bananas to be enjoyed. The expository method keeps the preacher off his hobbyhorse and leads him to provide a balanced diet for his people.

Systematic exposition also guards against using the Bible as a club. Sheep are known to be less than prim, proper, and brilliant animals. Shepherding these creatures will periodically give rise to the temptation to find a Scripture to rebuke an erring one in the public arena. Clearly, that is not a proper approach to preaching God's Word. Consecutively preaching its truths guards against that temptation. The expository method allows the Word of God, rather than our own inclinations, to speak to the current situation. As you faithfully proclaim the Word of God, the Holy Spirit will apply the truths to your listeners.

Stress Relief

Systematic exposition all but removes anxiety about what to preach. Topical, hit-and-miss preaching as well as a shotgun approach to exposition can create agony for the preacher. He can spend his whole week searching, scratching, and studying to find a topic or a text. Such stress often seeks relief by locating the latest hot topic from the best-sellers in the local Christian bookstore or by searching through sermon books by well-known preachers. The systematic expository method relieves this formidable problem. On Monday morning you know where you are going, and you can begin your preparation immediately. Should the Lord lead you to preach on another subject at some point during the week, you easily can make the adjustment. Next Monday you will be just that much ahead. You are better off having the entire week to study a passage rather than spending most of the week searching for one.

Appetite Development

An old proverb says, "Give a man a fish, you feed him for a day; teach a man to fish, you feed him for a lifetime." Believe it or not, every time the preacher stands to preach, he has a purpose that is higher than just teaching a lesson for that particular day. He must teach people to fish. Systematic exposition gives people an appetite for the Word that prompts them to go home and search the Scriptures for themselves. They become Berean Christians, who "were more fair-minded than those in Thessalonica, in that they received the word with all readiness, and searched the Scriptures daily to find out whether these things were so" (Acts 17:11). Such is the only way your people will continue to grow spiritually. You will be amazed at the knowledge of and excitement about God's Word that they will acquire as a result of a steady diet of good exposition. This approach is perhaps the best way to train people to become Bible teachers. Even general exposition creates an appetite and encourages others to teach the Bible. As you teach the Word of God, you are modeling how others can teach the Word in other contexts. Many fine Bible study leaders can be developed in this way.

God also uses exposition to prompt young men to answer the call to preach. As they listen to and observe your preaching, they will be challenged to minister the Word to others. Although a divine call to preach certainly must be present, much can be said about the importance of role models for the young people whom God may be calling to preach.

Spiritual Maturity

Charles W. Koller noted that nutritionists use the term "nutritional time bomb" with reference to certain deficiencies in one's diet that may remain undetected for years. Those deficiencies suddenly can manifest themselves in severe sickness. The same is true for those who are undernourished in their spiritual lives. Without a proper diet of Bible preaching and teaching, the stress of sudden catastrophe or unusual burden make the spiritually undernourished too weak to weather the storm.[27]

But as the pastor faithfully preaches the Word of God, the people receive strength. A reservoir of Bible truth is built within them that enables

27. Charles W. Koller, *Expository Preaching Without Notes* (Grand Rapids: Baker, 1962), 29–34.

DEFINING THE TASK ♦ 37

them to face times of crisis. God's people will come through with great triumph if they have been fed a solid Bible diet.

In addition, expository preaching has a way of broadening people's horizons. Listeners are enabled to glimpse the eternal. Bible truths such as justification, glorification, eternity, and the Spirit-filled life lift people to new heights of Bible knowledge and Christian experience. They are given the opportunity to see a world of Christian existence that they never dreamed possible.

The lack of moral strength and conviction that plagues our day is due to a large degree to the lack of Bible preaching. Even in the midst of today's compromising and conforming culture, however, multitudes of people do have a great heart hunger for the Word of God. Exposition speaks to that heart hunger. A return to strong, systematic preaching of biblical truth can do much to reverse the tide of immorality that threatens to engulf us. As believers understand the moral implications of biblical faith, they gain the adequate materials with which to build genuine, moral lives.

A careful study of successful ministries reveals that a high percentage of churches have been blessed by the ministry of a pastor who has spent many years with the same congregation. Most of those pastors also have been strong expositors. They actually have "preached through" their problems. Many of them started with very immature congregations, began preaching through books of the Bible, and so helped foster spirituality. As both pastor and people matured in the Lord, they were able to do His work together in a more harmonious and effective fashion. Bible preaching makes for a strong and healthy congregation.

THE DANGERS OF EXPOSITION

One of the facts of life is that people react against shoddy work. The majority of the criticisms raised against expository preaching are not justified with regard to the approach itself, but they are justified with regard to the approach poorly done. People do not disdain expository preaching; they disdain *poor* expository preaching. Some preachers have fallen prey to certain dangers in expository preaching and have, consequently, abused the approach. These abuses have caused expository preaching to fall into disrepute along the way. Like the careful driver on a well-traveled highway, the pastor will do well to avoid certain potholes along the road to exposition.

Dullness. Some believe expository preaching is merely making a few remarks based upon a long passage of Scripture. Still others understand it to be a lifeless, meaningless, pointless recounting of a Bible story. These perceptions have resulted from so-called expository preaching that always seems to be the same old thing. Sometimes the exposition is dull because of the sameness of approach. Perhaps the preacher becomes pedantic; every message has the same kind of introduction, the same predictable wording of divisions, and the same stale finish. Such will bore people out of their minds.

Constantly be looking for new ways to introduce your sermons. Search diligently for fresh, current illustrations. Be a student of people so that you can apply eternal truth to their lives relevantly. Make it a challenge to find striking ways to bring your messages to a close. Work on your delivery in order to get your whole self into your preaching. God's Word innately is alive and powerful. You will determine whether its presentation is dull or exciting.

Irrelevancy. Similarly, some critics even go so far as to suggest that expository preaching is irrelevant in today's world, containing no up-to-date application of truth to contemporary listeners. Expository preachers are sometimes charged with answering questions no one is asking. True expositors, however, are actually answering questions people *should* be asking.

Yet, the charge itself is not true. People are indeed asking the questions expositors are answering; they are just asking them in different words. Through intelligent, exciting, contemporary preaching of the Bible, you can elicit from your hearers a desire to hear answers to the right questions. You as the preacher can make exposition extremely interesting and positively relevant to your listeners. Remember, you are not preaching merely to expose your people to information but to give them truth that will transform their lives.

Monotony. Because of the similarity of content throughout a particular book of the Bible, the preacher must also work to avoid the danger of monotony. Many fine expositors have been able to sustain the interest of people through lengthy expositional series. Although some men naturally are more gifted than others in holding attention, a knowledge of certain aspects of delivery can make the sermon more interesting and exciting.

From time to time, preach from a shorter passage, maybe even a single verse. Remember, expository preaching depends not so much on the length of the passage as on the manner of its treatment.

Another good and needful practice is to identify an important doctrinal word in a paragraph and bring a message on that particular doctrine in an expository fashion. For pastors who preach multiple times each week, such a practice can get double mileage out of sermon preparation. As you systematically preach through lengthier passages during one service, use the overflow of your preparation to preach in another service a doctrinal sermon that is informed by a word or words found in the lengthier passage.

Another way to avoid monotony is to insert a brief series on another subject between book studies. You may preach a series on subjects such as great events in the life of Christ, great interviews in the life of Jesus, or the miracles of Jesus. These topics can be developed in an expository fashion and yet provide variety from week-by-week exposition of a Bible book.

Spiritlessness. Some have criticized the systematic exposition of Bible books as ignoring the leadership of the Holy Spirit in getting a message from God. Three observations deem this criticism defective.

First, all of the Bible is the Word of God. You ought never to be without a word from on high, even when you do not sense a particular direction from the Lord.

Second, the Holy Spirit is not limited in His guidance to one week at a time. He is more than capable of leading you to preach through a book of the Bible as well as leading you to a different text each week. Without question, the Spirit sometimes provides specific direction for particular messages on particular occasions. Just as easily, however, He may give clear direction to preach through certain books of the Bible. During these seasons you will be amazed at the appropriateness of the messages as He applies truth to current problems in the lives of your people.

Certainly, do not restrict yourself for weeks on end, even in the midst of a book series. If you sense the leading of the Holy Spirit to preach on a particular text, insert a parenthesis into your series and pursue the new direction. You always can return to your "home base."

Finally, the expositor can ensure the Spirit's involvement in his preaching by means of his ongoing personal communion with the Father. Nurture your personal worship of the One on behalf of whom you speak.

Formlessness. Some view expository preaching as an exhaustive and exhausting report of all the commentaries a preacher has read on a particular passage of Scripture. Indeed, often the expository approach is subjected to poor sermonic presentation. Such is the danger of the running commentary approach, which will be discussed later. The preacher who ventures here will face the temptation of doing little preparation beyond reading a few commentaries.

But an expository sermon at its very best is based upon thorough exegesis. The message is then built around a central theme that is communicated through well-organized divisions derived from the text. The sermon has good explanation, illustrations, argumentation, and application. Exposition is not done adequately unless you prepare in the most comprehensive way possible.

Detail overload. One of the biggest challenges the expositor will face is determining what exegetical material to allow into his sermon. You will make a grave mistake if you try to examine every minute part of every verse in a passage. This approach evidently was adopted by many Puritan preachers, who often preached many years on a single book. While their messages contained many rich Bible truths, the detail overload probably accounts for their very small congregations.[28]

You should *study* each minute detail of your preaching passage—grammar, verb tenses, prepositions, definite articles, and the like. But you must be intentional and selective regarding the amount of technical material you bring into the pulpit. Give the people the cream of your study—only what is necessary for understanding the Holy Spirit's heartbeat in the text. Avoid beating them to death with excessive material that is insignificant to the main thrust. Besides, all of our egos would be damaged if we knew how little of our sermons people actually retained.

THE HERITAGE OF EXPOSITION

The outstanding expository preachers past and present serve as additional rationale for the practice of exposition. The author of Hebrews said, "Therefore we also, since we are surrounded by so great a cloud of witnesses, let us lay aside every weight, and the sin which so easily ensnares us, and let us run with endurance the race that is set before us" (Heb. 12:1). The same can be said for the responsibility of rightly dividing the Word. The rich heritage of expositors who followed Jesus and Paul call upon us to be faithful with the sacred trust. A few of these torchbearers of exposition are mentioned in the following paragraphs.

Alexander Maclaren (1826–1910) spent forty-five years expounding the Scriptures at Union Chapel in Manchester, England. He subjected himself to a very rigorous study schedule. Each day of the week he would shut himself away in his study, giving little attention to visitation and administration. To read his sermons is to read messages of unusual clarity and strength. Maclaren's exegesis was thorough and accurate, his outlines were clear and to the point, his illustrations beautifully amplified the meaning of the passage, and his application was relevant to his hearers.

G. Campbell Morgan (1863–1945) has been called the Prince of Expositors. He served twice as pastor of Westminster Chapel in London. His ability to analyze a passage of Scripture continues to serve as a model for young preachers. Morgan was a master of studying a passage in its total context. He could analyze a text and then skillfully put it back together in a beautiful, logical sequence. Often he would read the Bible book from which he was preaching forty to fifty times during his preparation. In

28. George Henderson, *Lectures to Young Preachers* (Edinburgh: B. McCall Barbour, 1961), 88.

Morgan's opinion, determining an outline was the most important part of sermon preparation. Though his content was excellent, his ability to analyze the passage was the highlight of his work.

Donald Grey Barnhouse (1895–1960), who served as pastor of Philadelphia's historic Tenth Presbyterian Church, was a master at using the whole of Scripture to expose the meaning of a text. He would bring the entire Bible to bear on his particular preaching passage. Perhaps his greatest work is his multivolume set on Romans, a masterpiece of paragraph-by-paragraph exposition through a book of the Bible. He preached three and one-half years from this Bible book in the morning services, and his congregation grew continually until the building was filled. To read his work on Romans is virtually to give oneself a thorough education in the entire Bible.

W. A. Criswell (1909–), pastor emeritus of First Baptist Church in Dallas, has gained international recognition as a Bible expositor. After succeeding George W. Truett at the church in 1944, he preached systematically through the Bible on a regular basis. Criswell took eighteen years to preach through the entire Bible, during which time his congregation grew phenomenally. On one occasion he preached through the entire Bible in one twenty-four-hour period to a standing-room-only crowd. His books are veritable storehouses of information and guidance for the preacher who would preach expositorily. His volumes on Revelation are among the finest. His word study is excellent, and his interpretation is clear and concise. Though a clearly discernible outline often does not appear, the preacher will learn much about expository preaching by a careful study of his work.

As the sun sets on the twentieth century, a remnant of faithful Bible expositors is holding high the torch and paving the way for the next generation. In 1980, Stephen Olford, after a lengthy tenure as a pastor-expositor in both Great Britain and the United States, opened the Institute for Biblical Preaching in Memphis in an effort to restore expository preaching to the pulpit. W. Ian Barclay said of Olford, "He lays bare the truth so that the life and vitality of God's Word can be seen. He exposes the truth so that there is no doubt about its meaning."[29]

A further example of contemporary expositors is John Phillips, one of Olford's students in Great Britain, who also is known for his simple and clear exposition. Formerly associated with Moody Bible Institute, he remains active as a writer and preacher in churches and Bible conferences in North America and abroad. His many thorough yet understandable Bible commentaries are excellent resources for pastors, teachers, and stu-

29. W. Ian Barclay, "Stephen F. Olford—as a Preacher," in *A Passion for Preaching,* comp. David L. Olford (Nashville: Nelson, 1989), 33.

dents who desire to do good exposition.

Warren Wiersbe is a popular Bible expositor who served as pastor of the renowned Moody Memorial Church in Chicago from 1971 to 1978. He is known as "the pastor's pastor" for the encouragement and example he provides through solid, contemporary Bible exposition in conferences and seminars. In addition, he has written more than eighty books, most of which either demonstrate his own masterful expositional skills or highlight the same in the ministry of great preachers of the past.

Several pastors and educators join these men as fine contemporary models for biblical exposition. John MacArthur Jr. is president of the Master's Seminary and pastor-teacher of Grace Community Church in Sun Valley, California. A respected champion of biblical inspiration and authority, MacArthur is a master at laying open a text of Scripture to public view in order to set forth its meaning, explain what is difficult to understand, and make appropriate and relevant application. In addition to writing numerous books, including the MacArthur New Testament Commentaries, he is heard daily through his worldwide radio and tape ministry.

Charles Swindoll, currently president of Dallas Theological Seminary, is the former senior pastor of the First Evangelical Free Church in Fullerton, California. He is known for his ability to do fine biblical exposition, clothe it in contemporary style, and make relevant and piercing modern-day application. Like MacArthur, Swindoll is heard daily on worldwide radio broadcasts and is the author of numerous books.

Among African-American preachers, the name of Tony Evans stands out. Evans is senior pastor of Oak Cliff Bible Fellowship in Dallas and president of The Urban Alternative. His ministry is devoted to promoting a clear understanding and relevant application of God's Word in order to bring about changes in urban communities through the church. Evans is a popular Bible expositor whose ministry crosses both cultural and denominational lines.

In light of the tension we face to "do church" in a dramatically changing society, ignoring this heritage will be detrimental to kingdom work. Cautioning against the tendency to become man-focused in our efforts at contextualization, Kent Hughes said:

> Preaching . . . is often shortened to a 15- or 20-minute homily. Bible exposition is jettisoned as "too heavy" in favor of a lighter topical homily. And since the average TV-sotted American has a shrinking attention span, "sermons" become story-laden and sometimes a string of vignettes loosely related to a scriptural pretext.

Moreover, there is often such a strained attempt to be "relevant" that anything that has not come out of the last 20 years is consciously avoided. The great hymns of the church are shelved. A reverse elitism is instilled which is proudly cast. The end effect of this approach is to produce the unfortunate illusion that the evangelical church has come out of nowhere—without heritage or roots![30]

We cannot afford to be guilty of such a charge. Preacher, the baton has been passed to a new generation of kingdom servants. Take it up enthusiastically and continue the race faithfully!

30. Kent Hughes, "The Foundation of Our Vision," in *Vision 2000* (publication of College Church in Wheaton, Ill.), January 9, 1994.

CHAPTER TWO

LAYING
THE FOUNDATION

The preacher of the Word is not a salesman or a showman;
he is a spokesman! Hence our theology of proclamation must
be closely wed to our theology of devotion.

DAVID LARSEN

Understanding the task of exposition is only the beginning of a long journey toward good preaching. A wise builder may understand the concepts relevant to the construction of a building, but if he does not lay a proper foundation for the structure, his efforts are doomed to failure. Likewise, understanding the concepts that inform biblical exposition does not ensure that the preacher will preach with integrity and power.

The entire preaching event must be built upon certain spiritual foundation stones if it is to make a difference in the lives of people. First, the man himself must be called of God to the task of preaching. Second, he must have an unapologetic commitment to the nature and role of the Word of God. Third, he must be given passionately to the worship of God. Fourth, the preacher must be diligent in an unending quest for the anointing of God on his life and ministry.

THE CALL OF GOD

The New Testament speaks of the call to pastor in lofty terms. Three different words all refer to the same office in the local church. The word "elder" is the Greek word *presbuteros,* from which comes our word "presbyterian." The word refers to mature age or character. The word "bishop" is the Greek *episkopos,* from which comes our word "episcopal." This word means overseer or guardian and refers to what a man does. The most familiar word in the New Testament is the word "pastor." This Greek word is *poimēn* and means shepherd. The term emphasizes the pastoral role of caring and feeding. All three terms are used of the same church leaders, and all three identify those who feed and lead the church. All three terms are brought together in 1 Peter 5:1–3:

> The elders [*presbuteros*] who are among you I exhort, I who am a fellow elder and a witness of the sufferings of Christ, and also a partaker of the glory that will be revealed: Shepherd [*poimēn*] the flock of God which is among you, serving as overseers [*episkopos*], not by compulsion but willingly, not for dishonest gain but eagerly; nor as being lords over those entrusted to you, but being examples to the flock.

The apostle Paul wrote to young Timothy regarding the character of one called to such an office. The list of qualifications in 1 Timothy 3:1–7 is introduced with these words: "This is a faithful saying: If a man desires the position of a bishop, he desires a good work."

We live in a day when men are leaving the ministry in droves. The statistics are staggering. Tired of frustrations, emotional strain, controversy both inside and outside the church, and long hours, they are turning their backs on God's call and pursuing other things. One reason for the exodus is found right here in the word "desires." The term literally means to desire earnestly, stemming from an inward impulse, not from the object desired. If a man goes into the ministry for any other reason than the inward prompting of the Holy Spirit, he is doing it for the wrong reason. Chances are that he will not last.

If God prompts a man, and he desires to pursue that ministry, Paul goes on to say that he desires a "good work." What an exciting and awesome thought—a good work. Why would anyone want to walk away from a good work? Part of the reason is that too many focus on the "good" and forget about the "work." The two ideas cannot be separated. If a person looks for all the goodness but does not realize all the work involved, he ultimately will get discouraged. The ministry is hard work. It takes sweat to be a preacher of the gospel and the pastor of a local church.

Every preacher must have certainty about his call, a confidence that will make him willing and able to pay the price of hard work. Your perspective about your call to preach largely determines how you approach the pulpit. If you are going to be effective as a preacher of the gospel, you must understand that you have a prophet's call. Preach with an awesome sense that God is preaching through you. Some men go to the pulpit thinking that when they preach they merely are speaking *about* God. When you have a biblical message and are spiritually prepared, however,

God speaks through you. Such a perspective will change your whole appreciation for what is happening in the preaching event.

When you preach with this paradigm, you can be sure that God is speaking and that people will respond to His voice. This confidence equips you with an appreciation and enthusiasm for delivering God's message. Clovis G. Chappell described this wonder and the subsequent effect:

> He calls certain men to be his spokesmen because, knowing them, and knowing the world of which they are a part, he knows that they can do something for him that no one else can do. It is a thrilling and awe-inspiring thought that God has selected us for this high task in the knowledge that we can do this something that is essential to the salvation of men. In spite of all our handicaps, in spite of our limitations, if God has called us to preach, he has done so because he knows that we can do something for him that no one else can do.[1]

Each time you step into the pulpit, go believing that you are doing something no one else can do in that particular situation. God has called you to the task.

A study of pastoral work throughout history reveals an ever changing role for pastors. The turn of the twentieth century especially saw a subtle shift in emphasis from the preaching event to hands-on care of people and the administration of church programs. At the turn of the twenty-first century, more and more emphasis is being placed on executive leadership, vision casting, and needs-oriented teaching.

While all of these functions may have their proper place in pastoral work, consideration of the *biblical role* of the pastor cries out for reformation and specifically a return to the centrality of preaching. The primary scriptural analogy for the pastor comes from the word *poimēn*, or "shepherd." Though the word is used only in a few places in reference to the pastoral office, the picture permeates Old and New Testament teaching regarding the leadership of God's people.

Consequently, one must ask: What are the primary responsibilities of a shepherd? While the job certainly involves elements of administration and remedial care, the primary responsibility of the shepherd certainly is not to pet the sheep! Charles Jefferson asserted:

> That the feeding of the sheep is an essential duty of the shepherd-calling is

---

1. Clovis G. Chappell, *Anointed to Preach* (New York: Abingdon-Cokesbury, 1951), 25.

known even to those who are least familiar with shepherds and their work. Sheep cannot feed themselves, nor water themselves. They must be conducted to the water and the pasture. . . . Everything depends on the proper feeding of the sheep. Unless wisely fed they become emaciated and sick, and the wealth invested in them is squandered. . . . When the minister goes into the pulpit, he is the shepherd in the act of feeding.[2]

The primary role of the shepherd, then, is to feed and protect the sheep. In New Testament church leadership, both of these duties are accomplished by the same function—the preaching and teaching of God's Word.[3] The pastoral epistles are filled with exhortations to provide the flock with spiritual nourishment and to protect them from heresy, all through the instruction of right doctrine (see 1 Tim. 1:3–4; 3:2; 4:6–7, 13–16; 5:17–18; 6:1–5, 20–21; 2 Tim. 1:6–8, 13–14; 2:1–2, 8–9, 14–16; 3:14–17; 4:1–5; Titus 1:7–14; 2:1, 15).

If you will give yourself to Bible exposition, you will find you are in a field with no competitors. If you try to discuss politics with your people, someone else will be more knowledgeable. If you attempt to become an expert in the social questions of the day, you will discover your knowledge is limited. If you play the philosopher, you will find yourself speaking to an empty building. But if you give yourself to being a Bible expositor, you will be pleased to discover that people from all walks of life will come to hear you.

People deal with assembly lines, chemistry, computers, classrooms, mathematics, and kids all during the week. When they come to church on Sunday they want to know what God says. In your congregation may be doctors who are skilled in medicine, teachers who are experts in their field, and businessmen who are geniuses in finance. But chances are most of them are in kindergarten biblically and spiritually. They want to hear from a man who has been with God in His Word during the week. They want to hear a preacher who can proclaim from the Word the realities of life and answers for the deepest needs of their hearts. Be "a worker who does not need to be ashamed, rightly dividing the word of truth" (2 Tim. 2:15).

THE WORD OF GOD

Clear convictions concerning the Word of God are paramount in the

2. Charles Jefferson, *The Minister as Shepherd* (Hong Kong: Living Books for All, 1980), 59, 61.
3. John MacArthur Jr., "What Is a Pastor to Be and Do?" in *Rediscovering Pastoral Ministry*, ed. John MacArthur Jr. (Dallas: Word, 1995), 28.

preaching event. Many people believe just the opposite. They say that a preacher's view of Scripture is unimportant and not a factor in the effectiveness of his preaching. Such contentions are partially responsible for the sharp decline in biblical preaching during the twentieth century. On the contrary, your convictions about the Bible will directly affect both your motivation and the results of your preaching. If you lose your conviction that the Bible is trustworthy, authoritative, and dynamic, why should you bother to preach from Scripture? Merrill F. Unger rightly said:

> If the Bible is considered merely to contain the Word of God, rather than actually to be in toto the Word of God, there is naturally a decreased sense of responsibility to study its text minutely, or to systematize its theology, or authoritatively to declare its message.[4]

Your convictions about biblical inspiration, authority, benefit, and purpose are crucial in the matters of both sermon preparation and pulpit effectiveness.

INSPIRATION

The effective Bible expositor will have a high view of Scripture, beginning with a clear conviction about biblical *inspiration*. Many people regard the Bible as just one good book among many. More tragically, many preachers have failed to see the relationship between one's view of biblical inspiration and preaching effectiveness. Andrew Blackwood wrote, "Fortunately a man's effectiveness in the pulpit does not depend upon his theory of inspiration."[5] Nothing could be further from the truth.

Widespread rejection of the doctrine of verbal plenary inspiration of Scripture has permeated some theological circles for years. Some critics have insisted that the Bible is subject to error and human limitation. Others think the whole debate about biblical inspiration is merely a matter of semantics, a quibbling over words. On the contrary, the outcome of such arguments is eternally important to the people who sit in churches every week. The result of such contentions has been weak pulpits and weak churches.

If a preacher attempted to lecture from Shakespeare Sunday after Sunday, not many weeks would pass before he would lose his audience. On the other hand, systematic preaching through books of the Bible as

---

4. Merrill F. Unger, *Principles of Expository Preaching* (Grand Rapids: Zondervan, 1955), 18.
5. Andrew Blackwood, *Preaching from the Bible* (New York: Abingdon, 1941), 182.

God's inspired Word has filled many a church to overflowing through the years.

Verbal plenary inspiration suggests that "in the composition of the original manuscripts, the Holy Spirit guided the authors even in their choice of expressions—and this throughout all the pages of the Scriptures—still without effacing the personalities of the different men."[6] Inspiration is *verbal* because the words are inseparable from the message. Inspiration is *plenary* because it is entire and without restriction.[7] Frank E. Gaebelein said:

> The doctrine of plenary inspiration holds that the original documents of the Bible were written by men, who, though permitted the exercise of their own personalities and literary talents, yet wrote under the control and guidance of the Spirit of God, the result being in every word of the original documents a perfect and errorless recording of the exact message which God desired to give to man.[8]

Thus, the Bible is exactly and completely what God said.

Just as each individual is the greatest expert on his or her own background and experiences, so the Bible must be allowed to speak for itself regarding its own inspiration. The apostle Peter wrote that "prophecy never came by the will of man, but holy men of God spoke as they were moved by the Holy Spirit" (2 Pet. 1:21). This picture is of men being carried along by the Holy Spirit much as a sailboat would be carried along by the wind. The passage indicates that those men chosen to pen the inspired Word did so superintended by the Holy Spirit. Scripture has a dual authorship—the Holy Spirit is the divine author, and various men are the human authors. Peter verbalized this understanding in his Pentecost sermon: "This Scripture had to be fulfilled, which the Holy Spirit spoke before by the mouth of David concerning Judas" (Acts 1:16).

Some critics have erroneously suggested that verbal plenary inspiration implies a "mechanical dictation" on the part of the Holy Spirit. Refuting this assertion, J. I. Packer wrote:

> This "dictation theory" is a man of straw. It is safe to say that no Protestant theologian, from the Reformation till now, has ever held it; and certainly modern Evangelicals do not hold it. . . . It is true that many sixteenth and

---

6. René Pache, *The Inspiration and Authority of Scripture* (Chicago: Moody, 1969), 71.
7. Ibid., 72–73.
8. Frank E. Gaebelein, *The Meaning of Inspiration* (Chicago: InterVarsity, 1950), 9.

seventeenth-century theologians spoke of Scripture as "dictated by the Holy Ghost." But all they meant was that the authors wrote word for word what God intended. . . . The use of the term "dictation" was always figurative. . . . The proof of this lies in the fact that, when these theologians addressed themselves to the question, What was the Spirit's mode of operating in the writers' minds? they all gave their answer in terms not of dictation, but of accommodation, and rightly maintained that God completely adapted His inspiring activity to the cast of mind, outlook, temperament, interest, literary habits, and stylistic idiosyncrasies of each writer.[9]

To be sure, biblical inspiration was wrought through the unique personalities of individual writers. One can sense the burning sarcasm of Isaiah; the tender, earnest pathos of Jeremiah; the philosophical leanings of John; the sharp, crisp logic of Paul. Each of these writers truly was a man with his own mind. Each was like the individual pipe of a magnificent organ, so fashioned that each might give one unique note, yet all filled with the same breath. These holy men were fashioned by the circumstances of their lives and the genetic combination of their personalities so that each one might give out his own note. Yet, all of them were filled by the breath of the divine Spirit.

The effective preacher not only will believe that the Bible is inspired but that it is *totally* inspired. Paul reminded Timothy that "all Scripture is given by inspiration of God" (2 Tim. 3:16). This verse clearly speaks of plenary inspiration. All Scripture—the totality of Scripture—is inspired. Such inspiration extends to the words as well as to the thoughts.

While some people hold a conceptual view of inspiration, maintaining that the thought patterns but not individual words are inspired, they fail to explain how thoughts are possessed apart from words. Referring to the words of his message, Paul said, "These things we also speak, not in words which man's wisdom teaches but which the Holy Spirit teaches" (1 Cor. 2:13). The words the Holy Spirit teaches clearly are the words of Scripture. Underscoring the inspiration of even the smallest part of the letters of God's words, our Lord said, "For assuredly, I say to you, till heaven and earth pass away, one jot or one tittle will by no means pass from the law till all is fulfilled" (Matt. 5:18). Such a view is indeed a high view of inspiration. The preacher who is committed to the lordship of Christ surely must give careful attention to Jesus' view of Scripture.

The Bible also claims to be inerrant. The Holy Spirit overruled the limitations of the human writers so that they were able to write without

---

9. James I. Packer, *Fundamentalism and the Word of God* (Grand Rapids: Eerdmans, 1958), 79.

error. If the preacher can acknowledge the Spirit's power to overrule human limitation at any point, he must be willing to grant his superintendence over every matter in Scripture. A person may intelligently hold that there are no scientific errors, no historical errors, and no prophetic errors in the Bible. If the preacher cannot trust his Bible on those matters, neither can he have confidence in Scripture on matters concerning his soul's salvation.

Certainly, no person is obligated to immediately clear away every Bible difficulty in order to believe. Although areas exist where modern readership does not have final answers, ever surfacing information inevitably seems to evaporate many supposed difficulties. New archeological discoveries vindicate further the accuracy and integrity of the Bible. Such recent answers to issues that have perplexed scholars for years suggest that information regarding other, unanswered questions is still to come.

The inspiration of Scripture should be claimed only for the original manuscripts. Critics often use the unavailability of the originals as a reason for rejecting a high view of inspiration. They say accuracy cannot be determined by documents that have never been seen. This criticism overlooks the fact that unavailable documents can be recovered with accuracy from numerous available sources. The careful textual critic seeks to determine from a comparison of divergent documents which form of the text should be regarded as most nearly conforming to the original.[10] The objective of textual criticism is the enhancement of the integrity of the text. P. Kyle McCarter Jr. said, "The goal is the recovery of an earlier, more authentic—and therefore superior—form of the text."[11] In essence, all the various written forms are "witnesses to and evidences for the text."[12]

George Henderson illustrated how good textual criticism can produce reliable documents and, therefore, a Bible that can be trusted as the inspired Word of God:

> On January 1, 1863, President Lincoln set his name and seal on the proclamation which set four million slaves free. The proclamation was written on four pages of ordinary foolscap in the president's own handwriting. That document perished in the great Chicago Fire of 1871. Suppose some slave-owner should seize a former slave of his, challenge him to produce Lincoln's Proclamation as his charter of liberty, and say that if he did not produce the

10. Bruce M. Metzger, *The Text of the New Testament: Its Transmission, Corruption, and Restoration*, 3d. ed. (New York: Oxford Univ., 1992). Preface to the 1st ed.
11. P. Kyle McCarter Jr., *Textual Criticism: Recovering the Text of the Hebrew Bible* (Philadelphia: Fortress, 1986), 12.
12. Gene Tucker in the Foreword to McCarter, 7.

original, he would hold him still in slavery; what could the ex-slave do? He could not produce the original, for the original was destroyed by fire. Although he could not produce the original document, he could recover and produce the original text. How? By copies of the same in public documents; newspapers of the period; by translations of the text in French, German, and other languages; by quotations from the proclamation in speeches, periodicals and books. By comparing and combining all these, he could establish to the satisfaction of a court of law the original message which gave him liberty.[13]

Although the original scriptural documents are unavailable, the preacher can be confident that he possesses the correct text by way of the multiplicity of available manuscripts.

A strong conviction about the inspiration of Scripture naturally will inform the way you preach. A high view of biblical inspiration and inerrancy demands that the primary approach to preaching be the exposition of Bible books. If, in fact, one believes that the Holy Spirit inspired the text of the Bible, then it behooves him to present that text to people in a way that most closely resembles the way in which the Spirit gave it. The Spirit did not inspire principles that float around unrelated to the rest of Scripture. He inspired truths that are embodied within sentences. Those sentences are embodied within paragraphs. Those paragraphs are embodied within letters and historical accounts and other kinds of literature. Each of these components, along with related issues of chronology and background, must be taken into consideration when exposing God's truth to people.

Unwavering confidence in the inspiration of Scripture definitely will affect the preaching event. The preacher who seriously gives himself to the task of Bible exposition must hold a high view of the inspiration of Scripture. Please give earnest, prayerful thought to this matter. If you have doubts in your heart about the absolute accuracy and integrity of the Word, you most likely will have a difficult time doing exegesis—fervently seeking to know what the text actually says—and yielding your personal life to its commands.

AUTHORITY

A high view of biblical inspiration issues forth into a clear conviction regarding the Bible's *authority*. If the Bible is inspired by God and consequently void of error, then it can be trusted as the sole authority for matters of faith. The sparsity of good expository preachers at the close of the

13. George Henderson, *The Wonderful Word* (Edinburgh: B. McCall Barbour, n.d.), 13.

twentieth century is in part due to lack of conviction in this area. The preacher is assigned the responsibility to preach the Word of God. Jesus commanded Peter to "feed My lambs" (John 21:15). Paul urged young Timothy to "preach the Word" (2 Tim. 4:2). He admonished the elders of Ephesus to "shepherd the church of God" (Acts 20:28), which suggested providing the spiritual food of the Word. If the preacher's confidence in the authority of Scripture is shattered, he will have no sense of urgency to preach the Bible.

Some critics and skeptics try to make a distinction between the actual Word of God and the text of Scripture. But God's approach clearly has been to speak His Word and have someone record it for subsequent adherence and application. Moses wrote down God's words and instructed the Levites to preserve them as a witness (Deut. 31:24–26). God then commanded Joshua to abide by those same words (Josh. 1:8). Joshua later added God's new revelation to the Book of the Law (Josh. 24:26). And on went the process even into Jesus' day, when He verified the written Word's authority on the remaining generations (Matt. 5:17–20). The apostle Paul later verified the addition of the testimony of the apostles to the authoritative Word of God by describing it as the foundation on which the church is built (Eph. 2:19–22).

Still others try to distinguish between the authority of Jesus and the authority of the Bible. Someone says, "I worship Jesus and not the Bible." But the question must be asked as to whether or not it is possible to give allegiance to someone who is made known only through the pages of Scripture. Another response is leveled: "I know Him through my experience with Him." But experiences must be tested, and the only valid instrument for such a task is the written Word of God. Common sense tells us that no clear distinction can be made between the authority of Jesus Christ and the written Word that He Himself endorsed.

Every preacher must come to the place where he accepts the authority of the Bible by faith. Admittedly, a gap exists between empirical evidence and the acceptance of biblical authority. That gap ultimately can be crossed only by faith.

Many great preachers have wrestled to cross the gap. G. Campbell Morgan, the "Prince of Expositors," had such a personal crisis. Influenced by some of the critical theories of his day, he plunged into the darkness of doubt. Setting aside all his books, he determined to discover for himself if the Bible was indeed what it claimed to be. The result was not merely that he found the Bible but, as he said, "The Bible found me."[14] That experi-

---

14. Jill Morgan, *A Man of the Word* (Grand Rapids: Baker, 1972), 39–40.

ence resulted in a preaching ministry that blessed two continents during his lifetime and that, through his writings, continues to bless countless preachers and other Christians worldwide.

Billy Graham faced a similar crisis early in his ministry when he questioned whether or not the Bible was indeed the Word of God. In a time of deep spiritual commitment, he committed himself to the preaching of the Bible as God's Word to man.[15] Still today, his piercing statement "The Bible says" reflects the authority he embraces as his preaching ministry continues to impress, grip, and move myriads. When the serious student of the Bible considers all the evidence objectively and prayerfully, the gap between facts and certainty becomes ever so narrow. Confidence in the Bible's authority, then, becomes easy.

Your authority as a preacher lies solely in the authority of your message. Paul told the Thessalonians, "Our gospel did not come to you in word only, but also in power, and in the Holy Spirit and in much assurance" (1 Thess. 1:5). That sense of authority is neither a privilege to be abused nor a blessing to be minimized. Rather than spending your ministry trying to convince people of your own authority, you can simply rest in the authority of the One who sent you. Rather than submitting to the opinions of men, you can speak from a "Thus saith the Lord" standpoint. When you preach from that perspective, the authority of the Word becomes prominent in your pulpit ministry. Thus you experience the wonder and awe of being a fellow laborer with God, reaching people and changing their lives. As you preach out of a deep conviction that the Bible is God's living Word, listeners will receive the message more seriously and consider it more binding as the power of God works mightily through the preaching event.

The Word has survived through all the centuries. In A.D. 303, Diocletian commanded that all copies of the Bible be burned; yet the Bible still lives. The inscription on the monument to the Huguenots of Paris succinctly and accurately expresses the Bible's miraculous longevity: "Hammer away ye hostile hands; your hammers break; God's anvil stands." The transmission of the Bible through thousands of copies into modern print has not tainted its purity. No other book of ancient literature has been exposed to similar processes of propagation and maintained such accuracy of transmission. Only the sovereign control of God through the centuries can account for such an act. Careful study of the Bible and its history will convince the reader that it is a miracle book, one that man could not have

---

15. Billy Graham, *Just As I Am: The Autobiography of Billy Graham* (New York: Zondervan, 1997), 138–39.

written if he would and would not have written if he could. Truly, the Bible can be trusted and preached as the authoritative Word of God.

BENEFIT

The effective preacher also will have a clear conviction about the *benefit* of Scripture. If you do not embrace that conviction, then you will not be able to preach as though your preaching makes any difference in the lives of those who listen. A high view of the inspiration of Scripture and an unshakeable dependence upon its authority will give you confidence in its ability to transform lives. If, in fact, the Bible is the inspired Word of God, then it can be trusted to provide and accomplish that which it claims.

A cursory survey of just some of the claims of God's Word regarding its benefit is quite astounding. In the Old Testament, Joshua 1:8 promises *prosperity* and *success* for the one who digests and obeys the Law. Psalm 19:7–11 says it *converts (restores)* the soul, makes *wise* the simple, gives *joy* to the heart, and *enlightens* the eyes. The same passage describes the Word as *everlasting, true* and *righteous, invaluable,* and *sweet* to the taste. The writer goes on to claim that the Law provides both *warning* and *reward.* Psalm 119:9–11 states that the Word of God is the agent for *cleansing from* and *avoidance of sin.* Verse 105 of the same chapter says the Word provides *guidance* and *direction* for the future.

In the New Testament, Jesus Himself is equated with the Word in John 1:1, 14 and therefore embodies all of its power and benefits. While praying for His disciples in John 17:17, He defined the Word of God as *truth* and implied that it was God's primary *sanctifying* agent. Romans 10:17 says that it results in *faith.* Regarding the Holy Scriptures, 2 Timothy 3:14–17 claims they give wisdom for *salvation, teaching* about what is right, *rebuke* when one is wrong, *correction* for getting back on the right track, and *instruction* for living righteously, all for the purpose of *maturation* and *preparation* for service. Hebrews 4:12 describes it as *alive* and *sharp, penetrating* human nature and *detecting* and *analyzing* a person's most intimate and personal thoughts and feelings. First Peter 2:2 describes the Word of God as the milk that is necessary for spiritual *nourishment.*

The list could go on and on. The benefits of God's Word are endless. Its riches are inexhaustible. Furthermore, when looking at such a list, one sees that the most basic desires and needs of human existence are addressed. In a day in which churchgoers are crying out for relevant, application-oriented, and need-directed messages, why should you go anywhere else to find preaching subjects and content? The Word of God by nature is relevant, dynamic, and effectual. It will take root and radically affect the lives of those who receive it if you will faithfully expound it.

PURPOSE

The preacher also must have a clear conviction regarding the *purpose* of the Bible. Confusion at this point is a serious problem in the modern pulpit, even in the most conservative circles. Just because the Bible is inspired by God, authoritative by nature, and effectual for life change does not mean that it was intended for any and every purpose. Neither was the Scripture intended to address every question that arises in life. If you overlook this reality, your theology may be right while your preaching makes the Bible do and say things it was never intended to do or say.

Peter greeted his readers with a revealing reminder:

> Grace and peace be multiplied to you in the knowledge of God and of Jesus our Lord, as His divine power has given to us all things that pertain to life and godliness, through the knowledge of Him who called us by glory and virtue, by which have been given to us exceedingly great and precious promises, that through these you may be partakers of the divine nature, having escaped the corruption that is in the world through lust. (2 Pet. 1:2–4)

These verses contain several truths that are relevant for a consideration of the purpose for which God has given His Word. First, He desires that we know Him through Jesus Christ. Second, God's revelation contains everything that we need for gaining that knowledge. Third, such knowledge is possible because we have inherited the divine nature. Fourth, that knowledge is fleshed out through godly living. In other words, God has given us everything we need to know Him and be transformed into His likeness.

From beginning to end, the Bible has one overarching theme: the redemption of God's creation. Scripture opens in Genesis with the story of man's fall from the likeness of God. Scripture closes in Revelation with the ultimate restoration of that likeness in His eternal presence. Everything in between describes God's plan of re-creation through Jesus Christ, a relationship with whom involves the process of transformation into His likeness.

The Bible reveals the salvation process as a three-phased journey involving justification, sanctification, and glorification. Thus, God's Word was not given to answer every question under the sun or to provide specific direction for every circumstance that might be encountered in life. Such is the work of God's Holy Spirit, who applies the wisdom and knowledge of the Word to the plethora of everyday life experiences (see Luke 11:9–13; James 1:2–8). Instead, the Bible was given to lead people to a saving knowledge of Jesus Christ and to transform them into His likeness through godly living.

The effect of confusion about the preaching event is ever so subtle at this point. The preacher is a minister of grace and desires to meet people's needs and heal their hurts. But what happens when the specific answers for which people are asking in order to deal with certain issues in life are not specifically spelled out in the Bible? The preacher then is tempted to make the Bible say things it does not say. He ends up offering practical and even helpful information but neglecting the truth that the Holy Spirit inspired in order to transform people into Christ's image. That which the preacher gives is not heresy or blatant error, but neither is it the truth that people need in order to work out their salvation.

This subtlety may be described as the difference between *good stuff* and *God's stuff*. Good stuff is information or principles that are gleaned from observation. When Aristotle delineated his principles of rhetoric, for example, he developed his assertions by engaging in one particular activity: observation. He watched enough public speakers that he was able to glean certain "truths" for speaking effectively. Those principles have had profound impact on preaching and all other forms of public speaking. To say the least, those principles are good stuff. They are both helpful and useful. Those principles, however, will not make anyone look more like Jesus.

Although no preacher would think of preaching on how to do good public speaking, many other doctrines of "good stuff" appear more relevant to contemporary churchgoers and debut as the feature in many sermons. If a person observes enough people dealing with stress in the workplace, certain helpful principles can be gleaned for addressing the issue. If one observes enough people journeying through divorce recovery, guidelines can be developed that are helpful for that crisis. The observation of enough parents rearing their children will produce much practical benefit for such a task. While certain truths in Scripture certainly can be applied to these and other life experiences, to say that God provides a specific treatise for such would be a stretch. Common sense reveals that to address all the scenarios that result from the possible combinations of factors related to these and similar issues would require multiple volumes much larger than the Bible.

God's stuff, on the other hand, is the truth that is revealed in the Bible as part of the salvation process. Though that truth may inform certain principles that might be categorized as good stuff, its primary intent is to bring people to Jesus and mold them into His likeness. The faithful expositor will rightly interpret, exegete, and expose the mind of the Holy Spirit in every text of Scripture so as to give people the information God deemed necessary for life and godliness. When the preacher relegates God's stuff to secondary status by focusing on good stuff, a serious problem arises. The tragedy is not what people are *getting*, because they likely are getting some helpful information. The tragedy is what people are *not* getting, which is the truth that is necessary to transform them into Christ's image.

Much helpful information gleaned by observation is easily accessed in the plethora of Christian psychology and counseling materials. Such material, however, should not be the primary subject matter of your sermon except in such cases where it is the primary intent and content of a text of Scripture. Sermon content should be driven by the Spirit's intent in every individual passage in view of the larger intent of the Bible. You must be most careful about standing up to say "Thus saith the Lord" when the Lord did not saith.[16]

THE WORSHIP OF GOD

The preacher must know intimately the Author of the message he proclaims, if his ministry is to be built on a strong foundation. A book that at first seems dull and uninteresting suddenly becomes exciting when the reader becomes personally acquainted with its author. If the preacher falls in love with the Lord, he will love His Word. Such love of the Lord and for the Bible will be conveyed enthusiastically to listeners in the preaching event. But just as the scientist may lose God in his test tube, so the preacher may lose God in his study. He may become so involved in the mechanics of sermon preparation that he loses his awareness of the presence of God in his personal life. Consequently, the preacher must develop and nurture a vibrant practice of personal worship.

A NEEDED DISTINCTION

The term *personal worship* is used to describe the intimate communication, or communion, between God and one of His children. Whether it is called quiet time, daily devotions, or some other name, every believer must make it his first priority. At the risk of oversimplification, personal worship can be described as the integrated disciplines of Bible reading, prayer, and praise. God speaks to us primarily through His Word. We speak to Him through prayer. Praise is our response to His revelation of Himself to us. These practices are matters that we can ill afford to confuse with other aspects of our ministry.

---

16. See Haddon Robinson, "The Heresy of Application," *Leadership* (Fall 1997): 20–27.

PERSONAL COMMUNICATION AND MINISTERIAL TRAINING
A Personal Testimony

The importance of a personal devotional life was brought home to me during my freshman year in college. Since my call to preach at the age of sixteen, I had maintained a brief morning time for Bible reading and prayer. Upon my arrival at college, I immediately delved into my preparatory studies for the ministry. I was majoring in Bible, and my days were filled with reading many, many chapters from the Bible, sometimes as many as thirty nightly. The next day I would be expected to take an examination on those chapters. In addition, I was studying Greek, philosophy, and additional liberal arts courses.

I found time to be at a premium. So I convinced myself I was reading the Bible as much as I needed. I failed to understand there is a difference between reading the Bible to take a test and reading God's Word to feed one's heart. I also had some brief prayer time. Frankly, my prayers primarily included urgent appeals to pass the examinations! As a result of my neglect of a daily devotional time, my heart became cold to the things of God. I found myself becoming very critical and judgmental of others. On the outside, everything seemed fine. No one would have known I was far from God. On the inside, however, matters were quite different.

Through a citywide crusade preached by a lay speaker, I was awakened to the fact that my problem came from neglecting a daily quiet time. I asked God's forgiveness and reestablished my quiet time. Since then, my daily devotional life has been the highlight of my Christian life. I cannot do without a daily time for Bible reading and prayer. On those rare times when I have been unable to begin my day this way, the day has not gone far until I am consciously aware of a poverty of spirit and a depletion in power.

Jerry Vines

One may easily rationalize that the preacher spends much time with the things of God—reading his Bible in sermon preparation, studying commentaries, leading prayer meetings, constantly talking the language of Zion. But the accumulation of this "holy work" can dull the preacher's awareness of his need to be alone with God. A fundamental difference exists between communion with God and service to others. The former is ministry to the Lord; the latter is ministry to people. The expositor of the Word must learn that he will never be able to minister to people effectively if he does not practice ministry to the Lord.

As one reads the biographies of great preachers, a strong practice of personal worship surfaces as a common denominator. Their public preaching gave evidence of private communion with God. Many otherwise gifted men miss the mark here. They assume their natural and spiritual giftedness will suffice. But even God's gifts, exercised in the energy of the flesh, breed death instead of life. Highlighting the relationship between effective expository preaching and personal worship, Unger wrote:

> It takes a long while for many otherwise able expositors to discover this simple fact. Others never realize it. As a result their ministry is characterized by intellectuality rather than spirituality. The letter of Biblical truth is illuminated, but not properly combined with the Spirit and power of the Word.[17]

Never forget—good exposition and meaningful worship can never be separated.

Obviously, daily time for personal worship is foundational for all believers. This reality makes it paramount for preachers, who claim to speak for God. How can we possibly communicate the reality of God to those who listen to us preach unless we have been in God's presence ourselves? Speaking for God effectively demands that we first spend time alone with Him. Effective expositors cannot afford to minimize the need to develop a sense of humble dependence upon God. We must draw regularly from the strength that comes only from Him, a strength that is derived as we wait before Him on our knees with an open Bible.

Personal worship, then, is not a time for looking for sermons. Although many ideas and helpful insights for sermons may be born there, it is the time for listening for the voice of God to the preacher's personal life. In the closet of communion he learns of God's love, promises, and instructions. Such is a precious time of growing in the Lord. Discipline at this point will enable the preacher of the Word to leave his knees with the joy of the Lord bursting from his heart. The tone of the day will be set, and he then will be ready to give himself to sermon preparation. After meeting with the Lord and basking in the sunshine of His love, the preacher is right with Him and ready to prepare sermons to grow God's people. Such a daily practice keeps the heart free of unconfessed sin and reminds the preacher of the primary business at hand.

SOME HELPFUL HABITS

In his fresh and inspiring book *Fellowship with God,* Jerald White recalled the keen observation of a respected friend who said, "A godly life is

---

17. Unger, *Expository Preaching,* 61.

the result of establishing godly habits."[18] The expositor must discipline himself to develop certain healthy habits regarding communion with the Father if he is to walk in godliness. The following paragraphs contain several suggestions for establishing and maintaining a daily practice of personal worship.

Seek inspiration. Seek regularly the inspiration of those who beckon us to prioritize personal communion with God. In addition to White's volume, numerous works are available that can be used over and over again to inspire you to personal worship. Joseph S. Carroll's *How to Worship Jesus Christ* is a powerful call to the priority of personal communion with God. The books of A. W. Tozer, especially *The Pursuit of God,* are invaluable in developing the practice of private worship. Ruth Paxson's three-volume *Life on the Highest Plane* is another challenging work dealing with the spiritual life. Both James Gilchrist Lawson's *Deeper Experiences of Famous Christians* and Raymond Edman's *They Found the Secret* report the experiences of many great men and women who learned to walk with God in a deeper way. For a book specifically related to prayer, consider reading E. M. Bounds's classic *Power Through Prayer* on a yearly basis in order to remind you of the direct relationship between prayer and the power of God in preaching. The many volumes by Andrew Murray such as *With Christ in the School of Prayer,* John R. Rice's *Prayer: Asking and Receiving,* and the anonymous work *The Kneeling Christian* all will challenge you to pray and help you to properly channel your prayers.

Calendar God. Someone has said that you can determine a man's priorities by looking at his checkbook and his calendar. To be sure, the things on which we spend our money and the things for which we reserve time in our schedules are the things that are dearest to our hearts. If you want to be a man of God, you must put your appointments with Him on your calendar as religiously as you do meetings, counseling sessions, study time, family time, meals, recreation, and other needful activities. He must be your first priority. The difference, furthermore, between communion with God and the other activities on your schedule should be evident in the time allotted. While certain time constraints may affect your daily time with Him, do everything in your power to buffer your meetings with God so as to avoid hurriedness. Take time to enjoy Him, to minister to Him, and to get your life in touch with Him in preparation for subsequent service.

Read intentionally. Although daily devotional guides such as *Our Daily Bread, The Daily Walk,* the works of Mrs. Charles Cowman, Oswald Chambers's *My Utmost for His Highest,* and others can be helpful in nurturing personal worship, the Bible itself should serve as your primary source material.

---

18. Jerald R. White Jr., *Fellowship with God* (Denham Springs, La: Barnabas, 1995), 66.

The Bible is read most profitably when approached in some kind of systematic fashion. Many different methods have been developed and employed. You may read through the Bible systematically during the course of a year. You may choose to read several chapters from the Old Testament and several chapters from the New Testament each day, covering the Old Testament one time and the New Testament several times during a year. Many helpful reading guides that focus on selected passages are available, but the expositor must be careful not to take Scripture out of context even in devotional reading. Regardless of the approach, avoid haphazard and random reading of the Word. Instead, be intentional about hearing His voice.

Let nature take its course. Bible reading is more exciting at some times than at others, but you should not allow the presence or absence of excitement to dictate your motivation. God's Word is daily nourishment. A person's enthusiasm—or lack thereof—about food does not affect nature's growth process. Parents are not able to observe from day to day the growth of their child. When looking at a year-old picture, however, they certainly are able to see how much the child has grown as a result of receiving proper nourishment. Such is the case with Christian growth. The pastor and his church members will grow as they feed on the milk of the Word (see 1 Pet. 2:2). In his helpful booklet on the devotional time entitled *Manna in the Morning,* Stephen Olford describes this practice as the provision of manna for the hungry soul.

Practice "high yield" praying. Like Bible reading, much prayer is done randomly, haphazardly, and selfishly. Get in the habit of intentionally praying in a God-honoring way so as to make the most effective use of your efforts. Talk to Him as you would any other close friend, but be sure to avoid any unjustified familiarity. Begin by loving and adoring Him. At the heart of true worship lies the privilege of believers to be a blessing to God and to minister to Him (see Acts 13:1–2). Thank Him for your salvation, your call to the ministry, the opportunity to serve Him, and all the sources of gratitude that fill your heart on that particular occasion.

Since no Christian can pray for everything that merits prayer, prioritize interceding on behalf of those with whom you have personal contact and to whom you may minister personally as God's answer to prayer. Pray for family members, church members, congregational needs, and fellow preachers. Pray for lost people, boldness for witnessing, and open doors for evangelistic opportunities. Above all, pray the Word of God so as always to be praying according to His will. For example, consider praying through one proverb each day for yourself and your family members, and pray through your weekly preaching text for yourself and your congregation. According to the Bible, this kind of praying is sure to be heard and answered (see John 15:7; 1 John 5:14–15).

THE ANOINTING OF GOD

As the preacher grows confident in God's call and builds upon that foundation strong convictions about God's Word and the practice of intimate personal worship, divine anointing will not be far behind. Such is the lifeline of effective preaching. The anointing is the spiritual fervor that flows through a man in the preaching event. Though the effects of this divine work often are not noticed until the delivery of the sermon, the man of God must build his entire preaching ministry on its presence. Consequently, attention must be given to the need for this anointing long before the sermon-building process begins.

UNDERSTANDING THE ANOINTING

In the area of speech communication, the gospel preacher has an advantage that separates him from all other public communicators. Even secular public speakers can be passionate about their subject matter, but one particular ingredient is reserved solely for the one who speaks the words of God. This ingredient enables the preacher's words to be pointed, sharp, and powerful. This ingredient has been called *anointing*.

Anointed preaching places God into the sermon and on the preacher. When a preacher preaches in the power of God, the results are remarkable. He preaches with inspiration and fullness of thought. He has both freedom and simplicity of utterance. This element of the divine in preaching must be foremost in the preacher's preparation and delivery if he is to be lastingly effective. Criswell retold a story about when the devil was once preaching the gospel. When a saint became alarmed, his fears were quieted with the words "Have no fear, the preaching of the devil will do no good; there is no power in it."[19] No one can preach with power apart from the anointing of the Holy Spirit.

Several Scripture passages describe the role of the Spirit in preaching (e.g., Matt. 10:19–20; 1 Cor. 12:3; Acts 11:15). Of all the references in the Bible, however, the words of Paul in 1 Corinthians 2:1–5 are classic concerning the connection between preacher and audience. Paul began by saying that he did not come to the Corinthian believers with "excellence of speech or of wisdom declaring . . . the testimony of God." In those days the Greek orators were famous for their eloquence and rhetorical display. Beyond question, Paul was well trained and quite capable of eloquence. Yet, he indicated that he did not depend upon an eloquent manner of

19. W. A. Criswell, *The Holy Spirit in Today's World* (Grand Rapids: Zondervan, 1966), 78.

LAYING THE FOUNDATION ♦ 65

speaking to attain results. The naturally gifted preacher must guard against using his own eloquence to get the message across. The result may be that he so adorns what he says that he says nothing at all.

R. G. LEE AND THE HOLY SPIRIT'S ANOINTING

Dr. R. G. Lee, for many years pastor of Bellevue Baptist Church in Memphis, related a personal experience with God's anointing. The incident took place on a Sunday in 1955. About that morning Dr. Lee said: "It seemed as though Someone had wrapped a warm blanket about me. There was a sensation as though Someone's tender fingertips were caressing me, up and down my body." Never before had Dr. Lee experienced such a mysterious feeling. He said to someone that morning: "There is going to be a great day at Bellevue today."

During the service Dr. Lee preached an uncharacteristically brief sermon from John 1:42. He spoke simply, with quiet intensity, and with directness. When the sermon was over, the whole congregation was under the spell of the power of God. The entire body was visibly moved. The invitation was given, and people started to respond. People streamed down the aisle. The service was not concluded until 12:45 P.M. When the day was over, 126 persons had made some kind of decision. That evening Dr. Lee baptized 52 new converts as a result of the morning service. He said: "Nobody can go through a day like this and doubt the reality of the Holy Spirit and His work in convicting people of sin, of righteousness, and of judgment. The movement among people today was as when, in Ezekiel's day, the Valley of Dry Bones became a living army."[20]

In verse 4, Paul continued by saying, "My speech and my preaching were not with persuasive words of human wisdom, but in demonstration of the Spirit and of power." Corinthian speakers were known for their persuasive words and powers of poetic expression. They were spellbinders, able to mesmerize listeners with their learning and oratorical skills. A preacher may impress his hearers with his logic and skill but actually leave them unmoved at the deepest level of their existence. Paul made emphatically clear that effective sermon delivery does not depend upon the skill of the preacher. While we can and must yield our gifts of speech to the Lord, genuinely effective preaching comes only in the demonstration of the Spirit's power.

20. John E. Huss, *Robert G. Lee* (New York: Macmillan, 1948), 196–201.

Spirit-anointed preaching does something to both preacher and people. The anointing keeps the preacher aware of a power not his own. In the best sense of the word, he is "possessed"—caught up in the message by the power of the Spirit. He becomes a channel used by the Holy Spirit. At the same time the people are gripped, moved, convicted. When the Holy Spirit takes over in the preaching event, something miraculous happens.

Serious contemplation of the responsibilities of preaching can be overwhelming. Every sincere preacher is aware of his own weakness and finiteness. He must say with Paul that he has this treasure in a jar of clay (see 2 Cor. 4:7). Only as the Holy Spirit comes upon him can he even dare to attempt this high and noble calling. Few would disagree that Charles Spurgeon preached with such anointing almost weekly in the Metropolitan Tabernacle. Fifteen steps led up to the pulpit. Spurgeon is said to have slowly and methodically mounted those stairs, each time muttering to himself, "I believe in the Holy Ghost."[21]

Anyone who has preached for any period of time knows what it means to preach with and without the power of the Holy Spirit. When the anointing is present, there is power and blessing. When human strength and skill are at the helm, there is nothing. A preacher may preach the same hermeneutically sound and skillfully exegeted sermon on two different occasions with drastically different results. One occasion, clothed in the Spirit's power, is marked by blessing and response. The other occasion, void of His touch, breeds dryness and inaction.

The difference, of course, is the anointing. Nothing is as exhilarating as preaching when the Spirit's anointing is evident. The message soars, words come easily, and the desired results occur. Nothing is harder or more frustrating, however, than when the preacher preaches in his own strength.

This anointing is not something that happens one time and remains upon the preacher forever. The anointing must be sought day by day in the pastor's walk with God, in his preparation process, and in each individual preaching event. As you learn to seek God's anointing, you also will learn to recognize its reality in your life. You may learn to recognize it more by its absence than by its presence. You will know of its presence in your inmost being. As you preach, you will be cognizant that you are a man possessed. You will know God is at work. The people to whom you preach will be aware of the anointing as well. The difference will be immediate and dramatic. They will be gripped by what you say. Conviction, a deep sense of God's presence, and a stirring of their hearts will be evident.

21. John R. W. Stott, *Between Two Worlds* (Grand Rapids: Eerdmans, 1982), 334.

A SPECIAL MEASURE OF DIVINE ANOINTING
A Personal Testimony

In 1976 I was assigned the responsibility to preach at the Alabama Baptist State Evangelism Conference. Several months prior to the meeting I had a definite impression from the Lord to speak on the subject of the ascension of Jesus Christ. I studied every passage in the Bible that dealt with that theme, gathered every bit of information I could on the subject, and read every sermon I could find on the topic. I exhausted every possible resource in preparing this message. Within a month of the time I was to deliver this message, I became aware that God was working in my heart and life in a peculiar way. The theme consumed me. I could hardly stay away from my study. Many nights I stayed up into the wee hours studying and preparing this message. Many, many times God's presence was so overwhelming as I prepared that I actually would weep.

The day came for me to deliver the message. The conference to that point had been average and nothing unusual had happened. I approached my assignment with great fear and trepidation—I almost had a sense of dread. When I began to preach, however, something happened. When I was barely five minutes into the message, the Spirit of God seemed to take complete possession of me. The congregation of mostly preachers was caught up as well. I felt as if I were actually in another world looking on the event. The conference of preachers seemed to be swept along in a flood tide of joy and spiritual excitement. When I finished, we were all aware that God had visited us. Never before nor since have I been so stirred and moved by the Holy Spirit.

In the days and weeks after I preached, the tapes of the message were sent into every state of the Union and many foreign countries. When preachers heard the tape in distant places, the same spiritual phenomenon occurred. Phone calls and letters began to pour in. Preachers at the point of despair were lifted and encouraged. Since that memorable day, hardly a week has passed that I have not heard from someone who has been blessed by the message.

Why has there been such unusual blessing as a result of that sermon? The answer lies in nothing that I did. I have listened to the tape numerous times. The sermon has many flaws, and its delivery is far from good homiletical, rhetorical, and psychological standards. I have only one explanation for the results and effectiveness of the message. The Holy Spirit of God anointed me in a special way on a special occasion for a special task.

OBTAINING THE ANOINTING

The things of the Spirit often are undefinable and, therefore, elusive. Spiritual awakening, for example, is characterized by both the sovereignty of God and the readiness of mankind. The best we can do in longing for it is to align ourselves with those factors that have been present every time it has come in the past. Divine anointing is a similar concept. No one can provide a guaranteed formula for ensuring it in our preaching. The best we can do is look for common denominators that seem always to be present in the lives of those who preach with such spiritual fervor. Several factors can be identified with which the preacher can align himself in order to experience divine anointing.

Be sure and pure. Anointing in the preaching event obviously is reserved for the genuinely born-again preacher. More than one man has preached several years only to discover that he was preaching a message he had never experienced himself. Be sure of your own personal relationship with Jesus Christ.

As one of His children, be sure to walk in purity. Anointing is not reserved for when you stand up to preach. This quality is born as you walk day by day with the Lord and with people. The Bible says, "Be clean, you who bear the vessels of the Lord" (Isa. 52:11). God's Holy Spirit will not anoint and inspire an unclean, unsanctified life. Do not go through even one day without doing a spiritual reality check, and never go to the pulpit without earnestly praying that you will be emptied of all sin and self. You want your life to be clean so that the Lord can work freely through you.

Commune with God regularly. If the Holy Spirit is to come upon you in great power in preaching, you must maintain communion with Him through regular Bible study and prayer. No preacher can be used effectively apart from daily time with God. Spend time alone before the Lord. Let your sermon become a sacrifice. The great Athenian statesman Pericles often said that, so solemn did he deem the act of speaking, he could not begin without an anxious invocation to the immortal gods for their assistance. Surely the gospel preacher should approach the sacred pulpit with as much prayerfulness as would Pericles. To preach a sermon is a great and awesome task. Pity the man who approaches such a holy calling with poor spiritual preparation and a prayerless heart. Bounds lamented:

> The preacher who has never learned in the school of Christ the high and divine act of intercession for his people will never learn the art of preaching, though homiletics be poured into him by the ton, and though he be the

most gifted genius in sermon-making and sermon delivery.[22]

In all your learning, learn how to get hold of God in prayer.

Keep asking for it. Earnestly seek the Spirit's anointing and the passion that comes from His inspiration. Bounds said, "This anointing comes to the preacher not in the study but in the closet."[23]

Diligently ask the Spirit to come upon you and your message. Allow Him to manifest His power in and through you. Never be satisfied with anything less in your preaching. You may not always experience the power of the Holy Spirit in equal measure. For reasons in the realm of the mysterious, there are times when the anointing of the Spirit will come upon you in larger measure than at other times. Sometimes you will be more passionate about certain subjects than about others. That reality is beyond question. But there should be such surrender of life to the Spirit that every time you preach there is the evidence of God's blessing upon you.

And do not think that the Spirit's anointing and inspiration come by means of short, flippant prayer.

> Prayer, much prayer, is the price of preaching unction. Prayer, much prayer, is the sole condition of keeping this anointing. Without unceasing prayer, the anointing never comes to the preacher. Without perseverance in prayer, the anointing, like overkept manna, breeds worms.[24]

Tarry long in asking God to give you His divine anointing.

22. E. M. Bounds, *Power Through Prayer* (N.d.; reprint, Grand Rapids: Baker, 1991), 76 (page citation is to the reprint edition).
23. Ibid., 69.
24. Ibid., 74.

CHAPTER THREE

DEVELOPING
THE PREACHER

*The key question for the shepherd, then, is, How can
I position my life and ministry to break down the
encasements that surround hearts and minds, capture
their attention, and effectively lead them to personal
growth and communal development?*

JOSEPH STOWELL

Preparation is an important element in good expository preaching. The preacher must not only spend time preparing the message, but he also must prepare himself. As the definition of preaching in the first chapter indicates, God's Word is not preached apart from human instrumentality. Both what the preacher is and what he believes play vital roles in sermon preparation. On the foundation of God's call, the Word, worship, and anointing, the preacher must build certain qualities in order to be a healthy expositor.

Consideration of several aspects of personal preparation will make this possible. The contemporary preacher must give attention to the issues of character and integrity, intellectual development, physical fitness, and study habits. The right application of these qualities will serve to make you a better messenger, which, in turn, will enable you to prepare better messages.

A HEALTHY HEART

Effective delivery and reception of the Word are tied to the related concepts of character and integrity. It is interesting that *Merriam Webster's Collegiate Dictionary* uses similar terms to describe both words.[1] *Character* refers to moral excellence and firmness. *Integrity* is the firm adherence to a

---

1. *Merriam Webster's Collegiate Dictionary* (1994), s.v. "character" and "integrity."

code of moral values. In Christian ministry the two words together describe the degree to which a person adheres to God's standard of moral excellence. The preacher must decide whether or not to embrace the biblical emphasis on matching the manner with the message, the life with the lips, what the man is with what the man says. Great strength exists in the silent sermon of a godly life.

CONSEQUENCES OF A HEART CONDITION

Preaching the Bible is an altogether unique enterprise, for God's Word cannot be preached effectively when something is awry in the personal life. God wants His vessel to be clean all the way to the innermost being—all the way to the preacher's heart. A man might teach algebra adequately and yet not pay his bills, but he cannot expound the Word of God effectively and fail to meet his financial obligations. A person might do a great job as a grocery store clerk while living in sexual immorality, but no person can live that way and preach the Word of God with life-giving power. A man's personal life and discipline can make or break his preaching ministry.

To carry it a step further, neither will the Word be *received* effectively when the deliverer is polluted. The author of Proverbs wisely observed that "a righteous man who falters before the wicked is like a murky spring and a polluted well" (Prov. 25:26). Anyone who has lived where wells are the primary source of water knows what happens when one becomes contaminated. The well is not purified. The water is not filtered. Only one thing happens when a well becomes polluted—it is capped! No more water is drawn from a ruined well. That is exactly what happens in ministry. When a preacher—a conduit for the Water of Life—becomes contaminated with the pollution of the world. People stop drinking. Actually, the question is not whether a "fallen" minister ought to be restored and allowed to return to the pulpit. Reality is that people stop listening.

QUALITIES OF A HEALTHY HEART

The Bible is not silent regarding the character and integrity of the preacher. Paul charged young Timothy, "Take heed to yourself and to the doctrine" (1 Tim. 4:16), admonishing him to give attention to these matters as well as to his teaching. First Timothy 3:1–7 and Titus 1:5–9 both provide a heart checkup for the pastor/preacher. Maybe the most intimate and intensely personal passage, however, is found in 1 Thessalonians 2:1–12. Here, the apostle Paul set forth his own convictions about the benchmarks of pastoral leadership characterized by character and integrity. Take a moment to open your Bible and look at that passage. Use the following qualities from Paul's exhortation as your own spiritual benchmark.

God-given mission. Today's image of the successful pastor and effective preacher is of a man who is unusually handsome. He has the voice of an actor and the mind of a scholar. Not so, according to Paul. In the first two verses, Paul indicated that he felt a strong sense of mission. His previous tribulations in Philippi were enough to send weaker men scurrying for home. Why did Paul not give up the mission? The reason is obvious. He felt a commitment to the gospel of God that made him bold under the most difficult circumstances. The work of preaching is no easy task. No shortcuts are acceptable. When you set out to serve the Lord, you can be sure you will encounter many difficult obstacles along the way. Only a sense of mission such as Paul expressed can keep you from going under such circumstances.

Genuine motivation. When Paul referred to "our exhortation," he was not talking simply about a particular message or about his delivery. He was going to the depths of his own motives. In Paul's time, false teachers often moved from place to place, preying on the people. Sadly, we face the same problem today. Charlatans on television and radio have caused large numbers of people to be skeptical of preachers in general. Consequently, our motives must be right. Paul emphatically stated that his preaching was "not of deceit, nor of uncleanness, nor in guile" (v. 3 KJV). He was saying that his message was true, his motives were pure, and his methods were above question.

Nor was he attempting to please men by using flattering words (v. 5). Someone has said that flattery is soft-soaping a person until he cannot see for the suds. Too much flattery is present in modern preaching. Though there is a right place for compliment, we must never flatter those to whom we preach for the sake of personal gain or praise. We must search our hearts to the depths. We must carefully ask ourselves at all times, "Is my preaching genuinely motivated?"

Gentle manner. Paul conducted himself in a "gentle" manner. He had a compassionate and loving heart. The true preacher, like Paul, will assume the following threefold role.

First, Paul was like a *mother* to the people (vv. 7–8). The picture here is actually of a mother in the nursery. She caresses, feeds, and hugs her babies. In the spiritual sense, the true preacher acts in the same manner toward his people. The mother will gladly give her life for her children. Paul would gladly have given his own soul for the people. Real preaching is not only the delivery of a message but a life as well. Preaching is not the performance of an hour; preaching is the outflow of a life.

Second, Paul was a *laborer* (vv. 9–10). His ministry was not confined to a forty-hour week. He poured his life into his labors. The preacher with integrity knows no office hours and punches no time clock. Certainly, you need time for family, recreation, and other vital activities. But personal integrity demands that you be a hard worker. No member of your congregation should work harder at his job than you do at yours.

Third, Paul compared himself to a *father* (vv. 11–12). Along with the tenderness of a mother, the preacher must provide the firmness of a father. Personal integrity demands that you be truthful. Speak lovingly but firmly. Among other things, a father teaches the child how to walk. God's people are children in a royal family. Preachers have a responsibility to teach them how to live the Christian life. Such is a sacred responsibility.

A HEALTHY MIND

A toolbox contains many tools—of all shapes and sizes for all kinds of tasks. The more tools a man has in his toolbox, the more tasks he will be able to accomplish. So it is with the intellectual development of the preacher. Because you have been called upon to preach the Word of God, you must prepare yourself intellectually to the fullest extent of your abilities. No preacher should be satisfied to use only bits and pieces of the intellectual ability with which God has blessed him. Of the many avenues for intellectual development, the effective Bible preacher certainly should give attention to education, examples, and experience.

FORMAL EDUCATION

Certainly, a man may have unusual gifts and bring tremendous blessing without formal education. Many great men of God through the ages had very little formal training. Peter and John were "uneducated and untrained men" (Acts 4:13), indicating that they never attended the schools of the rabbis. Yet who can doubt the spiritual power that flowed from their ministries? John Bunyan, Charles Spurgeon, G. Campbell Morgan, and many others were greatly gifted preachers who had little training in formal schools. No one will ever know, however, the degree of effectiveness these men may have attained had they acquired more tools for their toolboxes through formal training. We may be confident that all of them would urge the would-be preacher to take advantage of every possible means to train himself.

Formal education is a wonderful opportunity for you to hone the gifts God has given you. You will benefit from a broad, general education. Comprehensive studies in the arts and sciences will prove invaluable. Study psychology, history, biology, and sociology. Remember that all truth is God's truth, even though it may not be that which He ordained to be a part of the sanctifying words of Scripture. You need not fear God's truth even when it is found in what may be considered secular sources. Take advantage of every opportunity to receive a thorough liberal arts education. It will provide you with a wonderful intellectual and cultural background for preaching and will prove invaluable in years to come. Academic training will provide a storehouse of useful information for preaching. You will gain a broader understanding of life, and illustrations and methods for applying biblical truth will be stockpiled.

Many theologically sound Bible colleges are enabling students to receive excellent Bible training. Be careful, however, not to let Bible college education deprive you of the breadth needed in your training. In other words, the Bible-college-trained preacher should not confine himself to biblical and theological studies. Such does not have to be the case, for more and more professors who teach in Bible colleges are urging their students to widen their scope of outside reading. Many of these colleges provide in their curricula courses covering a wide range of subjects such as literature, philosophy, psychology, and science.

The preacher should, however, acquire as much specific education in the area of theology and Bible as he possibly can. Herein is the value of Bible college and seminary training. At the heart of expository preaching is the act of "exposing" the truth that has been covered up by differences in language, time, culture, and worldview. The faithful expositor will gain as much knowledge as possible about these and other areas so as to convey the intent of Scripture. For example, acquiring a working knowledge of the original biblical languages is of tremendous value.[2] Being able to find the truth for yourself is fresh and exciting. Confidence and a sense of authority flow out of your study. It certainly is possible to preach effectively without a knowledge of biblical languages, but you will have a great advantage if you are able to use Hebrew and Greek.

The preacher also should be trained in theology, both systematic and biblical. Systematic theology is the correlation of biblical revelation as a whole in order to exhibit systematically the total picture of God's self-revelation.[3] This approach has value in that you are given a framework for understanding Bible doctrine. Biblical theology issues forth from the historically conditioned progress of the self-revelation of God in the Bible.[4] This approach will make you aware that you are dealing with the very

2. Many helps are available today for the preacher with little or no knowledge of the biblical languages. Such volumes as W. E. Vine's *Expository Dictionary of New Testament Words* and A. T. Robertson's *Word Pictures in the New Testament* can be greatly beneficial, but they leave the preacher entirely dependent upon secondary sources.
3. Charles C. Ryrie, *Basic Theology* (Wheaton: Victor, 1986), 14.
4. Ibid.

mind of God in the Holy Scriptures. Biblical theology also will help you avoid the danger of putting all Bible doctrine in neat little compartments.

Formal study in the area of hermeneutics, or Bible interpretation, also is needful. As you learn proper principles of Scripture interpretation, you will learn to avoid "off the wall" interpretations. You will learn the importance of studying Scripture in context. Becoming aware of different interpretations offered for controversial passages will help you avoid enslaving yourself to any man's particular system of interpretation. This area of study also will make you aware of the main interpretations that have been embraced through the years.

Formal training also can provide help in the areas of sermon preparation and delivery. Advances in science and technology have ushered us into a day of fascinating insights and helpful resources in matters of biblical exegesis and sermonic composition. Many new and helpful materials are available to the preaching student. The plethora of Bible study materials on computer, used rightly, can assist in more effective and efficient preparation.[5] The multimedia resources available today can powerfully augment the exposition of God's Word. The wise man will avail himself of every new tool that will help him explain the meaning of the biblical text and persuade people to respond to it.

FAITHFUL EXAMPLES

One of the discouraging trends in theological education today is the increasing number of students who attend Bible college or seminary without having sat under healthy examples of biblical exposition. The church where the young preacher is called to the ministry plays a crucial role in his preparation. A strong, warm church led by a faithful expositor of the Word creates an atmosphere conducive to launching a youthful preacher toward a successful ministry. A cold, skeptical, liberal church, which is accustomed to sermons void of significant Bible content, may greatly cripple a young preacher as he attempts his first steps in the ministry. The pastor should be a positive role model for the budding young man of God. To sit under the ministry of a good, faithful expositor gives a young man a head start in his ministry. The pastor can train him, encourage him, and point him to a good choice for his formal schooling.

---

5. David Lang ("Taming Bible Study Software," *Computing Today*, March/April 1998, 22–24) provides some helpful guidelines for harnessing the power of electronic exegesis and avoiding embarrassing mistakes. Lang counsels students to (1) study verses in context, (2) avoid looking for secret word meanings out of context, (3) study root words carefully and with integrity, (4) check programs for credible sources, and (5) avoid depending upon computers as a substitute for diligent study.

If you are a student in training for ministry, seek out a church where the pastor faithfully expounds the Word of God with integrity. Such a setting is equally as vital (or more so) as finding a place of service in a church while you are in training. The opportunity to listen to and learn from a fine expositor is invaluable for your ministry.

If you are a pastor, seize the opportunity given you by faithfully modeling good Bible exposition for those sitting under you who have been called to ministry or who may yet be called. The mentoring relationship that takes place in the local church cannot be duplicated in the context of formal theological training.

FIELD EXPERIENCE

Regardless of your past intellectual training, you should spend all the days of your ministry studying and preparing to preach. Every day should be a search for general materials for preaching. Be a student of culture and of contemporary life. Read widely and study in as many areas as possible. Keep abreast of the times. Read regularly a good newspaper and several respected magazines that expose you to current events in the local, national, and worldwide arenas. Although you will never be able to read all the books you would like, you can read the book reviews.

Be aware of what is going on in the world of literature, music, movies, and television. You certainly do not need to expose your eyes to any of the trash, but, once again, reviews on all of these media are available. Read biographies and good novels. Read fiction and nonfiction. Stretch your mental capacities. You will be amazed at how this will help you in your sermon preparation and delivery. Read everything worthwhile that you can get your hands on. Francis Bacon said, "Reading maketh a full man." Alexander Whyte, a Scottish minister, advised, "Sell your shirt and buy books."[6]

Be a student of preaching throughout your ministry. Study the lives of the great preachers.[7] Regularly read a book on some aspect of preaching, so as to glean helpful insights as well as to stay abreast of any unhealthy trends in the field. Be constantly studying your own work. Look for new ways to go about your task of preaching. Talk with other preachers. Glean from them their methods of sermon preparation and delivery. Your entire

---

6. William Evans, *How to Prepare Sermons* (Chicago: Moody, 1964), 31.
7. Warren Wiersbe's books *Walking with the Giants* and *Listening to the Giants* are helpful volumes for getting acquainted with some of the great preachers and sermons of the past. Clyde Fant and William Pinson Jr.'s *A Treasury of Great Preaching*, formerly *Twenty Centuries of Great Preaching*, is a classic multivolume set that provides a more extensive look at these areas.

life is a process of intellectually preparing yourself to preach. Bring your finest intellectual efforts to your sermon preparation. Koller rightly said, "A preacher must not preach out of the fullness of his heart and the emptiness of his head."[8]

A HEALTHY BODY

A positive trend has emerged in recent years, especially in America. People are getting into shape. Everywhere you go, you see men and women jogging alongside the roads. Health spas, exercise rooms, tennis courts, and other fitness facilities are doing a booming business. People are more conscious of their eating habits. A proliferation of books is available on the subjects of good physical conditioning and proper diet. Men and women are counting calories, pushing away from the table, and controlling their weight. In the last several years there has been a renewed interest in good health.

This new interest has a good biblical foundation. The Bible teaches the sacredness of the body. The believer's body is the temple of the Holy Spirit, and the well-instructed believer understands he has a responsibility to keep the temple in good shape. The better we care for our bodies, the better we will be able to serve our Lord. Consequently, Christians should be concerned about physical fitness. Several essentials are necessary for such a task—intentionality, exercise, healthy eating, and plenty of rest.

INTENTIONAL EFFORT

Physical fitness is a neglected area for many preachers. Too often the preacher is so involved in the Lord's work and the myriad of activities at his church that he does not take adequate time to tend to the needs of his body. In fact, his message oftentimes loses credibility because of the poor condition of the vessel that is being used to deliver it. Some preachers minimize the importance of physical fitness. They claim that a minister should not waste time in exercise or other forms of recreation. Although you do not have to become an amateur athlete to attend to your physical needs, you are wise to spend some time keeping your body in good condition.

Experience proves that, if you do not find time to maintain physical fitness, you will have to find time for physical illness. Someone has said that the body and the soul live so close together they catch one another's

8. Charles W. Koller, *Expository Preaching Without Notes* (Grand Rapids: Baker, 1962), 44.

diseases. Modern physiology bears out this statement. You cannot benefit one part of your life without benefiting the whole. God intends his servants to have sound minds and healthy bodies. A prepared body helps the preacher to deliver a prepared sermon. The body is the vehicle God uses to communicate His Word to men. Keep your body in good condition. Make it a finely honed tool for God.

REGULAR EXERCISE

We already have determined that many, many hours of your time each day must be devoted to study as part of the sermon preparation process. Most of those hours will be spent in intensive mental labor, a most tiring form of work. One may bounce back from strenuous forms of physical work in a relatively short time. To recover from mental labor quickly is not so easy. For this reason, the preacher needs to plan definite blocks of time for exercise.

Without regular exercise, your body will tire more easily. You will find yourself with no energy. Some form of regular exercise will benefit your cardiovascular system and give you more stamina. Many people enjoy jogging. Thirty minutes per day at least three days per week is a good minimal routine. Other forms of exercise are just as good. Swimming, for example, is a great form of exercise for the entire body, both inside and out. Certain team sports such as basketball give you the benefit of a strenuous workout plus the enjoyment of being with others. Some people like racquetball or golf (no carts, please!). The issue is not so much the form of exercise you engage in as it is that you just do something. Before you begin, go to your doctor for a complete physical. Get his permission to do whatever form of exercise you choose. Even most people who are in poor physical condition can begin to walk for exercise. Walking is a good opportunity for the preacher to be with his wife.

The time you spend exercising will not be wasted time. You will be more productive in your working hours because you take a few minutes each week for physical exercise. You will be able to think more clearly and will find your creative powers heightened.

GOOD EATING HABITS

Eating correctly also helps your physical well-being. The preacher needs to keep his weight under control as well as develop healthy dietary habits. A balanced diet, including all the daily requirements from the various food groups, should keep your weight where you desire. Eat only when you are hungry and avoid snacking between meals. Be careful not to eat excessively after you preach. Normally, tensions are being released immediately after preaching, and greater hunger and thirst often are experienced then more than at any other time. These factors can lead to overindulgence. Also, eating large portions at late hours can contribute to poor sleep and overweight. Keep sweets and breads to a minimum. Cutting down on sugar intake not only will be healthier but also will be very helpful to your throat. Sugar and milk have a tendency to form mucus, which can give you difficulties with your speaking voice. Eat plenty of green, leafy vegetables and be sure you have an adequate intake of bulk.

You do not have to become a health-food faddist; simply give attention to proper eating habits. Not only will these habits be good for your physical well-being, but their effect also will be a positive testimony. How can we tell others Christ can give them power over drugs and alcohol when we seem to have no control over our eating habits?

Numerous Christ-centered dietary programs have been developed in recent years. These have helped many people get a handle on healthy eating habits. Many of them have different areas of concentration. *First Place*, for example, is a program that encourages the development of a healthy diet along with regular exercise and personal Bible study. *The Weigh Down Workshop* is a program that places more emphasis on self-control and adequate portions than on the nature of the foods eaten. This program also incorporates regular Bible study. Regardless of what approach you may take, be aware that resources are available to help the Christian minister develop healthy eating habits.

ADEQUATE REST AND RELAXATION

Most preachers do not get enough rest. For whatever reasons, many are night owls and seem to come alive in the late hours. Such practice obviously makes it harder to get up early in the morning. A conscious effort to go to bed earlier will pay off the following day. Some experts have said that every hour of sleep before midnight is worth two hours after midnight. This theory proves to be true for most people.

The pastor especially needs to get adequate rest on Saturdays. Try to take Saturdays off. Relax your mind completely. Do some things you enjoy doing. Spend some leisurely time with your wife and children. Try not to think too much about your Sunday sermons. Before you go to bed, get alone for a brief time to go over your morning message. Try to saturate your soul with the content of the sermon. Spend some time in prayer, talking to the Lord about the message. Then go to bed for a good night's rest. When Sunday morning comes, you will be rested and ready.

A story is told about the apostle John. A young hunter at Ephesus, returning from the chase with an unstrung bow in his hand, entered John's house. To his amazement, he found the beloved John engaged in playing with a tame dove. The young man expressed his astonishment that the apostle was so lightly engaged. John, looking gently at him, asked him why he carried his bow unstrung. The young man replied that it was only in this way that the bow retained its elasticity. Even so, John told him, mind and body will not retain their elasticity or usefulness unless they are at times unstrung.

Even if fictitious, this story aptly illustrates the importance of physical rest, relaxation, and recreation. Prolonged tension destroys the power of mind and body. Be diligent about giving your body time to unwind. Such effort will improve the time you spend on sermon preparation.

A HEALTHY ROUTINE

Probably the most familiar aspect of sermon preparation takes place in the preacher's study. The work that is done there is paramount for solid Bible exposition. Paul urged young Timothy, "Be diligent to present yourself approved to God, a worker who does not need to be ashamed, rightly dividing the word of truth" (2 Tim. 2:15).

Again, a word of balance is in order. All theory and no experience makes for an unreal preacher. Do not cloister yourself in your study and fail to relate to the outside world. The preacher who comes from his ivory tower to the pulpit on Sunday morning will lack the ring of reality in what he has to say. Constantly test your studies in the crucible of daily life and ministry. But keeping this caution in mind, be sure to prioritize and protect the time to do the hard work of biblical exposition. You will do well to develop discipline for study, protect your time and place for study, and intentionally build a personal library of functional study tools.

DISCIPLINE

Discipline for study is a nonnegotiable. At the risk of sounding trite, let it be said that the primary thing the Bible expositor must remember is to approach this part of the process *prepared* to study. The easiest thing in the world for a preacher to do is waste time under the guise of studying. You face the constant danger of laziness within your study walls. Although most preachers are free to plan and organize their own daily schedules, many hours can be wasted in the study. Just because you are sitting at your desk for a period of hours, do not suppose this guarantees that you are actually studying.

Stott tells the story of a young preacher who did not study as he should. He frequently bragged to his deacons that his messages were prepared between the time he left the parsonage in the morning and the time he arrived at the door of the church. No wonder his deacons decided to buy him a new home five miles away![9]

Take whatever steps necessary to develop the discipline of study. Read materials on time management. Use some kind of monthly, weekly, and daily planner to schedule specific times and tasks for studying. As you read the biographies of great preachers, note the various ways they mapped out their study time. Then develop an approach that works for you.

One approach might be to prepare on Monday morning a half sheet of paper divided into the days of the week. At the bottom of the page put down your study requirements for the week. You may have a Sunday morning and a Sunday evening message to prepare. In addition, you may need to prepare for an outside speaking engagement. Then arrange on a daily basis the time you will spend preparing for each message.

You may set aside two hours each morning for the Sunday morning message, one hour for the Sunday night message, and another hour for the other speaking engagement. Or you may schedule longer times of preparation for different messages on different days. Though you may not necessarily follow the schedule to the minute, you are preparing some kind of time structure for each day. You may have to experiment with several methods before landing on one that fits your personality and ministry context, but arranging a schedule will be helpful as you prepare to study each day.

A good preacher will continue to be a student throughout his life. Spurgeon said, "He who has ceased to learn has ceased to teach. He who no longer sows in the study will no more reap in the pulpit."[10] Continue to study, and you will continue to be fresh and interesting. As you study, you will find messages springing from your soul like water bubbling from a fountain. Many preachers have expressed regret toward the close of their ministries that they had studied so little. Donald Grey Barnhouse said, "If I had only three years to serve the Lord, I would spend two of them studying and preparing."[11] If you give yourself to study, you will never lack something to say. Your people will know it and appreciate it if you do, and they will quickly know it and resent it if you do not. A workman not ashamed is a workman who disciplines himself to study.

In addition to your scheduled study time, find all the additional time you can. If you can snatch an extra hour in the afternoon, do it. Though

9. John R. W. Stott, *Between Two Worlds* (Grand Rapids: Eerdmans, 1982), 211.
10. C. H. Spurgeon, *An All-Round Ministry* (Carlisle, Pa: Banner of Truth, 1960), 236.
11. Donald Grey Barnhouse, quoted in Stott, *Between Two Worlds*, 181.

you will keep most of your books in your study, you will want to have books at other places. Have a good book in your church office. Keep a book at your bedside. When you travel, throw a book into your suitcase. Strive for variety in your reading matter. Everything you read will be helpful information for your sermons.

As you grow in your experience as a Bible expositor, both the amount of time needed for study and the way that time is spent may need to be adjusted. The more you study the Bible systematically, the more you will grow in your general knowledge of God's Word. That knowledge will begin to inform your study of every passage in every sermon. You will discover that you will depend less and less on commentaries and study tools as you store up knowledge gleaned from previous study of the same passages, themes, authors, and doctrines. Such is another advantage to following the expository process.

Do not be too quick to assume such knowledge, however. Let this process run its natural course. Furthermore, though the amount of time you need to analyze a text may decrease, the amount of time you spend bridging the gap to the contemporary world, praying, and doing other spiritual preparation likely will increase.

PROTECTION

Disciplined study habits will be enhanced greatly if the preacher's time and location for study are protected. Often the structure of the particular church and home will determine this matter. Most congregations provide a study at the church that doubles as the pastor's office. Such a locale can be used if no other place is available, but you will find study extremely difficult when much activity is going on. Well-meaning members of the congregation inevitably will come by to visit for a few moments, which often stretch into an hour or more. A better situation is to have your study in a secluded place, away from the traffic flow.

Some men use an out-of-the-way place at the church as a study. Or, if an extra room is available and your church leadership is agreeable, use a room at your house. There you will be away from the activities at the church. Whichever is the case, find some way tactfully to protect yourself from phone calls and other interruptions. Answering systems make this possible even when no secretary or family member is available.

Most congregations are willing to accommodate the preacher's study needs, especially when they begin to reap the benefit of good Bible exposition. Lovingly and patiently explain to your people the nature of and reason for your study needs. Tell them you want to be the best preacher for them you possibly can be and that you desire to preach God's Word faithfully to them. Explain that in order to do so you need uninterrupted study time. At the same time, assure them of your availability in case of emergency and prove to them your diligence in ministry when you are not studying. The people likely will be understanding and patient. They gladly will adjust to whatever changes need to be made. The obvious difference in the pulpit will give them an understanding of the value of your protected study.

You need to establish regular times for study. Mornings seem to be best for most preachers. For years, W. A. Criswell wisely has counseled young preachers to "keep the mornings for God."[12] He calls on pastors to protect the first hours of the day for study, prayer, and preparation. Martyn Lloyd-Jones, however, was correct when he said that no universal rules exist about the time of study. Each man must know himself. Many a preacher seems to do best at night. Each man's body will differ in these matters.[13]

The morning hours do have some definite advantages, especially if you have children who are in school. Studying in the morning will make you more accessible to them after school and in the evenings. If you have preschool children, however, just the opposite may be true. Time given to the kids early in the day may be a better investment, allowing you to study in the afternoon during their nap time or in the evening after they have gone to bed. The afternoon and evening hours also are better for tending to administrative matters and making home visits.

RESOURCES

You will need several items in the study to make your time most efficient and effective. A good desk obviously is important. See that you have plenty of shelves for your books. Make sure the lighting is the best possible. The walls should be thick enough to keep out noise. All circumstances cannot be ideal in every situation, but do your best to make your room as conducive to good study as you possibly can.

Constantly be in the process of building a good library. Be careful not to neglect the many helpful resources that serve as tools to help you mine the treasures of Scripture. To claim with a hyperspiritual attitude that all one needs is the Bible and the Holy Spirit in order to preach is a grave error. To be sure, these two resources are nonnegotiables for solid exposition, and God certainly may choose to use them alone under certain circumstances. But such a claim demands that God speak only on our terms and conditions. Furthermore, this arrogant suggestion all but de-

12. W. A. Criswell, *W. A. Criswell's Sermon Preparation in His Study* (Dallas: The Criswell Foundation, 1997), videotape.
13. D. Martyn Lloyd-Jones, *Preaching and Preachers* (Grand Rapids: Zondervan, 1971), 167.

nies His ability to have spoken to students of the Bible who have gone before us or who serve as our contemporaries. In reality, the preacher who makes such a claim usually is making advance excuse for laziness and poor preaching. Spurgeon warned preachers about such negligence:

> Of course, you are not such wiseacres as to think or say that you can expound Scripture without assistance from the works of divines and learned men who have labored before you in the field of exposition. If you are of that opinion, pray remain so, for you are not worth the trouble of conversion, and like a little coterie who think with you, would resent the attempt as an insult to your infallibility. It seems odd, that certain men who talk so much of what the Holy Spirit reveals to themselves, should think so little of what he has revealed to others.[14]

Because the expositor is interested in finding out what the Holy Spirit is saying in every passage of Scripture he studies, he should use every available means in order to make such a determination.

Several resources are basic for general Bible study. One foundational tool is probably already lying around the house of every Christian—*various Bible translations.* You can begin your library by gathering these different versions of the Bible. Work as much as possible with the text of the original languages and your own translation of them. Beyond those texts, work primarily with several literal translations that best maintain the basic syntax of the original language. The King James, *New King James,* and *New American Standard* are all good for this purpose. Use some of the newer translations for clarity of meaning and intent. The *New International Version* and the *New English Bible* are good in this area. Good paraphrases such as *The Living Bible,* J. B. Phillips's *Paraphrase of the New Testament,* and Eugene Peterson's *The Message* can give additional insights and provide new understanding of familiar passages. While you do not have to endorse everything in paraphrases, they can be helpful when used alongside literal translations. One of the many multitranslation volumes available can enable you to see at a glance what several major translators have done with a particular passage.

An *exhaustive Bible concordance* will enable you to search out each word in a particular verse as well as locate other places in the Bible where a particular word is used. This tool is helpful in doing cross-reference work on a particular passage. A *Bible atlas* is important for understanding the geography of the Bible lands and certain other kinds of Bible facts. A

14. Charles H. Spurgeon, *Commenting and Commentaries* (Edinburgh: Banner of Truth, 1969), 1.

Bible dictionary is helpful for understanding the meaning of particular words. If you do not understand the meaning of a word, you are likely to misunderstand the meaning of the verse where the word is used. A *Bible encyclopedia* is a similar tool, used for acquiring information on a broader range of subjects. Although some of these works are also called "dictionaries," they provide more detail about Bible terms, places, people, and backgrounds in the form of articles.

Basic *English language tools* are always needful at various stages of the sermon preparation process. An English dictionary sometimes is needed in conjunction with more technical theological works. A dictionary of synonyms and a thesaurus will provide you with variety in the words you use in your sermons. *Word study tools* provide more information on word meanings, etymology, and usage. Lexicons furnish similar information but with more technical and exhaustive detail. Other *specialized tools* are designed to supply more detailed or focused study. Books on figures of speech in the Bible, Bible characters, and other topics are also available to assist with specific studies.

Various *Bible commentaries* are beneficial for gleaning the insights God has granted other individuals. The beginning Bible expositor will no doubt want to purchase at least one complete set of Old Testament commentaries and one complete set of New Testament commentaries to ensure that he has something on every book of the Bible. The best way to buy commentaries, however, is to purchase individual books by good expositors. When preaching on Romans, for instance, try to find the best volumes available on that book. No one man has done the best work on every book of the Bible. To be sure, some of the classic volumes are found within commentary sets. Many of the best works, however, are individual volumes. Find the best books on the particular Bible book from which you are preaching.

Consult lists of suggested works by respected expositors. Look for other book lists provided by seminaries and within volumes on preaching. Call acquaintances who practice Bible exposition and ask for the names of their favorite works. Survey the shelves of the bookstores, especially the used ones. Tap into the many discount book clubs via subscrip-

15. For a thorough discussion of study tools for expository preaching, including a list of suggested works for building a beginning expositor's library, see James F. Stitzinger, "Study Tools for Expository Preaching," in John McArthur Jr., *Rediscovering Expository Preaching*, ed. Richard L. Mayhue (Dallas: Word, 1992), 177–208. A similar list may be found on the Internet at http://www.mastersem.edu/750books.htm. Also, see Bruce Corley, Steve Lemke, and Grant Lovejoy, *Biblical Hermeneutics: A Comprehensive Introduction to Interpreting Scripture* (Nashville: Broadman & Holman, 1996), 385–416, and D. Edmond Hiebert, *An Introduction to the New Testament*, vols. 1–3 (Chicago: Moody, 1975/1977.

tion, newsletters, and Internet. Find every available means to get your hands on the best works on the Bible book you are studying.

Be intentional and methodical about acquiring the best tools for study.[15] Some pastors take pride in acquiring large numbers of books that serve no purpose other than to look impressive in one's study. If certain books are never read or do not contribute to the preacher's work, they simply take up space that could be used for something more functional. Fill your shelves with books that are helpful and needful. Such intentionality is both good stewardship and common sense.

The preacher who does expository work will constantly be adding information to his store of knowledge. Everything you see, read, or hear is potential material for sermon preparation. Continually be filling your sermon barrel. Harper Shannon said that preaching from the overflow was an artesian well where the water flows steadily but the great reservoir of water is underneath the earth. If the well flows year in and year out in the small stream, one can rest assured that there are hundreds of thousands of gallons of water underneath the earth that are never seen. This is a good description of the process of studying to preach.[16]

As the years go by, you will develop a great reservoir of sermon material. As you prepare sermons week by week, you will be able to draw from this ever increasing supply. This discipline is one way the preacher can avoid the problem of being set aside in the latter years of his ministry. The preacher who maintains his study habits will have something fresh and relevant to say. He will never lack an audience.

---

16. Harper Shannon, *Trumpets in the Morning* (Nashville: Broadman, 1969), 58.

PART TWO

THE PROCESS OF EXPOSITION

CHAPTER 4: Analyzing the Text

Instigation
Investigation
Interpretation
Implication

CHAPTER 5: Unifying the Theme

The Intended Audience
The Central Idea of the Text
The Proposition
The Purpose
The Title

CHAPTER 6: Designing the Structure

The Necessity of Structure
The Creation of the Design

CHAPTER 7: Maturing the Ideas

Amplification
Incubation

CHAPTER 8: Building the Sermon

Writing the Manuscript
Developing the Parts

"Thus saith the Lord . . ." That phrase frequently has been used to summarize the preaching event—and rightly so. In one sense, preaching simply is speaking on God's behalf. Such a task has huge ramifications. Every word the preacher speaks, whether he attributes it to God or not, is received by the audience as being the mandate of heaven. What a responsibility! The implications, then, demand that the preacher do everything within his power to ensure that his sermon reflect accurately that which God actually has spoken. In other words, an extremely close relationship must exist between the text of Scripture and the sermon.

This part of Power in the Pulpit is aimed at helping the preacher maintain a high degree of similarity between text and sermon. Our interest here is good exegesis that culminates in good homiletics. Exegesis draws out the meaning of a passage and correctly represents it. Homiletics takes that representation and packages it in a clear and persuasive manner. The process of exposition begins with solid exegesis and winds up with an appealing sermon, one in which the preacher confidently can claim, "Thus saith the Lord."

CHAPTER FOUR

ANALYZING
THE TEXT

And now the end has come. So listen to my piece of advice:
exegesis, exegesis, and yet more exegesis! Keep to the Word,
to the scripture that has been given to us.

KARL BARTH

The expositor's first and highest responsibility in dealing with the biblical text is to discover—insofar as possible—what the Holy Spirit was saying when He inspired a particular passage of Scripture. The first stage of the process of exposition is given to this end. Many different approaches have been proposed for analyzing a Scripture passage. To simplify this part of the process of exposition as much as possible, we will adopt a fourfold approach: instigation, investigation, interpretation, and implication.[1]

INSTIGATION

The first stage of analyzing a text of Scripture is *instigation*. At the beginning of the process, we are asking the simple question, Where do I

---

1. Irving L. Jensen, *Enjoy Your Bible* (Chicago: Moody, 1969), 60. Jensen suggested analyzing a passage in three stages: (1) Observe, asking, "What does the passage say?" (2) Interpret, asking, "What does the passage mean?" and (3) Apply, asking, "How does this apply to today?" Another helpful approach can be found in Walter C. Kaiser Jr., *Toward an Exegetical Theology* (Grand Rapids: Baker, 1981), 43. Kaiser provided the seven steps in the analysis of a passage as arranged by Victor Paul Furnish: (1) Formulate the main points of the passage. Discover from the passage itself the main points. (2) Either note what is problematical in the passage or compare various translations to see if there is any major disagreement. (3) Identify key words or concepts found in the passage. (4) List any historical, literary, or theological problems that are apparent in the text. (5) Prepare a tentative outline for the passage in keeping with its overall context. (6) Refer to parallel Bible passages or other related literature where ideas similar to the ones found in the passage appear. (7) Record in note form whatever wider implications the passage may contain.

start? The process of exposition begins with preparing your people for expository preaching and then choosing the text you plan to expound.

STEP #1: PREPARE YOUR PEOPLE

After you have committed yourself to preach expositorily, your eagerness to be about the task may cause you to overlook an important step of preparation. While mentally *you* are ready to go, your congregation may never have heard such preaching, especially if you are going to preach systematically through a Bible book. Many congregations have been fed through the years a regular diet of topical preaching. Unless your people have been blessed with a Bible expositor for their shepherd, you may be the first pastor they have ever heard who actually preaches what the Bible says.

This adjustment will stretch your people. Expository sermons will be a different kind of sermon to them. Many may not even be in the habit of bringing their Bibles to the services. You will have to train them to do so. You can do this by asking them at the beginning of your message if they have their Bibles. After a period of time, as you preach paragraph by paragraph, you will know the joy of watching people habitually carry their Bibles. You also will experience the thrill of hearing the sweet sound of rustling pages as you announce your sermon text.

Understand, however, that a congregation that has been accustomed to topical preaching at first may not seem thrilled with this new approach. The different method may be a radical change for them. It may take several weeks or even months for them to get on the same wavelength. Nonetheless, stay the course! Before long they will make the adjustment and be completely hooked. Jesus said that kingdom citizens continually hunger and thirst after righteousness (cf. Matt. 5:6). As you feed them the truth of God's Word, that nourishment will incite a longing for more and more. Furthermore, once a congregation gets accustomed to systematic exposition through books of the Bible, they will never again be satisfied with anything else. Be assured, you will always have an audience when you preach expositorily.

STEP #2: CHOOSE YOUR TEXT

After preparing your people, the time has come for you to choose the text from which you will preach. The way you choose a preaching passage will largely depend upon whether you are going to do general or systematic exposition.

General exposition. We previously determined that general exposition involves preaching expository sermons on Bible texts that are not necessarily consecutive passages or exhaustive treatments of an entire Bible book.

This preaching approach usually begins with a sermon idea. Sermon ideas may originate from almost any arena as long as the preacher determines that the subject is addressed substantively by some biblical text. Several of the most common sources for finding sermon ideas are discussed below.

The *biblical text* itself obviously provides the richest and safest treasury of appropriate preaching subjects. As long as the passage is treated rightly, you can choose any Bible passage and be sure that you have a legitimate word from God (even if you do not have a warm, fuzzy feeling!). Texts that inform the great doctrines, stories about real people, and numerous spiritual and practical themes all provide rich material for general exposition.

Human needs are another fine source for sermon ideas. The problems and struggles that people face on a day-to-day basis often are directly addressed in the Word of God. The preacher must constantly be a student of the human experience through his daily encounters with people, counseling situations, church-related activities, and current events on a local, national, and worldwide basis.[2]

Several words of caution need to be offered here, however. Make sure the Bible speaks to the human need you want to address. Remember, do not dare to put words in God's mouth! Also make sure that particular human need is shared by a significant number of people in your congregation. Some human situations are better addressed in individual or small-group contexts. Finally, do not turn your pulpit into a therapy session. Though counseling has a legitimate place in Christian ministry, it is distinct in many regards from the preaching event. Everyone would agree that one of the worst things a pastor can do in a counseling session is to "preach" to the person who has come for counseling. At the same time, an equally detestable act is for that pastor to go into his pulpit and conduct large-group counseling. The primary purpose of the preaching event is not to ask a lot of questions but to give a lot of answers.

A third arena from which sermon ideas can be drawn is *congregational situations.* Part of the prophetic office and gift has always involved addressing the corporate life of God's people with His Word. As the pastor leads his congregation, certain situations will arise from time to time that need to be addressed with a message from God. These situations might involve crisis, tragedy, or disobedience. Whatever the case, you as pastor will want to bring God's perspective to bear on the situation. The corporate life of the body of Christ frequently will drive the preacher into the Word in search of God's voice.

2. Al Fasol, *Essentials for Biblical Preaching* (Grand Rapids: Baker, 1989), 29–30.

The preacher's *personal experience* will also provide him with a wealth of possible preaching ideas. To be sure, the preacher never speaks on the authority of personal experience but on the authority of God's Word. His personal experience, however, may serve as a springboard to discovering what God says about a particular issue. Personal devotions, spiritual victories and failures, crises, flashes of inspiration, reading, and general lessons about life all may serve as a seedbed for preaching subjects. As the Word of God is allowed to measure and evaluate each experience, the personal flavor heightens the preacher's understanding and passion regarding the subject.

In considering all the possible arenas in which sermon ideas may be discovered, you must keep one important truth in mind:

> A SERMON IDEA IS NOT NECESSARILY
> EQUIVALENT TO BIBLICAL TRUTH!

The preacher of the gospel has not been called to speak on every issue under the sun. He has been called to proclaim God's truth as it is revealed in Scripture. Consequently, just because you have a sermon idea does not necessarily mean you have a preaching subject. Always take your sermon idea to the biblical text to see whether or not God has spoken on that particular subject in some definitive way. If He has spoken, then locate the relevant text or texts and move ahead with your preparation process. If He has not spoken, then avoid sacrificing your preaching ministry on such a subject.

Furthermore, if you think the Bible addresses a particular subject in a text but discover in your study that the text does not say what you thought it said, then you have two options: (1) set your subject aside and preach the text, or (2) find another text that truly addresses the topic. The action you must avoid at all costs is making a text say something it does not say.

Systematic exposition. Systematic exposition, we determined, is the consecutive and exhaustive treatment of a book of the Bible or extended portions thereof. Once again, going through the Bible books chapter by chapter and paragraph by paragraph will be the best preaching you do. Plan to dedicate at least one of your pulpit times each week to such a study. Your other preaching times may be given to general exposition on doctrine or other Bible topics. The systematic approach, however, is foundational for the local church pastor. Consequently, we will assume the systematic approach from this point forward in our discussion. Essentially, all of the principles for systematic exposition of a Bible book apply to general exposition from different passages.

Instead of finding a sermon idea and locating a text that addresses it, the first task in systematic exposition is determining which book of the Bible to use. The following guidelines will be helpful in this task.

Choose your book carefully. Your best starting point will be with a book that is relatively simple and comparatively short. Do not start with Revelation or Ezekiel! Choose a practical book rather than a doctrinal one. For example, think about the book of James. That book has only five chapters and abounds with practical application to today's world. Or you might want to use Philippians, which has only four chapters. There are few doctrinal nuts to crack, and you can move on to something else in four to six weeks if you get in trouble!

AVOIDING BOOK BOGDOWN
A Personal Testimony

One of the reasons I took several years to get into the expository method was an unfortunate experience in my first pastorate. My home pastor preached through books of the Bible. I really enjoyed hearing that method. In my first rural church, I decided I would follow suit. However, I was an eighteen-year-old boy. I owned only one book beside the Bible. I had never done more than speak at a few youth gatherings. I decided to begin a series of messages through the book of Romans. I had no commentaries on Romans. All I had was a Bible and an eager heart.

The first week I read and read and reread Romans 1. Although I struggled, a twenty-minute message was prepared from the first chapter. The next week was even harder. It was all I could do to get something to say from the second chapter. Those sixteen weeks, preparing one message per chapter through Romans, were the most miserable weeks of my life. I was scared away from book-by-book preaching for many years. I tell you this to urge you to choose the book carefully.

Jerry Vines

Choose your book according to need. Ask yourself, *What do my people need?* As you study your congregation, you will see many areas where they need Bible teaching and admonition. Find a Bible book that addresses those needs. This approach enables you to preach to the problems of your people without singling out individuals. As you proceed through a book of the Bible, the people will expect you to interpret and apply the book as it stands.

Choose your book prayerfully. Just as you ask God to lead you to prepare one message, so you should ask Him to lead you to prepare a series of messages from a book in the Bible. Go to Him in prayer and see if there is a particular book He wants you to use. If so, He will direct you accordingly, and you can be confident of His guidance to the particular place in His Word. If not, you can be confident that He gives you the freedom to preach from any part of the Bible. Whichever is the case, your people will be edified and blessed. As you move through the book, you will be thrilled to see God work. Needs you never dreamed would surface in the lives of your people will be addressed by the passage of Scripture from which you are preaching.

One other matter in beginning a book series needs to be noted. The introductory sermon is highly important. That message helps prepare the people for the entire series. Here the pace is set for all the messages. Sometimes a bird's-eye view of the book is a good way to begin. Arouse as much interest as possible in the book. Whet their appetites but do not give them the entire message of the book in the first sermon. Throw in just enough tidbits to create a sense of anticipation.

As you preach through books of the Bible, a new adventure in Bible study with your congregation will be yours. Both preacher and people will be caught up in the awareness of coming in contact with the very mind of God. You will discover that God is alive and is speaking in your day. The people to whom you introduce the expository method will rise up and call you blessed.

INVESTIGATION

After you have prayerfully examined the needs of the people and selected an appropriate book, you come to the second stage of the expositional process—*investigation*. Here we are answering the question, What does the Scripture passage say? This stage is fundamental in the process, for we cannot determine what Scripture means until we know what Scripture says. Three steps are suggested for investigating what a passage says.

STEP #1: DO A BACKGROUND STUDY

Whether you are preaching from a single passage or systematically through a Bible book, always begin with the "big picture" of the preaching text. Such a picture is gleaned from a thorough background study of the book in which your passage is located and that book's relationship to the rest of the Bible.

A common problem in expository sermonizing is that too much exegesis has failed to "map the route between the actual determination of the authentic meaning and the delivery of that word to modern men and women who ask that that meaning be translated into some kind of normative application or significance for their lives."[3] The expositor, therefore, must bridge the gap between exegetical studies and the preparation of a message that will be helpful and practical to contemporary listeners. The only way to accomplish this task is first to understand the historical side of the bridge. The historical setting, the customs of the times, the political and religious conditions all are involved in an adequate understanding of a passage of Scripture.

To do a background study, consult six to eight good sources on each of the areas discussed below. These might include commentary introductions, Old and New Testament surveys, Bible dictionaries, Bible encyclopedias, Bible handbooks, and even some good study Bibles. As you read each author's treatment of the subject, summarize helpful information from each work. Then step back and compare your summaries to see where the weight of the evidence lies. Look for common emphases, helpful insights, and pertinent details. Record these observations in a concluding paragraph under that particular category. Follow the same procedure for each of the following categories of background information.

Biblical context. The expository preacher should have a working knowledge of the various books of the Bible.[4] Knowing the particular stage of revelation of a particular passage affects proper understanding. God's truth is unfolded progressively throughout the Bible, and failure to recognize that is the cause of many tragic misinterpretations. Bible doctrine is not built on Old Testament revelation alone but on the entire revelation of God. Consequently, we must be keenly aware of the stage of revelation in which our particular Scripture passage is found.

A book's location in the canon may be crucial for understanding its nature. Bible books often are divided into certain categories that provide clues to their respective makeup. The first seventeen books of the Bible

---

3. Walter C. Kaiser Jr., *Toward an Exegetical Theology*, 88.
4. Several books are helpful in gaining an overview of each Bible book. John Phillips's *Exploring the Scriptures* is a good one-volume survey of the books of the Bible. He gives a brief, pertinent introduction to each book as well as a helpful outline and a few brief paragraphs summarizing the book's contents. A larger, more extensive work is J. Sidlow Baxter's four-volume *Explore the Book*. Baxter provides helpful introductory material on each book as well as valuable insights and clues that aid in understanding.

(Genesis through 2 Chronicles) are historical in nature. The next five books (Job through Song of Solomon) are books of poetry. The last seventeen books of the Old Testament are books of prophecy (Isaiah through Malachi). In the New Testament, the first five books (Matthew through Acts) are historical. The next twenty-one are letters (Romans through Jude). The last book (Revelation) is apocalyptic in nature.

Authorship/speaker. Determining who wrote the book under consideration, whenever possible, can be tremendously helpful. Ask yourself, Who is the speaker? Who wrote the words I am reading? What kind of person was he? Because each writer wrote in the context of his personality, environment, and culture, understanding these factors frequently will provide the key to understanding the meaning of certain passages.

For example, knowing that Matthew was a tax collector is helpful information. His practice of dealing with details probably contributed to his detailed notes on the Sermon on the Mount. As a Jew, Matthew naturally sought to relate Old Testament prophecies to the coming of the Messiah.[5] Such information becomes important when you try to determine the reason for his detailed genealogy (1:1–17) and other attempts throughout the book to prove that Jesus of Nazareth had the legal right to the throne of Israel.

As you begin to deal with individual passages within the book, you also will want to ascertain the particular speaker in each passage if the individual is different from the author of the book. For instance, to remember that Jesus is the speaker in the Sermon on the Mount is as important—or more important—as understanding that Matthew recorded the words.

Date. Knowing the time period in which a particular book was written can help the expositor avoid gross misunderstanding. Ask, What is the importance of the subject matter's being written at that particular time? The date of Isaiah, for instance, will determine whether the material (especially chapters 40–66) is viewed as messianic or reflective. Words in 1 John take on an entirely new significance when you learn that they were written during a period when Gnostics were claiming special knowledge. John's emphasis upon "know" appears in a different light altogether. Although the time of writing is not as crucial as some other aspects of the background study, awareness of where the book fits into history can provide some important clues for understanding. The date of the book is especially important for understanding passages that deal with specific cultural settings.

Setting. Knowing something about the *people* who first read the pas-

5. Fasol, *Biblical Preaching*, 53.

sage also is pertinent data. Matters such as the place of writing and the reason for writing often make the text come alive. Ask, To whom were these words originally addressed? Who were they? What do I know about them? Why was it important for them to read these words? For example, to know that Paul's second letter to Timothy was written to a struggling young pastor highlights the many exhortations and words of encouragement in the book.

Be concerned about the *place* in which the passage was written or takes place. Ask, Do we know where it was written? Is there any significance to that particular place? When you know that Bethel means "the house of God," the fact that Jacob spent the night at Bethel (Gen. 28:10–22) has increased significance. To know that the letter of 2 Timothy was written from a prison dungeon from which Paul likely was never released helps the emotion and passion of the writer to surface.

The *occasion* that called for the verses to be written is also important. Try to determine the circumstances surrounding the book's writing. Paul's letter to the Galatians becomes more intelligible when we understand that his apostleship was under attack. We are better able to understand the change from his normal introduction when we know this information. Be interested in the purpose of the passage. Ask, What is the writer trying to accomplish? What truth is he seeking to convey? What error is he seeking to correct? What encouragement is he trying to give?

Knowing the writer's particular *interest* is always important. Robinson said, "What a writer means in any specific paragraph or chapter can be determined basically by fitting it into the larger argument of the book. This is the broad context."[6] Do not attempt to expound a book of the Bible without first understanding the basic truths and emphases that are made. Know the plan of each Bible writer in putting his book together. To understand that Paul, a Jewish Christian, wrote Ephesians to Gentiles who were feeling inferior makes the first three chapters of the epistle make so much more sense. When you understand the author's plan and his approach, many otherwise obscure details will become understandable.

Literary genre. When you are studying in a particular book of the Bible, know its literary form. An awareness of a book's location in the canon often is a clue to its type of literature. The historical books obviously recount God's activity with man in narrative fashion. The books of poetry have literary nuances all their own. The books of prophecy contain specific literary devices. The letters are still another form of written communication. The apocalyptic literature is probably the most complicated

6. Haddon W. Robinson, *Biblical Preaching* (Grand Rapids: Baker, 1980), 58.

of all the genres. When you are studying a particular book of the Bible, always spend some time familiarizing yourself with its literary form.[7]

THE LITERATURE OF THE BIBLE

Prose—This form is the normal daily speech of mankind. Most of the conversational texts in the Bible as well as the epistles fall into this category.

Poetry—One third of the Old Testament is poetry. Old Testament poetry does not rhyme. Rather, the expressions contain a parallelism of ideas. The Psalms and the Song of Solomon are poetic books.

Historical Narrative—This type of literature is present in the four gospels and in the book of Acts, as well as in several books in the first part of the Old Testament.

Wisdom—Much of this literature is reflective and philosophical in nature. Such books as Proverbs and Ecclesiastes fall into this category.

Apocalyptic—This kind of literature is rich in symbolism. We are specifically told that the book of Revelation is written in this manner (see Rev. 1:1). Parts of Ezekiel and Daniel also contain such material.

Prophetic—Although prophetic material can be considered a species of prose, this literature has a nature of its own. Making up approximately 22 percent of the Bible, prophetic material is largely sermonic in nature and can have both immediate and future relevance.

Parables—Parables are a type of comparative literature that utilizes story. These stories contain an element of reality and are intended either to clarify a spiritual truth or deliberately leave the hearer with a certain amount of confusion.

Special subjects. Other background subjects germane to individual books may arise as you begin your study. For example, some familiarity with the political and religious conditions during the time of Judges will make that book much more understandable. In Judges 21:25 we are told, "In those days there was no king in Israel: everyone did what was right in

---

7. Some helpful resources for studying the various literary genres of the Bible include Kaiser, *Toward an Exegetical Theology;* Gordon D. Fee and Douglas Stuart, *How to Read the Bible for All Its Worth* (Grand Rapids: Zondervan, 1982); Sidney Greidanus, *The Modern Preacher and the Ancient Text* (Grand Rapids: Eerdmans, 1988); and Donald L. Hamilton, *Homiletical Handbook* (Nashville: Broadman, 1992).

his own eyes." This statement illuminates all of the material in the book. A study of 1 Corinthians may lead you to investigate the mystery religions. The backgrounds of Colossians and 1 John may prompt you to read up on Gnosticism. Do as much backgrounds study as you possibly can. All these details will combine to enhance and inform even your general reading of the biblical text. Furthermore, once you have done a background study on a particular book, you will need only to review and update it next time you preach from that book.

STEP #2: CARVE OUT THE CONTEXT

After you have looked at the background of the Bible book, consider how your passage relates to the book's overall organization. To illustrate, imagine yourself looking at a block of wood. Pick up the block and turn it from side to side, over and over. Examine it carefully. Upon close examination you will find certain natural divisions in the block. When the natural divisions are found, crack the block of wood at those places. Perhaps you find two, maybe three, maybe four natural divisions in the wood. Following the natural divisions, you are able to crack the block into those sections and divide it according to its nature.

An entire book of the Bible, such as Romans, can be analyzed like a block of wood. A careful study of the sixteen chapters of Romans reveals three main divisions, just like the natural divisions in the wood block. Chapters 1–8 group together, chapters 9–11 make up a second group, and chapters 12–16 comprise a third group. The first division (1–8) may be labeled *doctrinal,* the second division (9–11) may be labeled *parenthetical,* and the third division (12–16) may be labeled *practical.* This gives us a neat, simple analysis of the entire book of Romans.

Now back to our block of wood. Take one of the smaller sections, such as chapters 1–8, and look further for natural divisions. Look for the natural divisions of subject and thought patterns. Again, crack the block of wood into these smaller divisions. Likely, you will find three major subdivisions, which might be labeled *sin* (1–3), *salvation* (3–5), and *sanctification* (6–8). Each of these subdivisions may be broken down into even shorter preaching passages. When the process is over, our block of wood is now in neat piles of kindling.

Take some time to see how your preaching text is related to the larger context of the book. The observations you glean here likely will set you on a solid path toward good interpretation.

STEP #3: READ, READ, READ!

Once you see the big picture of the book from which you will be preaching, the third step in your investigation is to read the Scripture. At this point, no reference books will be consulted. No word study will be done. The process involves only you, God, and His Word. You merely are giving yourself to a thoughtful and thorough reading of your text. Often the preacher rushes on to do the technical work and passes over the simple, apparent truths of the passage. Richard Moulton commented:

> We have done almost everything that is possible with these Hebrew and Greek writings. We have overlaid them, clause by clause, with exhaustive commentaries; we have translated them, revised the translations, and quarreled over the revisions. . . . There is yet one thing left to do with the Bible: *simply to read it* [italics added].[8]

As you read, jot down insights that you glean. Approach your reading in the following ways:

Read repeatedly. If you are going to preach through a book, read that book again and again before starting your series. G. Campbell Morgan, remember, often read a book fifty times before starting his expository work. As you read the book over and over, you will begin to get a feel for the content, a sense of the author's flow of thought, and an awareness of the main arguments.

Once you have read the book enough to get an overall impression of its contents, begin your week-by-week work with a particular preaching paragraph. Normally you will find several verses that seem to hang together and give promise of a helpful message for your people. The paragraphs will vary in length according to the flow of ideas in them. You may find help at this point in a good reference Bible that divides the text into paragraphs. Many Greek New Testaments also have the text divided in this way. You may or may not use these paragraph divisions, but choose your passage based upon the author's unified thought blocks.

Once you have determined your preaching passage, read it repeatedly as you did the entire book. If you are able, translate the verses from the original language and read that translation over and over again. If your knowledge of the biblical languages is more limited, find several reliable English versions and use them.

Read prayerfully. Because the Bible is the inspired Word of God, your reading should be done with the deepest reverence. The same Holy Spirit who inspired men to write the Bible will illuminate your mind, assisting

---

8. Richard G. Moulton, *A Short Introduction to the Literature of the Bible* (Boston: D.C. Heath, 1901), iii–iv.

you to understand what you read. Before you read, pray for guidance. As you read, remain in an attitude of expectant prayer and allow this exercise to be a time of communion with the Father.

Now take your prayerful reading a step further. As you begin to glean what the Holy Spirit is saying in a passage, pray the truth of the text for yourself and for those who will hear you. Such a practice does three things. First, you begin to internalize and personalize the truth that you will proclaim. Second, you begin early in the preparation process to identify the text with your listeners. Third, you engage in the most powerful kind of prayer—that which is according to the will of God. This kind of reading and praying lays the foundation for some powerful preaching!

Read carefully. Do not be in a hurry. Take as much time as is necessary. Read the text as a traveler. The traveler journeys slowly in order to absorb everything available to his senses. He looks at the magnificent scenery, the interesting sights, and the people of the land. When the journey is over, he knows where he has been and what he has seen. The preacher must read his Bible this way.[9] As you read, revisit the information you dug up in your background study. Learn to ask questions of your Scripture passage. The six words *who, what, when, where, how,* and *why* are indispensable tools as you read. Answer as many of these questions as possible with the information you learn about authorship, date, purpose, occasion, audience, and the like.

Read contemplatively. When reading your passage, stop from time to time and put your mind to work on it. Allow your thoughts to travel down many avenues. Suck the verses as a child does an orange. Chew on the passage as a cow does its cud. Give time for subconscious incubation. During the reading process, take time to meditate and allow your mind sufficient time to really work into the passage.

Read imaginatively. Use your imagination as you read. Imagination can take a familiar truth, bring it to life, and give a new sense of impact and excitement.[10] Put yourself into the passage and imagine you are actually there. Role-play the different characters involved. Read the verses aloud and try to imagine the tone of voice and the inflection of each speaker.

Do not go to the extreme of being frivolous or concocting details that become determinative for understanding the passage. Simply allow yourself to live what is being taught. Employ sanctified imagination by clothing the passage with contemporary points of reference. If you are reading the parable of the Prodigal Son, bring him into the contemporary culture. Visu-

9. Ibid.
10. Chevis F. Horne, *Dynamic Preaching* (Nashville: Broadman, 1983), 52.

alize him as he gets into his Lexus and drives away from his father's west Texas ranch on his way to Las Vegas. The use of imagination can make the difference between a good preacher and an average preacher.

Read purposefully. As you read, remember that you are moving toward a particular purpose—that of finding out what the passage means and how it applies to you and your people. See if you can begin to identify the subject of the passage. In a preliminary way, your reading should point you toward discovering the unifying theme and basic structure of the passage.

The unifying theme is the central idea that controls, or drives, the whole thought of the passage. The structure is determined by those natural divisions in the text (remember the block of wood?) that likely will serve you well later as a sermon design. Normally, the unifying theme and main divisions will become clearer later in the process, but do not hesitate to begin looking for them at this point. Many times a clear design begins to emerge after a few readings.

Several clues will be useful as you move toward a discovery of the meaning of the passage. Look for repetitions of terms, phrases, clauses, or sentences as seen in 1 Corinthians 13 with the word "love." The word "therefore" always will point us backward or forward. The word "but" is often a *corner* word in Scripture. You are walking down one road in Scripture, then you come to this "corner" and suddenly find yourself on another road. In Ephesians 2:1–3, for example, Paul makes a radical change in verse 4, where we read, "But God . . ." What a change! Quite frequently these kinds of clues will be the hinges upon which turn beautiful interpretations and explanations.

Look for other kinds of movement in the passage as well. Sometimes transitional statements conclude one argument and introduce another. Also be aware of any change of person speaking or being spoken to. Look in the passage for any progression or successive stages of argument. Often a change in time, location, or setting will be a clue to understanding a text, especially in the narrative passages in the Bible.

Purpose clauses, indicated by words and phrases such as "that," "in order that," and "so that" frequently point toward a natural flow of thought and a very good sermon design. Philippians 3:8–11 contains a couple of purpose clauses that are followed by lists of desired conditions. Sometimes the purpose clauses are progressive; they reveal different stages culminating in a particular intended goal. Ephesians 1:15–23 and 3:14–19 both contain successive series of purpose clauses that lead to a more mature knowledge of God.

Other helpful information can surface in a careful reading of the text. Be watching for any naming of examples or instances. Look within the passage for illustrations of the truth that is being presented. Sometimes a passage will give a cumulative selection of ideas or teachings. Often, ideas are compared or grouped together in a passage. Look for contrasting ideas. Sometimes a passage will give cause-and-effect relationships. Sometimes your reading will reveal a rhetorical question used effectively. For example, Malachi's repeated use of "Wherein?" is an important clue to determining what he is saying.

Be looking for what details the particular Bible writer has selected and how those details are arranged. In the four gospels, no single writer includes all the details in the life of Christ. Ask yourself, Why did each writer choose what he did include? What purpose is he seeking to accomplish by the inclusion or exclusion of certain details?

Sometimes the writer himself will give us a clue as to the meaning of the passage. John, for example, tells us why he included the particular miracles in his gospel (John 20:30–31). The reader is helped if he will remember John's purpose as he reads each of the miracles recorded. In his first letter, John states several reasons for that epistle's composition. These reasons provide vital clues to the meaning of his material. John also gives the key to the meaning of Revelation at the very beginning of that book (see Rev. 1:19).

Read obediently. Once you begin to get a preliminary idea about the gist of the passage, one final approach should be employed in your general reading. Read the text obediently. As you read the Scripture, your own heart will be confronted with many truths. The preacher must never confront his people with Bible truths that he himself has refused to face in his own life. The Bible admonishes, "Be doers of the word, and not hearers only, deceiving yourselves" (James 1:22). Studying the Word of God in order to preach it to others is a deeply searching matter. The pastor's own life will be rebuked, challenged, and expanded weekly. Be willing to allow your soul to be exposed to the teachings of the Word of God.

INTERPRETATION

After determining what the passage says, we turn our attention to the third stage of analysis. Here we will seek to answer the question, *What does the passage mean?* This question takes us into the area of hermeneutics, or interpretation. At this stage, our expository work will become very detailed. Every conceivable method of interpreting the meaning of the passage will be explored.

No stone must be left unturned. Remember, our purpose is to find—insofar as possible—the Spirit's intended meaning of the Scripture passage. We must never be satisfied simply with what we *think* the passage means. Paul said in 2 Timothy 2:15 that we are to divide rightly the Word of truth. The phrase *rightly dividing* actually means "cutting straight." The phrase was used in classical Greek of a surgeon's use of a knife. The least deviation meant death to the patient.[11] We are dealing with issues of life and death to those who listen to us preach.

STEP #1: MINIMIZE THE SUBJECTIVITY

The first step toward properly interpreting a passage of Scripture actually is not something you do but something you embrace. The expositor must be careful to approach the text of the Bible with a sound exegetical paradigm if he is to interpret it with integrity. Tremendous care must be taken in order to attain biblical integrity.

The goal in determining how to approach the process of interpretation must be to minimize subjectivity as much as possible. To be sure, as long as God chooses to use human instruments in the preaching event, some element of subjectivity always will be present. Because we are imperfect beings, we forever will bring to the biblical text certain biases, preconceived ideas, cultural influences, limited worldviews, and other factors that shape our hermeneutical paradigms.

Some have suggested that the presence of such variables prevents any man's being certain about the meaning of any text. The best we can do, they say, is to determine what a particular text "means to me." Nothing could be further from the truth.

Would a loving God, who desires to redeem His creation, call His messengers to say "Thus saith the Lord" and then make it impossible (or even a long shot) for them to know what He is saying? After inspiring His holy Word, could God actually be seated on His throne amused by His chosen servants' efforts at solving an unsolvable puzzle? Such suggestions are preposterous and strike at the character of God.

Although proper interpretation is hard work and requires careful consideration, the vast majority of texts in the Bible can be understood clearly and certainly. Consequently, God's preachers can stand and confidently proclaim His Word. The expositor's task, then, is to reduce the subjective element—the human element—as much as possible during the interpretation process.

Many older hermeneutics and homiletics textbooks often referred to the *grammatico-historical* method of exegesis as being best for reducing subjectivity and arriving at proper interpretation. The aim of this method

---

11. Merrill F. Unger, *Principle of Expository Preaching* (Grand Rapids: Zondervan, 1955), 164–65.

was to determine the meaning of the text by application of the laws of grammar and the available facts of history.

Kaiser proposed a new name for the process: the *syntactical-theological* method. He suggested that two key parts were crucial for proper understanding: (1) The way the words are put together in a passage as well as the meanings of the words themselves aid the interpreter in the discovery of the author's meaning; (2) biblical theology helps the interpreter know how antecedent revelation informed the understanding and intent of the writer of the passage under consideration.[12]

The expositor should not be concerned as much with what the method is called as with the concerns that inform the methodology. In fact, Kaiser himself admitted that if the term were not so awkward and clumsy, the truth of the matter is that the method should be called *grammatical-contextual-historical-syntactical-theological-cultural* exegesis, for each of these concerns, and more, must participate in the exegetical venture [italics added].[13] In other words, the subjective element in the process of interpretation is reduced to the greatest degree when the interpreter takes each of these components into consideration.

Each of these concerns will help you to rely on objective rather than subjective information in understanding your preaching text. The grammar and syntax of the original languages are the primary vehicle through which the revelation was given. The historical and cultural settings, which you already have identified in your background study, provide the backdrop for understanding what the words meant to the original audience. Both biblical and systematic theology serve to align your interpretation with the rest of Scripture.

The context of a particular passage holds you accountable for extracting meaning from a passage in its relationship to other revelation. All of these components will be considered as you continue the process of interpretation.

STEP #2: STUDY THE CONTEXT

A key ingredient in determining the meaning of a passage of Scripture is contextual analysis. Exposition demands that we be familiar with all aspects of the context in which a particular element of truth was given. You must determine how your passage fits in with the overall context of the book in which it is found, as well as with the total revelation and message of the Bible. Someone has rightly said, "A text without context is pretext."

12. Kaiser, *Toward an Exegetical Theology*, 89–90..
13. Ibid, 90.

Many doctrinal errors occur because the context of a Scripture passage is ignored or misunderstood.

The word *context* comes from two Latin words: *con,* meaning "with" or "together," and *texere,* which means "to weave." The context has to do with something woven together. For the purpose of this study, context is defined as that part of a discourse in which the passage occurs. The context guides us in explaining the meaning of the passage.[14] The part must be seen in relationship to the whole.

In order to accomplish this task, first revisit any notes you made during the investigation stage of your exegetical process. Your background study, general reading of the Bible book, and closer reading of the preaching text all will contribute to your understanding of the immediate and larger context of the passage. Your background study may have turned you on to particular theological or doctrinal developments as well as to historical and cultural nuances. Your repetitive reading certainly provided you with an awareness of the flow of the book and the connectedness of its component parts. All of this information will help you to see your particular preaching paragraph in proper perspective.

Next, give close attention to the connection of your passage with the immediate context. No member or part of an organism, however minute, can be explained adequately apart from its relation to the whole. Even so, every paragraph of Scripture has a connection with its totality. Carefully consider the verses immediately preceding and following the passage. Never lift a paragraph or individual verses from their contextual setting. A paragraph must be studied in relation to the thought that runs through an entire section. Sometimes a text will appear to be totally unrelated to what has been previously said. Careful examination, however, will reveal that the idea is indeed related in some way.

At this point, broaden your consideration of the passage's context. If you have not already done so, consider the entire chapter in which the passage is located as well as the surrounding chapters. Look for the same kinds of connections as before. Then review the context of the entire Bible book to see if your background study informs the passage in any way.

Finally, study your passage in relation to the whole revelation of the Bible. Donald Grey Barnhouse illustrated this by means of an inverted pyramid. He said the particular passage you are studying is like a point on a straight line. The entire revelation of the Bible is like an inverted pyramid that is brought to bear upon that single point. Consequently, if your interpretation of a particular passage contradicts the clear teaching of the

14. Unger, 142.

whole Bible, you may safely assume that your interpretation is astray.

CONTEXTUAL CONNECTIONS

Milton S. Terry suggested four types of connections between a passage and its immediate context.[15] Look for these connections when analyzing the context of a passage:

Historical. Look for connections of events or facts in the passage. Certain times of the year, for example, can give insight into the meaning of a Scripture passage. If the events in a particular passage occurred during the Passover, you should gather some information on the Passover. Then you can determine the significance of such a reference.

Theological. Some doctrine may be stated in this particular section. Your preaching paragraph may be an integral part of this theological argument. Paul's statement "You have fallen from grace" in Galatians 5:4 easily becomes a proof text for a whole new system of theology unless it is considered in its proper context. Paul is arguing that someone who embraces justification by the Law must be prepared to keep the whole Law in detail in order to maintain salvation. That person cuts himself off from the system of grace, which Paul here simply describes as "grace." Thus, the reference is not to the personal experience of God's free, unmerited mercy and life but to the gospel system of salvation in Christ.

Logical. The writer may be building a particular line of truth. The paragraph under your consideration may be part of this development.

Psychological. Something stated in the verses prior to the paragraph under consideration may have led the author to the particular thought now being expressed in your preaching paragraph.

This understanding is very helpful in explaining the meaning of certain obscure passages in the Bible. What is obscure must be interpreted by what is clear. That which is briefly mentioned must be interpreted by that which is distinctly, clearly, and abundantly expressed throughout the Word of God. Never allow yourself to be robbed of the value of what you

15. Milton S. Terry, *Biblical Hermeneutics: A Treatise on the Interpretation of the Old and New Testaments* (New York: Phillips & Hunt, 1890; reprint, Grand Rapids: Zondervan, 1964), 218–19.

do understand by something that you do not understand. The one is founded upon knowledge; the other is based upon ignorance.

STEP #3: EXAMINE THE STRUCTURE

The consideration of context prepares the expositor to examine the structure of the text. Consider the block of wood discussed earlier. You have "carved out" the entire book; now try to carve out your particular passage in the same manner. Look at your passage as a smaller block of wood to be divided into its natural divisions. Finding those natural divisions actually will give you a head start on sermon construction. Now imagine yourself as a shade-tree mechanic in an auto parts store. As you look for a part for your car engine, consider the exploded diagram found in the automotive reference book. This diagram shows each part of your motor separately as well as how each one fits with the whole motor. Because each item is labeled, you are able to locate your part quickly and determine how it fits into your engine. Look at your text as an exploded diagram. As you analyze it, explode the whole into constituent parts and label each one. This process of analysis gives you an overall view of the contents of your text.

For this task, utilize what has been called variously a structural diagram, block diagram, mechanical layout, or syntactical display. The idea is to re-create the text visually, phrase by phrase, in its exact word order. This exercise helps to show the relationship of various ideas in the text in graphic form.[16] Such a representation enables you to see the thought flow of the biblical writer as it was given by the Holy Spirit. If you are not able to do the exercise using the original language, be sure to use a literal English translation such as the *King James, New King James, American Standard,* or *New American Standard.*

Because of the distinctive nature of the various literary genres, ideas are communicated through language in different ways. The structure of the discourses found in Bible speeches and epistles, for example, must be viewed differently from that of narrative or verse. Therefore, analyzing the structure of a text may require different approaches. The general guidelines below should be employed for the primary Bible genres. Examples of each process may be found in Appendix 1.

---

16. Wayne McDill, *The 12 Essential Skills for Great Preaching* (Nashville: Broadman & Holman, 1994), 27.

SCRIPTURE SCULPTURING

For Prose:

Begin independent clauses in the paragraph at the left margin of a sheet of paper.

Place supporting phrases, clauses, and words directly under (or over) the words to which they relate.

Vertically line up any series of parallel words, phrases, or thoughts.

Place connectives (*and, but, or,* etc.) in brackets above or adjacent to the respective clause.

Place parentheses around italicized words and forms of address.

For Story:

Begin each verse of the story at the left margin of a sheet of paper.

Underline and label the major components (setting, scenes, characters, plot, etc.).

Circle connectors and other transitional indicators (*and, then, but, now,* etc.).

Divide the text according to movements in the plot (life situation, conflict, climax, resolution, application).

For Poetry:

Begin each verse of the poetry segment at the left margin of a sheet of paper.

Identify the type of Hebrew parallelism within each verse, and vertically line up any series of parallel ideas.

Divide the text into groups of ideas, mood changes, or other apparent shifts of thought.

You may choose to modify your approach in order to accomplish the same purpose. For example, try to determine the core of each sentence in your preaching paragraph by identifying the main subjects, verbs, and objects. Lay out the entire paragraph in visual form by diagramming each sentence. This representation will enable you readily to see the structure of each sentence. Indent, underline, or circle such clues as repetitions, comparisons, and progressions; then, tie them together by drawing lines from one to another.[17]

17. Jensen, *Enjoy Your Bible,* 77.

The layout will give you a picture of the entire passage. Often such a visual re-creation will help you to see the unifying theme and supporting divisions very quickly. The procedure is especially helpful in showing the repetitions that occur as well as the relationship of each section to the whole paragraph.

One of the expositor's most difficult assignments is analyzing the manner in which the supporting propositions in a paragraph relate to one another around a single theme. Some kind of structural analysis often supplies many clues that lead toward the discovery of this single idea. Time spent doing such work will pay rich dividends. Frequently, a sermon design will begin to appear at this point in the analysis process. Your best preaching will be done when your sermon design flows directly out of the structure of the text. Remember, if the Bible is the inspired and inerrant Word of God, preaching should reflect that revelation as closely as possible.

STEP #4: DO WORD STUDIES

Once you have a handle on the structure of the text, give attention to specific words and the relationships between words in the text. Word studies can help the expositor determine the literal meaning of the text by revealing the simple, plain, obvious, and literal sense of the words, phrases, clauses, and sentences of the passage. Never minimize the use of a particular word. Jensen said,

> Just as a great door swings on small hinges, the important theological statements of the Bible often depend upon even the smallest words, such as prepositions and articles. Using another picture, one writer has said that as the smallest dewdrop on the meadow at night has a star sleeping in its bosom, so the most insignificant passage of Scripture has in it a shining truth.[18]

Therefore, follow the steps below when doing word studies:

First, read through the passage in the original language in keeping with your ability. Greek especially abounds in beautiful word pictures. A veritable treasure-house of preaching material may be found in the meanings of some of these words.

Depending upon the length of the text, you may want to examine each word. If the passage is lengthy, however, simply look for the main words. If you do not have a working knowledge of the original languages, do not be dissuaded. Simply identify the words in a good English text and

---

18. Ibid, 96.

utilize some of the many tools available to help in word studies (see note 15 in chapter 3 for suggested resources).

Second, look up the meaning of the words in the original languages, using lexical aids, theological dictionaries, and other tools. Find the definition of each term in the passage and exactly how it is used in the present context. Sometimes the original meaning of a word is absolutely essential to the interpretation of the passage.[19] Also look for root meanings to determine the presence of any preaching suggestions.

Third, determine how the word was used by the person who wrote it. Many times this usage can be discovered by comparing it with other passages where the writer used the same word. Be aware that the same words frequently are used with different meanings in different books of the Bible and by different authors. Each writer may have a particular way in which he uses a word.

Fourth, determine the grammatical use of the word. See if a particular word is used in contrast with other words in your passage. The contrast between "flesh" and "Spirit" in Romans 8:5–8, for example, provides a fruitful preaching passage.

Fifth, be aware of cultural usage. Your background study may have enlightened you to particular cultural terms used in the book you are studying. Be aware of special idioms and rare words employed in your text. Every language has particular modes of expression and methods of phrasing that are peculiar to that language. In Genesis 2:17, for instance, we read, "You shall surely die." Literally translated, the phrase means "a dying you shall die." This expression is an idiom, peculiar to the Hebrew language, that affects our understanding of this passage.[20] Sometimes insight can be gained even by finding a word's usage in extrabiblical literature.[21]

Sixth, determine the biblical emphasis on a word. Using an exhaustive concordance, check the number of occurrences in the Bible. Try to find how the word is most frequently used. Compare Old and New Testament usage. See how much import Scripture places on the term.

Seventh, analyze figurative language. Figures of speech add warmth, color, and life to any language, including that of the Bible. Always begin by taking words in their literal meaning. Unger wrote:

> When the plain sense of Scripture makes common sense, seek no other sense; therefore, take every word at its primary, usual, literal meaning, unless

19. Unger, *Expository Preaching,* 120.
20. Ibid.
21. A good resource for extrabiblical word usage is James H. Moulton and George Milligan, *The Vocabulary of the Greek New Testament.*

it is patently a rhetorical figure or unless the immediate context, studied carefully in the light of related passages and axiomatic and fundamental truths, clearly points otherwise.[22]

FIGURING OUT THE FIGURES

How Do I Know If It's Literal or Figurative?[23]

♦ Does the literal understanding create a mismatch in the sentence? (In the statement "God is our Rock," the animate subject God is identified with the inanimate predicate noun Rock.)

♦ Does the literal understanding make the statement absurd or contradictory to the rest of revelation or the usual order of creation? ("The mountains clapped their hands.")

♦ Is there a reason for using a figure of speech at this point in the passage? A heightened feeling? Some dramatic emphasis? A mnemonic device?

♦ Is there an example and/or corresponding explanation of the figure of speech elsewhere? In the same sentence? (". . . the sword of the Spirit, which is the word of God.") In the same passage? (The "seven golden lampstands" in Revelation 1:12 are defined in verse 20 as the "seven churches.") In the same book? (The "Root of David" in Revelation 5:5 is identified as Jesus in 22:16.) In other writings by the same author? (Paul's employment of athletic and military imagery is best understood by reading his usage throughout his writings.) In another passage of the same literary genre? (A hint to the meaning of the sealed scroll throughout Revelation can be found in the apocalyptic literature of Daniel 12:8–9.) In another part of the Bible? (The "light of the world" metaphor in Matthew 5:14 is clarified in John 8:12.)

What Do I Look For?

Simile—an imaginative comparison usually using *so, like,* or *as.* ("As the deer pants for the water brook, so pants my soul for you"; "He shall be like a tree planted by rivers of water.")

Metaphor—an implied likeness in which *so, like,* or *as* are omitted. ("You are the salt of the earth"; "You are the light of the world.")

22. Unger, *Expository Preaching,* 176.
23. Adapted from Kaiser, *Toward an Exegetical Theology,* 122–23. Further help in interpreting figurative language can be found in E. W. Bullinger, *Figures of Speech Used in the Bible: Explained and Illustrated* (1898; reprint, Grand Rapids: Baker, 1968).

Paradox—a seemingly absurd or contradictory statement that catches the attention. ("Whoever desires to save his life will lose it, and whoever loses his life for My sake will find it.")

Hyperbole—an exaggeration used to emphasize a point. ("It is easier for a camel to go through the eye of a needle than for a rich man to enter the kingdom of God.")

Synecdoche—a part used for the whole or the whole used for a part. ("All the world should be registered.")

Metonymy—one noun exchanged for a related noun. ("They have Moses and the prophets" = the books these men wrote.)

Irony—words used to convey the opposite meaning. ("The man has become like one of Us.")

Euphemism—an exchange of earthy words or concepts for gentler ones. ("Attending to his needs" = going to the bathroom.)

Sometimes the words cannot be taken literally, as when an understanding proves to be absurd and inconsistent with the other parts of the sentence. Other times, the literal understanding does violence to the nature of the subject being discussed. When this occurs, look for a figurative meaning in the terminology. Ask yourself: If I take the meaning to be literal, will this be consistent with the general content of the passage? Does a literal meaning coincide with the historical material or the doctrinal subject found in the passage? This process will help you to avoid some absurd interpretations.

After you have thoroughly considered selected words and phrases in the passage, give some attention to grammar. Words do not occur in isolation but in relation to one another. Look to see if the verbs are in the past, present, or future tense. Be sensitive to the relation of the words to one another. If you are unable fully to understand the syntactical relationships of the passage, check a word-study volume such as A. T. Robertson's *Word Pictures in the New Testament*. The way the words are put together may reveal the author's meaning.

STEP #5: CHECK CROSS-REFERENCES

One of the best methods of interpreting Scripture is to allow Scripture to interpret itself. A good way to accomplish this goal is to check cross-references. This task will enable you to discover what other passages of Scripture say about the subjects discussed in your passage. At this point, the concept of contextual analysis is carried to its practical application.

You are drawing from the entire Word of God what is said about any particular subject.

If the theme of your Scripture passage is grace, find out what other texts have to say about grace. Check the word grace in your exhaustive concordance, topical Bible, or some other specialized tool such as *The Treasury of Scripture Knowledge* (Revell, 1973).[24] Read all the references on grace and allow Scripture to interpret Scripture. A learned Bible scholar gave a copy of his commentary on Matthew to his gardener. A few days later the scholar asked the man, "What do you think about my commentary on Matthew?" His Bible-taught gardener replied, "Doctor, the Bible sure does throw a lot of light on your commentary!" Very few passages in the Bible cannot be explained or made much clearer by other passages.

STEP #6: CONSIDER PRINCIPLES OF REVELATION

Now determine how the text under consideration relates to the rest of biblical revelation. A failure to do so can cause the expositor to go astray in adequately expounding what the passage actually means. Several principles are helpful for rightly understanding a text.

The *ethnic division* principle is important for understanding the primary audience and determining proper application. In 1 Corinthians 10:32, the entire human race is divided into three categories: the Jew, the Gentile, and the church. All Scripture is addressed to one of these three categories. Always ask when reading a passage, To whom was this written? Much misinterpretation is due to a failure to distinguish between passages written specifically to the Jews and those written to the church. Although all Scripture has bearing on our lives, not all is necessarily addressed to us. The ethnic division principle will help you avoid misapplying the many Old Testament prophecies addressed to the nation Israel. Literal promises were given to the Jewish people, and they have been or will be fulfilled literally. Although those things written in the Old Testament are helpful for our learning and bring patience and comfort to our lives (see Rom. 15:4), we must not appropriate promises that were given specifically to the Jewish nation.

The *first mention* principle reminds the interpreter that often the first time a subject is mentioned in Scripture is the key to its meaning. In Genesis 3:1 the Bible mentions the serpent, or Satan, for the first time. We are told that he is very "cunning." This reference sets the tone for scriptural information on Satan throughout the Bible. Furthermore, the first men-

---

24. This work lists 500,000 Scripture references and parallel passages and is an extremely helpful book for doing cross-reference work.

tion principle becomes important throughout the entire book of Genesis. Consequently, some scholars have referred to Genesis as the seed plot of the Bible.

It becomes necessary to employ the *full mention* principle when subjects are given one comprehensive treatment somewhere in the Bible. A fairly comprehensive understanding of faith can be gained from a careful study of Hebrews 11. Love is mentioned quite comprehensively in 1 Corinthians 13. Sometimes God declares His full revelation on a particular subject in one place in the Bible.

The *proportionate mention* principle calls the interpreter's attention to the amount of space given in Scripture to a particular theme. Because truth out of proportion can become error, we must be sure that we magnify those truths that Scripture magnifies. We also must avoid dwelling on truths that are mentioned only briefly. Many false doctrines, and even entire denominations, have resulted from failing to maintain this balance.

The principle of *repeated mention* reminds the interpreter that sometimes God's truth is revealed in an evolutionary fashion in the Bible. Often the Holy Spirit will first give only the bare outline of a subject. Then, as the subject is repeated again and again, added details are included. The reader will be fascinated to see how the recurrence of certain truths adds new information throughout the total revelation of the Bible. Many, many doctrines open up like a flower throughout various passages of Scripture.

The *gap* principle often sheds light on otherwise confusing passages. On occasion God ignores certain periods of time, leaping over many centuries without comment. Isaiah 61:1–2, for example, obviously is messianic in nature. These verses give a beautiful picture of the characteristics of the ministry of our Lord. In verse 2, Isaiah says the Messiah would come "to proclaim the acceptable year of the Lord, and the day of vengeance of our God." But between the phrases "to proclaim the acceptable year of the Lord" and "the day of vengeance of our God" many centuries would pass, as indicated by Jesus' use of the prophecy in the synagogue in Nazareth (see Luke 4:17–20). When He came to the phrase "to preach the acceptable year of the Lord," He closed the book and said, "This day is this Scripture fulfilled in your ears" (Luke 4:21 KJV). By so doing, Jesus clearly indicated that His first coming fulfilled only the first part of the prophecy. The second part will be fulfilled when He comes again.

The *salvation/fellowship* principle frequently helps the interpreter to determine whether a passage should be applied to Christians, non-Christians, or both. Scripture distinguishes between being in God's family and in God's fellowship. If a Scripture passage deals with salvation, we understand the verses in one way. If the verses have to do with the matter of fellowship, however, we understand them in another way. This principle is important in accurately interpreting such passages as John 15. Is this a salvation or a fellowship passage? If we are dealing with a salvation passage, then the verses suggest that a person can lose his or her salvation. But that implication most surely contradicts one of the greatest, most fundamental truths in the entire Scriptures. Obviously, then, the passage is about the matter of fellowship. Jesus is not talking about the loss of salvation. He is speaking about maintaining fellowship with Him, an activity essential to bearing fruit.

The *threefold* principle recognizes that God's great truth of salvation is presented in a threefold way: *justification* presents the past aspect, *sanctification* presents the present process, and *glorification* sets forth the future dimension. A person can be biblically correct in saying, "I have been saved; I am being saved; I will be saved." Looking closely at a passage to determine which stage of the salvation event is being referenced can prevent the expositor from creating doubt and confusion in the minds of the listeners. Paul's instruction, for example, to "work out your own salvation" (Phil. 2:12) could suggest the need to earn one's salvation, if the particular stage being referenced is not clarified.

The *recurrence* principle will serve you well as you interpret passages in which a subject is repeated from a different viewpoint and with a different purpose. Failure to understand this principle of interpretation has caused some to miss the intent of Genesis 1 and 2 and view a contradiction between the two chapters. In Genesis 1, the Holy Spirit sets forth Creation from a chronological point of view. The emphasis is upon God's creative power. The name used for God is that which emphasizes His majesty and might. In the Genesis 2 account, the same subject, Creation, is presented from a different viewpoint. The emphasis here is not upon chronology but theme. God's grandest creative work, the creation of man, is given the prominent place. The name used for God is that which emphasizes His covenant relation to man. No contradiction exists between the two accounts, only an instance of the recurrence principle.

STEP #7: CONSULT COMMENTARIES

After analyzing the text from all of the aforementioned standpoints, only then should the expositor consider the observations that others have made about the same passage. The use of commentaries is mentioned last because such sources must not be allowed to sway you unduly. Our goal is to reduce subjectivity in the exegetical process as much as possible. Because commentaries are written by other human beings, they bring a high degree of subjectivity to the table.

At the same time, commentaries can provide a rich resource of information that God has taught other servants who have traveled before us. Do not be afraid to use commentaries, but avoid the temptation to consult them prematurely so that they become crutches upon which you lean.

Commentary work should be done in similar fashion to background study. Instead of categorizing your work by various elements of background information (i.e., authorship, date, etc.), break your passage into verses or even phrases. Then consult six to eight commentaries on each verse or phrase.

Be sure to consult a balance of quality *critical, homiletical,* and *devotional* commentaries. Critical works will give you insight into the technical aspects of the biblical language. Homiletical works will offer exegetical help with a view toward application. Devotional works will convey introspective thoughts about the passage. As you read each, summarize helpful information from each author. Then step back and compare your summaries as you did in your background study. Look for the common emphases, helpful insights, and pertinent exegetical details. Record these observations in a concluding paragraph under that particular verse or phrase. Follow the same procedure for each verse, group of verses, or phrase.

What others have written on a Scripture passage provides several benefits. Commentaries can serve as checkpoints for your own interpretation. If your interpretation leads you far afield from respected expositors, carefully revisit your conclusions. To be sure, from time to time your understanding will differ from most or all of the commentaries. If you arrive at an interpretation that is diametrically opposed to the consensus of reputable commentaries, however, let that be a red flag that you carefully heed.

Very often commentaries will shed additional light on your passage. God does not give all insight to any man; His truth is the property of His church. Furthermore, when it comes to biblical truth, the expression "There is nothing new under the sun" certainly applies. So look for helpful insights on your Scripture passage from a variety of sources. All truth that God gives to mankind can be used in preaching truth to others. Commentaries also will help you think through the truths you confront in Scripture. They will trigger your thinking.

Several warnings about commentary use should be heeded: (1) Do not lift another man's expressions of thought and merely place them in your message. Take his insights into the fertile soil of your own mind, allow them to become part of you, and then express them in a way that is consistent with your own understanding and personality. (2) Avoid becoming enamored with a particular Bible commentator. Sometimes you will find a writer whose views so closely coincide with your own thinking that you find yourself constantly referring to his work. Do not allow yourself to become a slave to any man. Even the best Bible expositors may occasionally go astray in their interpretations, so do not sell your soul to any of them. (3) Discipline yourself to bring every commentary to the judgment of Scripture. Even though you may benefit from the writings of a particular man, do not regard them as the final word on the Scriptures. (4) Furthermore, do not restrict yourself to reading only those commentators with whom you agree. Your own thought processes may be stimulated by reading authors who take an opposing view. Their conclusions may either provide helpful insight or serve to confirm your conviction about the interpretation you have found.

IMPLICATION

At this point (if not before!), you probably will be tempted to begin sermonizing—taking all this information, organizing it, finding illustrations, and figuring out how it applies to your people. Though the expositor ought to have his sermon and his people in mind throughout his preparation, shallowness and even heresy can show up in a sermon because another crucial phase has been overlooked in the analysis of the text. This phase involves determining the theological implications of the passage.

In other words, before the preacher can apply the text to the modern world, he must determine what it says to all people of all time. Haddon Robinson said, "Application must come from the theological purpose of the biblical writer."[25] Practical application must be driven by theological implications, and the former can be done with integrity only when the latter is known.

This reality makes the fourth and final phase of analyzing the text so vitally important. Although somewhat shorter than the other three phases, the work here is indeed crucial. We have investigated the passage in order to determine what it *says*. Next, we interpreted the passage to find out what it *means*. We are now ready to determine the implications of the text. Here, we want to ask the question, *What does the passage say about God and man?*

STEP #1: DETERMINE THE THEOLOGICAL SIGNIFICANCE

The Bible is a book of unified theology. Although there is a progressive unfolding of revelation found in the Bible, the Old Testament and

---

25. Robinson, *Biblical Preaching,* 91.

the New Testament agree on theological truths. The great theme of redemption runs all the way through the Scriptures. One might say that the entire Bible is an unfolding of the simple message of John 3:16. All the way through, we read of God's great love for man, His grief at man's sin, and His determination to send a Savior to make possible man's redemption from sin.

The Old Testament's history, typology, and prophetic pronouncements were a preparation for the coming of the Lord Jesus Christ. The Old Testament could be summarized in one brief statement: "He is coming!" For this reason, the Old Testament cannot be separated from the New Testament. Likewise, the New Testament must always be studied in light of the Old Testament. The New provides us with a commentary on the Old. We must always give attention to the teachings of the New Testament as we search for correct interpretation of the Old. Paramount to determining theological significance is the consideration of revelation already given. Kaiser contends that there is always in a passage of Scripture a theological content that has its roots antecedent to the passage.[26]

A thorough examination of biblical theology is essential to accurate interpretation. The words in a passage, for example, should be examined in light of their historical usage *up to that time* in God's revelation, not according to meanings that evolved subsequent to the revelation under consideration. Thus, the good exegete should keep on hand a volume on biblical theology as well as other tools germane to theological analysis.[27]

As you consider the antecedent revelation, Kaiser suggested looking for several clues: (1) Look for terms that already have acquired particular meanings, especially related to salvation (e.g., *seed, servant, rest, inheritance, kingdom, gospel, mystery*). (2) Note references to previous events (e.g., the Exodus, the epiphany on Sinai, the outpouring of the Holy Spirit). (3) Consider direct or indirect quotations that might have bearing on the new situation (e.g., "Be fruitful and multiply . . ." and "I am the God of your fathers"). (4) Notice references to God's covenants and promises, especially regarding their contents, what has been added, and details ("I am the Lord your God, who brought you up out of the land of Egypt"; "I will be your God; you shall be my people, and I will dwell in the midst of you").[28]

In addition to considering antecedent revelation, Robinson suggested

---

26. Kaiser, *Toward an Exegetical Theology,* 131–46.
27. For a good bibliography of helpful works on theological analysis, see Kaiser, *Toward an Exegetical Theology,* 147.
28. Ibid.

that the expositor ask some important questions of the text in order to determine theological significance.[29]

First, are there any indications of purpose, editorial comments, or interpretive statements? The statement "Now there arose a new king over Egypt, who did not know Joseph" in Exodus 1:8 provides a telling commentary on Israel's conflict with Pharaoh. The explanation that "these are written that you may believe that Jesus is the Christ" in John 20:31 is helpful in interpreting many texts in that book, especially the miracle passages.

Second, are theological judgments made? The comment "In those days there was no king in Israel; everyone did what was right in his own eyes," found in Judges 17:6 and 21:25, provides a sad commentary on the spiritual climate in Israel reflected in that book. The note in 1 Kings 11:6 that "Solomon did evil in the sight of the Lord, and did not fully follow the Lord, as did his father David" highlights a theological implication often overlooked in the life of the wisest man who ever lived. Matthew's numerous references to Jesus' fulfillment of Old Testament Scripture suggests his purpose in writing.

Third, for narrative texts especially, is the story told as an example or warning? Is the incident a norm or an exception? What limitations should be placed on it? When compared with other texts dealing with sin in the church, the Ananias and Sapphira story in Acts 5:1–11 appears to be an exhortation for unity and purity in the church as opposed to a disclosure of the normative way in which God deals with erring members.

Fourth, what message was intended for the original readers (or hearers) as well as those the writer knew would read or hear later? The genealogy in Matthew 1:1–17 may appear to have little relevance for contemporary culture until we understand that it was the obvious starting place for a writer who wanted to prove that Jesus of Nazareth had the legal right to the throne of Israel and, consequently, the right to claim to be the Christ.

Fifth, why would the Holy Spirit have included this account in Scripture? When this question is asked of texts in 2 Timothy, it becomes apparent that even God's choicest servants sometimes want to quit and that there is available encouragement and motivation to stay the course.

Asking such questions may at first appear monotonous and time-consuming. Yet, it is at this point that so many preachers hurry to be relevant and end up building application on a weak theological foundation. Remember, the only thing that is going to change people's lives is the truth of God's Word. Take time to make sure your message to modern listeners is based upon solid theological assertions.

---

29. Robinson, *Biblical Preaching,* 92–93.

STEP #2: IDENTIFY THE TIMELESS TRUTHS

Preachers always get into trouble when they try to be relevant without good theological foundation. In an effort to avoid "irrelevancy," many become involved in spiritualizing a passage, giving a "Bible editorial" on some selected passage of Scripture, or looking for a few moral lessons that can be drawn from the verses. All of these inadequate attempts to derive practical lessons from the Scriptures can be avoided. Look for the timeless truths in the Scripture passage you are studying—truths that issue forth from the theological foundations you discovered.

To identify the timeless truths, continue to ask certain questions of your passage, this time concentrating on matters that relate to all people of all time. What is God doing in the text? What does the passage teach about the person or character of God? What does it say about the nature and need of man? What about God's activity with humanity? These issues have bearing on the life of every person in every generation. Finding these timeless truths will help you relate in a practical way to your congregation.

Truth is truth whenever and wherever found. The great theological truths that spoke to the hearts of Bible people can speak to our own day as well. As you find these timeless truths, state them in principles that apply to the needs of all people of all time, including those of your contemporary audience. Kaiser called this process "principlization."[30] You are identifying spiritual principles that will help bring people to God through Christ and mold them into His image.

The Bible addresses in some way all the major issues of life—human identity, the reason for existence, the future, guilt, love, marriage, relationships, death, eternity, and more. Although specific guidelines for each subject are not always delineated, Scripture speaks to these issues as they relate to the redemption of mankind and the transformation of individuals into Christlikeness. Thus, the expositor must address these issues from the timeless truths he finds in his Scripture passage.

As he moves through the passage, he will draw from its verses rebukes, challenges, appeals, and encouragements. Because the issues are timeless, these responses from God's Word are timeless. This kind of "preliminary application" is vitally more important than the secondary application made to the nuances of each generation. In other words, what God has to say to all people is foundational for what He has to say to each individual situation.

---

30. Kaiser, *Toward an Exegetical Theology,* 152.

Later, when you put together the introduction to your message, you may seek to arouse interest in the hearers by indicating some of the human needs that will be dealt with in the sermon. In the exposition part of the sermon, you can state your main divisions in such a way as to apply to those human needs. As you develop each division, you can apply the principles of the text to the unique situations and circumstances of your particular listeners. When you bring the message to a close, you can gather all the practical ingredients of the passage and relate them to your hearers in one final, stirring appeal to their hearts. This way, your sermon is not driven by specific, changing situations of the human experience but by God's eternal truths.

STEP #3: INTERNALIZE YOUR DISCOVERY

As you conclude analyzing your text, be sure to allow God's truth to impact *you*. The transition from Bible study to sermonizing causes many to miss out on the work of God in their own lives. Although you will not start making specific application to the potential listeners until later in the process, it is important for you to begin the application process here. Now is the time intentionally to examine yourself in view of the truths you have discovered. Do not proceed with the sermon preparation process without encountering God personally and acting on His truth. As God's chosen vessel, you have no right to sermonize until you internalize.

This step becomes a deeply soul-searching experience for the preacher. Week by week, as you prepare expository sermons, you will be confronted personally with God's truth discovered in the preaching passage. Face God's truth in your own life. Never deal in unfelt truth, for you cannot preach to others what has not been first preached to yourself. To do so is to face the danger Paul expressed in 1 Corinthians 9:27, "Lest, when I have preached to others, I myself should become disqualified." If you have not done so already, allow your study to become a meeting place with God. Often your heart will be rebuked by the truths that become increasingly apparent throughout your study. Honestly face the ramifications of what you have uncovered. Only as you internalize the truths of God's Word in your own life are you able to apply them to the lives of your people.

If you will be faithful to this activity, your preaching will be infused with spiritual power. It is here that you largely will determine whether or not God's anointing will rest on this particular preaching event. As an expositor, you are able to make practical application to people because the Bible is a real book preached by a real person. Remember, the message of the Word of God does not come to the listener apart from a living personality. You flesh out the truth of Scripture as you deliver the message.

Preaching that is able to apply most powerfully to the listeners is incarnational—the living Word of God communicated through human flesh. Nothing is so potent and applicable as the message of salvation communicated through the life of a redeemed man.

CHAPTER FIVE

UNIFYING
THE THEME

I have a conviction that no sermon is ready for preaching,
not ready for writing out, until we can express its theme
in a short, pregnant sentence as clear as crystal.

J. H. JOWETT

If you have done your exposition work correctly, all the necessary data with which to build an effective expository sermon is before you—material that can be put together to present a message from God to your people. Analysis, however, is not the end of your work. Attention now must be turned to synthesis. You have dissected the text through the process of analysis; synthesis involves putting the pieces of the passage back together in an orderly, systematic manner. This process starts by pulling your material together in a unifying way.

Bridging the chasm between Bible study and the sermon begins with the task of unifying all of the exegetical material you have uncovered. This exercise will set you on the road to developing a good structure upon which to build the sermon. Unifying the material and using it to design your sermon will organize it into an attractive, usable form with which to communicate God's Word.

Begin by using some kind of summary sheet like the one found in Appendix 2 to record the work that you do in this part of your exposition. As you determine each component of the process, you will be moving gradually from text to sermon.

THE INTENDED AUDIENCE

The first step in moving from text to sermon is to identify the primary audience in the passage. Only two kinds of people live in the world—those who are lost and those who are saved. Although many passages of Scripture address issues that are equally applicable to believers and unbelievers, most texts address either the people of God or unregenerate mankind. The preacher must be very clear in his mind regarding the primary audience of his particular text, so that he can relate it rightly to the modern audience. Much poor theology and subsequent confusion has arisen because a preacher has failed to clarify the kind of listener who is being addressed.

Again, if the intended audience of Jesus' teaching on fruitless branches in John 15:6 is not clarified, the suggestion of losing one's salvation easily can be entertained. Both believers and unbelievers can become confused. Likewise, pointing out that Ephesians 2:8–9 initially was intended for Christians can help those listeners learn an exciting concept that often is overlooked due to the passage's secondary (but most frequent) evangelistic application.

Some have identified the major objective of the text as either *Evangelistic* or *Christian Life*.[1] We will use the terms *Salvation* and *Fellowship* correspondingly. Recognizing that a few selected passages in the Bible may simply be addressing moral issues related to all mankind, we may add a third description called *General*. The preacher, however, should select this third description only after exhausting all possibilities of designating the intended audience by one of the first two descriptions. After you have identified the primary audience in your text, note that description on your summary sheet.

Do your best always to let the primary intended audience inform the application of your sermon. It is always best to relate a text to the same kind of people as those to whom the words originally were written or spoken. Certainly it is possible to preach a salvation, or evangelistic, sermon from a passage originally intended for the people of God and vice versa. Your best preaching, however, will come when the Holy Spirit's original intent is preserved as much as possible, including the nature of the audience that first received or heard it.

THE CENTRAL IDEA OF THE TEXT

The next step to unifying your Bible study material is to capsulize the mind of the Holy Spirit in the text. A good expository sermon always is developed from the "big idea" of the passage on which it is based. This idea has been described in various ways. Robinson called it the *exegetical idea*.[2] Harold Bryson and James Taylor labeled it the *essence of a*

---

1. Al Fasol, *Essentials for Biblical Preaching* (Grand Rapids: Baker, 1989), 57.
2. Haddon W. Robinson, *Biblical Preaching* (Grand Rapids: Baker, 1980), 66.

text in a sentence (ETS).[3] Stephen Olford referred to it as the *dominating theme.*[4] We will employ the terminology suggested by Al Fasol, who called this summation the *central idea of the text (CIT).*[5] Regardless of terminology, a good sermon must be given a one-sentence statement that summarizes the central idea of the Scripture passage being preached.

THE NECESSITY OF THE CIT

A survey of preachers would reveal a frightening reality at this point. Most—including many who are quite proficient in sermon preparation—never take time to write out a one-sentence statement that summarizes the subject of their text. This failure may be attributed to several factors.

First, stating the main subject of a Scripture passage may be the most difficult area of sermon preparation. Broadus said, "To state one's central idea as the heart of the sermon is not always easy, especially in textual and expository preaching."[6] To do the necessary word study, to gather the needed background data, and to study the contextual considerations is not difficult. But to pull together in one succinct statement the essence of a paragraph of Scripture can be a most rigorous assignment.

Second, most pastors are extremely busy. They are preaching several times a week. That demand places severe strain upon the time available for preparation, and most men find it difficult to find time to think through each sermonic passage in this manner.

Third, some preachers simply are lazy and refuse to do the hard work of identifying the subject of the text.

The absolute necessity of doing this work is related directly to the nature of preaching itself. If the preacher's responsibility is to communicate what God already has said, then the central idea of any given sermon must reflect the central idea intended by the author himself. As Donald G. McDougall rightly said:

> Our task is NOT to create our own message;
> It is rather to communicate the author's message.
> Our task is NOT to create a central theme;

3. Harold T. Bryson and James C. Taylor, *Building Sermons to Meet People's Needs* (Nashville: Broadman, 1980), 61.
4. Stephen F. Olford and David L. Olford, *Anointed Expository Preaching* (Nashville: Broadman & Holman, 1998), 75.
5. Fasol, *Essentials of Biblical Preaching,* 56.
6. John A. Broadus, *On the Preparation and Delivery of Sermons,* 4th ed., rev. Vernon L. Stanfield (1870; revision, New York: Harper & Row, 1979), 38 (page citation is to the revised edition).

It is rather to
1. find the author's central theme
2. build a message around that theme, and
3. make that theme the central part of all we have to say.[7]

DEFINING THE CIT

The concept of the central idea of the text may be defined as follows:

Def'ə-nish'ən

central idea of the text (CIT) *n.* A 15–18-word past-tense statement interpreting what the text meant then.

This definition contains several words that provide clues for developing a good theme statement. The *15–18-word parameter* is intended merely to be a guide for being concise yet thorough. If you find yourself with less than fifteen words, you probably are not saying enough. If you have more than eighteen words, you likely are saying too much and should make an attempt to be more concise. Avoid being legalistic, however. Say what needs to be said.

The term *past-tense* is a reminder that the big idea of a given text is the same today as it was when the Holy Spirit first inspired it. At this point in the expositional process, you simply are concerned with synthesizing that meaning. The word *interpreting* describes the primary purpose of the CIT, which is to summarize the meaning of the text. The word *then* underscores the reality that significance for contemporary culture begins with a right understanding of historical meaning.

IDENTIFYING THE CIT

Operating with this paradigm, you can begin the work of identifying your CIT. At this point, revisit the insights you gleaned from every part of your analysis. Review especially the conclusions you drew regarding each verse or thought block in the passage. As you synthesize this material, ask

---

7. Donald G. McDougall, "Central Ideas, Outlines, and Titles," in John MacArthur Jr., *Rediscovering Expository Preaching*, ed. Richard L. Mayhue (Dallas: Word, 1992), 229.

yourself, What's the "big idea"? McDougall suggested three primary ways for accomplishing this task.[8]

First, *identify the CIT from a single statement in the passage*. Many times one sentence in the text will contain the nucleus of the text. Contrary to the traditional approach to basic English composition, the main thought of a paragraph in the biblical languages is not always found in the first sentence. For example, after Paul established growth in Christlikeness as the goal of the church, he called upon the Ephesians to stop acting like the rest of the Gentiles and start acting like Christ (4:17–32). The central idea of this passage is found in 4:22–24, where he tells them to put off the old man and put on the new. The CIT might be stated as "Paul instructed the Ephesians to stop acting like their fellow Gentiles and start acting like Christ."

Second, *identify the CIT from the larger context*. Sometimes the CIT is found sandwiched between two related ideas. In 2 Timothy 1:3–2:2, for example, Paul conveyed the main idea that Timothy was to be faithful in passing on the gospel to the next generation. In 1:3, Paul referenced the investment of his own forefathers. In 1:5, he noted the investment of Timothy's grandmother and mother. Then, in 2:2, Paul charged Timothy to invest the gospel in faithful men who would be able to pass it along to others. In between these related ideas are several exhortations, or ways, to stay the course faithfully amid suffering. The CIT might be worded "Paul charged Timothy to faithfully pass the gospel to the next generation in the face of opposition."

Third, *identify the CIT from recurring ideas*. The recurrence of certain words may be the clue for which you are looking. You often will be able to discover the author's emphasis by noting a particular idea (or group of ideas) that continually surfaces. When the mantle of leadership was passed from Moses to Joshua in Joshua 1:1–9, God instructed the new leader three times to be strong and courageous (1:6, 7, 9). This repeated exhortation serves to highlight the central idea. A good CIT might be stated thus: "Because of His faithfulness, God encouraged Joshua to be strong and courageous in leading the Israelites into Canaan."

In many Scripture passages the CIT is not immediately apparent. In such cases, take time to think through your passage. Force yourself to process carefully all that you discovered in your analysis of the text. Your previous reading and analyzing of the passage should give you sufficient clues to identify the CIT.

---

8. Ibid, 229–33. McDougall discusses several excellent scriptural examples of each of possible approaches to identifying the central idea of a text.

With few exceptions, a CIT can be found in a passage of Scripture, however difficult the search may be. Robinson said finding it is not easy, but he also contended that the achievement is worth the effort. Even when a text presents several ideas, all of which should be incorporated in the sermon, it is desirable to find for them some bond of unity, some primary idea that will serve as focus or axis or orbit. One may fix attention on one of the ideas as the subject and consider the others in relation to it.[9] If you will take the time to give your best thought to the search, that unifying idea eventually will surface.

Once you have identified the CIT, summarize that main thought in one brief, pointed sentence. Write it down in your own words, using the guidelines noted above. Some seasoned preachers have become so accustomed to grasping the essence of the passage mentally that they have moved beyond the point of writing it down. The process has become second nature to them. Do not be too quick to move in that direction, however. Be intentional about finding the central idea of the text and expressing it in a well-written sentence.

BENEFITS OF THE CIT

The importance of identifying the CIT cannot be overemphasized. Having a clearly stated "big idea" in mind produces several benefits that build upon one another.

Structural foundation. Having a clear understanding of the central idea lays the foundation for good organization. Critics of the expository method often say that expository sermons do not have a discernible structure—no clear-cut beginning, no carefully prepared points, no discernible conclusion. An unorganized expository sermon appears to be a combination of several little sermonettes haphazardly tied together with no obvious relation between them. This lack of healthy organization understandably gives the impression that the sermon is a rambling, structureless, never ending message. Identifying the main thrust of the passage will give the sermon focus and clear direction.

Mental organization. Good structure built around a central idea will provide you with a better understanding of the truths you will be sharing with your people. Robinson said:

> An exegete does not understand the passage until he can state its subject and complement exactly. While other questions emerge in the struggle to understand the meaning of a Biblical writer, the two—what is the author

9. Robinson, *Biblical Preaching,* 33.

talking about and what is he saying about what he is talking about—are fundamental.[10]

The CIT will crystallize in your mind the single, controlling idea of the passage. "A sermon should be a bullet not a buckshot. Ideally each sermon is the explanation, interpretation, or application of a single dominant idea supported by other ideas, all drawn from one passage or several passages of Scripture."[11]

Intentional sermonization. Clear comprehension of the passage's big idea will help you cut unnecessary material from your sermon. More than likely, at the conclusion of your analysis you will have more material than you possibly can include in one sermon. Too much detail—or the wrong choice of detail—can cause you to miss the controlling purpose of the Scripture paragraph. A well-thought-through theme sentence will help you remove unnecessary material by giving you a standard by which to determine what you let into your sermon. Finding the central theme will enable you to choose intentionally those parts of the paragraph that make that theme the clearest and most emphatic.

Directed reception. Identifying the CIT will also enable you to give direction to those who eventually hear your message. They will be able to understand more easily what you are saying, because you give them a point of reference for the details of your sermon. People who come to listen to you have given you some of their valuable time. They deserve to have a well-arranged, thought-through message, including a mooring to which to tie the specific truths and applications you give them. A clearly stated central idea will be the mooring that keeps contemporary application anchored to the truth of God's Word.

THE PROPOSITION

When a songwriter writes a song, he or she usually works out the refrain before writing the different verses that accompany the refrain.[12] All the verses, then, support and develop that refrain. The third step in moving from Bible study to sermon development is to transform your CIT into a proposition for your sermon. This proposition becomes the refrain of your message.

10. Ibid., 41.
11. Ibid., 33.
12. James C. Humes, *The Sir Winston Method: The Five Secrets of Speaking the Language of Leadership* (New York: William Morrow, 1991), 45. Humes's work on Winston Churchill's approach to public speech making and presentation is an extremely helpful work for preachers.

UNDERSTANDING THE PROPOSITION

Most experts on formal speech preparation strongly emphasize the importance of having a central subject. Some refer to the subject as the main object of the talk. Others call it the central idea; still others, the theme of the speech. Homileticians almost unanimously agree. In fact, throughout the years, numerous teachers of preaching have referenced J. H. Jowett's words during the 1912 Yale Lectures, which are cited just under the title of this chapter.

Again, different writers have used different terms to describe this "pregnant sentence." Farris D. Whitesell called it the sermon theme and described it as "the whole sermon in a nutshell. It is a one-sentence statement of the content of the message."[13] Robinson dubbed it the homiletical idea.[14] Bryson and Taylor said it was the essence of the sermon in a sentence (ESS).[15] Koller and Fasol referred to it as the thesis.[16] In most of these discussions, however, the word "proposition" has been used at some point to describe the concept. This statement is what you are "proposing" to the audience regarding the given text of Scripture. In similar fashion as the CIT, we may define the proposition as follows:

Def'ə-nish'ən

proposition *n.* A 15–18-word present- or future-tense application of the CIT to the contemporary context.

Once more, the definition contains several words that provide clues to developing a good thesis. The *15–18-word parameter* again serves as a guide for striking the balance between conciseness and comprehensiveness. Avoid legalism, but let the word count hold you accountable. The terms *present-tense* and *future-tense* help us to bring the Holy Spirit's original intent from the biblical world into the modern world. The word *application* reminds us that we no longer are looking to discover meaning but

---

13. Farris D. Whitesell, *Power in Expository Preaching* (Old Tappan, N.J.: Revell, 1963), 60.
14. Robinson, *Biblical Preaching*, 97.
15. Bryson and Taylor, *Building Sermons*, 63.
16. Charles W. Koller, *Expository Preaching Without Notes* (Grand Rapids: Baker, 1962), 72; Fasol, *Biblical Preaching*, 57.

simply to apply the previously determined meaning to the current situation. The phrase *contemporary context* presses us to communicate the original idea to our audience in an understandable way.

FORMULATING THE PROPOSITION

Begin the process of formulating your proposition by looking closely at your CIT. Identify those components that need to be contemporized. Such elements may include certain biblical names, dated terminology, specific circumstances, and cultural nuances. For example, consider how some CITs mentioned earlier might be contemporized:

CIT	PROPOSITION
Paul instructed the **Ephesians** to stop acting like their fellow **Gentiles** and start acting like Christ.	**Christians** should stop acting like the **lost culture** around them and start **acting like Christ.**
Paul charged **Timothy** to faithfully pass the gospel to the next generation in the face of opposition.	**Christian leaders** must faithfully pass the gospel to **the next generation** even in the face of opposition.
Because of His faithfulness, God encouraged **Joshua** to be strong and courageous in **leading the Israelites into Canaan.**	The **people of God** can have strength and courage to **serve Him obediently** because of His faithfulness.

Notice that in each example the boldfaced type represents components that have been contemporized from the CIT to the proposition. Remember, here we are intent upon moving from *then* to *now* without losing the Holy Spirit's intended meaning. Be careful to communicate that meaning in language that is relevant to your listeners.

When you are moving from CIT to proposition, the degree to which you need to contemporize may vary. For example, when the CIT applies to anyone at any time, the proposition may be very similar (if not identical) to the CIT. Other CITs simply will need to be personalized. The truth being taught may be applied directly, but the author/speaker and the listeners/readers need to be translated to your situation. Further still, some propositions may be less tied to the wording of the CIT as long as the same truth is conveyed.[17]

Work hard at formulating your proposition. Work it, rework it, and then work it again until you have the best possible wording. Robinson un-

17. Robinson, *Biblical Preaching,* 97–99.
18. Ibid., 99.

derscored the import of such toil when he said the language of the proposition should be both winsome and compelling without being sensational. Does it sparkle? Does it grab hold of a listener's mind? Can I remember it easily? Is it worth remembering? Does the language communicate effectively to modern men and women?[18]

Moving from an intensive analysis of the historical text to a creative statement of its relevance for contemporary listeners could be the most difficult work you do in the expositional process. But "when the idea rises in the preacher's mind 'clear as a cloudless moon,' he has the message to be preached."[19]

PUTTING YOUR PROPOSITION TO THE TEST!

The following are checkpoints for evaluating sermon propositions. They are adapted from Charles Koller's *Expository Preaching Without Notes*.[20] Use these qualities to evaluate the propositions you formulate.

Promising. The proposition should indicate the course of the discussion that is to follow, promising information that the sermon must fulfill. It must be deliverable!

General. A good proposition should be a generalization reflecting the timeless, universal truth of the passage.

Simple. Generally, the proposition should be a simple sentence.

Clear. The proposition should be very clear.

Comprehensive. The proposition should comprehend the entire thought of the message—it is the gist of the sermon in one sentence.

Important. The proposition should be important enough to deserve the elaboration that follows in the main body of the sermon.

Sermonic. The proposition should express or imply some response or change on the part of the audience.

THE VALUE OF THE PROPOSITION

To appreciate the value of the proposition, take a moment to process

18. Ibid., 99.
  19. Ib
  20. Koller, *Expository Preaching*, 72–

what is happening. Because you have been called as a preacher to speak "Thus saith the Lord," you have analyzed a text of Scripture in order to know the mind of the Holy Spirit and discover precisely what God has said. Then, you capsulized your discovery in one concise, yet thorough, statement. At this point you are not coming up with a new statement but rather transferring that statement into the here and now in order to develop a sermon. In reality, this process ensures that what you are proposing to your people in a sermon is actually the same as what God is proposing to them in His Word. Such is the essence of expository preaching—you are exposing the very mind of God to contemporary culture.

A well-worded proposition also will assist you as you organize your entire message. It will give a sense of direction to everything that follows. The discussion on sermon designs in the next chapter will reveal that the main divisions of your message actually should be found in your text. When you have formulated a proposition based upon the CIT, you can arrange those main divisions more easily. The introduction of the sermon obviously is easier to put together when you know where you are going. Likewise, the concluding parts of the message can be built more effectively when you know where you will have been. In fact, Koller suggested that the proposition of the sermon actually is the conclusion in reverse. The proposition looks ahead, anticipating the conclusion; the conclusion points back to the proposition.[21]

THE PURPOSE

Dwight Eisenhower always incorporated what he called the "QED" in his speeches. The letters stood for *quod erat demonstrandum*—the bottom line.[22] After formulating your proposition, begin to think about your sermon's purpose. Every message ought to have a specific purpose aimed at a particular group of people. This purpose defines what you want the audience to take away with them—what you want them to do.

DISTINGUISHING THE PURPOSE

Like the proposition, the purpose of your sermon ought to be informed by the CIT. At the same time, do not confuse the proposition with the purpose. The purpose of your message is what you desire in terms of audience response. You know what the sermon is about, including its central thrust. You even know the primary audience to which it should be applied. But what do you want your listeners *to do* about that subject? If the

---

21. Ibid., 7
22. Humes, *The Sir Winston Method,* 46.

preacher does not know what he wants the people to do about the message, he cannot expect them to do anything. Many sermons never give the faintest notion to those who listen what the preacher wants them to do. If people are going to respond favorably, they must know what they are expected to do.

In addition to identifying the major objective of the text, Fasol encouraged the preacher to develop a major objective of his sermon, which he described as "a statement of what the preacher hopes to accomplish with this one message, from this one text, for this one congregation, at this particular time."[23] Building on this concept, we may define the sermon's purpose as follows:

Def′ə·nish′ən

purpose *n.* A brief statement of what the preacher specifically hopes to accomplish in the lives of his primary listeners with this particular message on this particular occasion.

Consider the nature of this purpose statement. It should be a concise, simple sentence. It should identify what specific action you want your listeners to take. It should specify whether you are primarily addressing believers or unbelievers. God can and does speak to both the lost and saved through the same preaching event, but a specific target will give your application clarity and pointedness. Finally, your purpose should take into consideration the nuances of the particular preaching event in which you intend to preach this sermon, including the particular people and time.

STATING THE PURPOSE

The actual wording of the purpose statement will vary according to the nature of the sermon. The purpose statements for most *Salvation* sermons will be similar, since the primary action for which the preacher is calling is commitment to Christ. Certain aspects of the biographical status of the listeners may vary depending upon the context (i.e., "I want these

23. Fasol, *Biblical Preaching,* 57–58.

students to accept Jesus Christ as Lord and Savior," or, "I want these *senior adults* to give their lives to Christ"). The purposes of *Fellowship* sermons to believers, however, will tend to vary in more areas. Below are some possible purpose statements developed from the propositions noted earlier:

CIT	PROPOSITION	PURPOSE
Paul instructed the Ephesians to stop acting like their fellow Gentiles and start acting like Christ.	**Christians** should stop acting like the **lost culture** around them and start **acting like Christ.**	I want these **Christian young people** to commit to replace **worldly ways** with **Christlike qualities.**
Paul charged Timothy to faithfully pass the gospel to the next generation in the face of opposition.	**Christian leaders** must faithfully **pass the gospel** to **the next generation** even in the face of opposition.	I want our **church leaders** to commit to becoming intentional about **discipling** the **people for whom they are responsible.**
Because of His faithfulness, God encouraged Joshua to be strong and courageous in leading the Israelites into Canaan.	The **people of God** can have strength and courage to **serve Him obediently** because of His faithfulness.	I want **church members** to know that our faithful God will give strength and courage as we **obediently start this new ethnic mission.**

Notice the correlation between the boldfaced words. The purpose statement gets more specific with certain aspects of the proposition. The target groups are narrowed, and the action being proposed is defined more precisely. You will discover that these details in your purpose statement may change slightly each time you preach from a particular text without changing the timeless truth of God's Word reflected in your CIT and proposition.

When you think about the purpose of your message—especially those sermons addressed to Christians—consider several possibilities. Sometimes your purpose will be to *inform* people about the vital doctrines in Scripture. You will tell them about these doctrines in order to lead them to be more grateful to God for what He has done for them, to build these truths into their daily habit patterns or to communicate them to others. Sometimes you will purpose to *comfort* your people with a positive message from God's Word. These sermons will seek to encourage and strengthen them in times of need. At other times your purpose will be to *challenge* the people with the call of Scripture to total surrender or complete dedication. Whether you seek to inform or to inspire, motivate or challenge, encourage or rebuke, get the purpose of your sermon clearly in mind.

THE TITLE

The final stage in unifying your Bible study material is to take a preliminary stab at a title for your sermon. The CIT capsulizes the mind of the Holy Spirit in the text. The proposition applies that truth to the contemporary situation. The purpose asserts the desired response to that truth from a particular group of listeners. The title pulls it all together in a memorable, attention-getting way. This effort is described as "preliminary" simply because your title may undergo many revisions prior to its final form.

THE PURPOSE OF THE TITLE

The most important issue regarding the sermon title is not when the title is conceived but the reason for having a title in the first place. The title of a message differs from the subject and the purpose. A title has a threefold purpose:

TITLE TALES

1. **Attention.** The sermon title is primarily designed to get attention. It is the primary public relations agent for the sermon. You are seeking to arouse interest on the part of those who may hear your message.

2. **Reinforcement.** The title also provides a shorter, looser rendition of the sermon proposition, which can reinforce the thrust of the message in the listeners' minds.

3. **Memory.** The sermon title serves as a mooring to which the listener may tie the content of the message for easy recollection. After a sermon is heard, a well-worded title may help to jog the listener's memory of the sermon substance.

Because of the title's public relations benefit, every effort should be made to get it in front of people prior to the preaching event. Perhaps you can list your sermon titles in a weekly church ad, the regular church newsletter, or special mailings. Church marquees and web sites can be used for publicizing sermon titles. If you are able to prepare far enough in advance, next week's title may be printed in this week's bulletin or order of service. Even sermon titles printed in the current day's bulletin or listening guide can arouse interest in the minds of those persons who are preparing for worship. Stating the title at the beginning of the message also can help gain attention at the moment of delivery. All of these ways will serve as advance publicity and stimulate interest in the upcoming sermon.

QUALITIES OF GOOD TITLES

Several qualities make for effective sermon titles. Use the following characteristics as benchmarks in the development of your titles:

TITLE TONES

Tantalizing. Develop titles that whet the appetite of potential listeners. Just as a good advertisement causes a listener to crave a piping hot pizza at lunchtime, so your sermon title should cause people to want to hear your message.

Brief. Capsulize your sermon in a word, phrase, or short sentence. Make it easy for people to remember. "Seventeen Reasons Why the Modern Church Is Not Getting the Job Done as It Should Be Getting It Done" is not a good title. "The Breakdown of the Modern Church" would be a better effort.

Catchy. Try to capture the gist of the sermon in a catchy word or phrase that will stick in the listeners' minds. Good titles will grab the attention and not let go.

Appropriate. Make sure your title has taste and integrity. Avoid sensational and offensive wording as well as ridiculous suggestions. Titles such as "Seven Dips in a Muddy Pond" for a sermon on Namaan the leper really becomes absurd.

Deliverable. Do not promise more than you can give in a message. Neither "The Second Coming" nor "How to Solve All Your Problems" are good titles—the former because it is too broad and the latter because it is impossible. Some preachers have lost credibility because the substance of their sermon did not fulfill the enormous claims of the title.

Related. Each title must be related closely to the proposition of the sermon. Do not promise something that the Word of God does not provide.

TYPES OF TITLES

A variety of kinds of titles can be used to label sermons. The particular type should be employed based upon the nature of the message, the occasion, and the audience.

TITLE TYPOLOGY

Key word or phrase—a word or phrase that describes the essence of the sermon proposition

> **Title:** "First Team Christianity"
>
> **Text:** Ephesians 3:14–21

Imperative statement—a statement that emphasizes an action or command that the sermon will put forth

> **Title:** "Go for the Gold!"
>
> **Text:** 1 Corinthians 9:24–27

Interrogative statement—a probing question, which the sermon promises to address

> **Title:** "What's So Amazing About Grace?"
>
> **Text:** Titus 2:11–15

Declarative statement—a statement of claim, which the sermon proposes to support

> **Title:** "The Yoke's on You!"
>
> **Text:** Matthew 11:28–30

Remember that an idea for a sermon title may be conceived at any point in the sermon preparation process. You may or may not have your title at this point in sermon organization. You may not find it until the end of all your preparation. On the other hand, a good title may flash into your mind in the midst of your study as you do your expository work. At any rate, at least attempt to hang a title on your sermon before you begin to structure your message.

CHAPTER SIX

DESIGNING
THE STRUCTURE

*If a man did not know how to preach, he might choose
a paragraph which is pure gold, and yet bring out a
sorry substitute for a sermon. Like Aaron, the would-be
biblical preacher might complain: "I cast it into
the fire, and there came out this calf!"*

ANDREW BLACKWOOD

Many pitfalls exist along the road to good expository preaching, not the least of which is trying to move from a unified theme to a good sermon package ready for delivery. Anyone who has preached much at all knows the frustration of digging up exciting truth from God's Word and then struggling with how to communicate it to His people. What we are talking about here is good sermon structure, or organization. Without clear, logical development and organization, a sermon does not have the effect and power it could have. Herbert Spencer said, "When a man's knowledge is not in order, the more of it he has, the greater will be his confusion of thought."[1] Avoiding that confusion demands understanding the necessity of sermon structure and knowing how to design it.

THE NECESSITY OF STRUCTURE

A wide gulf exists between good exegesis and a good sermon. In fact, failure here has fostered much ridicule from critics of expository preaching. Simply taking exegetical material and even a central theme into the pulpit with no organization frustrates those who listen. You cannot afford to take your Bible bullets and toss them at your congregation. You must organize them and then systematically fire them. If you structure your sermon well, you will be far ahead in your attempt to get the biblical message across to a contemporary audience.

---

1. Josh McDowell, "Syllabus on Communication and Persuasion" (© Josh McDowell, 1983, mimeographed), 28.

THE CURRENT DEBATE

In the fourth century B.C., Aristotle systematized an approach to persuasive speaking in his *Rhetoric*. In the first century A.D., Quintilin pulled together and elaborated on the five classic canons of rhetoric in his *Institutes on Oratory*. After the Edict of Milan in A.D. 313 under the reign of Constantine, schools were opened to Christians.[2] The art of public and persuasive speaking had by then been reduced to principles and rules for study. Along with grammar and dialectic, these principles and rules were included as one of the three basic elements in classical education.[3] Partnered with these principles of ancient oratory and rhetoric, the various qualities of Hebrew prophecy and the Christian gospel ultimately shaped the development of sermon form. By the middle of the fourth century, sermons began to reflect a more intentional use of both structure and style.

In the last forty years, however, traditional approaches to sermon structure have come under increasing criticism from many scholars and practitioners who espouse a more existential nature for modern homiletics. This group has reacted strongly to outlined sermons and championed an emphasis on movement and experience. Much of the criticism is rooted in the accusation that traditional homiletics relies too much on propositional ideas. As David Larsen lamented, "It was only a matter of time before the new hermeneutic should be followed by the new homiletic."[4]

The door was opened for such criticism in the 1950s when H. Grady Davis introduced the organic nature of the tree as a new metaphor for the sermon in *Design for Preaching* (Fortress, 1958). Fred Craddock was more aggressive with his critique in *As One Without Authority* (Phillips University, 1974), calling for a process of discovery to replace propositional homiletics. David Buttrick pulled out all the stops in *Homiletic* (Fortress, 1987). He rejected what he considered the extreme punctilious approach to structure in traditional homiletics and championed a phenomenological sermonic style that consisted of a sequence of five or six plotted ideational units called "moves," which culminated in the sermonic conclusion.

As the twentieth century comes to a close, the movement has lost any form of subtlety. One essay reflecting the theories of Craddock, Buttrick,

---

2. Vernon L. Stanfield, "The History of Homiletics," in *Baker's Dictionary of Practical Theology*, ed. Ralph G. Turnbull (Grand Rapids: Baker, 1967), 50–51.

3. John A. Broadus, *On the Preparation and Delivery of Sermons*, 4th ed., rev. Vernon L. Stanfield (1870; revision, New York: Harper & Row, 1979), 10–11 (page citations are to the revised edition).

4. David L. Larsen, *The Anatomy of Preaching* (Grand Rapids: Baker, 1989), 65.

Henry Mitchell, and Eugene Lowry summarized their suggested homiletical paradigm shift as "the creation of an experience in which both speaker and audience are co-participants in an event of understanding."[5] Lowry himself commented:

> After hearing for years about constructing, assembling, building, and putting together sermons, the metaphoric tease of the term tree changed everything. And that was almost forty years ago!
>
> A lot has happened since then. The "New Homiletic," as it is often called, has evoked new images and new definitions about what preaching is all about—with such terms as inductive preaching, phenomenological sermons, storytelling, eyewitness biblical accounts, and narrative plots.[6]

Lowry hailed the common denominators of the "new homiletical family" as (1) a refusal to announce a conclusion in advance and (2) an intentional use of moving, sequenced form.[7] Both elements stand in opposition to time-tested rhetorical structure that calls for a clearly stated proposition and supported divisions.

Although huge theological blunder lies at the root of both the new hermeneutic and the new homiletic, the utter absurdity of such theory is especially blatant in these homiletical assertions. Consider several factors that often go unobserved—or at least unmentioned—when these new trends are discussed.

First, the contentions that fluidity of thought and inductive development have replaced traditional rhetorical structure as the primary effective means of communication have not been proven or even tested. Aristotle developed the principles of rhetoric primarily from simple observation, not from some philosophical or anthropological paradigm that no longer exists. He watched people—speakers and audiences. He observed that both learning and persuasion were enhanced by speeches with logical arrangement developed from a clear proposition. People are no different today in that regard. If they were, politicians and government leaders would have adopted these new forms of communication long ago. Nations are still moved by the power of the spoken word transmitted through propositional assertion and logical arrangement. Just because

---

5. Robert Reid, Jeffrey Bullock, and David Fleer, "Preaching as the Creation of an Experience: the Not-So-Rational Revolution of the New Homiletic," *The Journal of Communication and Religion* 18, no. 1 (March 1995): 1.

6. Eugene L. Lowry, *The Sermon: Dancing the Edge of Mystery* (Nashville: Abingdon, 1997), 12.

7. Ibid., 28.

someone writes a book, gives a lecture, or champions a new idea in some other way, the idea is not necessarily substantiated.

Second, many proponents of a less-structured homiletic have played the hypocrite by being inconsistent with their own methods of communication. It is interesting that the vast majority of works promoting this new homiletical approach are themselves based on some proposition stated early in the book and then developed by means of logical arrangement. Donald Hamilton has observed rightly:

> It is interesting to note that the same authors who condemn the concept of propositional truth do so almost exclusively through means of propositional argumentation. . . . Those involved in espousing a "new homiletic" seem to be contradictory in the way they communicate their ideas about preaching in comparison to the way they say sermonic ideas themselves must be communicated.[8]

If modern listeners learn best according to a particular means of communication, then it seems that such a means ought to be employed at every turn—not only in sermons but also in the books that teach how to develop them. Lectures by many critics of structure often are presented the same way. During a recent interview, a popular youth communicator was belittling the use of traditional outlining approaches in contemporary youth talks. He followed his sarcastic comments by saying, "Now let me give you four reasons why I don't think you should use an outline."

Third, and similarly, a structureless speech or sermon really does not exist. Every sermon will have some kind of structure. Even Buttrick, who orchestrated the attempt to dismantle the old homiletic, admitted that "all speaking involves sequence."[9] His "moves" themselves are a kind of structure. Lowry's own *Homiletical Plot* (John Knox, 1980) suggests certain movements and transitions that provide structure for narrative sermons. So the issue is not whether or not a sermon should have structure. As Hamilton said, "The issue is whether the structure chosen will benefit or hinder the communication process."[10]

Fourth, the majority of homileticians who espouse the new homiletic hail from church traditions where preachers preach for fifteen to twenty minutes one time a week. Such is a radically different preaching paradigm from that of many evangelical churches, where the preaching event is

---

8. Donald L. Hamilton, *Homiletical Handbook* (Nashville: Broadman, 1992), 28.

9. David Buttrick, *Homiletic* (Philadelphia: Fortress, 1987), 309.

10. Hamilton, *Homiletical Handbook,* 22.

more central and more frequent. Furthermore, the track record of church growth where this new homiletic has been practiced does not reveal any substantial evidence that such theory is actually affecting growth in the body of Christ. At the same time, a cursory look at local churches and denominations that have reflected consistent, substantial growth reveals that the majority have been exposed to a regular diet of exposition packaged in propositional development and logical arrangement.

The assault on sermon structure may be to a large degree a reaction to the many abuses of traditional homiletical structure. Larsen observed, "We would readily concur that much preaching is too boxy. It is in chunks and gobs, parts and pieces."[11] For many preachers, outlining has become a time-devouring art that produces attractive sermons with little substance. Others have become technicians and are overly concerned about matters such as alliteration or having a certain number of divisions. Such abuses frequently have led to imposition upon or altering of the text. "As a result," said Hamilton, "valuable time is taken away from exegetical study, attention-grabbing introductions, convicting conclusions, or even pastoral work other than preaching!"[12] Still others have fallen prey to routine, using the same kind of design week after week and desensitizing their audiences with boring predictability.

Some even have tried to substitute a mastery of sermon structure for holiness. Koller said, "Structural soundness cannot supply that life of holiness which is basic to pulpit power. There is an eloquence of the lips, and there is an eloquence of the heart." The former alone only frustrates listeners.

The proper response for the expositor is to avoid throwing out the baby with the bathwater. He must understand the role of sermon structure, so that it is neither neglected nor ignored. "Structure is not what preaching is all about. It is a vehicle meant to allow the substance—the content—of the sermon to be more effectively communicated. It is a means to an end."[13] The statement of the proposition announces the truth being proclaimed, lays it in the listeners' laps, and sets the direction for their understanding and subsequent response. A clear design enables the preacher to measure progress and movement. For the listeners, the design provides handles to grab during the course of the message.[14] Without question, good structure is indispensable in the preaching event.

11. Larsen, *Anatomy of Preaching*, 66.
12. Hamilton, *Homiletical Handbook*, 21.
13. Ibid., 21–22.
14. Alvin C. Rueter, "Issues Shaping Effective Proclamation," *Emphasis* 14 (February 1985): 9.

UNDERSTANDING SERMON DESIGN

As implied in the previous discussion, the traditional term used to describe the structure of the body of a sermon is the "outline." While Davis's assertions regarding the whole of sermon structure are lacking, his use of "design" to describe sermon development is helpful. He wrote:

> So I shall speak of sermonic design rather than of sermon construction. . . . I shall speak of the sketch or the design of a sermon rather than of an outline, for it seems more significant and closer to the nature of the work. But if we know the thing we are talking about, it can be called an outline or a plan just as well. It seems more natural to call it a design, because the word outline does not necessarily connote true seeing and shaping.[15]

Regardless of the terminology employed, such organization is crucial for effective sermon structure. We will adopt Davis's terminology but define the design as follows:

Def'ə-nish'ən

de·sign *n.* The arrangement and coordination of the main body of a sermon according to two or more divisions that support the development of the given proposition.

The subordinate ideas of a design frequently are called "main points." The term "divisions" seems more appropriate, however, because the structure of some sermons is better described in terms of descriptions, categorizations, movements, scenes, or some other idea that more closely reflects the nature of the given text. "Points" implies a more limited nature of sermonic design. The major issue here is that of structure, not whether the wording makes a particular "point." These divisions, then, are developed, supported, clarified, and applied with subdivisions or other supporting material that expounds the Word of God.

THE IMPORTANCE OF SERMON DESIGN

Good design will enhance the preacher's ability to communicate the CIT, proposition, and purpose. Designs are like road maps, enabling us to

---

15. H. Grady Davis, *Design for Preaching* (Philadelphia: Fortress, 1958), 21.

view where we are going and keeping us on the proper road as we journey toward our desired destination. They are the burrs that lodge themselves in the minds of our listeners.[16] A design also may be compared to an arrow. The shaft must be straight, the point must be penetrating, and the feathers must be in just the right proportion to steady the arrow in flight.[17]

The design of your message, then, is an extremely important part of its organization. Good organization requires the development of main divisions before you add explanation, argumentation, illustration, and application to your message. A well-planned design enables you to place all of these added ingredients into your message in the most appropriate and beneficial places. Excellent sermon design gives the preacher several advantages.

A clear design gives *structure* to the sermon. Too often the preacher takes a text, departs therefrom, and goes everywhere preaching the gospel. Design keeps him on course and enables him to summarize better what he has said for a final impression upon his listeners.

A clear design gives *guidance* to the listener. As the message is delivered, the hearer can better follow its logical unfolding.

A design gives the sermon a sense of *pace*. The message is journeying step by step through a passage of Scripture, moving toward an effective climax. This logical development will give your listeners a sense of expectancy and anticipation.

A design brings *unity* to the various parts of the sermon for both preacher and listener. It ties the different parts of the message together. Each division can be related to the others as the proposition of the sermon is unfolded.

A design gives *arrangement* to the abundance of exegetical material. It will help the preacher know how to organize his information and determine where each piece fits best.

Several dangers need to be noted when designing a sermon. First, if your design is very noticeable, it can become *distracting* from the substance of the sermon. Your design is just the skeleton of the sermon. Be careful that the bones of your message do not protrude to the point that the flesh is missed. Second, some designs are overly *sensational*. Although a sermon design should be clear and appealing, avoid the temptation to make it too clever or shocking. You may acquire a reputation as a skillful sermon designer but fail to give usable information to your people. Third,

16. John Phillips, *One Hundred Sermon Outlines from the New Testament* (Chicago: Moody, 1979), Introduction.
17. Charles W. Koller, *Expository Preaching Without Notes* (Grand Rapids: Baker, 1962), 41.

a design easily can be *imposed* upon a Scripture passage. If you have a propensity toward a certain number of divisions, for example, you may impose more or less than the Bible text dictates.

VARIETY IN SERMON DESIGN

Always be aware of the need to approach your sermonizing from a variety of angles. In the ensuing discussion, we want to establish some good principles of sermon design. Room exists, however, for a great deal of variety and originality in the arranging of sermon designs because of the variety of literary genres in Scripture.[18]

Because homiletics is the *art* of preaching, you should employ your artistic tendencies to create sermonic masterpieces. Some designs will be like ladders. Each division moves to the next like the rungs of a ladder. Other sermon designs will look more like a beautiful diamond. The proposition of the sermon is approached from several angles so that each facet of the idea's beauty may be seen. Still other sermon designs will appear like a skyrocket. The message begins on the ground, rises to magnificent heights, bursts into pieces, then gracefully comes to earth again.[19]

The novice preacher, however, would do well to master several basic methods of creating sermon designs before experimenting with other forms. James Braga wisely counseled:

> While the student is learning homiletics, it would not be wise for him to exercise this liberty. On the contrary, the beginner should apply himself rigidly to the rules until he has mastered them thoroughly. There will come a time later in his ministry when, under the leading of the Spirit of God, he may disregard some of these principles.[20]

Warren Wiersbe concurred:

> Homiletics is the science of preaching, and it has basic laws and principles that every preacher ought to study and practice. Once you've learned how to obey these principles, then you can adapt them, modify them, and tailor them to your own personality.[21]

---

18. Every student of preaching would do well to own a copy of Hamilton's *Homiletical Handbook* (Nashville: Broadman, 1992). He has done a superb job of putting together a practical guide to the development of eight different sermon structuring methods and their application to the various kinds of literature in the Bible.
19. John R. W. Stott, *Between Two Worlds* (Grand Rapids: Eerdmans, 1982), 229.
20. James Braga, *How to Prepare Bible Messages* (Portland: Multnomah, 1981), 90.
21. Warren W. Wiersbe, "Your Preaching Is Unique," *Leadership* 2 (Summer 1981): 32.

Three of these basic designs will be discussed later in this chapter.

Some preachers seem more gifted than others in being able to divide a passage into its main divisions. Lloyd-Jones discussed the obvious gift of Alexander Maclaren, the famous Baptist expositor in England. Maclaren seemed to have a kind of golden hammer in his hand with which he could tap a text, and immediately the text would divide itself into sharp, crisp divisions.[22] But most of us have to work hard at designing the main divisions of our messages. Do not hesitate to tarry at this task when necessary.

If you have difficulty and find yourself at the point of mental paralysis, do not waste your precious study time. Move on to some other aspect of preparation for a while, such as looking for illustrations or thinking about specific application of the certain truths in the text. The main divisions may very well emerge at some later point. Later, we will discuss some suggestions for breaking the mental tangle that sometimes arises during preparation.

THE CREATION OF THE DESIGN

Creating effective sermon designs can be accomplished in four phases: *identification, clarification, reiteration, and transition.* The expositor first must identify the design that is suggested by the structure of the text. Then he must work to express each division in the clearest way possible. Next, he should reinforce the divisions by means of various reiterative tools. Finally, the preacher should give a sense of cohesiveness to his divisions by developing good transitional sentences.

As you create a design for your sermon, you will want to lay it out on your summary sheet (see Appendix 2). The most common methods of doing this utilize some type of enumeration for organization purposes. For example, after beginning with the introduction, you may arrange the main divisions by Roman numerals (I, II, III, etc.). Under each main division you might use subdivisions A, B, C, and so forth. For the material under the subdivisions you could use numerals—1, 2, 3, and so on. Indent subdivisions under each main division. Then, indent the supporting material under each subdivision. This approach gives you an easy-to-read arrangement for your sermon design. Of course, you may choose to use any number of enumeration methods, including bullet lists. Find the method that is comfortable and functional for you.

---

22. D. Martyn Lloyd-Jones, *Preaching and Preachers* (Grand Rapids: Zondervan, 1971), 208.

PHASE #1: IDENTIFICATION

The first task of the expositor in developing a design is to *identify* the natural divisions in his passage of Scripture. This characteristic distinguishes expository sermons from most other forms. Rather than impose a design upon the text, the expositor allows the structure to emerge naturally from the passage at hand whenever possible.

Getting your main divisions from the passage itself dictates the number of divisions you will use. Some homileticians over the years have championed adamantly that all sermons have three divisions. The old joke "He had three points and a poem" is characteristic of many preachers. A sense of balance and beauty does seem to characterize sermons with three divisions, but do not allow yourself to fall into a numerical trap. The number of divisions will vary according to the substance of the passage. You may have two divisions or three or more. If you exceed four, you may be using too much Scripture for one sermon. At the same time, do not force divisions from the text if they are not present.

DIFFERENCES IN DEVELOPMENT

Several different approaches to designing expository sermons have been used throughout the history of preaching. Some are better than others, but each has made an important contribution to the preaching event. The approaches below are listed in order of preference with regard to expository preaching, because of the degree to which they employ good sermon structure.

Expository sermonizing. The finest type of expository preaching is the expository sermonizing approach. This approach reflects understanding of the passage on the part of the preacher. He prepares a logical presentation of the content of the text. He has a proposition, main divisions, an introduction, and a way to conclude. Using this structure as a guide, he explains, illustrates, argues, and applies the truth of the passage and establishes its relevancy to the lives of his listeners.

Pure exposition. With pure exposition, little attempt is made to give any balance or beauty to a scant design. Very little work is done in providing subdivisions under the main divisions. It is interesting that most of the men who do expository work tend to fall into this category. Preachers who have an obvious gift of teaching find pure exposition extremely adaptable to their purposes, as their unique giftedness compensates for little sermon structure.

Bible reading. The Bible reading approach involves the reading of a segment of Scripture (paragraph, thought block, etc.), giving some explanation and application, then moving to the next section. In this case, the sections of the Scripture that are read serve as the design, or sermon structure. These divisions may or may not be labeled.

Homily. Also called the running commentary, this approach is similar to the Bible reading approach except that the preacher explains, illustrates, and applies as he moves word by word, phrase by phrase, and/or verse by verse through the passage.[23] The approach has no discernable design, although the preacher usually identifies some benchmarks for his own aid in presentation. The primary danger of using this approach is that the preacher easily can depend upon his thoughts about the passage at the moment rather than giving himself to rigorous study of the text. Furthermore, the absence of a definite design does weaken the sermon's structure, lessening the listener's ability to retain the substance of the message.

Advanced homily. This approach is a species of the homily in which the preacher usually begins with a strong introduction and finishes with a strong conclusion.[24]

You may already have a germinal design in mind before you reach this point in the expositional process. Sometimes the natural divisions will begin to emerge during your general reading of the text. Those occurrences are so rewarding, especially when your initial observations later are confirmed in your thorough analysis. Sometimes the design gradually emerges as you come to the conclusion of your exegetical work. But at other times you will find yourself at this point looking more intently for a design.

Three foundational approaches are suggested for identifying the natural divisions of a text and developing corresponding expository designs. Each of these approaches is intended to focus the preacher's attention on the structure of the text. Sermon structure that reflects the structure of the given biblical text has been considered a distinguishing characteristic of expository sermons. After selecting the best method of development for your particular text, note it on your summary sheet in order to keep you focused as you develop your design (see Appendix 2).

---

23. James Cox, *A Guide to Biblical Preaching* (Nashville: Abingdon, 1976), 22.
24. H. C. Brown, *A Quest for Reformation in Preaching* (Nashville: Broadman, 1968), 222–23.

Key Word Method

One of the most helpful suggestions for developing sermon designs was championed by Koller and Whitesell in the early 1960s. This method has continued to serve expositors well, especially when the preaching text is no more than one paragraph in length. The approach calls for the use of a plural noun as the key word that characterizes the main divisions. The main sections of the message are arranged around this plural noun, using a lead-in sentence and creating parallel structure with logical, orderly development.[25]

The Key Word Method requires that you first revisit the structural diagram you did earlier in your analysis work. Now that you have completed your exegetical work and know the meaning of the passage, look again at the syntax to see if you can identify the natural divisions. You are looking specifically for any primary series of parallel or progressive ideas. You may notice a series such as reasons, examples, commands, steps, or phases, any of which may serve as your key word.

In a message from Colossians 2:8–23, for example, you may use the key word *substitutes* to describe certain philosophies that people embrace in place of Christ:

Lead-in: In this text, the Bible reveals four false substitutes for Christ that people embrace:

> Intellectualism (vv. 8–10)
> Ritualism (vv. 11–17)
> Mysticism (vv. 18–19)
> Legalism (vv. 20–23)

In a sermon taken from Titus 2:11–15, you might identify three *benefits* of God's amazing grace:

Lead-in: According to this passage, the following three benefits await everyone who receives God's amazing grace:

> Salvation (v. 11)
> Education (v. 12)
> Anticipation (v. 13)

---

25. Koller, *Expository Preaching*, 52–55. In addition to guidelines for employing the method, the author provides an extensive list of possible key words that will prove very helpful for the expositor.

Again, you may use the key word *actions* in a message exhorting people to give financially:

Lead-in: The apostle Paul challenges believers to take two actions regarding good financial stewardship:

Acknowledge Everything You Have as Belonging to God.
Appropriate God's Grace to Enable You to Give.

Make an effort to avoid using the word "things" as the key word in the development of the sermon. "Today, I want to tell you three *things* about getting your life on track" does not give the listeners anything concrete on which to hold. This word is much too general. Seek for a specific key word that can help you move into the main divisions of your message. To employ the Key Word Method, then, follow these steps:

KEYING IN ON A KEY WORD

☞ Revisit your structural diagram and identify natural divisions and parallel ideas.

☞ Ask a series of probing questions about your proposition. Who or Whom? What? When? Where? Why? Which? How?

☞ Determine which question is best answered by the primary series of parallel or progressive ideas in the text.

☞ Identify the key word that summarizes the answers to the question.

☞ Build your introduction and lead-in sentence around the key word.

☞ Develop your design as a series of answers to the question.

Now look at the Key Word process from beginning to end. Although preaching from one verse usually is not the best approach, let us use Hebrews 4:12 as an example of a preaching text. After thorough analysis of the context, an appropriate proposition might be: *People should respond obediently to God's rest because of the nature of His Word.*

First, look back at the structural diagram of Hebrews 4:12 in Appendix 1. Look for natural divisions and parallel ideas. Notice the series of descriptions of God's Word: *living, powerful, sharper, piercing,* and *discerner.* Once you have identified this series, ask the following questions of the proposition—*people should respond obediently to God's rest because of the nature of His Word:*

> *Who* should respond obediently to God's rest?
> *What* is the nature of His Word?
> *When* should people respond to God's rest?
> *Where* should people respond to God's rest?
> *Why* should people respond obediently to God's rest?
> To *which* rest should people respond?
> *How* should people respond obediently to God's rest?

Next, look back at the text to determine which of these questions is best answered by the series of parallel ideas. In this case, probably the second question (*What?*) or the fifth question (*Why?*) is addressed most directly by the text. The parallel descriptions of God's Word appear to delineate the nature of His Word as well as supply a justification for people's obedience. The key word that best describes the answers to the second question might be *characteristics* or *qualities.* The key word that best describes the answers to the fifth question is *reasons.* Any of these descriptions would be appropriate for this text. In other words, people should respond obediently to God's rest because His Word is living, powerful, sharp, piercing, and discerning! So your resulting lead-in sentence and subsequent design might look like this:

> *Lead-in:* In this text, the author provides five qualities of God's Word that merit our obedient response to God's rest:
>
> > Quality #1: Living
> > Quality #2: Powerful
> > Quality #3: Sharp
> > Quality #4: Piercing
> > Quality #5: Discerning

Or it may look like this:

> *Lead-in:* The biblical writer provides five reasons that people should respond obediently to God's rest:
>
> > Reason #1: God's Word Is Alive.
> > Reason #2: God's Word Is Powerful.
> > Reason #3: God's Word Is Sharp.

Reason #4: God's Word Is Piercing.
Reason #5: God's Word Is Discerning.

As you can see, this approach produces several benefits. (1) Your main divisions are kept in one category. (2) The plural noun form of the key word (*qualities, reasons*) points you in the direction you intend to follow throughout the development of your message. (3) Your sermon now has a sense of unity. (4) The singular form of the key word (*quality, reason*) helps to construct your main divisions in a parallel manner. (5) This key word allows you to test your main divisions to see if they fit with the other divisions in your design. (6) The main divisions of your sermon are tied together. (7) The key word will help you memorize the main divisions of your sermon.[26]

Koller summarized by saying that the great value of the Key Word Method is that it "opens a corridor down the length of the sermon structure, with direct access from the front entrance to every room, instead of leaving the preacher and his hearers wandering uncertainly from room to room."[27]

Analytical Method

Another approach to developing an expository design is the Analytical Method. This procedure is especially helpful when preaching from texts of two or more paragraphs in length. Along with the Key Word Method, the expositor should be able to use this approach to develop sermon designs from almost any passage in the Bible.[28]

The Analytical Method basically involves analyzing the proposition and breaking it down into component parts that are conducive to easy understanding. Analytical designs may be the most common type of structure utilized in expository sermons. Each major division normally reflects some category or subtopic of the primary subject.

Again, the Analytical Method involves revisiting the structural diagram to see if you can identify different categories that describe various segments of the text. You may notice some combination of an assertion, a reason, an example, a rationale, or a command. Maybe different actions are described, such as an explanation, an excuse, a defense, or an intent.

A sermon on the new birth from John 3 might be designed as follows:

26. Farris D. Whitesell, *Power in Expository Preaching* (Old Tappan, N.J.: Revell, 1963), 60.
27. Koller, *Expository Preaching,* 52–53.
28. Hamilton, *Homiletical Handbook,* 59. This method also has been suggested by R. C. H. Lenski in *The Sermon: Its Homiletical Construction* (reprint, Grand Rapids: Baker, 1968), 90; and Lloyd M. Perry in *A Manual for Biblical Preaching* (Grand Rapids: Baker, 1981), 90–95.

1. The Must of the New Birth
2. The Mystery of the New Birth
3. The Means of the New Birth

A message on the tongue from James 3:1–12 could be designed like this:

1. The Directive Nature of the Tongue
2. The Destructive Nature of the Tongue
3. The Deceptive Nature of the Tongue

A design for 1 Peter 1:13–21 regarding Christians being temporary residents in this world might read:

1. The Imperatives of Pilgrim Living
2. The Implications of Pilgrim Living

The Analytical Method is a very easy way to design expository sermons. Many possibilities usually exist in every preaching paragraph for dividing and categorizing the content. To summarize the use of the Analytical Method, consider the following steps:

ACQUIRING AN ANALYTICAL DESIGN

☞ Revisit your structural diagram and note the major aspects or facets of the text into which the proposition can be divided.

☞ Formulate your major divisions based upon some unique quality, characteristic, or category of the proposition.

☞ Word the major divisions according to the above qualities, characteristics, or categories.

Consider, for example, the structural diagram of Jeremiah 17:5–10 found in Appendix 1. After careful analysis of the passage, the following proposition might evolve: "Depend upon the Lord instead of yourself, because He is able to know your heart as well as your actions." You quickly will notice three prominent divisions that delineate the sayings of the Lord. He said, "Cursed is the man . . ." (v. 5), "Blessed is the man . . ." (v. 7), and, "I, the Lord . . ." (v. 10). From this passage, Kaiser formulated the following three major divisions for a sermon entitled "The Lord Who Knows Our Lives and Our Futures":

The Way of the Wicked—The Cursed Man (vv. 5–6)
The Way of the Blessed—The Blessed Man (vv. 7–8)
The Way of the Lord—The Examining God (vv. 9–10)[29]

With such a design, the preacher can analyze the central idea of the passage according to the actions and attitudes (i.e., "The Way of . . .") of each of the three characters mentioned in the text. The information in the corresponding verses would be used to support the treatment of each character's way.

Sermonic Plot Method

A third design, the Sermonic Plot, is especially helpful when preaching from narrative, or story, passages. Because 80 to 90 percent of the biblical text is in some kind of narrative form, preachers must become skillful at organizing sermons from such passages. Whereas the Analytical Method and occasionally the Key Word Method may be used with narrative passages, neither of the two is the best form for the genre, especially when those passages possess the natural qualities of story.

The common denominator of most stories is *plot*. Robert Roth said, "Stories begin once upon a time. They move through episodes to a climax and then come to an end. . . . Stories move. They have a plot."[30] Most biblical stories are no different. They contain the common elements of a life situation, episodes or movements, tension, climax, and resolution.

The Sermonic Plot, then, is a way of allowing these natural qualities of story to form the major divisions of the expository sermon based on a narrative text. The preacher simply uses the Bible story's natural movements to develop the proposition of the sermon. If, as expositors, we truly aim to allow the structure of the text to dictate the structure of the sermon, then this sermonic design must be considered for many sermons.

Technically, such a design does not infringe on logical arrangement, organization, propositional treatment, or even how the sermon looks when it is designed on a page. More important is the issue of understanding the progression of thought and moving accordingly from one division to another. As Calvin Miller noted, "Narrative sermons have a linear, not an Arabic numeral, outline."[31] Consequently, your design from a narrative

29. Walter C. Kaiser Jr. *Toward an Exegetical Theology* (Grand Rapids: Baker, 1981), 168–69.
30. Robert Roth, *Story and Reality* (Grand Rapids: Eerdmans, 1973), 23–24.
31. Calvin Miller, "Narrative Preaching," in *Handbook of Contemporary Preaching*, ed. Michael Duduit (Nashville: Broadman, 1992), 114.

text may progress something like this:

Introduction ➞ Scene ➞ Resolution ➞ Conclusion

Or, as Miller described it:

Once Upon ➞ Event ➞ Event ➞ Happy Ever ➞ Application
a Time   After

THE HOMILETICAL PLOT

Eugene Lowry's *The Homiletical Plot* (John Knox, 1980) can be very helpful for designing sermons from narrative texts. Though Lowry's work is born out of a much broader homiletic, he gives the expositor a good pattern for sermon structure based on story material. See if you can identify these components in narrative passages:

Upsetting the Equilibrium
(Oops!)—introduce the problem

Analyzing the Discrepancy (Ugh!)
—diagnose or analyze the problem

Disclosing the Clue to Resolution
(Aha!)—introduce the solution to the problem

Experiencing the Gospel (Whee!)—bring the gospel to bear on the problem

Anticipating the Consequences (Yeah!)—apply the gospel resolution to contemporary life

The expositor normally will be able to identify at least the first three movements and usually the fourth in biblical narratives. The last movement then can be developed as the preacher applies the truth of the text. After identifying the components and using them to structure your sermon, experiment with phrasing the divisions in other terminology.

Regardless of the terminology that is employed, the sermon—like the text—moves from an introduction (or setting) to a series of events (or scenes) in which tension evolves, to a resolution of that tension by way of God's truth, and finally to the application of that truth to the contemporary hearers.

Once again, many variations of the Sermonic Plot design are possible for just about every narrative passage. Once you have identified the major movements in the text and the major components of the story, you should be able to identify a good design rather quickly. To design a sermon using the Sermonic Plot, simply follow these guidelines:

PLODDING THROUGH THE PLOT

☞ Look at the flow of the passage and note connectors and transitional words that indicate movement (*and, then, now, but, however,* etc.).

☞ Identify the basic elements of plot in the text (setting, scenes, tension, resolution) as you reflect back on your analysis work.

☞ Identify the primary characters in the story.

☞ Formulate the major divisions of your sermon according to the movement from one element in the story to another.

Take a moment to look back at the literary representation of Mark 4:35–41 in Appendix 1. Notice the connectors *now, and, but, then, but,* and *and* at the beginnings of verses 36–41 respectively. These words are hints to the movements between the elements of the plot. An analysis of the text reveals that the passage emphasizes the deity of Christ and the subsequent faith people should have in Him. Verses 35–37 merely describe everyday events around the Sea of Galilee. The connectors *now* (v. 36) and *and* (v. 37) serve as transitions between the various descriptive elements. These verses present the setting of the story. The connector *but* in verse 38 introduces the tension, or conflict. The problem in the story is not the storm—that happened regularly on this sea. The problem in the story is that Jesus, who professed to be something more than mere man, was asleep during the storm, seemingly unconcerned about the fate of the crew. Next, the connector *then* at the beginning of verse 39 introduces the resolution to the problem: Jesus tells a real live storm to sit down and be quiet. Verses 40–41 describe Jesus' application of His deity to the disciples' lives, as well as their reflection on His identity.

Based on the previous discussion, several ways of structuring a sermon from this text emerge. The preacher simply needs to determine which way best communicates the truth of the passage regarding the deity of Christ without compromising the integrity of the narrative literature. Consider the following possibilities:

Verse(s)	35–37	38a	38b	39	40–41	
Design #1	Identity Assumed	Identity Confused	Identity Questioned	Identity Revealed	Identity Realized	
Design #2	The Stormy Life of Galilee	When Jesus Doesn't Act the Way He's Supposed To		That's a God-thing!	If He Can Do That, He Can Do Anything	
(Miller)	Once Upon a Time	Events		Happy Ever After	Application	
Design #3	Jesus is Never Around When You Need Him!	The Real Messiah Would Never Do That!	Look At What Jesus Did!	Only God Could Do That!	Since Jesus is God, He Can Handle Anything in My Life!	
(Lowry)	Upsetting the Equilibrium (Oops!)	Analyzing the Discrepancy (Ugh!)	Disclosing the Clue to Resolution (Aha!)	Experiencing the Gospel (Whee!)	Anticipating the Conse-quences (Yeah!)	

Keep in mind that using the elements of plot to design sermons from narrative texts does not imply an inductive approach to preaching. Many proponents of a contemporary narrative homiletic suggest that because story is inductive by nature, then the sermon should be inductive. This assertion, however, overlooks the reality that the preacher has not been called merely to *retell* the biblical story but to *explain* it. Consequently, use the narrative design to structure your sermons from narrative texts, but do not neglect your responsibility to expose God's truth through deductive reasoning. The two elements together can be a powerful combination.

PHASE #2: CLARIFICATION

The second phase in designing involves expressing each division in the clearest and most understandable form possible. Once the expositor has identified the natural structure of the text, he should work toward tightening up the design so that it is conducive to oral communication. Several qualities discussed below will aid him in expressing his divisions in a clear form. Exceptions to these qualities certainly exist (especially with some narrative designs), but you can use this checklist as a guide for developing clear structure. Several fictitious designs have been provided to illustrate the discussion. The respective designs are referenced along with the corresponding qualities.

Design #1	Design #2
1. God Is Good	1. God Is Good
2. God Is Great	2. God Is Great
3. Let Us Thank Him for Our Food	3. God Is Provider

Design #3	Design #4
1. Go into All the World	1. Go into All the World
2. Baptism	2. Baptize the Converts
3. What To Do with New Converts	3. Instruct the Disciples

Parallel structure. Make sure all the divisions in the same sermon are grammatically parallel. Avoid mixing verb tenses, phrases, imperative statements, and declarations. This effort will provide a sense of unity and symmetry as well as help your listeners follow you more easily. Compare #1 with #2 and #3 with #4. Note the difference in parallelism.

Mutually exclusive. Keep your divisions related to the CIT and proposition, but be sure each one is discrete and independent of the others in content and development of the central idea. In #1 or #2, for example, the preacher would need to make sure that the material in the first two divisions regarding goodness and greatness was not repeated in the material in the third division on provision.

Application-oriented. Use the present and future tenses as much as possible. Avoiding the past tense gives a sense of application to those who listen. The present and future tenses will help you get from the Bible world to the world of your listeners with a more contemporary ring. Without regard to the nature of the texts or the purpose of the sermons, #4 is better than #2 because of its application orientation.

Complete sentences. Make each division a concise, complete sentence. Most designs will be more effective, memorable, and relevant if they are worded in complete thoughts. Beside not being parallel with the first division, the second two divisions in #3 are not as effective as the first because they are sentence fragments instead of complete sentences.

Progressive. Develop a gradual heightening of interest in your main divisions. Avoid becoming unduly occupied with any single division and failing to give adequate attention to the others. Doing so will hinder any sense of movement in your sermon and foster slackening interest on the part of your listeners. Consider how #4 progresses from one division to the next in a logical manner.

Climactic. Move your main divisions toward a climax. Most Scripture passages build toward a climax and, consequently, will lend themselves naturally to such a design. Keeping your proposition in mind, word each division so that its contribution to the design is underscored. Notice how #4 builds toward the climax of maturing disciples.

Assertive. Word each main division as a declaration, not a question. The preaching event is intended to answer questions, not ask them. Although interrogatives may be used on rare occasions, work toward giving your people answers to questions that arise from the text and help in applying those answers. Both #2 and #4 are examples of assertive designs.

Simple. Concentrate on developing strong main divisions with an intentional effort to avoid subdivisions. Work toward holistic communication. Emphasize how the parts relate to the whole without distracting the listener with too much structural detail. You may use subdivisions for your own purpose but avoid announcing them any more than is absolutely necessary. Both #2 and #4 are good, simple designs.

PHASE #3: REITERATION

Once you have clarified your major divisions, always look to see if they can be reworded in such a way that repeats the proposition. When a sermon's structure can be expressed in an easy-to-follow, memorable way, the truth of God's Word has a better chance of being firmly planted in the heart.

The value of reiterative patterns. The kind of symmetry utilized in reiteration often gives major division statements "a beauty and force of expression."[32] George Sweazey observed:

> A sermon will be better grasped and remembered if the titles of its points have some sort of correspondence. They may have a similarity in sound, or in the first letter. . . . Such devices might seem fatuous, but even the best speakers use them because they can make the difference between a speech being lost and its being followed and remembered.[33]

When the preacher words his major assertions as beautifully as possible, listeners are assisted in loving and responding to the truth.[34]

Even biblical writers used reiterative tools. "Playing games with the

32. Wayne McDill, *The 12 Essential Skills for Great Preaching* (Nashville: Broadman & Holman, 1994), 150.
33. George E. Sweazey, *Preaching the Good News* (Englewood Cliffs, N.J.: Prentice-Hall, 1976), 74.
34. Glen C. Knecht, "Sermon Structure and Flow," in *The Preacher and Preaching,* ed. Samuel T. Logan Jr., 275–302 (Grand Rapids: Baker, 1986), 287.

alphabet was not too childish for the Psalmist."[35] Some evidence even exists of their employment by Paul in the closing verses of Romans 1. Reiterative patterns have played a prominent role in literature, especially in poetry. They have been used by many prominent figures in literary history such as Chaucer, Spenser, and Swinburne. Certain phrases that occur in common speech have evolved as a result of such devices: "might and main," "life and liberty," "wrath and wickedness."

Types of reiterative patterns. Four particular reiterative patterns enhance understanding and response: *alliteration*, or the repetition of consonant sounds; *assonance*, or the repetition of a dominant or concluding vowel or a vowel and consonant combination; *repetition* of key terms; and *parallelism*, or the use of a similar form in each principal division:[36]

- ♦ *Alliteration.* This can mean beginning a word with the same letter and even the same first syllable. Look back at the designs from John 3 and James 3 in the discussion of the Analytical Method on pages 157–58. These developments employ alliteration using the beginning letter. The design from 1 Peter in the same discussion is characterized by alliteration using the first syllable.

- ♦ *Assonance.* The pattern of assonance usually employs words that have similar endings. Look again at the discussion of the Key Word Method. The sermon design from Colossians 2:8–23, on page 154, is characterized by assonance. Each word closes with the same syllable—*ism*. The sermon design from Titus 2:11–15 in the same discussion is made up of words that all end with the syllable *tion*.

- ♦ *Repetition.* Repeating certain terms highlights key concepts. Once again, the designs from John 3, James 3, and 1 Peter 1, on pages 157–58, used in discussion of the Analytical Method contain key words that are repeated for emphasis. "New Birth," "Nature of the Tongue," and "Pilgrim Living" all are repeated in order to call attention to the focus of each message.

- ♦ *Parallelism.* This pattern, already addressed in the discussion regarding clarification, characterizes all of the designs cited above. All divisions in each sermon are grammatically parallel, providing a sense of unity and symmetry while helping the listeners to follow more easily.

Proper employment of reiterative patterns enhances communication, but their misuse distracts listeners and deters response. Nothing is as

35. Sweazey, *Preaching the Good News,* 74.
36. E. Eugene Hall and James L. Heflin, *Proclaim the Word!* (Nashville: Broadman, 1985), 205–7.

poor as a poor attempt at a reiterative design. For example, consider the following design from Matthew 24:35–44:

1. A Pertinent Contrast
2. A Pointed Comparison
3. A Paradoxical Crisis
4. Our Prospect Comparable
5. The Practical Challenge

Several flaws immediately are apparent. The first three divisions parallel one another, but the last two are not parallel. The first three divisions use adjectives that begin with p. The fourth uses a noun that begins with p and a verb that begins with c, in contrast to the nouns that begin with c in the first three divisions. The fifth division then jumps back to the structure of the first three. The fourth division does not seem to fit at all.

Another example of a poor reiteration is found in Kaiser's design on Nehemiah 6:1–19:

1. A God-Given Sense of Direction (6:1–4)
2. A God-Given Spirit of Determination (6:5–9)
3. A God-Given Heart of Discernment (6:10–14)
4. A God-Given Demonstration of Approval (6:15–19)[37]

Notice that the first two divisions are parallel in structure and employ alliteration and assonance. The third division has no alliteration consistent with the words *sense* and *spirit* in the previous two divisions, nor does it share the assonance. The fourth division is even worse. This division uses a word that begins with d and shares the assonance of the three previous divisions, but that word is out of place in the sentence structure.

Let it be noted that the expositor should never feel compelled to use reiterative patterns in sermon outlining. At the same time, the abuse of such devices by some is not an adequate reason to reject them altogether. Most of the criticism leveled against the use of reiterative patterns comes from ministerial students and preachers who have witnessed repeated abuse. The vast majority of the people who sit in our pews, however, appreciate and welcome the added assistance. So use *good* reiteration if you intend to use it at all. If a particular pattern comes naturally from the Scripture passage or seems to fit it well without being forced, do not hesitate to employ it.

37. Kaiser, *Toward an Exegetical Theology,* 208.

REHABILITATING REITERATION

The use of reiterative patterns is a controversial subject. Many of the finest teachers of homiletics frown upon their employment. On the other hand, many effective expository preachers both past and present have utilized such tools. Several dangers as well as advantages are present when using the various devices. An awareness of both will help the preacher employ them with integrity.

DANGERS

Abuse. Preachers who use reiterative patterns sometimes demonstrate a tendency to manipulate the subject matter in order to make the content fit a desired design. Such employment is an abuse of God's Word and hinders the proclamation of the truth of the text.

Addiction. Some pastors become so addicted to the use of reiteration that their designs become burdensome for the hearers. Many who become overly interested in alliteration not only alliterate the main divisions but also the subdivisions (and even further!). Such use can be very annoying for those who must listen.

Arrogance. Like excessively referring to the meaning of Greek words, some preachers use reiterative patterns to display their ingenuity and cleverness. After a time, audiences will detect such arrogance and react against the entire message.

ADVANTAGES

Interpretation. A reiterative design frequently is fitted to good interpretation, making reiteration conducive to sound Bible exposition. For whatever reason, the natural flow of a Scripture passage often lends itself to a certain design with reiterative qualities.

Instruction. Designs that are characterized by reiteration tend to guide listeners through the journey of the sermon more easily. A reiterative structure enhances the listener's navigation through the biblical text. Divisions that are easily recognized give people clear instructions about the information for which they are to listen next.

Internalization. Reiterative designs can aid the memory of both preacher and audience. The whole task of memorizing designs is simplified greatly. Reiterative patterns also have a way of making the main divisions of the sermon stick in the minds of the listeners. Impressions are created upon their minds that will not be forgotten quickly.

PHASE #4: TRANSITION

The final task of the expositor in designing good sermon structure is to determine how best to move from one division to another. Such movement can be accomplished with transitional statements. A good sermon will have clear, smooth transitions between its major divisions.

Transitions fulfill two primary functions. First, they assist the preacher in testing his logic. Second, they aid the listeners in their understanding of the preacher's logic.[38] Transitions give evidence that the preacher clearly understands each section of his sermon and knows how one section moves logically to another. They also alert listeners to the fact that he is moving from one thought to another.

Development. The development of transitional sentences will vary somewhat depending upon the particular sermon design. The transition from introduction to main divisions is perhaps the easiest, especially when using the Key Word Method. Your introduction should conclude with a transitional sentence using the key word that moves naturally into your main divisions. Consider the lead-in sentence from the Colossians 2:8–23 design in the discussion of the Key Word Method, along with some possible transitional sentences between each division.

> *Lead-in:* In this text, the Bible reveals four false substitutes for Christ that people embrace. The first false substitute noted by Paul is . . .
>
> Intellectualism (vv. 8–10)
>
> > *Transition:* In addition to intellectualism, another false substitute for Christ is . . .
>
> Ritualism (vv. 11–17)
>
> > *Transition:* The next false substitute for Christ mentioned in this text is . . .
>
> Mysticism (vv. 18–19)
>
> > *Transition:* The final false substitute for Christ discussed in this passage is . . .
>
> Legalism (vv. 20–23)

Because of the nature of the Analytical Method, developing good transitional sentences may take a bit more work. Analyzing the proposi-

---

38. Milton Dickens, *Speech: Dynamic Communication* (New York: Harcourt Brace Jovanovich, 1954), 141.

tion and breaking it down into component parts normally produces categories or subtopics that are not as conducive to easy movement from one division to another. With patient and thoughtful attention, however, the expositor can move smoothly through an analytical design. The sermon from John 3 on the new birth noted earlier might follow this movement:

> *Lead-in:* In this passage, the new birth is considered from three standpoints. Notice, first of all, . . .
>
> The Must of the New Birth
>
>> *Transition:* Now that we've looked at the Must of the New Birth, consider . . .
>
> The Mystery of the New Birth
>
>> *Transition:* In addition to the Must and the Mystery of the New Birth, this text reveals . . .
>
> The Means of the New Birth

The unique nature of narrative genre requires the expositor to move from one division to another with even greater skill and intentionality. Being true to the structure of narrative literature demands transitions that least break the flow of events, especially when dealing with Bible stories. Therefore, specific attention should not be called to the actual divisions to the same degree as in the other designs.

Although the preacher is not simply retelling the story, he must work toward maintaining its natural movement. This task means that the transitional statements themselves carry the weight of the sermon's structure. For example, the sermon from Mark 4:35–41 mentioned earlier might be designed as follows:

> *Lead-in:* The story of one group's discovery of Jesus' deity begins with their assumption of His identity . . .

Division	Identity Assumed (vv. 35–37)	Identity Confused (v. 38a)	Identity Questioned (v. 38b)	Identity Revealed (v. 39)	Identity Realized (vv. 40–41)
Trans-ition	But just as the disciples were getting comfortable with who they thought Jesus was, He did some-thing out of character . . .	When Jesus didn't act the way the disciples thought He should, they began to question His actions . . .	The disciples' question provided Jesus with the perfect opportunity to reveal His identity . . .	Having seen Jesus do something only God could do, they suddenly became aware of who Jesus actually was . . .	If Jesus is really God, imagine how that truth impacts anything and everything you face in life today . . .

TRYING OUT YOUR TRANSITIONS

Inconspicuous. Broadus said that transitions from one part of a sermon to the next are best when they are least noticeable. He further stated that ideal transitional statements enable the constituent parts of your sermon to fit together perfectly.[39] Formulate statements that serve their purpose but do not call attention to themselves.

Simple. Usually transitions can be made by a single sentence that alerts your listeners that you are moving from one thought to another. Often, helpful words such as *again, moreover, furthermore, in the next place* can make helpful transitions.

Smooth. Practice vocalizing your transitional statements between each division. This exercise will help you test the structure of your design. If your divisions follow a logical sequence, movement from one division to another should be smooth. If you encounter trouble connecting each major division, you may need to revisit your transitions and possibly even your design.

Varied. Avoid using predictable transitions between every division, especially excessive use of numerical notations. Vary the way you introduce each section. Listeners tire of "first," "second," and "third." Instead, try saying, "The next mark ," or, "An additional mark," or, "A further mark."

Brief. Transitions usually can be made very quickly. In addition to the words noted above, terms such as *next, let us consider, further, I call your attention to, in addition to, or consider* will move you rapidly to your next thought.

---

39. Broadus, 121.

Characteristics. The quality of your transitional statements is crucial. Poorly worded sentences can confuse listeners as well as cause them to miss the movement of the sermon. Use the checklist of characteristics on the previous page for developing good transitional sentences.

Most preachers give little attention to transitions, relegating them to mere afterthoughts. On the contrary, transitions essentially are the glue that holds all the material of your message together. They briefly forecast the next thought, quickly summarize the previous thought, and show the connection between one thought and another. A good transitional statement is like a sign that says "This Is the Way—Follow Me."

CHAPTER SEVEN

MATURING
THE IDEAS

*A scaffolding is essential in putting up a building, but when
you look at the completed building you do not see the
scaffolding; you see the building. . . . The same thing
precisely is true of the human body. There is the frame,
the skeleton, but it must be clothed with flesh before
you have a body. This is equally true of a sermon.*

D. MARTYN LLOYD-JONES

Like the developing human body, a sermon is not capable of realizing its full potential until it matures. Some homileticians refer to this maturing process as putting meat on the bones of the message. Some preachers make the mistake of presenting only the bare framework of a sermon as the substance of their messages. This practice is as unpalatable to a listener as unwanted bones in a good fish dinner. The people want and deserve more than just a design. They need other information that will intentionally support, amplify, and drive home the truths you have discovered in the Scripture. This process of maturation involves two phases—amplification and incubation of the ideas in your message.

AMPLIFICATION

After you have unified the theme of your Scripture text and structured the passage, the time has come to amplify the major divisions with the necessary exegetical information. This process of amplification will help add the support needed in your sermon design to expose the mind of the Holy Spirit in the passage. Amplification can be accomplished with two general tasks. First, you must determine what exegetical information should be included in your sermon. Then, you must use certain functional elements—explanation, argumentation, application, and illustration—to develop the truths of the text in the best way possible.

WHAT ARE YOU DOING IN MY SERMON?

The expositor must be intentional about what he lets into his sermon. Every word, sentence, and paragraph must have a purpose for being there. Time constraints, short attention spans, demands for relevance, and other factors call on the modern preacher to be saying *something* every time he opens his mouth. The use of certain functional elements in the construction of the sermon will ensure intentional content. Make sure everything you say in the main body of your sermon is characterized by one of these elements. Furthermore, use the elements to determine the content of your message by asking the corresponding question of your exegetical material:

 Explanation. What information won't my audience immediately understand?

 Argumentation. What assertion(s) won't my audience immediately **agree with?**

 Application. How are these truths **relevant** to my audience?

 Illustration. Which assertion(s) can be **enhanced** with additional light?

As you begin this phase of your preparation, keep in mind two important things:

In the first place, you still are only making notes as opposed to precisely organizing your material. Do not get bogged down just now in trying to find the exact wording you will use in your sermon. Simply note general ideas and thoughts that you will refine at a later point.

Then, realize that the functional elements often overlap. Developing sermon content is not as simple as "explain, illustrate, apply," as some have suggested. Sometimes you will explain with an illustration. At other times you may apply with an illustration. Just try to think in terms of the primary purpose for using certain material.

STEP #1: DETERMINE THE NECESSARY BIBLICAL MATERIAL

Not all the material you have gathered in your analysis will need to be used. Avoid taking all of the technical baggage to the pulpit. A helpful practice is to ask yourself, What information from my analysis is absolutely necessary for my listeners to understand the meaning of this text and apply its truths to their lives? As some wag said about her scholarly pastor, "If he doesn't Hebrew-root you to death, he will strangle you to death with Greek participles!" Most of the people to whom you preach likely will not be interested in the technical details of your study. Do all the spade work of exegesis in your study and then glean the preaching riches for your sermon.

As you revisit the results of your analysis, you probably will be loathe to exclude *any* of the information you worked hard to discover. Be absolutely unyielding, however, in eliminating irrelevant material. Any material that does not definitely amplify what you are seeking to say from the text must be discarded rigorously. Use *only* what applies directly to the proposition at hand. If you acquire information so good that you must use it, file it away for ready reference and use it to support another message.

To help decide what biblical material is necessary for a sermon and what should be held back for another day, the preacher must have a determinant. That determinant is his sermon proposition, which was developed from the central idea of the text (CIT). For every bit of exegetical information uncovered in the analysis stage, you must ask the following question:

THE CONTENT QUESTION

IS THIS INFORMATION ABSOLUTELY NECESSARY OR EXTREMELY HELPFUL IN SUPPORTING THE PROPOSITION OF THIS SERMON?

Answering this question honestly will yield much fruit. This practice will help to ensure that everything you say in your message has a legitimate purpose.

To determine the specific biblical truth that will be the foundation of your sermon, follow these two steps:

♦ Ask the content question as you thoroughly go through all of the exegetical material reaped from your analysis. If you drew substantive conclusions from your consideration of the background material and each verse or group of verses in the text, you should be able to revisit those conclusions and complete this work.

♦ Organize each bit of necessary information according to each major division you developed in your design when you moved from analysis to sermon structure.

STEP #2: DEVELOP THE BIBLICAL MATERIAL

Once you have determined the necessity of certain information, you then can begin to develop the specific biblical truth that eventually will be the meat of your message. This task can be accomplished by employing two of the functional elements in particular—explanation and argumentation—as well as helpful supporting material. To help with the process, use a separate sheet of paper for each major division of your sermon. Make notes under each division regarding elements of the text that you will need to explain or argue. Follow the guidelines below to determine such material.

Explain What is Unclear

Explanation is the process of making something clear or plain and therefore more understandable.[1] Explanation is foundational for expository preaching and is its primary distinguishing factor. Robert Thomas said:

> The point that differentiates expository sermons from other types is not the cleverness of their outlines or their catch clichés. Neither is it the relevance of the message to everyday life. These are helpful and necessary as communicative tools and devotional helps, but they do not distinguish expository preaching from other kinds of sermons. A sermon could still be expository without them, but if the explanation of what the author meant is missing, so is the heart of Bible exposition.
>
> The unique contribution of Bible exposition is its substantial enhancement of the listeners' comprehension of Scripture's intent.[2]

Explanation is the element that vaults the supernatural truth of God's Word into the mind of the listener, thus enabling life change. Bill Hull said, "Transformation comes through the commitment of the mind. Without the proper knowledge and thinking we have no basis for personal change or growth. The mind is the pivotal starting place for change."[3]

In one respect, the other functional elements—argumentation, application, and illustration—are servants of explanation. These other elements all hinge on a proper understanding of truth. You are able to argue a point only after the facts are understood rightly. You can apply to the life only that which is properly comprehended. You never just illustrate; you illustrate *something,* and that something is a right understanding of God's truth. Argumentation, application, and illustration all depend on explanation of God's Word. Though argumentation and application both can

---

1. Al Fasol, *Essentials for Biblical Preaching* (Grand Rapids: Baker, 1989), 73.
2. Robert L. Thomas, "Exegesis and Expository Preaching," in John MacArthur Jr., *Rediscovering Expository Preaching,* ed. Richard L. Mayhue (Dallas: Word, 1992), 138.
3. Bill Hull, *Right Thinking* (Colorado Springs: NavPress, 1985)

be made using illustrations, the primary role of all three elements is to serve explanation.

The use of explanation in the sermon is tied almost exclusively to the various details of the biblical text under consideration. From time to time, however, this functional element may be used in conjunction with certain nonbiblical information. To determine what material needs to be explained, simply ask the following question of all of your necessary exegetical information:

> *WHAT INFORMATION WON'T MY*
> *AUDIENCE IMMEDIATELY UNDERSTAND?*

Asking this question will help you avoid explaining things in your message that do not need to be explained. Many words, phrases, and concepts in the biblical text are obvious. They simply mean what they say. Other meanings are less clear and need explanation if the audience is going to grasp the mind of God. But the expositor impairs his preaching and wastes valuable time when he explains the obvious or the unimportant.

Much of your explanation will be taken from the exegetical material you gained during your analysis of the passage. Give your people some explanation of the meaning of the passage based on word studies, syntactical and grammatical nuances, relevant doctrines, background information, and contextual considerations. In addition to your logical division of the text in your design, you may communicate this explanation through several means:

EXPLANATION EQUIPMENT

Presentation of Facts—information drawn from the analysis of the text. "There are three different words in the language of the New Testament, all of which are translated with the English word 'know.' The word used in this verse means to know by experience."

Theological Statement—a conclusion or assertion. "Jesus is the only way to heaven."

Narration—a story based on the setting, characters, and action of the text. "Several hours before daylight, Jesus woke up before anyone else and went to a deserted place in order to be alone with the Father."

Cross-Reference—a supporting parallel passage. "Some help in identifying which rock Jesus was referring to in Matthew 16:18 can be found in 1 Peter 2:1–8."

Comparison—relation to a familiar concept. "One jot and one tittle would be similar to one serif and one period."

Visual Aid—object or other visual augmentation. "Putting on the new man in Ephesians 4:24 describes the same action as my taking off this jacket I've been wearing and putting on this new jacket" (actually do it as you speak).

Oral Interpretation—reading the text as the biblical author or speaker likely intended it. "Come to *Me* [emphasis], all you who labor and are heavy laden, and *I* [emphasis] will give you rest. Take *My* [emphasis] yoke upon you and learn from *Me* [emphasis] . . ."

Regardless of which means you use, explanation always should be presented in an appealing, nonpedantic manner with the intent of increasing the listeners' understanding of the text.[4]

Arguing What is Objectionable

Regrettably, explaining aspects of the text to some listeners is not enough. We no longer live in a day when people believe something just because the Bible and the preacher suggest it. In other words, just because people understand an assertion does not mean that they automatically believe it. Consequently, as modern culture becomes more steeped in pluralism and relativism, preachers of the gospel will need to become more skilled in the art of argumentation. Argumentation in preaching may be defined as persuasion with the intent of changing an attitude or action.

Though argumentation generally involves controversy and dispute as much as reason and discussion, the functional element in preaching should aim at the latter two qualities.[5] The skill calls for a keen sense of discernment. The expositor must identify issues that might hinder the audience from embracing the proposition and then discuss them in a logical fashion in the spirit of Christ.

Robinson suggested that expositors work on anticipating objections their listeners may make to the truths presented.[6] To determine what aspects of the passage need to be argued, ask the following question of all of your necessary exegetical information:

4. Fasol, *Biblical Preaching,* 7
5. H. C. Brown, *A Quest for Reformation in Preaching* (Nashville: Broadman, 196
6. Haddon W. Robinson, *Biblical Preaching* (Grand Rapids: Baker, 1980), 71–72.

> *WHAT ASSERTION(S) WON'T MY*
> *AUDIENCE IMMEDIATELY AGREE WITH?*

As you ask this question, be sure not to raise objections that no one else would raise! Further, determine always to show respect and consideration for those who may hold views contrary to your own.[7]

Whereas most of your explanation is taken from your exegetical material, argumentation normally is built upon logical reasoning. John Calvin and Charles Finney, both of whom were trained in law before they began to preach, employed argumentation effectively. The apostle Paul, having been trained in ancient oratory and rhetoric, also was competent in the art.[8] The following models will help you as an expositor to argue your assertions in an effective way:[9]

ARGUMENTATION APPROACHES

Authority—Citing someone whom the audience considers authoritative. "You can trust what the Bible says. Billy Graham has become known over the years for saying, 'The Bible says . . .'"

Rebuttal—Tactfully and diplomatically proving to be erroneous or false "Many of you parents encourage your children to memorize the Sunday school memory verse but you refuse to hide God's Word in your own hearts. One day, your children will grow to assume that if it's not important for Mom and Dad, then it's not important for them."

Direction/Stages—Direction involves showing that a contention is not necessarily wrong, but it might lead to undesirable consequences. "Taking one drink may not be sin in and of itself, but statistics show that the chances of a social drinker's becoming an alcoholic are very high." Stages involves leading to a conclusion in a progressive manner, when a more direct approach might be rejected. "Many people accept the fact that Jesus is God. And most would agree that God is eternal,

---

7. Ibid.
8. Fasol, *Biblical Preaching*, 79.
9. For additional discussion on models of argumentation, see Stephen N. Rummage, "Toward Contemporary Apologetic Preaching: An Analysis of the Argumentative Methodologies of Richard Whately, William Bennett, and Josh McDowell" (Ph.D. diss., New Orleans Baptist Theological Seminary, 1998). Additional information can be found in Brown, *Reformation in Preaching*, 65–66, and Fasol, *Biblical Preaching*, 80–81. Fasol based his discussion on Brown's contentions.

meaning He's still around today. And everybody knows that God is Lord over everything. That makes Jesus Lord over your life right now."

Causal—Showing how a cause leads to an effect or an effect is the result of a cause. "Since we have been justified through faith, we have peace with God." And, "No one would dispute that the intricacies of a Pentium computer chip suggest that someone made it as opposed to its just happening by itself. Likewise, the intricacies of our universe suggest a Creator."

Hierarchical—Appealing for something lesser in light of a greater example, or something greater in light of a lesser example. "If that widow gave everything she had, then surely you and I can give a tenth of our income." "If sinful human fathers give presents to their children, then it follows that a perfect and good God will give good things to those who ask Him."

Compatibility—Showing that two things either are or are not compatible. "You say that you don't pursue God today because religion was forced on you as a child. Let me ask you something: Didn't your parents have to force you to brush your teeth as a child? Certainly! But you still brush your teeth today, don't you? So being forced to do something beneficial as a child isn't necessarily a logical excuse for rejecting it as an adult."

Pragmatic—Among a variety of pragmatic arguments, appealing to personal interests, prejudices, or emotions is one of the most common. "Some practical reasons also exist for giving financially to kingdom work. Your grandchildren are going to need a church where they can be nurtured and where their children can be nurtured. Right now is the time to be laying the foundation for that provision."

Model/Anti-model—Appealing for action that is like or contrary to a given example. Model: "Let this mind be in you which was also in Christ Jesus." Anti-model: "You believe that there is one God. Big deal! Even the demons of hell believe that much, and they tremble when they think about it."

As you employ argumentation, remember one other important truth. A defense lawyer in a court of law does not have to prove his case beyond refute. He needs only to establish reasonable doubt in the minds of the jurors. Similarly, the defender of the faith in the pulpit does not have to prove his point beyond rebuttal but merely bring his listeners to the place of at least entertaining the possibility that his assertions are valid. Such is fertile soil in which the Holy Spirit can do His convincing work.

STEP #3: APPLY THE BIBLICAL MATERIAL

Just because the preacher explains the text clearly and makes a convincing argument does not necessarily mean the listeners will make the connection between the biblical text and their lives. To be sure, the Bible is relevant regardless of what people may think. But the Bible's being relevant does not guarantee that every person understands its relevancy. The responsibility of the preacher, then, is to establish that relevancy in the minds of his listeners through *application*.

Broadus described application in preaching as "that part, or those parts, of the discourse in which we show how the subject applies to the persons addressed, what practical instruction it offers them, what practical demands it makes upon them."[10] Here the preacher does the work of linking the importance of the truth of the text with the hearers' situation and need. They are urged to accept what has been stated and act upon its counsel.[11]

Application, then, involves the listeners in the sermon by showing them how to live out particular Bible truths. This functional element may tell them how to know God, how specific problems can be solved, how to grow spiritually, how to perform Christian service, or how to live a better life. After you have done everything you can to expound the meaning of the passage, ask yourself, *So what? What does this have to say to my people?*

The Need for Application

As the twentieth century closes, a great deal of concern has been expressed about the lack of moral convictions on the part of the average churchgoer. A George Gallup poll taken in 1984 revealed that more people were going to church than ever before, yet no lifting of moral standards in American society took place. In 1999, little has changed. Nine out of ten adults indicate a religious preference of one kind or another and say that they attend church on at least some occasions. Six out of ten say that religion is very important in their personal lives. Despite increased church attendance, however, recent surveys indicate that the average American perceives "religion as a whole" to be losing its influence on American life.[12]

Many have expressed concern about the lack of moral change on the

---

10. John A. Broadus, *On the Preparation and Delivery of Sermons*, 4th ed., rev. Vernon L. Stanfield (1870; revision, New York: Harper & Row, 1979), 167 (page citation is to the revised edition).

11. James Earl Massey, "Application in the Sermon," in *Handbook of Contemporary Preaching*, ed. Michael Duduit (Nashville: Broadman, 1992), 209.

12. The Gallup Organization. Gallup Poll Archives. "Religious Faith Is Widespread but Many Skip Church," December 17, 1998. Online. Available from CWIX@http://198.175.149.8/ poll_archives/1997/970329.htm.

part of the average church member. Somewhere along the way, multitudes of regular church attenders have failed to make the connection between the truths of the Bible and their moral implications for daily life. Although many factors likely have contributed to this lack of moral awareness, one problem has been the failure of those in the pulpit to apply Bible truth to the daily lives of those who listen to their sermons.

John R. W. Stott, in his book *Between Two Worlds,* made some astute observations about applying the truths of God's Word to modern congregations. He correctly affirmed that application is essential. Using the metaphor "bridge-building," he noted that through application we are able to span the gap between the world of the Bible and the world of today.[13]

Stott asserted that two extremes often characterize modern preaching. On the one hand is the tendency to live on the Bible side of the chasm. The conservative, expository preacher often falls victim to this danger. He is so interested in accurately finding the message of the Bible that he may neglect to "earth it out." He fails to build a bridge to the modern world. Such preaching may be clearly biblical, but it lacks contemporary application. Exposition without application never arrives at the doorstep of modern man.[14]

On the other hand, the mistake frequently is made of living on the contemporary side of the chasm. Many preachers—both liberal and conservative—are highly contemporary but lack a biblical base. They may give an up-to-date picture of contemporary life but fail to communicate authoritative Bible truth to their congregations. Such preaching demonstrates a healthy knowledge of contemporary problems but lacks the ability to offer God's fresh Word as a viable solution to those problems.[15] Expository preachers must be aggressive in bridging the chasm between the world of the Bible and the world of their listeners. The German theologian Tholuck said, "A sermon ought to have heaven for its father and the earth for its mother."[16]

The Nature of Application

Biblical truth is best applied when the preacher knows as much as possible about contemporary man. His knowledge of man as he lives life today makes possible a positive flow between the Bible world and the

---

13. John R. W. Stott, *Between Two Worlds* (Grand Rapids: Eerdmans, 1982), 137–38. Stott's fourth chapter, "Preaching as Bridge-Building," is a much needed discussion in this area. His suggestions help the preacher relate a particular message to the contemporary situation. His suggestions guide the preacher to "contextualize" the Word of God.
14. Ibid., 140.
15. Ibid., 138.
16. Ibid., 150.

modern world. This awareness will enhance his ability to preach the eternal Word in such a way that his people get the message.

Depending upon each individual sermon, application can be placed strategically at two primary places. It can be restricted *to an extended section after the main body of the sermon* and immediately before the invitation. Traditionally called the conclusion, this section would involve a restatement of the sermon's proposition followed by a call for action issuing forth from the theme that has been developed. Application also can be made by way of *key sentences and discussions throughout the message.* Within the body of the sermon, strategic links can be made between truths that have been explained and their relevance to the lives of listeners. Lloyd-Jones said:

> It is important that you should have been applying what you have been saying as you go along. There are many ways of doing this. You can close by asking questions and answering them or in various other ways; but you must apply the message as you go along.[17]

Thus, application can be immediate as the sermon develops. Such employment usually is best, because listeners can see relevance throughout the sermon instead of having to wait until the end.[18]

Naturally, application is ineffective if done poorly. Because many give no thought to the quality of the application in their sermons, what was intended to draw listeners in ends up driving them away. The following characteristics will ensure effective application:

APPLICATION ATTRIBUTES

Personal. Use first- and second-person plural pronouns ("we," "us," "you"). Such employment will make the truth of the text strong and direct. Avoid merely using the first-person singular pronouns ("I," "me"), which lessen—and sometimes nullify—the force of the application.

Varied. Use a combination of both direct and indirect application in each sermon. Though direct application is safest and best, do not hesitate occasionally to apply truth indirectly. In 2 Samuel 12, Nathan

17. D. Martyn Lloyd-Jones, *Preaching and Preachers* (Grand Rapids, Mich: Zondervan, 1971), 77.
18. Massey, 209.

used both approaches in confronting David. His initial story about the rich thief was indirect, but his final application was direct: "You are the man!" A study of the teaching methods of Jesus reveals the use of both methods.

Decisive. Call your listeners to some action. After all, such is the object of the sermon. Good application helps them to see that the message is intended to make a difference in their lives.[19]

Appealing. Do not hesitate to exhort. Make an appeal to your listeners. Much modern preaching is too impersonal. Some of the best application you will ever do will be the times you earnestly plead with your people to believe something or to act in a certain way.

The Approach to Application

Applying biblical truth in a sermon involves three important issues. (1) You must be ready to make application. (2) You must determine exactly what biblical material can and should be applied. (3) You must apply that material with integrity. Take great care when tackling all of these tasks in expository preaching.

The expositor should constantly be preparing to make proper application. Several practices will help enhance this skill.

To begin with, learn all you can about people today. Read widely. Get yourself outside of commentaries and lexicons and into the worlds where your people live. Read movie reviews in order to stay current in the entertainment world. Stay in tune with music trends. Visit airports, malls, and other places just to watch people. Do everything you can to be a student of modern culture.

Read current literature that is relevant to the text from which you are preaching. If you are preaching on the Beatitudes, peruse some books—both religious and secular—that tell people how to be happy.

Then apply the text to your own life. Nothing will be more beneficial in applying the text to others than having engaged it yourself.

To determine what truths in your text needs to be applied, simply ask the following question of all the biblical material you have determined to explain and/or argue:

> *HOW ARE THESE TRUTHS*
> *RELEVANT TO MY AUDIENCE?*

---

19. Ibid., 211.

As you ask this question of your biblical material, revisit the theological implications and timeless truths that surfaced at the close of your analysis work. What did you discover about the writer's theological purpose? What timeless truths did you determine the text revealed? What human conditions are addressed by the text that are characteristic of your people? What about contemporary equivalents in your congregation? What further insights can you glean from subsequent revelation? These implications should provide the parameters for any application you make to the contemporary context.

Determining the right material is only half the battle in making good application, however. Once you know what material can and should be applied, handle that information carefully as you bring it to bear on the lives of your modern listeners. Robinson said, "More heresy is preached in application than in Bible exegesis."[20] His statement underscores the struggle many have in knowing how to take a text and determine its meaning for today's listeners.

Failure at this point easily can lead the preacher to say "Thus saith the Lord" when in fact the Lord did not saith! Although the expositor's exegesis may be orthodox, such heresy in application affects the listeners adversely. Noting the negative effects, Robinson observed:

> One effect is that you undermine the Scriptures you say you are preaching. Ultimately, people come to believe that anything with a biblical flavor is what God says.
>
> The long-term effect is that we preach a mythology. Myth has an element of truth along with a great deal of puff, and people tend to live in the puff. They live with implications of implications, and then they discover that what they thought God promised, he didn't promise.[21]

Avoiding this danger actually begins with thorough exegesis. The expositor does not have the right to make a passage mean something today that it did not mean in principle in the biblical world. Once that meaning is determined, however, the preacher must apply it rightly.

Essentially, right application is done along a continuum, which begins all the way back at the implication stage of your analysis (see chapter 4).

Theological Implications ⟶ **Timeless Truths** **Practical Application** ⟶

20. Haddon Robinson, "The Heresy of Application," *Leadership* (Fall 1997): 21.
21. Ibid., 22.

Sometimes the best application of a truth is limited to the theological implications of the text. The preacher will be able to say no more with regard to relevance without stretching the text. At other times, certain timeless truths issuing from the theological implications will surface and serve as the primary application of the passage. In many cases, however, you will be able to apply the truth rightly with practical ramifications. With each individual text, the preacher must determine how far along the continuum he can go and still make application with integrity.

To help make right application of biblical truth, Robinson suggested using "The Abstraction Ladder." The use of such a tool helps ensure that the biblical situation and the contemporary situation are related at the points he makes them connect.[22]

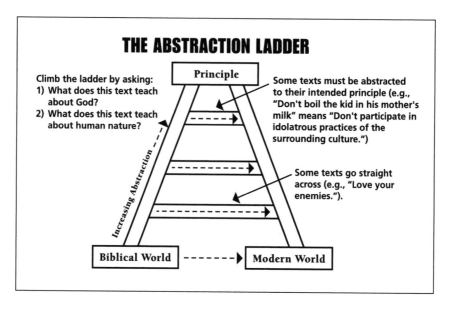

As the diagram indicates, the expositor should climb "The Abstraction Ladder" until he reaches the text's intent. In other words, increasingly move toward the *principle* underlying the text. Sometimes the connection between biblical and modern worlds will be specific and concrete. At other times, the connection will be more an abstract principle. Regarding the latter, Harold Freeman observed:

22. Ibid., 23, 25. For another helpful approach see Harold Freeman, *Variety in Biblical Preaching* (1987; reprint, Ft. Worth: Scripta, 1994), 41 (page citation is to the reprint edition). Freeman encourages the preacher to manage the middle between prior biblical revelation and the contemporary situation by *eternalizing*, then *universalizing*, and finally *principlizing* the text, also by asking a series of questions.

Many times the biblical statement will be a culturally conditioned particularization—provided for the people, time, and place of the textual situation—of a general principle. In that event, you would need to strip the text of its cultural specifics in order to get at the principle behind it.[23]

Once again, thorough exegesis will determine whether or not the text must be stripped of cultural nuances, thus determining how far up the ladder the expositor needs to move.

The preacher will move up the ladder toward principle by asking two questions. (1) *What does the text teach about God?* Look for some glimpse of Him in every Bible passage, such as God as Creator or Sustainer. (2) *What does the text teach about human nature?* Look for the depravity factor, that element of humanity that rebels against the glimpse of God.[24] The answers to these questions will issue from the theological implications gleaned earlier in the process.

As you seek to determine the contemporary equivalents to the shared human conditions, try visualizing specific members of your congregation. Ask yourself, What does this passage have to say to John Smith? or Pam Jones? or Billy Foster?

As Alexander Maclaren studied the Scriptures during his sermon preparation, he placed across from his desk an empty chair. He imagined a person sitting in the chair. He carried on a dialogue between himself and the imaginary person.[25] Such a practice would help keep us aware at all times that we are preparing our message for real people.

The Tension of Application

Both Robinson and Freeman noted the growing tension that exists in application as the preacher moves toward abstract principles and subsequent implications. "We want to have a 'Thus saith the Lord' about specific things in people's lives," wrote Robinson, "but we can't always have that."[26] Freeman warned, "Here we enter hazardous waters, and caution is in order."[27] Though the preacher has biblical authority for proclaiming the principles in a biblical text, he cannot speak with the same authority regarding exactly *how* those principles are to be implemented in the lives of the listeners unless Scripture delineates such. To do so is to put words in God's mouth.

As "The Abstraction Ladder" indicates, some texts do not need to be moved to application by principle. Some biblical statements are the prin-

23. Freeman, *Variety in Biblical Preaching,* 42.
24. Robinson, "Heresy," 24.
25. Chevis F. Horne, *Dynamic Preaching* (Nashville: Broadman, 1983), 137.
26. Robinson, "Heresy," 25.
27. Freeman, 42.

ciples that need to be applied. To identify such situations, look to see if essentially the same biblical idea can be found in different strata of biblical literature that cross different time frames and historical situations. If so, you probably are dealing with a principle. Also, rely on your exegesis to give you clues as to why a particular statement may have certain cultural restrictions.[28]

Regarding specific application of scriptural principles, Robinson challenged preachers to make a distinction between the principle of a text and the many possible applications of that principle. He suggested saying something like "This is the principle, and the principle is clear. How this principle applies in our lives may differ with different people in different situations."[29] He offered the following distinctions between various types of implications from a text: *necessary, probable, possible, improbable,* and *impossible.*[30] For example, the various applications of the command "You shall not commit adultery" in Exodus 20:14 might be as follows:

Necessary—You cannot have a sexual relationship with a person who is not your spouse.

Probable—You ought to be very careful of strong bonding friendships with a person of the opposite sex who is not your spouse.

Possible—You ought not to have lunch alone with a person of the opposite sex who is not your spouse.

Improbable—You ought not to be in a room alone with a person of the opposite sex who is not your spouse.

Impossible—You ought not to have dinner with another couple because you are at the same table with a person of the opposite sex who is not your spouse.

An honest treatment of the text reveals that only the *necessary* implication can be preached as "Thus saith the Lord." While you may have strong convictions about all or most of the other implications above, you may not present them as the words of God. "Too often preachers give to a possible implication all the authority of a necessary implication, which is at the level of obedience."[31]

Do not ever feel an obligation to address all of the specific questions and situations that your listeners face. The variables are infinite, and, con-

28. Ibid., 42–43.
29. Robinson, "Heresy," 26.
30. Ibid., 25.
31. Ibid., 26.

sequently, God did not purpose to treat each one in the Bible. Instead, the omniscient One has promised divine guidance through His Spirit regarding the specific situations and problems we face (see Phil. 4:6–7; James 1:5). Robinson asserted that

PAIN + TIME + INSIGHT = CHANGE

People often face difficult situations over time, but those situations do not necessarily change them. When insight is added to difficulty and time, however, change occurs.[32] Be faithful to concentrate on proclaiming divine insight, which flows from the necessary implications of God's Word—the "Thus saith the Lord." God's Spirit, then, will be faithful to make specific application to the listeners' lives in due time.

The Power of Application

The expository preacher has a powerful ally as he seeks creatively to communicate God's Word to the person in the pew. He has been promised the assistance of the Holy Spirit. This feature of the preacher's work separates him from other communicators. Beyond question, the modern preacher of the Word is facing what appear to be insurmountable difficulties. He is preaching to people who are accustomed to well-trained, fluent, polished communicators on television and radio. He also is trying to communicate to people who may have little Bible background. Much of the terminology of Scripture may be foreign to them. Relying on his own strength, he may yield to despair.

The role of the Holy Spirit in Bible preaching resolves many of these problems. The Spirit can arouse in the hearers deep desires to know the truth. He has been given by our Lord to bring men to an awareness of their sinfulness, the adequacy of the work of Christ, and the desirability of salvation through Him. The power of the Holy Spirit makes preaching effective and applicable. Paul stated in 1 Thessalonians 1:5, "For our gospel did not come to you in word only, but also in power, and in the Holy Spirit and in much assurance."

Our goal in preaching is to produce Christlike character in our people. As we interpret the Scripture, capture its practical and devotional nature, and bring its life-changing truths to bear on the daily lives and needs of our hearers, the Holy Spirit will bring about the desired transformation.

32. Ibid., 27.

STEP #4: ILLUSTRATE THE MATERIAL

The fourth step in amplification is to illustrate your sermon material. To illustrate means to enlighten or make clear.[33] The verb form comes from the Latin *illustrare,* which means "to cast light upon."[34] Likely, you have at least thought about using some form of illustration prior to this point in the exposition process. The expositor, however, should take some time at this stage intentionally to enhance his content with additional light.

Illustration Intentionality

You probably remember several outstanding sermons you have heard. As you reflect upon those sermons, you probably can remember some illustrations used in them. Someone has observed that people remember our illustrations but not our sermons. To be sure, illustrations often make the sermon—and even save some of them! To say the least, the use of a suitable illustration can be the difference between an average and an outstanding sermon.

Illustrations are mental photographs that illumine the ideas of our messages. We are preaching to a visually minded generation. For years, psychologists have claimed that we learn approximately 85 percent through sight, 10 percent through hearing, 2 percent through touch, 1½ percent through smell, and 1½ percent through taste.[35] Today, we must factor in the evolution of personal computers, the Internet, interactive media, and other technological advances that surely have heightened people's visual learning propensities. Thus the importance of illustrations in a sermon becomes apparent. We must make our sermons as lifelike as possible. Through the pictures that illustrations produce in the minds of our hearers, we can make the abstract come to life. The mind-set of today's modern congregations makes the intentional use of illustrations a psychological necessity.

The preacher, then, will determine where the illustration can carry the most force. You may want to begin your sermon with an illustration. You may want to amplify one of your main points with an illustration just as soon as you state the point. Or you may want to wait until the end of the point to use one. Avoid putting illustrations at the same place in each message.

33. Richard L. Mayhue, "Introductions, Illustrations, and Conclusions," in John MacArthur Jr., *Rediscovering Expository Preaching,* ed. Richard L. Mayhue (Dallas: Word, 1992).

34. Fasol, *Essentials for Biblical Preaching,* 24

35. Farris D. Whitesell, *Power in Expository Preaching* (Old Tappan, N.J.: Revell, 196 75.

Do not feel compelled to use an illustration for each truth you present. Although employing at least one good illustration for each major division of your sermon is a good practice, use illustrations more intentionally by determining what material needs to be illustrated. To determine what material in your sermon needs to be illustrated, simply ask the following question of all the material you have amplified to this point:

> *WHICH ASSERTION(S) CAN BE*
> *ENHANCED WITH ADDITIONAL LIGHT?*

A number of effective illustrations certainly can benefit the overall impact of your sermon. Well-chosen and purposefully placed illustrations can make for even greater effectualness.

Illustration Purposes

Illustrations, by nature, have an object. You do not just illustrate. You illustrate *something*. Illustrations are servants of the other functional elements. They cast light upon various facets of explanation, argumentation, and application. Overlooking this reality has caused many preachers and teachers of preaching to overrate and/or abuse the use of illustrations. If illustrations are, in fact, the most remembered parts of our sermons, then it is imperative that they be strongly related to the truths they are intended to illuminate.

Illustrations serve five primary purposes in their servant role. Illustrations *clarify*. They primarily help listeners understand what is being explained. Illustrations *intensify*. A simple, to-the-point illustration can drive home a truth and make it stick in the minds of the listener, thus enhancing memory. Illustrations *apply*. They help build bridges to your hearers. By means of an illustration you can create an awareness of need, stir emotions, move people to action. Illustrations *attract*. Though people may not be especially interested in what you have to say, you can create interest and a favorable hearing by means of a well-presented illustration. All preachers have experienced the power of an illustration to hold the attention of the audience or to regain lagging attention. And illustrations *argue*. They can demonstrate the validity of one contention and the fallacy of another.

Illustration Qualities

A number of qualities should be sought when choosing illustrations. The presence or absence of the following attributes can mean the difference between effective and ineffective employment:

A good illustration is *familiar.* A good illustration clarifies the truth you are communicating. The unknown is interpreted by the known. Consequently, if your illustration involves something with which your listeners are familiar, it will help them understand what you are trying to say. If not, the illustration probably will be ineffective. A preacher sometimes uses illustrations from rural life when preaching to suburban congregations. His people will miss the point completely if they do not understand the particulars involved in the illustration.

A good illustration is *persuasive.* Often a truth that is resisted initially can gain a hearing by means of a simple illustration. Furthermore, illustrations can be especially persuasive when they pull the heartstrings of people. This does not imply that the preacher must be melodramatic or sentimental. Little value can be found in telling a tearjerker just to work up the audience. A good illustration, however, will get to the hearts of the people. Once truth has been presented, most decisions are made in the heart, not in the head. Illustrations pry open the heart's door.

A good illustration is *colorful.* Make use of simile and metaphor. Use the mechanism of parable. Flavor your illustrations with historical references, biographical references, and an intelligent awareness of the contemporary world. Touch your people where they live by using illustrations taken from their life experiences.

A good illustration is *appropriate.* Work hard to see that your illustrations actually illustrate your point. Make them fit. An illustration may be a very good one but fail to cast light upon the subject you wish to illustrate. In addition, no illustration is good if it is inappropriate to the circumstances of the service. Some illustrations may be inappropriate because they do not match a particular audience. Others may be inappropriate because they are crude or disrespectful. Such illustrations have no place in the preaching event. Be sure every illustration you choose is employed appropriately and in good taste.

A good illustration is *believable.* An illustration that sounds farfetched will immediately produce questions in the minds of your hearers. If you are making up an illustration, say so. If the story is imaginary, do not hesitate to tell your audience at the appropriate time. Some fictitious illustrations can carry an impact if you wait until the end to tell the people it is fictitious. Such delay is within the bounds of proper use. Just be sure you are absolutely honest in your use of illustrations.

A good illustration is *frequented.* An often overlooked quality of good sermon illustrations is the frequency with which people will encounter the subject after the illustration is used. Many preachers have the false impression that phenomenal, almost unbelievable, stories make the best illustrations. A cursory look at the illustrations used by Jesus, however, reveal His simplistic use of things that were common to everyday life. The genius of this method was not only the familiarity people had with those objects but also the frequency with which they would see them after the sermon and thus be reminded of the truth that was illustrated. Everyday items such as a vacuum cleaner, a car, or a computer often will prove to be the most effective illustrations, because people will frequent them after the sermon is over, thus being reminded of the scriptural truth that was illustrated.

A good illustration is *visible*. For years, object lessons have been viewed as elementary and, therefore, relegated to children's sermons. But if the preacher's charge is to expose the text by explaining and applying it in the clearest fashion, and if the aforementioned statistics are true regarding the visual orientation of our culture, then the expositor will do well to employ appropriate visual illustrations. Such use certainly can be overdone, but the power of visual aids cannot be overestimated with any age group. Language alone should not be depended upon to create a picture in the mind if, in fact, the actual picture itself is available.

Illustration Sources

You will need to work hard to find illustrations, especially when you preach to generally the same people on a regular basis. Telling the same illustration several times can sap it completely of its vitality and appeal. Normally, you will not find enough usable illustrations in sermon illustration books to make them worth the money. Most of the illustrations from such books are canned and outdated. If you insist on having an illustration book, make sure it contains timeless illustrations or is updated regularly.[36] Good illustrations actually can be found anywhere. Be on the lookout for them. Keep an illustration notebook handy. Placed in alphabetical order, arranged by subject, note briefly the illustrations you find by observation, especially in the following places:

♦ The Bible
God's Word is a fruitful source of sermon illustrations. The many life experiences—good and bad—of real people across the ages serve as examples of every facet of life as well as the relationship between God and man. In addition, the use of biblical illustrations helps to deter the trend toward biblical illiteracy. Illustrating New

36. The following works may prove helpful from time to time: Paul Lee Tan, *Encyclop of 7700 Illustrations* (Rockville, Md: Assurance, 1979); Michael P. Green, *Illustrations for Biblical Preaching* (Grand Rapids: Baker, 1989); Raymond McHenry, *The Best of 'In Other Words'* (Houston: Raymond McHenry, 1996); Craig Brian Larson, ed., *Illustrations for Preaching and Teaching* (Grand Rapids: Baker, 1993); Charles Little, *10,000 Illustrations from the Bible* (reprint, Grand Rapids: Baker, 1981); and *The Treasury of Scripture Knowledge* (reprint, Old Tappan, N.J.: Revell, n.d.).

Testament truths with Old Testament experiences highlights the Bible's unity and underscores its relevancy. Furthermore, do not hesitate to use sanctified imagination when referencing Bible stories. In addition to Bible stories, the original words of Scripture are a good source of sermon illustrations. The Greek language is especially useful. Many Greek words are picturesque, the meanings of which serve as whole illustrations. Dig these out in your word studies during the analysis of the passage.

♦ Current Events

Some of the best illustrations will surface in your reading of the daily newspaper, weekly magazines, and other literature that reports current events. Such references connect the Bible with contemporary culture and establish its relevancy in the minds of the listeners. Even after you have chosen illustrations throughout the week, always be willing to sacrifice them to events that may appear in the Saturday or Sunday morning paper.

♦ Personal Experiences

Your own life experiences (or the experiences of others) provides one of your best sources. Do not hesitate to use them aptly to illustrate Bible truth. Your people can immediately identify with them. Several words of caution need to be noted, however. Be modest when relating personal experiences. Boastfulness will cause your audience to be resentful and resistant. Be careful not to refer to family members too frequently, as that can be annoying. Do not violate a confidence by taking matters told to you in private and using them as the basis of a sermon illustration. This mistake can be very painful to the one whose confidence is broken. And do not tell something that happened to another person as if it happened to you. You could be very embarrassed by such an act.

♦ Personal Reading

Reading in a wide range of topics will bring you across many illustrations for your preaching. As you read inside and outside the fields of theology and biblical studies, illustrations will surface that can illuminate biblical truth.

♦ Nature

Constantly keep your eyes open to the world of nature. Jesus was a master at using such illustrations. He referred to the fig tree, the lilies of the field, the soil, the wind, and other aspects of nature to cast light on spiritual truth.

♦ Language

Most illustrations are in the form of anecdotes—short narratives about interesting people or situations. The use of language in other ways, however, also can serve as illustrative material. Look back at the material on figures of speech in chapter 4 to see some language tools that can provide powerful support.

♦ **Internet and E-mail**

Modern technology serves the busy pastor well at many points. One such helpful tool in the search for illustrations is the Internet. In a matter of seconds, the touch of a search button can yield numerous stories and facts related to just about any subject. In addition, being on the e-mail lists of selected friends will bring your way a plethora of contemporary stories, poems, jokes, and other information, all of which can be stored instantly for easy access.

♦ **Sermons**

While listening to other preachers, you often will find illustrations you can use effectively in your own sermons. Whenever you listen to another preacher, have paper and pen on hand. As you later use such an illustration, be careful to give credit without being too specific. Stephen Brown observed that citing the details of the source can dull the edge of the illustration. Always note the complete source in your own notes, but do not feel constrained to reference it in detail when you preach.[37] An ethical guideline is simply to make clear that this is not your story. Brown's counsel should be applied to the use of all illustrations, not just those obtained from other preachers.

INCUBATION

All of us have faced those times when we cannot seem to get the sermon to "come together." We find ourselves mentally paralyzed. In reality, you may do all the necessary spade work, amplify the message well, yet still lack the creative spark that makes the sermon unique and effective. The solution to such a dilemma is found in allowing sufficient time for incubation. This brooding process allows time for your gathered material to mature by letting your creativity in on the action.

Several interesting studies have been done on incubation and the creative process. Rollo May, in his book *The Courage to Create,* defined creativity as the process of making or bringing into being. He points out that we use many different expressions to describe creativity. Such phrases as "a thought pops up" or "an idea comes from the blue" or "it suddenly hit me" all indicate different ways of picturing the experience of creativity. Somewhere beneath the level of conscious awareness, ideas break through into our experience. May described the phenomenon:

---

37. Stephen Brown, "Illustrating the Sermon," in *Handbook of Contemporary Preaching,* ed. Michael Duduit (Nashville: Broadman, 1992), 205.

Often when one works at a hard question, nothing good is accomplished at the first attack. Then one takes a rest, longer or shorter, and sits down anew to the work. During the first half hour, as before, nothing is found, and then all of a sudden the decisive idea presents itself to the mind. It might be said that the conscious work has been more fruitful because it has been interrupted and the rest has given back to the mind its force and freshness.[38]

Some of the most significant breakthroughs in all areas of life will take place in this manner. Four phases, adapted from the work of Horace Rahskoph in *Basic Speech Improvement,* are suggested as being necessary for the creative processes to develop fully.[39]

PHASE #1: SEPARATION

After you have assembled, digested, amplified, and comprehended all the relevant facts related to your text, separate yourself from your study for a time. In other words, leave your desk and engage yourself in other activities, whether they be recreational or some other aspect of your ministry that is less cognitive. The subconscious mind must be provided opportunity to work on the content that has been assembled.

This time is given to the germination and maturing of the main ideas. The previous preparation and the intensive labor involved may have led to a kind of mental indigestion. A time of rest or recreation is needed. The mind is allowed to digest and assimilate the gathered information. Though the length of this time may vary, the subconscious mind is reworking and reorganizing the gathered information. This rest or change of activity will release you from intensive effort and allow the creative impulse free rein. Eventually, new ideas will emerge. Periods of preparation and incubation may recur alternately as successive stages of work and rest.

This time of separation is important for the Holy Spirit's work. All through the preparation of an expository sermon, the preacher must keenly feel his dependence upon the Spirit. The divine Inspirer is the only One who can give the preacher understanding and insight into Scripture's meaning and application. Perhaps those times when we allow the subconscious to work on the sermon are those occasions when we have opened our lives to the direction of the Holy Spirit in a new and meaningful way.

PHASE #2: MEDITATION

Before returning to the mechanics of sermon preparation, spend

---

38. Rollo May, *The Courage to Create* (New York: Bantam, 1975), 70.
39. Horace G. Rahskoph, *Basic Speech Improvement* (New York: Harper & Row, 1965), 181–83.

some time meditating on your work. This activity may take place subsequent to or concurrent with your separation activity. As you meditate on the Scripture passage and the amplification material, you are preparing the way for the creative process. You can meditate on the fruit of your research at many times when you are not in your study—while you relax, walk, jog, or drive. Allow your mind to travel freely the many roads of the passage. Try to avoid familiar roads upon which you have previously traveled. Look for different, out-of-the-ordinary entrances into the text. You often will be amazed at what these brief times of meditation can do.

PLANNING FOR CREATIVITY IN YOUR WEEKLY PREPARATION
A Personal Testimony

In addition to brief snatches of meditation time, more extended periods must also be allotted for incubation to take place. In recent years I have found a helpful way to allow time for the creative process to work. I begin my sermon preparation on Monday morning. I plan to complete it at the end of my Friday morning study time. A very useful procedure for me is to use Thursday mornings for alternate study. I get the basic work done on my message in the Monday through Wednesday study times. On Thursday I set aside my sermon preparation for the coming Sunday. My attention is turned to outside reading, writing projects, and a variety of other study activities. I do not consciously give thought to the study of my sermons on that day. Later on in the afternoon or at night, in a different place, under a different set of circumstances, I look again at my sermon. Many times I am thrilled to see how much clearer the passage is after some time away from it. Very often, the sermon design arranges itself in a much more logical, clear manner. The sermon thesis appears in sharper focus than previously.

Terry Vaughn

As you meditate, put your imagination to work on the Scripture passage as an additional positive step toward creativity. Imagination is the capacity of the mind to receive a bombardment of ideas and impulses that well up from the subconscious mind. Imagination provides the capacity to "dream dreams and see visions."[40] You will be amazed at the insights and concepts that will emerge from the subconscious if you will allow your imagination time to work on your Scripture passage.

OPTIMUM OBSERVATION

1. **Broaden your sight.** Increase the breadth of what you have seen and observed. Take opportunities to visit art galleries and museums. Read literature that abounds in imagery. Poetry is especially good in this regard.

2. **Look, don't just glance.** Make the effort truly to look at things, not just glance over them. Take an object and examine it carefully. Notice every possible detail. What kind of materials were used in making it? What is its shape? How big or small is it? What is its color? its texture? Look at the object from every conceivable perspective.

3. **Listen, don't just hear.** Stand on a busy street corner. Listen to all the different sounds. Listen to voices as people crisscross around you. Listen to the sounds coming from stores nearby. Exhaust every sound that comes to your ears.

4. **Feel, don't just touch.** Pick up an object. Hold it in your hand. Feel the object. What is it made of? How does it feel? Is it smooth or rough? Touch the object in every possible way.

One way to strengthen the imagination is to improve your habits of observation. Spurgeon was noted for his ability to speak in picture language. His sermons literally abounded in sensory imagery. E. L. Magoon said of Spurgeon:

> He has rare powers of observation, recollection, assimilation and creation. . . . He seems to have opened his eyes to nature in all its varieties; to science in all its discoveries, and to literature in all its departments.[41]

Today's preacher can enhance his own preaching considerably by improving his powers of observation. This improvement can be gained in a variety of ways, some of which are noted at the top of the page. These activities are not something to be done for only a day or two. Rather, to

40. May, *Courage to Create,* 14
41. E. L. Magoon, *The Modern Whitefield* (New York: Sheldon, Blakeman, 1856), 11.

achieve maximum results in improving your imagination, make such habits of observation a way of life.

One more word about meditation needs to be noted. Some of your meditation time should be done on your knees in communion with God as another reminder of the paramount role the Holy Spirit plays in sermon preparation. Remember to saturate your entire sermon preparation with prayer, doing as much as possible on your knees. Someone has said, "Work without prayer is atheism; but prayer without work is presumption."

PHASE #3: ILLUMINATION

As you separate yourself from the mechanics of sermon preparation and meditate on your work, moments of illumination will occur. These moments are windows of insight. This dynamic flows out of periods of study, matures in the hidden subjective levels of thought, and springs into life with startling suddenness. These moments of illumination frequently will be accompanied by a deep sense of satisfaction and confidence.

Such moments may come at the break between preparation and incubation. An idea may emerge unexpectedly, without effort, often during the moments of relaxation, recreation, or even while you are attending a meeting. Sometimes the experience will occur while driving to work. Other times you may be awakened in the middle of the night with a burst of insight. You may even have a moment of inspiration in the shower! Whenever it takes place, your subconscious mind will work on the sermon, bring it all together, resolve the problems, and present the solution as a much-needed gift to your conscious mind. The time or place makes no difference. Consequently, be sure to keep pen and paper, cassette recorder, or palm pilot on hand so that when the creative moment comes you can record it.

PHASE #4: VERIFICATION

Subconscious work, flashes of inspiration, and other creative work cannot go unchecked. The creative idea must be developed and elaborated in terms of the surrounding context to ensure its validity. When the creative moment comes, quickly verify its accuracy in relation to the facts you have found in your expository investigation. Adjust your design accordingly. Restate your central idea and proposition, if necessary. The inspired concept must now be checked with the facts that have been brought forth in the previous period of preparation. This process enables you to validate the accuracy of your creative idea.

CHAPTER EIGHT

BUILDING
THE SERMON

*The time you spend working out your ideas and
beliefs on paper will make you sound in command,
clear and forceful—in the language of a leader.*

JAMES C. HUMES

Picture a construction site. A crew has just finished framing a house on top of a strong foundation. Lying around the site are all the necessary materials to fill out the structure and finish the home. Until that work is done, the facility is not ready to be inhabited.

Similarly, the sermon is beginning to take shape at this point, but it is far from being ready to preach. The work of analysis has been done. The theme has been unified and amplified so that it is potent for developing the proposition. Sufficient opportunity has been given to allow the creative process to unfold. The message now is more than just a set of facts. With the raw materials necessary and the spark of inspiration provided by the Holy Spirit, you finally are ready to build an expository sermon. Constructing the sermon involves developing certain key parts in written form.

WRITING THE MANUSCRIPT

Building a sermon demands writing out the message to some degree. One of the perennial discussions in homiletics is whether or not the preacher should write out his sermon in a *full manuscript*. Some do, but probably most do not. The average evangelical preacher preaches enough times each week that it becomes difficult to write each message in full. But every preacher is different. Many noted preachers—past and present—have written full manuscripts. Many others have not.

Although developing a word-for-word manuscript for every sermon may not be realistic for every pastor, such a practice certainly is a worthy goal. By doing so, the preacher is able to formulate his thoughts and be intentional about his expression. Another option is to write a sermon brief, which consists of summary paragraphs for each part of the message. Regardless of whether or not written materials are used in the pulpit during delivery, developing a full or partial manuscript on a regular basis is a healthy practice.

The young preacher would do well to discipline himself to write out at least one full sermon manuscript per week during the early years of his ministry. Such was the practice of the great expositor Lloyd-Jones. He said:

> Certainly it was what I did myself during my first ten years in the ministry. I tried to write one sermon a week; I never tried to write two. But I did try to write one for the first ten years. I felt that writing was good discipline, good for producing ordered thought and arrangement and sequence and development of the argument and so on. So my particular practice was to use both the written and the extempore methods.[1]

Without question, writing does enable you to work on ways to improve your style. The practice also serves to clarify your thinking and test the sermon for its practical application to your people. Some preachers dictate their sermon notes to a secretary, who then types them out in full. This avenue enables him to "talk out" his message and then evaluate the manuscript.

Probably a more common approach is to write out a full-sentence sermon design, or a *partial manuscript*. Within this design you may write certain sections in full. Illustrations normally are written word for word. Certain ideas about which the preacher wants to be deliberate can be written out in full. In any case, always strive to write a full introduction, summation, and invitation, because it is especially important to be pensive at these points. This practice enables you to work specifically on crucial sections of the sermon. Writing only part of the message also prevents your becoming too concerned about the exact wording at the moment of delivery. Additionally, writing a partial manuscript helps you avoid the danger of overpreparation. The sermon can be so overdone that it becomes a means within itself.

At the same time, some preachers err because their skeleton outline is never matured into particular words that convey complete ideas. The re-

---

1. D. Martyn Lloyd-Jones, *Preaching and Preachers* (Grand Rapids: Zondervan, 1971), 215.

sult is a sermon that is indefinite, abstract, and wordy. Their good content lacks a style that is most effective in getting the passage from the printed page into the hearts of the hearers.

A sermon is more than a disjointed compilation of Bible facts and practical applications. Some degree of thoughtful sermon composition that utilizes the basic ingredients of effective style must be done.

DEVELOPING THE PARTS

An expository sermon should be composed of certain necessary components. Each component plays a crucial role in bringing God's revealed truth to bear on the lives of listeners. Thus, purposefully build your message according to the following key parts:

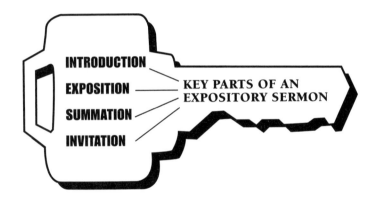

The general purpose that drives each part can quickly be identified. The purpose of the introduction is to *introduce* the sermon. The purpose of the exposition is to *expose* the meaning of the text for contemporary listeners. The purpose of the summation is to *summarize* the truth of the sermon. The purpose of the invitation is to *invite* people to respond to the message.

At this stage of the process, it is helpful to begin working from separate clean sheets of paper—one for the introduction, one for the summation, and one for the invitation. You will also need a separate sheet for each of the major divisions that make up your exposition. If you intend to use notes in the pulpit, you may even want to work with half sheets. Certainly a word processor is advantageous as you begin to manipulate information into a presentable form.

The composition of each key part, along with a corresponding desired quality, will be discussed below in the order in which each should be done. Basically, the parts should be composed in the order given above, except that the introduction is composed last.

PART #1: ENGAGING EXPOSITION

Technically, exposition is the act of presenting, explaining, or expounding facts or ideas, usually involving commentary and interpretation.[2] Often called the body of the sermon, this part is the heart of the expository message. Here the preacher *engages the listeners with the text* of Scripture. Using the functional elements and related homiletical devices, he develops the passage of Scripture according to his sermon design.

The Nature of the Exposition

This development can be likened to the activity in a backyard swimming pool. For some preachers, the text is merely a diving board and the pool is the sermon. These preachers jump off into the sermon and never return to the text. Other preachers use the text like pool furniture. They swim around in the sermon but make only casual and periodic visits to the Scripture text. The expositor, however, uses the text as the pool itself. He jumps off into it and takes his listeners for a swim. The text is the sermon.

Regarding the central role of the text in the sermon, Stowell's counsel to twenty-first century preachers must be heeded:

> The text must be preeminent in our preparation, and preeminent in our presentation. Sermons that deal only lightly and/or obscurely with the text cannot achieve the purpose of bonding people to God and His Word. Nor do they carry the long-term power that is needed to effect life-changing proclamation. Power is not in the clever creations of the communicator but rather in the intrinsic truth of the Word of God through him.
>
> It should concern us that, increasingly, preaching in America today is being postured as more of a self-help values lecture with periodic tips of the hat to Scripture references than it is to a clear exposition of the truth of the authoritative Word of God. This is not to say that there aren't some times when our communication is geared to certain audiences of seekers or secularists where a detailed exposition of the Word of God may not be an appro-

---

2. *The Reader's Digest Great Encyclopedic Dictionary* (1966), s.v. "exposition."

priate entrance into their hearts. It is to say, however, that when the church gathers as the body of Christ, it needs to be taught the Word of God. For in that is the only real power of transformational growth and development to the glory of Christ.[3]

The primary part of the sermon, then, is a journey into the biblical text where the preacher immerses both himself and his listeners in a rhetorical presentation of a passage of Scripture. And now you will begin to solidify the precise wording of what you intend to say to your audience about the biblical text.

The Development of the Exposition

To help develop the exposition part of your sermon, follow the process below, using a separate sheet of paper for each major division:

BODY BUILDING
Developing Your Exposition

♦ Revisit the amplification material you developed.

♦ Begin to organize the results of all your preparation thus far, including any pertinent thoughts you recorded during the incubation period.

♦ Under the appropriate divisions and subdivisions (if any), arrange every item of necessary and helpful material you have identified.

♦ Using as many complete sentences as possible, write out your notations logically, as if you were speaking directly to your audience.

Be aware that the ideas you record must become complete thoughts either now or at the moment of delivery. More will be said about expressing your thoughts in an effective style later.

One further important quality of the exposition needs to be considered. Stick to your theme. Stay focused. Do not let the audience get sidetracked from the main message by your meandering. You may have two, three, or four divisions, just as you might map out different routes by car, train, or plane, but you still have only one destination—one proposition.[4] Avoid confusing your audience with information that is not relevant to and necessary for the development of your proposition. Keep hammering

---

3. Joseph M. Stowell, *Shepherding the Church into the 21st Century* (Wheaton: Victor, 1994), 223.
4. James C. Humes, *The Sir Winston Method: The Five Secrets of Speaking the Language of Leadership* (New York: William Morrow, 1991), 48.

home that one idea.

The Support for the Exposition

As you develop the biblical truth in your message, consider the need to support it with additional material. Although you must be careful not to overload your sermon, added material can be helpful. Once again, be very intentional. As you explain, argue, apply, and illustrate, see if you notice any areas that could use an additional hand. Be careful, however, not to add material if it is not needed.

Assuming you find some areas that need support, do not limit your search to your own creativity. Totally original thinkers are few and far between (and not many of them are preachers!). Vance Havner once said, "At the beginning of my ministry I determined I would be original or nothing. I soon found out that I was both."

The preacher can access numerous sources for support material. *Statistics,* for example, can be valuable when trying to support some points in a sermon. *Quotations* can lend strength to your assertions. A quote from a well-known person in contemporary life or in history can provide a sense of authority to what you are saying. The *multiple approach* to a Scripture passage can supply additional material. Discuss portions of the passage from a variety of viewpoints—from the viewpoint of the reader or the other people who are involved.[5]

Commentaries can provide good support material. During your Scripture analysis, you consulted a variety of them and noted certain statements that amplify the truths of your passage. Make careful notations of them.

Read the *sermons* that other men have preached on the passage under consideration. Be careful how you borrow material, however. Plagiarism is rampant in almost every aspect of our society. Via the Internet, students and preachers alike now have access to complete research papers and entire sermons with the click of a mouse. Remember that the lifting of material word for word is improper. Be sure to give proper credit whenever you quote another preacher or writer. Jay Adams asserted that borrowing is permissible when you give new organization, new integration, and new expression to the materials you have read. He suggested that you mix the materials through your own mind, add them to your own experiences, then present them in your own way.[6]

Another source from which to draw supporting material is your *previous study.* Now is the time to look at some of your "overflow" material. Earlier we noted the necessity of saving certain unneeded information

---

5. Charles W. Koller, *Expository Preaching Without Notes* (Grand Rapids: Baker, 1962), 55–56.
6. Jay Adams, *Pulpit Speech* (Phillipsburg, N.J.: Presby. & Ref., 1971), 15.

from your analysis to be used in another sermon. Develop some way to organize sermon material you have gathered, maybe by topic or by Scripture reference. Certainly, computers provide infinite ways to store, organize, and access the fruit of previous study. Or you may want to keep a notebook for every book of the Bible, which contains all your sermonic preparation. However you choose to do it, find some easily accessible way to organize the used and unused material from every sermon you prepare.

PART #2: STRIKING SUMMATION

While the development of your exposition is still fresh in your mind, immediately begin to formulate your summation. Traditionally called the conclusion, the sermon summation *reinforces the proposition and reviews its relevancy*. At this juncture in the preaching event, your listeners are deciding on the issues at hand. Like a lawyer during closing arguments, the preacher will bring to focus as clearly as possibly the timeless truths exposed in the message into one final thrust upon their minds and hearts. Striking while the iron is hot, he must drive home the proposition and bring the whole thrust of the message to bear upon the people.

The Nature of the Summation

A brief glance at the four key parts reveals why we avoid the term "conclusion"—it is *not* the last part of the sermon! In reality, the sermon is not concluded until it is lived out in the lives of the people who hear it. Because the Word of God always demands a response, all biblical sermons should culminate in a call for such action. This invitation may or may not ask for an immediate, public expression of response, but the sermon still should culminate in some kind of challenge to respond. No sense can be made, then, of concluding the sermon and then having to jump-start that call, or "invitation."

Your sermon must not just dribble away into nothingness. The main theme of the message must be brought to completion. Greek orators sometimes expressed their view of this component by calling it "the final struggle which decides the conflict." For this reason, the summation may indeed be the most significant part of your sermon. Broadus said that rhetorically, psychologically, and spiritually this component "is a most vital part of the sermon."[7]

The Development of the Summation

Despite its important role, the development of a good summation of-

---

7. John A. Broadus, *On the Preparation and Delivery of Sermons*, 4th ed., rev. Vernon L. Stanfield (1870; revision, New York: Harper & Row, 1979), 108–109 (page citations are to the revised edition).

ten is neglected. Several reasons for this neglect are apparent. The preacher may run out of preparation time, causing him to tack on a thoughtless summary to the message. Then, many preachers are faced with time limitations in the delivery of their sermons. Whether due to radio or television deadlines or just the expectations of the congregation, the preacher may jettison his message prematurely. And third, the summation sometimes is neglected because the other work of the sermon has not been done properly. If the passage's unifying theme has not been clarified, or if the main assertions have not been developed logically, the preacher will find it difficult to arrange a strong summation.

Sermon summations may accomplish more than one purpose, but each will likely be characterized by one primary element. Several possible types are available to get the preacher started in the development of a good summation:

SUMMATION STARTERS

- ✦ **Recap:** A brief review of the sermon proposition and divisions
- ✦ **Illustration:** An anecdote that underscores or highlights the proposition
- ✦ **Application:** One or more ways in which the listeners can live out the truth of the text
- ✦ **Quotation:** A telling statement by a relevant source that drives home the proposition
- ✦ **Question:** A thought-provoking question that forces the listeners to ponder the proposition
- ✦ **Appeal:** A plea or exhortation for the listeners to act on the message

Qualities of a Good Summation

Certain qualities make for smooth summations. Let the following principles guide you as you flow from exposition to invitation.

First, the summation should reflect the exposition. Repetition is an important method of amplifying truth. A time-tested sermonic model has been "Tell 'em what you're going to tell 'em, tell 'em, and tell 'em what you've told 'em." Even if you do not repeat your divisions exactly in the summation, you probably will want to repeat certain phrases or words that summarize the main thrust of your exposition.

SUMMATION STOP SIGNS

Avoid several common flaws in your summations. The following were adapted from some suggestions made by Donald Demaray:[8]

Stop moralizing. Do not summarize your exposition by saying, "The moral of this sermon is . . ." This unclear thinking is too general and vague to be effective.

Stop when you're through. Do not press on after a good stopping point. William Jennings Bryan's mother leveled with him after an evening's address with the painful words "Will, you missed several good opportunities to sit down." Do not let your sermon ravel out at the end like a ball of yarn. When you are through, clip the loose ends, neatly tie them together, and leave your people with a well-developed message.

Stop only when you're through. The exposition should be developed fully before you move into the summation. Occasionally, every preacher will reach the climax of his sermon prematurely. At that point, the rest of the sermon is downhill. Careful organization and a sense of timing are the keys.

Stop dragging it out. Brevity is an important quality in summations. Say what you want to say. Say it briefly. Say it pointedly. Then be done.

Stop introducing new material. Systematic exposition especially lends itself to the temptation to summarize this week's passage by taking a peek into the green fields of next week's text. Such a practice will rob your sermon of force and power. Reserve any necessary comments about next week's sermon for the conclusion of the entire service.

Stop being the same. Summarizing every message in the same way robs your sermon of the positive benefits of an unexpected ending. This rut can let your listeners know you are wrapping up before you want them to know. Do something different. Be unpredictable. Keep them guessing.

Stop telling 'em you're coming. Normally, you should not begin the summation by saying, "In conclusion . . ." or, "Finally . . ." That completely destroys the element of surprise. The people should not have to be told you are wrapping up the exposition.

---

8. Donald E. Demaray, *An Introduction to Homiletics* (Grand Rapids: Baker, 1974), 98–101.

Second, a good summation should fit the exposition. Some summations have little to do with the material they supposedly culminate. If your sermon is one of encouragement, summarize with encouragement. If your sermon is corrective, summarize with firm correction. If your sermon is doctrinal, summarize with clear recapitulation.

Third, good summations should be characterized by clarity of thought and expression. Vagueness has no place in concluding the exposition. Your listeners must be able to understand without question what you are saying. If you are just beginning your ministry, be sure to write out your summations word for word, even when you do not prepare a full manuscript. This practice will force you to clarify what you are saying.

Fourth, reserve some strength and energy for your summation. Do not preach so that you expend all you have before you reach that point. Because the summation is building toward a climax in the invitation, reserve enough liveliness to carry your sermon to its proper ending. Broadus criticized energetic speakers who exhausted themselves before they reached this point and ended up "panting and hoarse and with no banner but a moist handkerchief."[9]

Fifth, relevance to your immediate audience is extremely important. Direct your remarks to the people that are present. No sense can be made of directing your message to those who are not present. Make use of the second person pronoun often. Appeal to individuals for a definite response. The summation should leave the people with a deep sense of personal responsibility. They should know beyond question what action they are being called upon to take. When you do this well, the foundation has been laid for a powerful invitation.

PART #3: INSPIRING INVITATION

The final part of the sermon—the invitation—is the preacher's *call for action.* Certainly, the invitation is not limited to the traditional "altar call" or any other form of immediate, public invitation. The invitation simply is the climactic call for listeners to commit themselves to acting on the truth that has been preached before they walk out the door. As you develop the summation, allow your thinking to flow directly into the development of an inspiring invitation. Now that you have exposed the listeners' minds to the truth of God's Word, the time has come for you to inspire them to act on it. Remember that inspiration does not suggest manipulation.

The Rationale for the Invitation

Unfortunately, most books on sermon preparation dedicate very little,

9. Broadus, *Preparation and Delivery of Sermons,* 111.

if any, attention to this vital part of the preaching event. Many homileticians do not even see the invitation as an integral part of the sermon. The summation—the "conclusion," as most call it—is considered the end of the sermon. In the last half-century the revival of audience analysis, a growing cynicism toward aggressive evangelism, and certain other factors have given birth to many questions about the role of public *expressions of response* in preaching. Even many preachers who embrace its validity have begun to lose confidence and aggressiveness in extending public appeals for *immediate* response.

Many discussions regarding the validity of the public invitation have centered on the biblical foundation (or lack thereof) of such an activity. Critics often claim that the frequently used "altar call" is a modern development with little or no biblical precedent. The problem with such an argument, however, lies in its failure to distinguish between the *function* of the invitation and the particular *form* of its employment. Certainly, because church architectural styles and even the logistics of worship are ever evolving, the same claim could be made regarding many contemporary practices (e.g., choirs seated behind a pulpit, pews for people to sit in, Communion tables, etc.). Thus, the claim that the absence of a biblical altar call negates the need for the public invitation is empty at best.

The Bible, on the other hand, does contain many examples of calls, appeals, and exhortations for individuals to respond to God. C. E. Autrey observed: "In many of the cases in Scripture, the exact idea of the present-day invitation is not intended, but the germinal idea is there. In some cases the basis for the modern invitation is there beyond any doubt."[10] While some models of the modern invitation truly are of comparatively recent origin, the spirit and principle of the activity is as old as the Bible itself.[11]

Secular and spiritual analysts alike have testified to the validity and the value of giving persons an opportunity to act immediately upon significant decisions. Amid all of the criticism Billy Graham has received regarding his evangelistic methodologies, the one component of his ministry that even secular analysts have hailed is his employment of the public invitation. Even secular psychologists agree that if you are going to call people to action, you ought to give them some immediate way to act.

Both psychological and spiritual value are attached to making some physical expression that will serve as a reminder of a significant commitment in days to come. Abraham built an altar to which he occasionally re-

---

10. C. E. Autrey, *Basic Evangelism* (Grand Rapids: Zondervan, 1959), 127–28.
11. Farris D. Whitesell, *65 Ways to Give Evangelistic Invitations* (Grand Rapids: Kregel, 1984), 15–16.

turned (Gen. 12–13). The people of Israel set up a monument of stones to remind them of certain covenants and works of God (Josh. 4). In response to Ezra's call for them to put away their pagan wives, the men of Israel gave a physical expression and made a covenant regarding their intent to obey (Ezra 9–10). Such expressions add accountability and heighten memory with regard to commitment to future action.

Yet the designation "public invitation" is not without some ambiguity. Does the designation refer to an invitation that *is being offered publicly* by a preacher or to an invitation offered by a preacher for persons *to respond in some public manner*? A difference does exist between the two, and proclaimers of the gospel must make the distinction before debating the validity of the role of the invitation in preaching. When the preaching event is traced through its biblical and historical development, the former appears to be a nonnegotiable part of the nature of preaching.

Proclamation of God's truth implies the call for decision, and proclaimers of the biblical text must call upon listeners to act upon the preached Word. Whether or not persons are asked to respond with some immediate, public indication of their decision every time preaching occurs is a different matter. In fact, the only determinant of whether or not a person truly acts upon the message is the changed life he or she lives long after the preaching event is over.

Preachers today, then, uncompromisingly must call upon listeners to act upon the message of the text. Regardless of the form of expression, every sermon should be intent upon fostering change in the lives of people. The entire message must move toward this purpose. We do not preach merely to hear ourselves talk or simply to convey information. We preach for a response. We are lawyers pleading our Lord's cause. We are calling for a verdict.

The gospel of Christ innately demands a response from those who are confronted with its claims. David L. Larsen rightly said, "The gospel is an invitation to which sinners are to R.S.V.P. A response is called for."[12] The invitation is the time when the people specifically and formally are called upon to commit to such a response. The particular avenues they are given to express their responses, however, must be open to constant revision and refinement in keeping with respective sermons and preaching contexts.

Possible Models for the Invitation

Recognition of the germinal idea of the public invitation in Scripture

---

12. David L. Larsen, *The Evangelism Mandate: Recovering the Centrality of Gospel Preaching* (Wheaton, Ill: Crossway, 1992), 102.

gives rise to several models that can prove valuable in the contemporary context. Each model innately possesses both advantages and disadvantages, which must be taken into consideration when applied to a particular sermon or worship event. Creative, intentional, and meaningful application of each model can resurrect a needed part of the preaching event that has become dead weight in many worship services.

◆ Verbal Appeal

The public invitation in its most basic, nonnegotiable form simply involves the verbal plea for people to act on the preached truth. Though many advantages go along with an immediate, physical expression of response, such an offering is not necessary for a sermon to have a strong invitation. The preacher simply may finish his sermon with an exhortation for people to go and practice what they have heard.

Such an invitation is best served when it is the last part of the worship service, just before people walk out the door. Exiting into the context of everyday life, then, becomes the expression of response as people leave to live out the message. Even if no other form of expression is called for by the preacher, this kind of invitation should be part of every sermon.

◆ Physical Relocation

Probably the most common model of the public invitation calls for listeners to respond immediately to a verbal appeal by moving from their seats to some other location within or near the meeting room. This model describes the traditional "altar call," which has been offered by many preachers during the twentieth century. At the altar or other designated new location, the responder receives further ministry from the preacher or a trained encourager.

The physical relocation model may serve as the "bread and butter" of many preachers, but consideration should be given to using it more meaningfully and intentionally. For example, a sermon about following Christ from Matthew 9:9–13 may best be served with a traditional call for persons to come to the altar area. The call may be prefaced, however, with an invitation to Christians in the audience to kneel at the altar as representatives of Christ. Lost persons then could be invited to come and kneel beside the Christians, "following" their example. Application from a text such as Matthew 5:21–26 regarding reconciliation with an offended brother or sister, however, might best be followed with a call for persons to move from their seats and go to others in the audience with whom they have grievances. The reconciled individuals could then be invited to the altar area together.

◆ Post-Meeting Ministry

Another age-old model calls for persons to respond to the verbal appeal by attending some kind of ministry session after the worship event has concluded. This response issues forth in a private or semi-private meeting with the preacher or other trained leader either immediately after the service or at some time in the near future.

Meaningful application of this model might include an invitation for persons to meet in a designated room on Monday night after a Sunday sermon about counting the cost of discipleship (Luke 9:57–62). Further instruction and challenge regarding discipleship would be given at that time. An invitation following a message from Psalm 101:3 (about not allowing the eyes to look upon wicked things) might ask persons to go home when the service is dismissed, collect in a paper sack items that fall into the said category, and return immediately with them to the church. Responders then could be led to discard the items in a meaningful way and be given help in following through with their commitments.

◆ Written Record

A fourth model of public invitation calls for the hearer to respond to the verbal appeal by recording his or her decision on a card or some other form. With this model, persons are asked to respond immediately but in a somewhat private manner. Of course, some easy means of collecting decision cards must be included in this model.

The written response model may be most effective following a message that calls for the confession of specific sins that do not need to be publicized beyond the realm of current knowledge. The approach is also helpful in contexts where large numbers of unbelievers are present who may be confused or hesitant about other forms of response. The written record especially is beneficial for persons who are not ready to make a decision but would like further information and help.

◆ Physical Gesture

A fifth model of public invitation calls for listeners to respond to the verbal appeal with some type of physical gesture while remaining at their seats. Such gestures may include standing, bowing, or raising a hand. Listeners may be asked to respond with the gesture while the audience is watching or while everyone's head is bowed.

Stationary gestures should be called for purposely. For example, a message about Shadrach, Meshach, and Abed-Nego from Daniel 3 (about not following the crowd) might be followed by dismissing the congregation and asking those who desire to make a commitment in this area to remain in their seats and receive counsel from designated individuals. A biographical sermon on taking a bold stand for Christ from the life of Onesiphorus (2 Tim. 1:13–18) may be driven home by a call for respondents to stand at their seats while everyone else remains seated.

♦ Multiple Approach

Most preachers who give a public invitation on a regular basis use the same model every week. But in addition to the variety mentioned above, think about offering more than one way of response within the same invitation.

For instance, a three-tiered invitation could involve a traditional altar call, followed by the use of a decision card provided for those who did not feel comfortable with going to the altar, followed by a third invitation for still others to meet with available encouragers at a designated place after the service.

Qualities of a Good Invitation

A fresh look at the qualities consistent with effective public invitations will help ensure that these opportunities for public response are offered in the most appropriate way. An examination of the philosophies of selected contemporary practitioners who are known to extend effective invitations reveals several prominent qualities that provide a healthy atmosphere for positive responses.

First, contemporary invitations must be *cohesive* with the sermons that precede them. Expressions of response called for at the close of some preaching events have become so routine that they often have absolutely no relationship to the message that has been preached. Some sermons dealing primarily with issues of the Christian life are followed with a call for persons to receive Christ.

Although an invitation for salvation always is appropriate, it may not best serve a sermon following a call for Christians to act upon the subject of the message. The invitation should never appear to be an addendum to the sermon but should flow naturally from its summation. Such an inclusion prevents the perception of a break between the invitation and the sermon.[13]

---

13. Robert L. Hamblin, "Evangelistic Preaching in Today's World," *Proclaim* 23 (January/February/March 1995): 49.

Second, in addition to being cohesive with the message, effective contemporary invitations are characterized by *simplicity and clarity* with regard to what respondents are expected to do. Intricacy and elaboration certainly are discouraged when it comes to giving instructions to people during an invitation. Many growing churches employ invitations that proceed directly to the point, avoiding verbosity and ornate terminology.[14] "Do not try to be profound, professional, and polished. Just be clear, simple, and concise."[15]

The invitation should be clear in several regards. Your listeners should be told exactly and specifically what they are being asked to do, why they are being asked to do it, and what will take place when they respond.[16] Also, make sure that you do not cheapen the appeal for response by making your invitation so broad and general that almost anyone can respond simply to maintain a sense of integrity.[17]

Avoid equating "walking an aisle" with a commitment to Christ. Clearly distinguish the call for repentance, belief, and public discipleship from the act of immediate physical response. At the same time, highlight the meaningful purpose of public expression, such as the availability of counsel, the provision of spiritual and/or psychological confirmation, and the presence of corporate affirmation and encouragement.[18] And, clearly distinguish between calls for salvation and other types of decisions.[19] A failure to do so can result in confusion for both respondents and counselors, as well as in unstable commitments.

Third, if you are going to invite people to make some immediate expression of response, make sure that what you ask them to do is *functional*. The offering of effective invitations, for example, can greatly be enhanced by the use of trained persons to offer encouragement and other ministry to respondents.

Churches and other ministry organizations should pay the price to investigate all related legal issues and then provide persons with adequate training. Such an investment may be the single most helpful element in making an effective public appeal. Although the use of the title "coun-

---

14. James Emery White, *Opening the Front Door: Worship and Church Growth* (Nashville: Convention, 1992), 125.

15. Ralph Bell, "Extending the Evangelistic Invitation," in *The Calling of an Evangelist,* ed. J. D. Douglas (Minneapolis: World Wide Publications, 1987), 188.

16. White, *Opening the Front Door,* 125.

17. Roy Fish, *Giving a Good Invitation* (Nashville: Broadman, 1974), 24–25.

18. R. Alan Streett, *The Effective Invitation* (Old Tappan, N.J.: Revell, 1984), 155–56.

19. Ralph Bell, *Giving a Successful Invitation: Preaching for a Verdict* (Minneapolis: North American Conference of Itinerant Evangelists, 1994), cassette S202A.

selor" probably should be avoided, the availability of such persons provides great advantages.

Fourth, effective invitations usually are characterized by some *decisive* element. In other words, potential respondents most often should be called upon to make a decision and express the intent of such a decision in some immediate way. Subsequent life change is enhanced when persons are given an opportunity to act immediately upon their intentions. The decisive nature of invitations that call for immediate expressions of response might be called the "altar advantage." Psychologically, public response serves to confirm the decision in the life of the responder.

Such a quality issues from the conviction that preaching is decisional in nature. The sermon does more than make the gospel known. It also calls for response.[20] When it comes to trusting Christ for salvation, for example, public invitations underscore the fact that it is absolutely necessary for a person to make a definite choice in order to become a Christian. Fish observed, "One does not become a Christian by osmosis. Nobody 'oozes' into the kingdom of God."[21]

Some contemporary practitioners have discouraged regular employment of the public invitation on the grounds that such significant decisions merit careful consideration. Windows of opportunity for spiritual decision making, however, are not always accommodating.

The Spirit of God is not limited or bound to human reasoning, nor is He obligated to continue or repeat His work in a person's life. If a man is beating his wife, he need not be encouraged to "think about" repenting. If a woman is living in adultery, she does not deserve the privilege of "contemplating" the ramifications of leaving such a lifestyle. One would be hard-pressed not to consider the immediate obedience of Matthew, Zaccheus, the woman of Sychar, and others.

Some contend that persons must be asked to respond immediately only when they are spiritually prepared to do so.[22] What preacher of the gospel in even the smallest congregation, however, can discern which people in his congregation on any given occasion are spiritually ready to make a decision? A better approach seems to be to offer opportunity for immediate response regularly, but to do so with integrity and clarity so as not to manipulate premature decisions.

20. Charles S. Kelley Jr., *How Did They Do It? The Story of Southern Baptist Evangelism* (New Orleans: Insight, 1993), 56–57.
21. Roy Fish, *How to Give an Evangelistic Invitation* (Produced by the Baptist General Convention of Texas. 44 min. Dallas, 1991), videocassette.
22. Bill Hybels, Stuart Briscoe, and Haddon Robinson, *Mastering Contemporary Preaching* (Portland: Multnomah, 1989), 40–41.

Fifth, the demeanor of those offering public opportunities for response must be both *nonmanipulative and nonthreatening*. This issue is one of integrity. Potential respondents should not be coerced, pressured, or made to feel guilty during the moment of decision.[23]

Some people have a natural fear simply of being in public situations. This fear is no different from other natural fears, such as the fear of heights, enclosed places, or water. The public invitation should be handled in such a manner that when a person responds to the given opportunity, he or she is not devastated by being thrust before a crowd without proper preparation or by being forced into some other embarrassing situation.

In addition to invitation models that are threatening to certain temperaments, any kind of manipulative approach also must be avoided. For example, some preachers employ a deceptively progressive invitation often called the "bait and switch technique." The congregation is asked to respond in one way, and then the first response is used to lead to a second and sometimes third response. Other tactics such as intentional embarrassment, being untruthful about how many stanzas remain to be sung, wrongfully playing on people's emotions, and lowering houselights also smack of lack of integrity. Abuse at these points causes many people to react against all kinds of public appeals.

Sixth, like the application made throughout the message, the invitation should be made *personal* to every listener. Each individual ought to feel that the preacher is talking specifically to him or her.

As you move into the invitation from the summation, become very direct. Such a personal touch will force each listener to contemplate the challenge. If at no other time during the sermon, every person in attendance should realize "This is for me" during the invitation.

Seventh, every invitation you offer should incorporate an *evangelistic* twist. Always turn the message at some point toward an appeal to the unsaved in the audience to receive Jesus Christ as personal Lord and Savior. All Bible preaching issues forth into evangelism. Regardless of the Bible content of your message, the subject should include an evangelistic appeal.

Certainly you should always begin your invitation with a call upon the primary intended audience to respond. If your text mainly is speaking to believers, invite them first to act upon the given truth. Do not fail, however, to transition the invitation to an evangelistic appeal before closing.

---

23. White, *Opening the Front Door,* 126.

PART #4: INTRIGUING INTRODUCTION

The final step in building your sermon is to prepare the introduction. This is the initial part of the sermon in which the preacher is attempting to *buy a hearing* from the audience. In essence, you must buy the right to take your listeners to the next step. The introduction, therefore, should be intriguing, gaining listener interest and seizing their attention.

Some difference of opinion exists concerning when the introduction should be prepared. Though each preacher may have his own preference, the best place seems to be at the end of the sermon preparation process. Most preachers find it rather difficult to introduce something before they know what they are introducing! Now that you have developed your exposition, tied it together in your summation, and called people to respond to it in your invitation, you likely have a more informed perspective regarding how to introduce it.

Purposes of the Introduction

The introduction of the sermon should be very intentional. The expositor should purpose to accomplish the following goals at the outset of his message:

First, *gain their interest*. You either have your listeners with you or you do not in the first few minutes of the sermon. In these early minutes the stage is set. The mood of the audience is determined. We cannot assume that those who sit in our congregations are automatically interested in what we are going to say. We must create that interest. Robinson referred to a Russian proverb as counsel concerning the introduction: "It is the same with men as with donkeys; whoever would hold them fast must get a very good grip on their ears!"[24]

Take time to prepare your introduction well. Write out a strong opening sentence that prepares people for a strong introduction. Someone has said, "Light your match on the first strike."[25] Songwriters use what they call a "hook" somewhere in the song to catch the listeners' attention. Use that first sentence to place a "hook" in your introduction and arouse the interest of your hearers.

---

24. Haddon W. Robinson, *Biblical Preaching* (Grand Rapids: Baker, 1980), 160.
25. Adams, *Pulpit Speech*, 54.

INTRODUCTION INSIGHT

Adrian Rogers, pastor of New Bellevue Baptist Church in Memphis, has a useful formula for putting together a sermon introduction. Rogers thinks in terms of four words: Hey! You! Look! Do!

Hey!—Get the attention of the listeners in the introduction. Catch the essence of the sermon in a sentence. Gain their interest.

You!—Indicate that the subject matter at hand applies to the listeners. "This is for you! I have something you need to hear."

Look!—Give some information about the subject to come. Briefly show what will be shared with them in more length and depth in the exposition of the message.

Do!—Tell them what they are expected to do as a result of hearing the sermon.

Second, *introduce your text.* If an expository sermon purposes to expose the truth of a text, then the introduction to that sermon should introduce the preaching passage to some degree.

On the other hand, setting up the text in detail should be done only selectively. The danger of textual overload in the introduction is that it can become very boring to those who regularly listen to expository sermons.

Third, *state your proposition.* You know what you want to say, but those who sit before you have no idea what you intend to say. In your introduction let your audience know the central idea of the text and the proposition of your sermon. The introduction lays the big idea before the people and prepares them for its development.

Emory A. Griffin, in his volume *The Mind Changers,* said:

Is it wise to present *this main point* at the start of the message, or would we be better off to wait until the conclusion? We'd do well to follow the advice of a successful country preacher. When asked the secret of his success he replied, "It's simple. I tell them what I'm going to say. I say it. Then I tell them what I've said. Let people know where you are headed right from the start. This way they will have a mental hook on which to hang all the illustrations and evidence you can muster to support your thesis. If they don't know where you are headed, they might unconsciously twist an example you give and see it as bolstering a different point of view.[26]

26. Emory A. Griffin, *The Mind Changers* (Wheaton, Ill.: Tyndale, 1976), 134.

To be sure, some narrative texts may be served better by an inductive development in which the proposition is not stated until the summation. Most passages, however, naturally will call for a strong, clear statement of the central idea at the beginning of the sermon. Several brief, well-worded sentences of introduction usually can make this theme unmistakably clear.

Fourth, *establish the relevancy.* The chances of gaining interest will be greatly enhanced if the preacher establishes the relevancy of the sermon in the minds of his listeners. Be sure to gain a favorable hearing by showing your audience that your message is important for their lives. Your purpose is to move the listeners to action, to help them make certain decisions on the basis of the sermon you deliver. That goal cannot be accomplished if they are not inclined favorably to the import of your sermon.

Someone has said there are three kinds of preachers: those to whom you cannot listen, those to whom you can listen, and those to whom you must listen. A good introduction will help you be the latter.

Fifth, *promise the "Take Away."* The introduction should display the fruit of listening to your people on a regular basis. As you discern both their expressed needs and the needs that lurk beneath the surface, incorporate them into the launch-pads of your sermons. The introduction should establish in word and attitude your empathy and care, as well as a statement of what benefit the listeners will be able to "take away" from the sermon.[27]

Sixth, *state your expectations.* The summation and invitation actually should begin with the introduction. Early in the sermon make clear where you are going, what you expect of the audience, and how you want them to respond. Begin in the introduction to drive toward the invitation, keeping your purpose in mind throughout the development of your exposition.

No paragraph of Scripture is without a personal appeal to the heart. Find that appeal and begin pressing it home at the beginning of your sermon.

Qualities of a Good Introduction

There are several marks of a good introduction. Building these qualities into the beginning of your sermon will heighten its effectiveness.

---

27. Lloyd John Ogilvie, "Introducing the Sermon," in *Handbook of Contemporary Preaching,* ed. Michael Duduit (Nashville: Broadman, 1992), 176.

Brevity. In most cases, the introduction should be short. A preacher easily can get carried away as the sermon begins. Avoid every word that is not absolutely necessary. Several years ago the distinguished senator and orator Albert J. Beveridge suggested, "If you can't strike oil in three minutes, you should quit boring."[28]

An elaborate, lengthy introduction may promise your listeners more than you are able to deliver. R. G. Lee used to talk about preachers who built chicken coop sermons on skyscraper foundations. An introduction is the porch, not the house. Make it long enough to introduce the subject and no more.

Variety. Make use of a variety of introductions. When your listeners know you are going to begin each sermon the same way, they will be prepared to give you only their inattention, not their attention.

Choose just the right kind of introduction for the message you have prepared. Because texts, audiences, and occasions vary, the sermon introductions that serve each one should vary as well.

Relevancy. Turn the introduction quickly to the needs of the hearers so as to establish relevancy. The introduction should arouse in them a sense of need. You cannot sell them something they do not know they need. Someone has said regarding this need, "Always grab the reader by the throat in the first paragraph, sink your thumbs into his windpipe in the second, and hold him against the wall until the tag line."[29]

If you can begin with felt needs in your introduction and then connect them with spiritual answers throughout your message, you will be far along the road toward being an interesting preacher.

Tension. Introductions should have a sense of tension. Create the awareness that your sermon will complete what you have begun in the introduction. Indicate that the questions you have raised in the introduction will be answered in the exposition of your Scripture passage. The needs you have identified in your introduction will be given Bible solutions in the message. The introduction sets the pace for the entire message.

Appropriateness. The introduction also sets the mood for the sermon. Texts and corresponding subjects vary in mood—some are happy and optimistic, others more serious in nature. Match the mood of your introduction with the text and its subject. You do not want to begin in a frivolous manner when you will be discussing something serious.

---

28. Judson S. Crandell, Gerald M. Phillips, and Joseph A. Wigley, *Speech: A Course in Fundamentals* (Glenview, Ill.: Scott Foresman, 1963), 169.
29. Robinson, *Biblical Preaching,* 160.

Conviction. The people should be aware from the very beginning of the sermon that you yourself are interested in the subject matter. If *you* are interested, the congregation likely will be interested as well. Put yourself into the introduction with your best thought and energy. Some preachers seem to care very little whether or not they are heard. Their messages seem to be soliloquies, intended for themselves alone. They might just as well be preaching to the trees and stars.

The preacher who is interested in communicating God's Word to people will be most interested in securing their attention. The majority of people who come to hear you preach really want to attend to what you say. Be sure you do not stifle that desire in the opening minutes. "People don't care how much you know unless they know how much you care!"[30]

Types of Introductions

Several kinds of introductions can be effective. The particular type you employ should depend upon your text, purpose, and audience.[31] You may use a straightforward *statement* of a contemporary problem and how the biblical text addresses that problem. Come up with your own quotable line or "zinger" that will shock or impact listeners. Just be sure the statement in not so startling that everything thereafter is anticlimatic. Other introductions may make use of a well-worded *question* or series of questions that get to the core of a human need or situation, followed by a statement of how the biblical text reveals God's response to that dilemma.

An *illustration* in the form of an anecdote or parable from contemporary life or history may be used. The narrative would expose the central idea of the text A *personal experience* from your own life to which you apply the given text can be used to set up your corresponding proposition. Better beginnings are hard to find. A *life situation* also can be used. A real-life story or circumstance often can get to the essence of a text effectively. Great introductions may include a positive believe-it-or-not case history from your own congregation or a feature story clipped from a magazine reflecting Christian values.

---

30. Humes, 25.
31. These types were adopted and expanded from Ogilvie, "Introducing the Sermon," 177–85. In addition to listing the types, Ogilvie provides excellent examples of each one.

INTRODUCTION ICHABODS

Beware of several undesirable ways to introduce a sermon. Avoid these kinds of introductions at all costs:

Hem-and-haw. Do not neglect your preparation so that you beat around the bush in your introduction. The preacher who is not really sure what he is going to say evidences that he has prepared neither the exposition of the sermon nor the introduction. He is unclear in his thought and his speech. An audience will notice this lack of preparation very quickly and will respond with corresponding inattention.

Apologetic. Do not introduce your message by telling the people how poorly you have prepared or how little you know about the subject. Probably you will never feel as prepared as you would like. But when a speaker makes excuses, "he is not taking out an insurance policy in case he flops; he is only planting in his audience's mind the likelihood of his failure."[32] If you are not prepared, they will know soon enough! Moreover, do not apologize for the nature of the subject you propose. If your sermon truly is expository, no apology is needed for any truth found in the Word of God.

Trite. Do not fill your introduction with meaningless statements that do not point toward your subject. Make your introductory remarks weighty. You are seeking to arouse attention. You must give your listeners enough substance in your introduction to merit that attention. If you are trite, they will not be impressed. Usually, praise for the audience is trite. If you must praise the audience or someone in it, use that praise in the middle of your sermon to support a point. Churchill contended that praise in the introduction of a speech comes off as flattery, whereas the same praise in the middle of the speech comes off as sincerity.

Funny. Humor can be used effectively in the sermon, but jokes rarely serve the preacher well at the beginning. If you lack the wit of a Jerry Clower or the timing of a Jay Leno, you can bury your sermon and embarrass both yourself and your audience. Again, turn your joke into humor by saving it for the body of the sermon where it will be unexpected and can be used to make a point.[33]

32. Humes, 18.
33. Ibid., 37.

Pedantic. Do not introduce your sermon in an academic way. A belabored, routine beginning soon will bore the listeners. Let your introduction be characterized by freshness and variety.

Misleading. Avoid promising something that you do not intend to deliver or cannot deliver. When the preacher proposes one subject and preaches on another, the people feel betrayed. Introduce your subject, then stick to it.

Still other introductions may center on a *felt need*. Powerful beginnings can be built around a sympathetic reference to a need expressed by many listeners and a promise to show how the biblical text addresses that need. A *current event* news item that is on people's minds can highlight the contemporary focus of the biblical text. Even an offbeat story, sharp quotation, editorial, or description of a key sporting event from the daily news can launch your message. Taking the paper into the pulpit and reading from it can also be effective.

Narrative material provides another strong beginning. A dramatic retelling of the story line of the biblical text with a "you are there" flavor, followed by a statement of connection to the parallel contemporary situation, often will seize listeners' attention. Or you may use a *textual* introduction. This approach involves a direct statement of the biblical text or a clearly stated paragraph describing its context, followed by application to contemporary life. Finally, a *quotation* from a person well-known to your listeners, followed by a statement of how the biblical text relates to that quote, can grasp attention. Avoid a long quotation that rambles on for a paragraph, however. Narrow it to one or two sentences at the most.

The Development of the Introduction

Once you have determined the type of introduction that is best for a particular message, you can develop your sermon beginning. The following process is suggested for building effective introductions.

Agonize. Spend time meditating on your exposition, summation, and invitation. Also, empathize with your people by reflecting on their life situations. Wrestle with these realities until you are able to identify the major point or points of intersection.

Verbalize. Write out your thoughts word for word, exactly as you would like to convey them to your people. "Writing is the expression of refined and polished thought."[34] Even if you do not write out in full the other parts of the sermon, write out the introduction to ensure a strong, clear beginning.

Criticize. Once you have written your introduction, put it to the test. Go back and see if it accomplishes the six purposes discussed earlier: gains interest, introduces the text, makes the proposition, establishes relevancy, promises a "take away," and states expectations.

Editorialize. Based upon your critical review, make any changes or refinements needed.

Memorize. Commit the final product to memory so that you will be able to look your people in the eye and establish communication. Your memorization may not be word for word, but repeated readings and oral recitations will fix it in your verbal memory patterns.[35]

Never underestimate the importance of toiling over the introduction. This crucial part can make or break your message. Spurgeon said, "You must attract the fish to your hook, and if they do not come you should blame the fisherman and not the fish. Compel them to stand still awhile and hear what God, the Lord, would speak to their souls."[36] Introduce your sermon as if it were life or death to your hearers—because it is!

34. Ogilvie, 177.
35. Ibid.
36. Charles Haddon Spurgeon, *Lectures to My Students* (London: Marshall, Morgan and Scott, 1954), 128.

PART THREE

THE PRESENTATION OF THE EXPOSITION

CHAPTER 9: Expressing the Thoughts

Understanding Preaching Style
Using the Elements of Style
Enhancing Your Style
Ensuring Persuasive Style
Incorporating Dramatic Style
Evaluating Your Style

CHAPTER 10: Playing the Voice

Understanding the Voice
Mastering the Voice
Improving the Voice
Caring for the Voice

CHAPTER 11: Making the Connection

Visualizing the Sermon
Vitalizing the Sermon
Communicating the Sermon

CHAPTER 12: Preaching the Word

Holding the Ear
Speaking with the Body
Augmenting the Message
Delivering without Notes
Proclaiming from the Heart

James Humes, who has written speeches for every Republican president since Eisenhower, made the following assertion: "Every time you have to speak—whether it's in an auditorium, in a company conference room, or even at your own desk—you are auditioning for leadership. The difference between mere management and leadership is communication. And the art of communication is the language of leadership."[1] What a great description of preaching—"The language of leadership!" The preaching event has life-changing ramifications, for by it the preacher leads people into a lifelong process of transformation into the image of Jesus Christ. If anything is needed in today's pulpit, it is men who will lead effectively with the Word of God. The importance of a quality presentation in the preaching event, then, cannot be underestimated.

This third and final part of the book is dedicated to helping preachers speak the language of leadership. The tragedy of all tragedies is for the man of God to have exegeted a text accurately, and then to have packaged it beautifully in sermonic form, only to dull its sharpness and dilute its potency with poor delivery. Effective delivery, on the other hand, will go far in enabling the preacher to lead his people to take new ground for the kingdom.

---

1. James C. Humes, *The Sir Winston Method: The Five Secrets of Speaking the Language of Leadership* (New York: William Morrow, 1991), 13–14.

CHAPTER NINE

EXPRESSING
THE THOUGHTS

Give me the right word and the right
accent and I will move the world.

JOSEPH CONRAD

The preacher speaks the Word of God in the words of men. Thus, preaching is the most important kind of public speaking known to mankind. The expression of the sermon ultimately will be manifested via oral communication during the delivery of the message. Although various elements of nonverbal communication are important matters, the preacher's first attention should be given to the quality of his verbal expression. Before stepping into the pulpit, you need to dedicate some time to polishing the style of your verbal communication. Some preachers work on style as they write out a full or partial manuscript. Others simply review their sermons mentally. Ideally, you will employ both methods to some degree.

Whether your review is through writing, mental review, or a combination of both practices, your effectiveness at the point of delivery largely depends upon your intentional development of expression prior to getting up to preach. In one sense, the effective preacher must be an artist. Such art may not be reduced to a step-by-step formula. Several useful considerations, however, can increase the effectiveness of your sermon.

UNDERSTANDING PREACHING STYLE

In recent years many homileticians have adopted a tendency to disparage rhetorical studies as they relate to sermon delivery. Few textbooks on the subject give much help in this area. Rhetoric, generally defined, is the art of using words effectively in speaking to influence or persuade others. This description obviously suggests that rhetoric is a legitimate area of study for the pastor who desires to preach effectively. The obvious dangers involved in such a consideration must not deter the preacher from investing time in this field. Broadus defined rhetoric as the art of extemporization, appropriate expression, and moving appeal.[1] Such a description underscores the importance of style, one of the five basic canons of classical rhetoric outlined by Quintilian in his *Institutes of Oratory*.

Style essentially is the preacher's characteristic manner of expressing his thoughts.[2] Broadus emphasized that the grammatical processes were the working tools of rhetoric and, therefore, could not be neglected by the preacher. Style also involves the way the preacher's self is being expressed. George Sweazey contended that effective style is a combination of the preacher's personality and craftsmanship. In addition, the preacher has to combine his skills of expression with "a message he [is] burningly eager to express."[3]

Because of its rhetorical role, style must have regard for the time in which it is employed, following the customs and tastes of different peoples and different ages. One of the great characteristics of Christian preaching is its ability to adjust to the people of a given time period and relate itself to them effectively.[4]

William Kooienga described style as the manner in which the preacher chooses to bring the message to a particular audience. He contended that style is dictated by rhetorical principles shaped by preaching's distinctive task. According to Kooienga, the style of preaching takes the shape of one of three intentions: instruction, persuasion, or movement to response. In other words, he believed that a sermon's intention should dictate the particular style that is to be employed.[5]

Style also is a matter of the heart. Elizabeth Achtemeier asserted that words flow naturally in a pleasing rhythm when the heart of the preacher is engaged with a passion to communicate the Word of God to his congregation. When the heart is engaged, she said, even words become concrete and pictorial. In summary, Achtemeier said, "Style is the man!"[6]

1. John A. Broadus, *On the Preparation and Delivery of Sermons*, 4th ed., rev. Vernon L. Stanfield (1870; revision, New York: Harper & Row, 1979), 10 (page citation is to the revised edition).
2. Ibid., 200–201.
3. George E. Sweazey, *Preaching the Good News* (Englewood Cliffs, N.J.: Prentice-Hall, 1976), 125.
4. Broadus, *Preparation and Delivery of Sermons*, 204.
5. William H. Kooienga, *Elements of Style for Preaching* (Grand Rapids: Zondervan, 1989), 51–52.
6. Elizabeth Achtemeier, *Creative Preaching: Finding the Words* (Nashville: Abingdon, 1980), 92.

All preachers have a style, whether good or bad. Your verbal style is your choice of words that express the truths of your sermon. The power of these words cannot be overestimated. The words you choose can render your sermon powerfully effective or miserably inept. Robinson said:

> Of all people an expository preacher professing a high view of inspiration should respect language. To affirm that the individual words of Scripture must be God-breathed and then to ignore his own choice of language smacks of gross inconsistency.[7]

The man of God who would be an effective communicator must give attention to the use of words in sermon style.

Style, like delivery, actually is not something we cultivate to make our preaching more effective but to prevent its being ineffective. The supernaturally powerful Word of God does not need our polished style to become more potent. We have a responsibility, however, not to dull the Word's sharpness with our poor style. Broadus said:

> Style is the glitter and polish of the warrior's sword but is also its keen edge. It can make mediocrity acceptable and even attractive, and power more powerful still. It can make error seductive, while truth may lie unnoticed for lack of it. Shall religious teachers neglect so powerful a means of usefulness?[8]

The obvious value of good sermon style should make it a matter of careful attention for the expository preacher.

STYLISTIC SHOWSTOPPERS

Poor style usually can be identified by several qualities. Work toward eliminating them from your sermons.

Verbosity. Using too many words to express your thoughts can hinder the desired effect and actually produce weariness on the part of the listeners. This quality is common among preachers. Work toward eliminating every unnecessary word as much as possible.

Lack of clarity. Sentences that are too long, ideas that are poorly arranged, phrases that are too complicated all cloud the truths you intend to convey.

7.   Haddon W. Robinson, *Biblical Preaching* (Grand Rapids: Baker, 1980), 175–7
8.   Broadus, *Preparation and Delivery of Sermons,* 202.

Circumlocution. This error involves saying many words but never really saying what you intend to say. As was said of one preacher with this problem, "If our dear brother had anything to say, he could certainly say it!" This defect is almost always fatal. The words promise the point but never seem to arrive.

Dullness. Lack of dramatic quality is a mark of poor sermon style. The words have no alluring quality; they do not arouse a sense of interest and expectancy.

Roughness. Absence of flow and rhythm greatly hinders good sermon style. The jerky sentence, the clumsy phrase, the hesitant expression are all indicative of poor style.

Sameness. Closely akin to the absence of rhythm is the prominence of rhythm, a quality that becomes monotonous. The sentences are all the same. The movement is always predictable. No variety is present in what the preacher says and in the way he says it.

USING THE ELEMENTS OF STYLE

A significant difference exists between the oral use of words and the written use. The writer has an advantage in that written words may be reviewed by the eyes of the reader. The oral communicator, on the other hand, must use words that can be understood at the moment of hearing. Certain elements of preaching style are crucial for helping the preacher bring this about. In the composition of your sermon you should strive to include the following qualities.

SIMPLICITY

Preachers should strive to be as simple as possible in their speech. A healthy goal is to work toward preaching so that the children in the congregation can understand what you are saying. One of the greatest compliments you will ever receive is when a mother says, "Billy likes to hear you preach because he can understand what you say." Martin Luther said:

A preacher should have the skill to teach the unlearned simply, roundly and plainly; for teaching is of more importance than exhorting. When I preach I regard neither doctors nor magistrates, of whom I have about forty in the congregation. I have all my eyes on the servant maids and the children. If the learned men are not well pleased with what they hear, well, the door is open.[9]

9. Quoted in D. Martyn Lloyd-Jones, *Preaching and Preachers* (Grand Rapids: Zondervan, 1971), 129.

When the little children can understand the words you use, you do not have to wonder if the grown-ups are getting it. If you put the cookies on the bottom shelf, the rabbits can eat them as well as the giraffes. Simplicity can be achieved in several ways. Consider the characteristics at the bottom of the page.

The words of a sermon should be simple rather than artificial, technical, theological, and impressive. Complicated words may impress a few people but will confuse the majority of them.

On the other hand, some people suggest that simple language demands the avoidance of all unfamiliar Bible terminology. Such a contention should be embraced cautiously, however. To be sure, the unbelieving world will never be able to understand Bible language on the surface. The words of the Bible are special to those who know and love the gospel. The preacher, however, has the responsibility to teach people the meaning of Bible terms. This task may be accomplished with words that are simple and easy to understand. When you must use big words, be sure to explain them clearly. The sermon must be spoken in words the people know.

SIMPLE SAYINGS

Short words. Words do not have to be long and complicated to be effective. Notice how short and simple are the immortal words "Four score and seven years ago"; "The Lord is my Shepherd"; "To be or not to be"; "We have nothing to fear but fear itself." A study of the sermons of Dwight L. Moody revealed that approximately 79 percent of the words he used were one-syllable words, 16 percent were two syllables, and only 4 percent were three syllables.[10] That undoubtedly is one of the biggest reasons the common people of Moody's day heard him gladly. The preacher should think with the theologians and scholars but talk to the common man.

Few words. Use only enough repetition to convey your assertion adequately. Beyond this point, people will become bored. Select words with a definite purpose in mind. Some preachers toss words around so freely that there is nothing left to be used when something really big is to be described. Government agencies are famous for the complexity of their directives. The rule seems to be "Never use a hundred words if a thousand will do." The delightful story is told of the plumber who wrote a government bureau in Washington to inform them that he had discovered clogged drains could be cleared by using hydrochloric

10. Kenneth McFarland, *Eloquence in Public Speaking* (Englewood Cliffs, N.J.: Prentice-Hall, 1961), 78.

234 POWER IN THE PULPIT

acid. The bureau wrote back: "The efficacy of hydrochloric acid is indisputable, but the corrosive residue is incompatible with metallic permanence." How much easier it would have been for them to say, "Don't use hydrochloric acid. It messes up the pipes."[11]

Plain words. Similarly, avoid loading your sermon down with pompous terms. Lighten up your expression with one-syllable equivalents. Use "so," not "therefore"; "but," not "however"; "still," not "nevertheless." Leave out heavy words such as "notwithstanding," "inasmuch," and "nevertheless." Some preachers seem to be afflicted with "elegantitis." Seemingly unable to use simple, clear, to-the-point words, they seek to clothe their language in a false elegance. Instead of saying "go to bed," they speak of "retiring." Rather than "getting up" in the morning, they "rise." They do not "eat," they "dine." Plain language is void of certain forms that Adams calls "word wax."[12] To avoid word wax, remove unnecessary superlatives such as "greatest," "best," "most phenomenal," and "quintessential." Rarely use "colossal," "thrilling," "exciting," "amazing," "wonderful," "splendid," "worthwhile." Eliminate trite and stale words. People get tired of hearing the same words over and over again. Do your best to cut out certain phrases that have a way of sticking in the preacher's vocabulary. Refrain from using the additives "such as," "and so forth," and "in the next place." Avoid weasel words, which unnecessarily qualify what you say.

CLARITY

Preachers often are amazed at what some people think they heard them say. Clear words will lessen the degree of misunderstanding. At the outbreak of the Franco-Prussian War, a general said to his officers, "Remember, gentlemen, that any order that can be misunderstood will be misunderstood."[13] The preacher has to be understood if people are expected to respond. Broadus explained:

> The success of a message depends on its being understood. If the message is not grasped, then all else is lost. Clarity has to be the beginning point and the most important point of style.[14]

Spoken style must be instantly intelligible to the hearer. The reader may pause to ponder the meaning of a word. The listener, on the other hand,

11. Ibid., 80.
12. Jay Adams, *Pulpit Speech* (Phillipsburg, N.J.: Presby. & Ref., 1971), 123.
13. Quoted in McDowell, 2.
14. Broadus, *Preparation and Delivery of Sermons,* 210.

is not given this luxury. He or she must understand in an instant what is being said. Clarity can be achieved in several ways:

CRYSTAL CLEAR

Specific words. The correct choice of a word can make the difference in conveying your thoughts. Mark Twain once said that the difference between the right word and the nearly right word is the difference between lightning and lightning bug. Strive for accuracy. Use words that convey your meaning correctly. Avoid words that can refer to a variety of qualities or feelings. Such words as "nice," "wonderful," "terrific," "fine," "cute," and "pretty" say little. Your words will have more weight when you say "Waycross, Georgia," instead of "a small Southern town." To say, "A fox terrier chased the boy," is clearer than to say, "A dog chased the boy."

Simple sentences. Your sentences should be short. Make them as uncomplicated as possible. Rudolf Flesch asserted that clarity increased as sentence length decreased. He determined that a clear speaker averaged seventeen or eighteen words in every sentence and never allowed any sentence to exceed thirty words.[15] Demaray said that sentences averaging eleven words are understood easily by 86 percent of American adults. Seventeen words per average sentence normally will communicate with 75 percent of American adults. More difficult speech, containing twenty-nine or more words in a typical sentence, will communicate with only 4.5 percent of the average audience.[16] Also, eliminate run-on sentences. Learn to use an abundance of periods in your speaking.

Active voice. The passive voice robs your sermon of life and action, turning colorful words of aggression into aloof suggestions.[17] Do not say, "The Word should be preached." Instead, say, "Preach the Word!"

Word combinations. Give attention to the way words are put together. Some words fit together, whereas other words do not. When words clash, understanding is difficult.

---

15. Rudolf Flesch, *The Art of Plain Talk* (New York: Harper, 1946), 38–39. Flesch c tended that oral and written style should be the same. His works were employed by many homileticians to measure certain qualities of preaching style. See Brown, Clinard, and Northcutt, *Steps to the Sermon*, 147–50; Broadus, *Preparation and Delivery of Sermons*, 213–14; J. Daniel Baumann, *An Introduction to Contemporary Preaching*, 161–63; Sweazey, *Preaching the Good News*, 154; Kooienga, *Elements of Style for Preaching* (Grand Rapids: Baker, 1972), 73–74; H. Grady Davis, *Design for Preaching* (Philadelphia: Fortress, 1958), 67; Ralph L. Lewis, *Persuasive Preaching Today* (Ann Arbor, Mich.: LithoCrafters, 1979), 144, 207, 222.

16. Ibid., 132–33.

17. Ibid., 54.

Clarity is indispensable for the decisional end of preaching. Obscure language deters people from response. Speaking about the lack of clarity, A. J. Gossip said,

> That is what kills many a sermon, and the truths they blur and smudge! In much preaching the great Christian verities fall dully on bored ears, largely because the language used is so opaque, so colorless, so unarresting.[18]

William Kooienga agreed, saying that "a sermon designed to persuade stumbles without the light of clarity."[19] You would be wise to listen carefully to the advertisements on radio and television. Read the ads in magazines and the words on billboards. Advertisers are interested in selling a product. They want to get their message to the people as clearly as possible. The preacher can learn from them. Though you rarely should resort to slang in preaching God's Word, you should aggressively attempt to use clear words.

FORCE

Force, or energy, is the quality of propelling your thoughts into the minds of the listeners. Your language should be such that listeners are impacted noticeably by the things you say. Several steps can be taken to add impact to preaching.

MAY THE FORCE BE WITH YOU!

Believe in your subject. You must deem important what you are saying if you desire to make an impact on your audience. Forceful speaking is prefaced by the speaker's enthusiasm about his subject.[20] Reflect back on your prepared message and see if your conviction about its magnitude is evident.

Be personal and direct. Address your listeners personally. Use the personal pronoun "you" often. This quality will make your sermon much more appealing to those who listen.

Be relevant. Adequately bridging the gap between the ancient text and the modern world also will increase the force of your message. Kooienga observed that the preacher's mind-set determines how he expresses himself. If you show remnants of Ramian-inspired Puritan

18. A. J. Gossip, in W. M. MacGregor, *The Making of a Preacher* (Philadelphia: Westminster, 1946), 12.
19. Kooienga, *Elements of Style for Preaching*, 63.
20. Broadus, *Preparation and Delivery of Sermons*, 210–11.

methods, you likely will use the Scriptures as a theological resource book. Your preaching will major on explanation without providing adequate application.[21] As you look back at your sermon, see if you truly bring biblical history into the contemporary world so that your message has a sharp edge.

Respect your listeners. A healthy attitude toward your congregation is a must. Lack of respect and appreciation for the congregation usually will be manifested in the pulpit through negative force. Sweazey observed that because most preachers are better schooled than their listeners in the subjects on which they preach, they may come to think of the congregants as retarded in their knowledge and primitive in their views. He encouraged preachers humbly to be aware of their listeners' abilities and character. If in private you think of them as clods or deficient Christians, such an attitude surely will come out in your sermon.[22] Similarly, be extremely careful not to fall prey to the tendency of some, who take out their personal frustrations on their audiences. Discouragement, resentment, impatience, hostility, sarcasm, and other attitudes are elements that can ostracize a congregation.

Enjoy preaching. The minister's personal enjoyment of his preaching, and his relaxation, confidence, and spiritual vitality all serve to build bridges of communication between him and his listeners.[23] Because the emotional response to a sermon is connected closely to the emotional response to the preacher, every pastor must cultivate a deep love for preaching and a subsequent affection for his people. You must develop a compassion for God's call on your life that is coupled with a desire to meet the deepest spiritual needs of those persons who listen to you preach.[24]

Achieving force may demand that the style of the sermon vary with the occasion. As you review your message for the particular preaching event at hand, take time to pray over and evaluate your use of the above guidelines. Force easily can be manifested with a negative character that will hinder rather than enhance the sermon.

INTEREST

Interest is the quality that secures and holds people's attention.[25]

21. Kooienga, *Elements of Style for Preaching*, Kooienga, 104–5.
22. Sweazey, *Preaching the Good News*, 298.
23. Ibid., 298–99.
24. Brown, Clinard, and Northcutt, *Steps to the Sermon,* 146.
25. See Brown, Clinard, and Northcutt, *Steps to the Sermon,* 151; Kooienga, *Elements of Style for Preaching,* 73.

More plainly, Sweazey described it as the quality of being other than dull.[26] The greatest fear that many preachers have is of boring their listeners. The writer of a book has the advantage of knowing that, under normal circumstances, the reader brings to his book some initial interest. The author is not faced with the need to create as much interest on the part of the reader as the preacher must create on the part of his listeners. Careful attention to certain stylistic features will help strengthen your ability to hold people's attention.

Identification with real life is one factor that will directly affect the preacher's ability to communicate with interest. As you expound the theological truths in your text, allow them to address subjects that portray God and mankind's relation to Him. Talk about the meaning of the cares and sufferings that people know. Achtemeier aptly said that "simple words about these things get down to the nitty-gritty of our people's lives and deal with them in the profound terms with which God has dealt with them."[27]

Do not be afraid to relate some of your own *personal experiences* that reflect your understanding of real-life problems and challenges. Achtemeier warned that "if preachers have not known God to deal with those things in their own lives, their preaching will not dip below the surface of sentimentality." You can avoid such an impression by carefully relating personal experiences with God along your spiritual journey. Such testimonies should not dominate the sermon, but rightly used they can heighten interest because people can identify with them.

Be aware that your *pastoral experiences* can make your sermons appear to be more relevant to the congregation. Staying in close contact with your flock prevents your speaking to your congregation as a technician who is an expert in religion. Instead, people will perceive you as a loving friend who knows them, cares about them, and enjoys them.[28]

The use of *contemporary language* heightens interest. The conviction that religious matters deserve a special style usually is a major hindrance to an audience's interest in a sermon. The use of words from the nineteenth century or from older versions of the Bible such as "wrought," "even so," "like unto," "beseech," "nigh," and "hast" can communicate to listeners that biblical truths are as archaic as the words being used to convey them. Kooienga noted that a preacher who delights in employing this kind of verbiage "risks making his sermon a museum piece."[29]

26. Sweazey, *Preaching the Good News*, 134.
27. Achtemeier, *Creative Preaching*, 93.
28. Sweazey, *Preaching the Good News*, 299.
29. Kooienga, *Elements of Style for Preaching*, 80.

Vivid language is interesting language. Certain words conjure up meaningful images in the minds of your people. They reach out and grab the interest of the listeners. This kind of expression has several key features:

VIVA VIVIDNESS!

Suspenseful. Words are more vivid when they carry a feeling of suspense. They arouse a sense of uncertainty. Sometime try presenting arguments on the other side of your sermon as though they were your own. This approach immediately will make your words come to life. Keep in mind that a reader is able to look at the previous sentences and even anticipate the words to follow. The listener does not have that privilege. Therefore, you must use words that build a sense of excitement, expectancy, and eagerness.

Climactic. Effective style has a sense of eagerness about it. Try arranging your thoughts in order of their ascending power. This effort eases mental fatigue and provides a method of measuring your final conclusions.

Energetic. Words are more vivid when they are energetic. Do not mistake energy for fury. Simple, specific words phrased effectively will provide tremendous energy. Give your statements a sense of movement. Let your words indicate you are going somewhere.

Concrete. The use of concrete rather than abstract words will make your sermon more vivid. Talk about "heaven" instead of "paradise." Refer to "a burning hell" instead of "eternal punishment."

Varied. Do not allow your sentences to get into any kind of pattern. Vary their length and type. This will help you maintain high interest on the part of your people and help create in them a sense of expectancy and suspense.

Figurative. The preacher must use figurative language to make connections with his listeners. The sermon should have comparisons and contrasts, for the listeners must be able to understand what is being said in relation to ideas and concepts that are familiar to them.

So, instead of saying, "A small Southern town . . ." say, "Homersville, Georgia." Instead of saying, "The beggar walked down the street," say, "The beggar stumbled down the busy street." This kind of vivid expression will allow your words to get up and walk.

BEAUTY

Your sermon style should have some degree of beauty or elegance. In many ways a sermon properly composed is a work of art. Beauty is not a quality that you can create but one that simply results from an effective use of the other elements of style.[30] As the preacher employs those other qualities, beauty and elegance will be the natural outflow.

Although this artistic expression primarily stems from the other elements of style, some small steps can be taken to ensure its presence. For example, sermons need a sense of rhythm and smoothness. In effective delivery, the words selected should glide easily on the preacher's lips and fall pleasantly upon the listeners' ears. Some combinations of words are difficult to articulate smoothly. For this reason, the preacher will do well to experiment with different ways of saying what he wants to say. For instance, "John the Baptist taught repentance" is harder to say smoothly than "John the Baptizer taught repentance." The latter expression removes the problem of using a word that ends with a *t* just before one that begins with *t*.

Beauty also is dependent upon the preacher's perspective of God. When God is seen as a God of incomparable glory and majesty, language conducive to worship will be used to describe Him. Furthermore, a realization of your love for Jesus Christ will enable words to flow in some semblance of eloquence and harmony. Your language will mirror the engagement of your heart.[31] These touches of beauty throughout the message make it much more appealing to those who listen. Give your sermon a touch of art.

ENHANCING YOUR STYLE

Several means of enhancing style already have been noted in discussions of other matters. In chapter 6, we determined that the proper development and expression of the major divisions contribute to good style. Earlier in this discussion, we observed that the preacher's choice of language raises the quality of style. In addition to these elements, several other tools are available to augment one's preaching style.

VISUAL LANGUAGE

Visual language paints pictures in the minds of the listeners, enabling them to see what they hear. An Arab proverb states, "He is the best speak-

---

30. Broadus, *Preparation and Delivery of Sermons*, 211.
31. Achtemeier, *Creative Preaching*, 96.

er who can turn the ear into an eye."[32] Man's mind is more like an art museum than a chalkboard. The preacher who desires to communicate adequately must use words that have sensory appeal.

Language that appeals to the senses is colorful. The sounds of words, for example, are important in transmitting your message. The combination of the sounds of vowels and consonants to help achieve a particular effect is called tone color.[33] For this reason, some prefer the term *color words*.

Colorful pictures painted in the mind move people. One picture may be worth a thousand words, but words themselves can paint powerful mental pictures. Jesus painted pictures with His words that called images to mind. He talked about seed sown in the soil; He spoke of a treasure hidden in the field; He spoke of tares sown among wheat. Use words to help your listeners call to mind the same images you have in yours. Listen for the sound suggestiveness of words. Speak of the *hum* of bees, the *thud* of a log, the *buzz* of flies, the *moaning* of the wind. In listening to words you will notice that their very sound sometimes conveys the meaning of the word. The word "smooth" is slow and quiet. The word "sharp" is abrupt and to the point like a knife. Think of "slow" and "swift," "bright" and "drab," "crisp" and "soggy," "gloomy" and "radiant." Think of the images they paint in your mind.[34]

Work hard to speak in the language of pictures. Try your best to lay aside words that are colorless and abstract. Good preachers help people to live out what they are saying. They portray the truth with such vividness that the people feel as if they themselves actually are involved in what is going on.

RELATIONAL LANGUAGE

Sermonic style is enhanced when the language of the preacher relates to the audience. Confusion abounds if he fails to understand his hearers. Avoiding such confusion demands that the preacher "acquaint himself with the point at which his hearers are, and begin from there, and not from uninformed assumptions about the situation."[35] As you look back over your sermon, see if you detect the following qualities that contribute to relational language.

32. Quoted in Donald E. Demaray, *An Introduction to Homiletics* (Grand Rapids: Baker, 1974), 107.
33. Charlotte I. Lee and Frank Galati, *Oral Interpretation* (Boston: Houghton Mifflin, 1977), 215.
34. Winston E. Jones, *Preaching and the Dramatic Arts* (New York: Macmillan, 1948), 68.
35. Donald O. Soper, *The Advocacy of the Gospel* (New York: Abingdon, 1961), 35.

Appropriate. Effective style follows the customs and tastes of different peoples and different ages. One of the admirable characteristics of Christian preaching is its ability to adjust to the people of a given time period and to relate to them effectively.[36] Lloyd Perry observed:

> The language the preacher employs should be contemporary and readily recognizable by the average man or woman. The phraseology used should be in terms of present needs and problems. Jesus Himself used a language of life that confronted people where they were and then awakened positive response. The people always knew what He was talking about because He used terminology that was familiar to them.[37]

Use words appropriate to the occasion. Be keenly aware of your audience, as well as the type of message to be delivered. Choose a level of vocabulary fitting the time, place, and purpose of the gathering. Use one level of word selection for a sermon to children or young people and another level for a speech to the senior adult group. Relational language consists of terms and themes with which the audience can identify. Such familiarity enhances the possibility of positive response.

Conversational. Because preaching is an oral event, your sermon should be expressed in accepted conversational English as opposed to formal written English. In other words, express your sermon the way you talk in a conversation with another person, not the way you write a term paper. Split your infinitives. End sentences with prepositions. Use contractions. Include sentence fragments. After reading and listening to many speeches as a young lieutenant, Winston Churchill recorded this key lesson about speech: *It must be geared to the ear.*[38]

Personal. Conversational style also is enhanced by the use of personal words and sentences. Personal words are personal names, personal pronouns, words of definite masculine and feminine gender, and words of definite personal description such as "men" or "children." Personal sentences are questions, commands, sentence fragments, exclamations, sentences addressed directly to the audience, and also direct or indirect quotations.[39] Frequent use of personal references makes speech more dramatic, thereby increasing human interest.[40] The preacher must use words that create a sense of rapport with the audience. Talk *to* your listeners, not

---

36. Broadus, *Preparation and Delivery of Sermons*, 204.
37. Lloyd M. Perry, *A Manual for Biblical Preaching* (Grand Rapids: Baker, 1981), 190.
38. James C. Humes, *The Sir Winston Method: The Five Secrets of Speaking the Language of Leadership*, 32.
39 Flesch, *Art of Plain Talk* (New York: William Morrow, 1991) 79.
40. Ibid., 150–52.

at them. Use the personal pronouns "we" and "you" to put persuasion in your application and appeal. Use "we" instead of "church leaders" and "you" instead of "church members." Be careful not to use "I" to note accomplishments or give instructions.[41]

IMPERATIVE LANGUAGE

The use of imperative language as a way to enhance style is often overlooked in contemporary preaching. If the preacher has good rapport with his people, however, he buys the right to speak frankly with them and challenge them to action. Seek to use words and phrases that explicitly call for action or response. Without being arrogant or authoritarian, speak with language that clearly demands that listeners either embrace a truth or act on a truth. Both intentions imply an aggressive response on the part of hearers.

Again, this employment of imperative language is consistent with the decisional nature of the preaching event. The intent of the sermon naturally is related to the call for action. Sweazey even used the term "decisions" to describe one of the primary purposes of preaching.[42] Broadus said the sermon objective was concerned with actions, changes, and verdict by answering the question, "What life changes should result from the sermon?"[43] The aim, then, is what we desire the truth of the sermon to do to the hearer, or what we desire the hearer to do in response to the truth. True preaching intrinsically purposes to lead people to make some kind of change. This change manifests itself as the listeners act in some new way or embrace some new concept. The preacher will use language, then, that calls upon listeners to dedicate all their time, talent, and personality to God.[44]

Jesus and the apostles frequently used imperative language. This employment caused listeners to recognize Jesus' teaching as authoritative, distinguishing it from the teaching of the scribes.[45] Achtemeier charged:

> Let us never mistake doubt in the pulpit for humility. Sometimes preachers are so worried about taking notice of every point of view and so fearful of imposing their own thoughts on their people, that they preach a gospel framed in the terms of "it may be." . . . We know whom we have believed, and there is no doubt about his victory. Only if our style conveys that certainty can our people have any hope at all.[46]

41. Humes, *The Sir Winston Method*, 57–58.
42. Sweazey, *Preaching the Good News*, 22.
43. Broadus, *Preparation and Delivery of Sermons*, 49.
44. Brown, Clinard, and Northcutt, *Steps to the Sermon*, 17.
45. Davis, *Design for Preaching*, 1958), 210.
46. Achtemeier, *Creative Preaching*, 95.

Be aware that imperative language can have a negative impact in some situations. Lewis said the imperative sermon is often unwelcome, authoritarian, and futile.[47] Davis advocated that imperative language be disguised, saying that the bald form was "so unwelcome as to be ineffective."[48] Careful and discerning use, however, will enable you to challenge people firmly and lovingly.

EMPHATIC LANGUAGE

Stylistic expression also can be enhanced through the use of emphatic language. Emphasis can be gained in several ways.

Place the emphasis where it should be. Be judicious in your choice and placement of words. Not all thoughts are of equal importance. The preacher must stress the truly important things. The big things in his sermon should be really big. The things that ought to be emphasized should be emphasized. One way to emphasize words is by their placement in the sentence. Normally, putting a word at the beginning or the end of a sentence emphasizes it.

Avoid throwaway words. Placing emphasis on some words reduces the emphasis of what is being said. Such words are seen frequently in the Scriptures. For instance, in Luke 2:10 we read: "Fear not: for, behold, I bring you good tidings of great joy, which shall be to all people" (KJV). To place the emphasis upon "behold" is to give wrong emphasis to the sentence. It actually takes away from what the sentence is intending to convey. Other "throwaway" words are "and," "for," and "saying." To emphasize these words is to throw off balance the intended meaning of what you say. Use strong nouns and verbs. Avoid overworked words and hackneyed expressions. Avoid using superlatives indiscreetly and qualifiers unnecessarily.

Restate key ideas. The preacher can emphasize a particular thought by the amount of time he devotes to it. Restatement is a positive way to increase the clarity of your message and underscore what you are trying to say. Again, words stated on the pages of a book are capable of being revisited by the reader. In spoken style, the preacher must ensure that his listeners have clearly heard what he wants to say.

One way to restate an idea is simple *repetition,* or saying the same thing again and again. Often a repeated phrase packs a significant punch. Martin Luther King delivered a message that has become world famous, built around the repetition of the phrase "I have a dream." Repetition of a particular phrase periodically throughout the sermon can help the mes-

---

47. Lewis, *Persuasive Preaching,* 211.
48. Davis, *Design for Preaching,* 210.

sage build to a tremendous climax.

Another way to employ restatement is *rewording,* or repeating a thought or phrase with an air of freshness. Be constantly on the lookout for new ways to say what you want to say. A catchy literary device may help you give what you are going to say a new, interesting twist. While preaching on the Bible word "glory," for example, you might discover the Bible teaches that the glory of God is behind, above, before, and within the believer. In trying to convey this comment in a fresh way, you might consider using the familiar tune "Old McDonald Had a Farm." You might say, "For the believer there is glory everywhere. There is glory here, glory there; here a glory, there a glory, everywhere a glory, glory." You would be saying what you wanted to say in a fresh, new way.

Be careful not to overuse restatement, however. Too much restatement becomes tiresome and actually lessens the emphasis intended.

EPIGRAMS AND WITTICISMS

An epigram is a bright or witty thought tersely or ingeniously expressed. A well-known definition of an epigram is:

> The qualities rare in a bee that we meet,
> In an epigram never should fail;
> The body should always be little and sweet,
> And the sting should be felt in its tail.

Similarly, a witticism is a witty saying, sentence, or phrase. Epigrams and witticisms are some of the oldest and most effective forms of expression. Even as early as 200 B.C. the Greeks were using epigrams that had brevity and unity of thought. Such noted writers as Sir Thomas More, Ben Johnson, George Bernard Shaw, and Oscar Wilde used them. Epigrams can be used very effectively to point out failures, to prod people to action, to puncture pride, and to cause laughter. Both epigrams and witticisms may be sarcastic, satirical, or humorous. They may express criticism or praise.

These tools can help communicate truth in a brief, pointed, catchy manner. They can enliven the message and sharpen its applications. They provide color. Familiar truths may be stated in different ways. They can capture your meaning in a brief statement. For instance, "A faith that can't be tested, can't be trusted" says a great deal about faith in one brief sentence.

Epigrams and witticisms also can help your listeners better remember what you are trying to say. They give your hearers something to turn over in their minds. The truth is more understandable to them. Instead of saying, "Possessions can wreck a life," try saying, "It isn't wrong to have possessions; it is wrong for them to have you."

By means of these devices you can even destroy an unsound argument, using only a few words gently clothed in tasteful humor. To be sure, epigrams and witticisms should not be just cute or funny. They should be used only when they are pertinent to what you are saying.

Some speakers are especially gifted in wording epigrams and witticisms, yet just about anyone can use them effectively. Listen for them in the sermons of other preachers. Look for them in your regular reading. They can be found in many sources.[49] As you run across epigrams and witticisms, file them in a notebook. Try memorizing a few each week.

Humor

Another effective way of enhancing your message is the use of humor. Some people consider the use of humor in the pulpit to be making a joke of sacred things. Though we definitely do not want to joke about or speak lightly of sacred things, humor can have a legitimate place in the preaching event.

Scripture places its approval upon appropriate expressions of humor. Proverbs 17:22 says, "A merry heart does good, like medicine." Proverbs 15:15 says, "He who is of a merry heart has a continual feast." Certainly, we must not strip ourselves of this God-given faculty. If we leave laughter and humor to the comedians and amusement places of the world, we are in a sad state. This is not an appeal for an overly lighthearted or frivolous approach to preaching. Rightly used, however, humor can be another tool in preparing effective messages.

Humor may serve several purposes in a sermon. First, the ultimate purpose of sermon humor is not to get laughs but to drive home a point in an entertaining way. Humes said, "What entertains endures—longer."[50] The best television commercials employ humor, not simply to get laughs but to sell products. Second, humor can be used to break the tension of the moment. People cannot maintain attention for a long period of time. Neither can they endure highly emotional material indefinitely. Humor can provide needed relaxation that buys the right to be intense at other points. Third, humor can tear down barriers that people may have erected between themselves and the preacher. Although you normally should avoid beginning your message with detached humor, your listeners are

---

49. See Herbert V. Prochnow, *Speaker's Handbook of Epigrams and Witticisms* (Grand Rapids: Baker, 1955), and E. C. McKenzie, *Mac's Great Book of Quips and Quotes* (Grand Rapids: Baker, 1980). Also, Vance Havner's sermons are filled with epigrams and witticisms.

50. Ibid., 135.

more likely to be receptive if you can get them to laugh.

THE C-R-E-A-M OF THE CROP
Making Words Memorable

James Humes, in *The Sir Winston Method: The Secrets of Speaking the Language of Leadership,* identified five ways notable leaders such as Winston Churchill, Franklin Roosevelt, John Kennedy, and Martin Luther King made their words memorable.[51] The preacher would do well to employ these tools in stylistic expression:

Contrast—Kennedy said, "If a free society cannot help the many who are poor, it cannot save the few who are rich." Churchill said, "If we open a quarrel between the past and the present, we shall find we have lost the future." The Beatitudes and the Proverbs ring with such paradox and contrast. *Poor Richard's Almanack* is filled with adages using antonyms such as rich/poor, spender/saver, old/young, dark/light, mountain/valley, present/future, and winter/summer.

Rhyme—Lincoln said, "Let us have faith that *right* makes *might* . . ." Nixon said, "Let us move from the era of *confrontation* into the era of *negotiation.*" Moms in the nursery and songwriters have the patent on rhyming. They use rhymes because they forever ring in the ear.

Echo—Franklin Roosevelt said, "The only thing we have to *fear* is *fear* itself." Jimmy Carter said, "America did not invent human rights, but in a sense, *human rights* invented America." Kennedy said, "Ask not *what your country can do for you*; ask *what you can do for your country.*" This technique requires repeating a word or phrase.

Alliteration—Franklin Roosevelt said, "The truth is *found* when men are *free* to pursue it." Martin Luther King spoke of a day when people "will not be judged by the color of their skin, but by the *content of their character.*" Although alliteration can and has been abused by preachers and politicians, it does ring a bell in the memory.

Metaphor—Churchill said of the Soviets, "From Stettin in the Baltic to Trieste in the Adriatic an iron curtain has descended across the Continent." Roosevelt said of Nazi Germany, "When you see a rattlesnake poised to strike, you do not wait until he has struck before you crush him."

51. Humes, *The Sir Winston Method,* 88–92.

Josh McDowell identified several kinds of humor that can be employed in effective communication: exaggeration, deliberate understatement, sudden change of thought, surprise thoughts, afterthoughts, the twisting of ideas, misinterpretation of the facts, intentional errors, restatement of a well-known quotation with a humorous twist, pantomime, poorly timed gestures, facial grimaces, anecdotes, impersonation of a character, and clever wording.[52] Five cardinal rules should be followed when employing such devices in a sermon:

YOU MUST BE JOKING!

Avoid opening jokes. Jokes before your sermon almost always will rob you of a stunning introduction. Laughter reaped by such beginnings usually is perfunctory.[53] Breaking down barriers and establishing rapport between speaker and audience usually can be accomplished with a confident, powerful introduction as opposed to ice-breaking humor.

Turn jokes into anecdotes. Jokes in sermons usually are tacky and awkward. Wit and humor, on the other hand, can be helpful when used rightly. Jokes are fiction, while anecdotes are possibly true at the very least. Weave jokes into anecdotes in the body of the sermon when they are not expected. That way, if they do not reap laughter, they still serve their supporting purpose.[54]

Use good timing. Learn to time the punch line. Avoid running past the punch line and causing the people to miss the humor altogether. Watch the response of your audience and adapt to it. Sometimes, your remark after their response can be funnier than what you said at first. Also, do not announce your efforts at humor. Let them come naturally. To signal the impression you are striving at humor will usually ensure that you are not humorous.

Make humor realistic, relevant, and retellable. Humor should add to your sermon, not detract. Make sure your humor is believable, appropriate to the subject at hand, and tasteful. Do not tell something funny just for the sake of telling it. Make the humor point toward what you are trying to communicate, and never be crude.[55] If you are going to take advantage of anyone in your humor, be sure it is yourself.

52. McDowell, 18.
53. Humes, *The Sir Winston Method,* 136.
54. Ibid., 137, 140.
55. Ibid., 146.

Stay within your level of ability. Humor must be natural. If you are to use it effectively, let your humor be spontaneous. If you cannot employ humor naturally, do not try to use it. Most of us do have a humorous side to our personality that should be developed. Even if you cannot locate the witty person within you, though, a sense of humor can be cultivated. Do not fail to see the humor in your own life. To be able to laugh at yourself is a sign of maturity. Very often, the humorous things that happen to you can be used effectively in your sermons.

Many of God's great preachers have used humor effectively. Warren Wiersbe, who is quite a humorist himself, wrote about Dwight L. Moody and Gypsy Smith:

> These men were not comedians; they were ambassadors—but joyful ambassadors. And because of their sanctified humor they were able to touch men for Christ. Not every preacher can do this, but those who can use humor should not bury their talent.[56]

We certainly must not dehumanize ourselves or our listeners when we come to the house of God. Laughter is a part of life. Humor is natural to man. God has given us the ability to laugh. Seize that privilege in your preaching when appropriate.

ENSURING PERSUASIVE STYLE

As you work on expressing your thoughts, remember that your ultimate goal is persuasion. Persuasion involves all ethical methods the preacher may use to induce people to make the right decisions and do the right things. This end often is overlooked in discussions about preaching. A review of the definition of preaching in chapter 1 reminds us that the motive of our preaching must be to *enable a positive response*. Preaching aims to persuade the hearers to act upon the truth that was shared. Persuasion actually is the overlapping point of all the functional elements as well as the actual delivery of the message. At this point in the expositional process, revisit your sermon and yourself to make sure your message will be as persuasive as possible.

UNDERSTANDING THE ROLE OF PERSUASION

Many of the older textbooks on preaching, such as Broadus's classic

---

56. Warren Wiersbe, *Walking with the Giants* (Grand Rapids: Baker, 1976), 220.

work, have a great deal to say about persuasion as a part of sermon preparation and delivery. In more recent years, however, most homiletical writers have devoted little attention to persuasion. Perhaps one reason persuasion is more likely to be ignored today is that people are persuaded on the basis of different considerations. Lengthy and technical arguments do not seem to move people to action at the turn of the twenty-first century as much as they did in previous generations. They now are swayed more by feeling.

However, though some methods may need to be adjusted, the techniques of persuasion definitely still have a vital place in effective pulpit communication. The wise preacher will learn to use many of these techniques and avoid resting his case with a single appeal. The preacher is wasting his time when he attempts to persuade people merely on the basis of obligation or duty. Scolding or fervent entreaty will benefit little. If the preacher uses a combination of persuasive techniques, however, he may be able to help those who listen to him see and feel for themselves something that is most desirable and worthwhile for their lives. The minister will have accomplished his desired intention when his listeners join him in saying, "I am persuaded."

AVOIDING MANIPULATION

Some question the validity of any use of the techniques of persuasion in preaching. They question the moral and ethical basis for the use of any persuasive technique. This contention, however, may be a reaction to the preachers who have become more like manipulators than persuaders. These preachers have taken the attitude "I don't care what method I use, just so it brings people to Christ. If it works, then fine. The end justifies the means." The fallacy of this kind of reasoning is that it equates being effective with being ethical. To take the position that any method of influence is good if it has positive results is questionable at best. Such manipulation certainly should raise concern among the righteous.

Although certain aspects of these devices play a part in the role of Christian persuasion, the preacher must remember that he is not merely involved in influencing behavior. His goal is to influence character and change destinies. The techniques of persuasion he employs must be in keeping with larger, more complex, and nobler purposes.

The gospel preacher may be tempted to say, "I won't try to persuade at all." But this position is untenable for the sincere Christian preacher. You are commanded by the Lord Jesus Christ Himself to win men. For this reason, you cannot refuse the responsibility to persuade others. But neither can you look upon a person as just another scalp on your belt or notch on your gun. This form of manipulation merely uses people as part of a numbers game. The preacher must never seek to persuade others in order to make himself appear to be successful.

ADVERTISING APPEAL

The four basic methods of persuasion used in the field of advertising are well known. In terms of modern advertising techniques these four devices are like the four sides of a square within which all persuasion is contained.[57]

Virtue. This device associates the product in question with everything a person may regard as good and desirable. We are urged to buy a certain brand of soap because it will make us smell good. We cannot be without the latest toothpaste because it will give us sex appeal. Such a device calls attention to the person's interest in some desirable, achievable goal.

Poison. This device associates failure to use the "desirable" product with everything people consider to be objectionable and harmful. If you do not use a certain shampoo, you will have dandruff. In turn, that dandruff will make you unappealing to members of the opposite sex. Therefore, you must purchase the new shampoo.

Testimonial. This device seeks to induce us to accept or reject a product on the basis of persons with reputation and personal appeal. Certain brands of cereal are to be eaten because sports heroes eat them. If you really want to be a hero, you will eat this particular brand.

Multiple approach. The fourth device combines the other three to operate by means of group pressure.

The preacher also may be tempted merely to "show them only the silver lining." Shading the truth and failing to present the total picture often is seen in the testimonies of the successful, famous, or beautiful people who have become Christians. The impression is given that to come to Christ will make a person one or all of these things. Such a method of persuasion is untrue to the gospel. Very often becoming a Christian means losing wealth, fame, and other perks of this world. Methods of manipulation that promise worldly success are unworthy of the sincere preacher who desires to bring men into the Christian life.

57. Winston E. Jones, *Preaching and the Dramatic Arts* (New York: Macmillan, 1948), 39.

As we learn the techniques of persuasion, we must embrace the words of Paul: "But we have renounced the hidden things of shame, not walking in craftiness nor handling the word of God deceitfully, but by manifestation of the truth commending ourselves to every man's conscience in the sight of God" (2 Cor. 4:2).

USING LEGITIMATE TECHNIQUES OF PERSUASION

Several legitimate means of persuasive application are available to the expository preacher:

The Word of God. The Bible is authoritative by nature and, therefore, persuasive and powerful. Billy Graham, the man who has preached to more people than any other in the history of Christianity, is characterized by his constant use of the phrase "the Bible says." Much of Graham's effectiveness is due to the persuasive way he uses the Word of God to support the substance of his messages. Such an employment of Scripture combines application with the elements of explanation and even argumentation to persuade listeners to act on the message. As you review your own sermon for delivery, make sure you place heavy emphasis on biblical authority.

Personal character. Aristotle called the element of character *ethos*. It answers the audience's question, "Why should I believe *you?*" As the pastor delivers his message, his own modesty, sincerity, intensity, and yieldedness to the authority of Scripture will add substantially to the credibility of the message. Though these qualities do not add to the *content* of the message, the very sincerity of the preacher is a factor in amplifying the sermon's main assertions.

Pause to evaluate whether or not you are ready to preach with a sincere heart. The testimony of the preacher—if he is credible—will provide strong personal appeal. The endorsement of a "satisfied customer" is powerful. Be careful, however, not to turn every sermon into a personal testimony. You may choose to augment your own testimony with the testimony of others. Personal accounts of answers to prayer, salvation experiences, and God's work in the lives of individuals can be used most effectively in sermons. A good store of information about Christian personalities throughout history and on the current scene can be used to persuade others.

Logical reasoning. Aristotle called the element of logical reasoning *logos*. It answers the audience's question, "What do you mean?" As you utilize certain approaches to explanation and argumentation, you will be helping your listeners understand the Scripture by appealing to their logic. A variety of logical appeals to reason already have been discussed in other aspects of the sermon preparation process. For example, facts and statistics may be helpful in influencing people to make a desired commitment. Anticipating and answering objections that might arise in the minds of your listeners is very persuasive. Also, a well-organized sermon will be more persuasive than one that is unorganized. The human mind thinks logically. If you are able to present your message in a clear, logical manner, it will have much more persuasiveness about it. Give your sermon one final look regarding these areas.

Emotional appeal. Aristotle called emotional appeal *pathos.* It answers the audience's question, "Is it significant?" Be sure that there is ample emotional content in your sermon to reach out and grab the heart. Whitesell said that people are not moved so much by lengthy or involved arguments as they are by illustrations, humor, and emotion. He maintained that people are more likely to be moved by emotions than reason.[58] Certain emotional appeals have great strength, such as the ones listed on the following page.

Fresh imagination. The Christian persuader may cease to be himself for a few moments and adopt the view of the character he is portraying. This technique enables the persuader to create in the minds of his listeners certain desirable or undesirable pictures. By inducing our listeners to imaginatively share with us a new position or pattern of thought, we stand a better chance of influencing them in that direction.[59] We already have discussed some of the uses of imagination in effective preaching. The imagination is a powerful persuader, and by role play we can activate the imaginations of our listeners. If we can get them to live out in their own imaginations the truths we are seeking to convey, we will be better able to change their attitudes and behavior. Check to see if there are places in your message where you might strategically use role play or some other imaginative technique to persuade the audience.

WINNING A HEARING

The Constitution guarantees you freedom of speech, but it does not guarantee you a listening audience. The right to be heard must be earned. Here are a few suggestions to help you win a hearing for what you say.

Know your stuff. Be sure you know what you are talking about. This necessity points us back to the importance of adequate sermon preparation. If you are poorly prepared, you will not have to tell your listeners. Lack of preparation is painfully and even disgustingly apparent. The peo-

58. Farris. D. Whitesell, *65 Ways to Give Evangelistic Invitations* (Grand Rapids: Kregel, 1984), 63.
59. Emory A. Griffin, *The Mind Changers* (Wheaton, Ill.: Tyndale, 1976), 82.

ple who listen have given you precious moments of their time. They have a right to know that you have prepared to the point that you are up on the subject you are addressing.

EMOTIONAL ENGAGEMENT

The Christian life. The Christian life should be presented in such a positive way that the listeners will want to become Christians. Heaven should be made so appealing that any thinking person would want to go there. Learn to make the destiny of the redeemed human soul so vivid and compelling that people will desire it. The psalmist put it quite well when he admonished: "Oh, taste and see that the Lord is good" (Ps. 34:8). To create this type of response in an individual has within it the power to change character and create desire for a nobler life.

Fear. The appeal to fear is not unworthy in and of itself. In our day many people have minimized and even scoffed at the appeals to fear made by some preachers. Certainly, no unreasonable or excessive use of fear should be used. Scare tactics as manipulative tools are unwarranted. Yet fear is an emotion of the human heart. The Bible presents in the plainest terms the dire consequences of the life that rejects Jesus Christ. Either we accept the Bible truth about these matters or we do not. If we do, then in faithfulness to the truth and love for those to whom we preach, we must give adequate warning. The doctor who seeks to cause his patient to abstain from smoking does not hesitate to use an appeal to fear. The Bible still says: "It is a fearful thing to fall into the hands of the living God" (Heb. 10:31).

Love. The preacher may also use an appeal to love. In one sense, all persuasion is an appeal to love—love of self, love of others, or love of God. We appeal to the Christians in our congregation on the basis of their love for Christ and desire to serve and please Him. We also appeal to all men that a response of love to Him is based upon His love for us. John wrote, "We love Him because He first loved us" (1 John 4:19). Paul said, "For the love of Christ compels us" (2 Cor. 5:14).

Love your audience. If the preacher has feelings of hostility toward his people, the listeners will pick up on it immediately. As you preach, you must communicate to your people—more by manner and attitude than by words—that you really love them and care for them. Get to know your people. Spend as much time with them as you possibly can. The more you are around them, the better chance they will respond favorably to you.

Be open. Let the people know you are a real person. Admit your failures. People are more responsive to a person who conveys human warmth and reality.

INCORPORATING DRAMATIC STYLE

From the viewpoint of the dynamics of speaking, sermon delivery may be viewed as a science. From the perspective of effective communication with a listening congregation, the preacher must be an artist. He must be an artist in his use of words, in his ability to use the principles of persuasion, and in his employment of dramatic technique. He must utilize all three elements if he is to convey the truths of the Bible effectively. Robinson asserted, "While a preacher is more than an actor, he should not be less."[60]

REFORMING THE PREACHING EVENT

Probably no generation has experienced such a vociferous attack upon preaching as has the present generation. For many years during the middle of the twentieth century, no end seemed in sight regarding objection to the traditional Sunday morning sermon. Many people thought preaching had outlived its usefulness, was not relevant to the present day, and only served to bore the people upon whom it was imposed. Obviously much of this criticism stemmed from a bias against the very nature of the Christian evangel itself. If people desired to eliminate the message of the gospel, no better way existed than to silence its voice in the pulpit.

Now, at the turn of the new century, the attack on preaching from outside Christian circles has somewhat subsided. From within our own ranks, however, the reaction against traditional preaching has adopted a new and subtle form. Many ministers are taking great pains to make preaching more relational and less confrontational. The prophetic aura of preaching frequently is replaced by the therapeutic atmosphere of a counselor's office. New approaches of delivery often are employed to make preaching more entertaining and less monotonous.

In all fairness, we must admit that some criticism against preaching as well as numerous efforts to redefine it have been due to the lack of interesting and stimulating pulpit delivery. The painful reality is that conservative, evangelical preachers have done much to invite the negative reaction of critics because of drab content and poor pulpit performance. All of us who have been brought up in the church know what it is to endure a dead, dry, long sermon.

---

60. Robinson, *Biblical Preaching*, 207.

The preacher can do much to relieve the problem of congregational boredom by understanding the role of dramatic technique in sermon delivery. Although the preacher does not deal in unreal subject matter or merely act out something that is not a genuine part of his own life, he must employ dramatic technique if he is to preach the meaning of his message in the most effective manner possible. Effective preaching must utilize the techniques of drama if it is to be all God intends it to be. The preacher's message may be well prepared. The points may proceed with the clearest possible logic. Sound principles may abound. All of these qualities are of little effect, however, if human life is not touched. No message will exert lasting influence unless it comes to bear upon the *emotional* lives of the people who listen to it.

Do not ever forget that listening to a sermon preached from the Bible is an emotional experience. The old adage "A person changed against his will is of the same opinion still" is true. Logic and argument are only temporarily effective. Permanent change in the hearts of men can be accomplished only as the emotions are moved. What a person feels about what is said is much more determinative than some people may realize. Consequently, whether or not a sermon is accepted or rejected is largely due to the emotions that are produced in regard to it.

As the preacher, you are the controlling factor in the preaching situation. The architecture of the building, the makeup of the congregation, the nature of the song service, the general atmosphere of the speaking situation are all factors in the preaching event. The key element, however, is the preacher himself. You must not only convince the intellect, but you must stir the emotions. This task can be done most effectively when you understand the techniques of drama.

Understanding the Dramatic Arts

The dramatic arts include those areas of human expression that are vivid, moving, and impelling. The preacher may learn from them how to convey his sermon more effectively. The dramatic arts re-create experiences in the minds of the people who view them. For this reason, all dramatic art gives a primary place to feeling. The artist releases a variety of feelings in those who behold his work of art. The same holds true for the preacher. By use of words he fulfills the function of an artist. Whereas the artist creates feelings with paint on a canvas, the preacher does the same by his use of words. He stirs the imagination of his hearers. He makes visible for his congregation that which is invisible. He enables his listeners to receive information through vicarious experience.

The writer who effectively uses words enables his reader to go places he has never been before. By means of his writing skill he enables the reader to sense how others must have felt even though they may have lived many miles away and long centuries before. The preacher does the same thing with oral words. As he stirs the imagination of his listeners, he brings home to them the meaning of events and experiences beyond the orbit of their lives. He transmits information and insight from himself to his listeners by inducing imagined experience.

By means of dramatic technique, the preacher gives his hearers an opportunity to react to life's situations in terms of their own emotions. He pictures vice in such a way as to make it ugly to those who practice it. He paints virtue so beautifully as to make it desirable even to those who do not possess it.

Much modern preaching misses the mark due to the lack of the dramatic element. Life itself is drama. People are involved in dramatic situations daily. People are loving and hating. They are struggling and surviving. They are living and dying. Life is not dull and drab. For this reason, to preach truthfully is to preach dramatically.[61] We who preach God's living Word to living people must do so in terms of real-life experience. We preach a book filled with the experiences of people who actually lived, spoke, struggled, and faced eternity. No reason exists for the preacher not to be able to preach such a book in a vivid, exciting manner. Painters do it for their viewers. They see the world around them. Then, through the medium of their own souls, they pour out on canvas for all the world to see. The preacher must do the same when he preaches.

Study the life and ministry of Jesus. In the grandest sense of the word, He was a verbal artist. He enabled men to see truths and values they had long forgotten. As He moved among men, He stopped to observe playing children. From that point on, His disciples saw children as they had never seen them before. He stopped to talk with an outcast woman. Thereafter His disciples saw the hidden potential in the lowest of people. He stopped at the temple treasury to view a poor widow drop her two mites into the receptacle. From that day on, the giving of the least to the Lord was sanctified and magnified in the minds of His disciples. He spoke of the lilies of the field and forever painted them with indelible strokes upon the minds of His followers. You can and must do the same in the delivery of your sermon.

INCORPORATING DRAMATIC TECHNIQUE

By means of dramatic technique the preacher helps his people see what

61. Jones, *Preaching and the Dramatic Arts*, 24.

they never saw before. As you work on the expression of your message, make sure you include elements that accomplish the following directives.

Capture attention. You must be able to capture the attention of your listeners. If you fail to gain attention at the beginning, the difficulty of gaining attention at other points along the way greatly increases. Every preacher should study the way a playwright designs his play. The playwright has an express purpose, an intended effect. The audience before whom the play will be performed always looms large in the design and fashion of the play. Make sure your sermon is arranged and built in the same manner. The people must be kept in mind throughout the entire preparation process.

Use variety. A good play incorporates change, suspense, and surprise. The script is written to build to a definite climax. Throughout the play there will be alternating moods and differing rhythms of interest.[62] Check to see if your sermon can be delivered with the same kind of arrangement in mind—including a great deal of variety. Preaching is often an intense matter. For this reason there must be variety and alteration in mood in the sermon. Neither the preacher nor his hearers can keep up a high level of excitement for an extended period of time.

Begin strikingly. A sermon may be compared to a one-act play. Within a single span of time the play must present itself, move through its various ingredients, and come to conclusion. Though a sermon generally conforms to this pattern, the preacher generally does not have the privilege of intermissions between his divisions. Therefore, he must prepare his introduction with the definite purpose of securing and maintaining attention. Double-check your sermon beginning and see if you begin in a striking manner.

Build to a climax. Drama is characterized by the development of climax. The logical, orderly development of your sermon theme should create the same effect. This theme should be developed throughout your message with a gradual heightening of interest. For that to be achieved, movement constantly must be occurring. Do not dwell upon any single point longer than is actually necessary. Sometimes you will discover you have lost your audience. Heads begin to move. Whispering and shifting around begin to occur. When these things start to happen, you may notice that you are saying over and over again what you already have made clear.[63]

Good drama has a distinct crescendo. Correctly done, a sermon too will reach a climax in interest and intensity. In order to achieve such

---

62. Ibid., 53.
63. H. A. Overstreet, *Influencing Human Behavior* (New York: Norton, 1925), 82.

crescendo, be sure to include conflict and suspense. The element of surprise must be part of your sermon. Adams said, "Cultivate in your sermons what is called 'the surprise power.' Don't say what people expect you to say. Let your thunderbolt drop out of a clear sky."[64]

Let there be a clash of forces throughout the message. In a good play there will be conflict between personalities. The outcome should remain in doubt until the conflict is resolved. The preacher can do the same in terms of the crucial issues of life and the answers people give to these issues. Depict persons who have lived on both sides of the issues raised. You can accomplish this scenario easily in a biographical sermon. The same technique may be used by introducing biblical or modern personalities into the various themes of your message.

A good play reaches its climax, then closes quickly. The same should be true of a sermon. All of us have experienced preaching past the best stopping point. When that happens, a definite letdown always occurs on the part of the people. When you reach your climax, bring your sermon to a graceful but quick close. Failure to do so will lessen the force and total impression of the message. You actually may undo what you have achieved earlier in your sermon. Wrap up the essence of what you are saying in a few brief, summary sentences. Leave the message with your hearers and call them to act upon it.

MAKING THE BIBLE WALK

Using dramatic techniques can help the Bible come alive as you preach. The Bible is not a dead book, although some preachers make it appear that way. You can make Bible characters come alive through imaginative dialogue. Allow the Bible characters to speak. If you are preaching on the three Hebrews in the fiery furnace, do not just recount the facts of the Bible narrative. Put the three young men in the flames. Put words in their mouths. Let them speak in the language of today.

The effect of your sermon can be enhanced greatly through an understanding of how to use story material. Stories must be so told as to induce a feeling of reality in those who listen. To induce this feeling, the artist uses illusion. He does not paint every tiny detail of a tree or flower. Rather, he leaves enough detail missing so that the viewer can fill in the details for himself. Do the same as you use story material. We grow impatient with the person who gives us too many details. We want to use some imagination ourselves.

64. Adams, *Pulpit Speech*, 36.

Preachers must learn the art of selection in storytelling. Certain items must be included, but others must be excluded if we are to be effective in telling stories. When drawing a picture of a character, use only enough description to activate the listeners' imagination. Eliminate all details that are not essential. Describe the personalities in your story in such a manner that your hearers can see them. Use dialogue freely, a technique that makes elaborate explanation unnecessary.

Make use of slanting when telling a story for illustrative purposes. You perhaps are familiar with the use of slanting in news reporting. Such slanting is not considered justifiable when the purpose of the report is to be objective, although it is considered perfectly acceptable in an editorial. A sermon is more like an editorial than a report of a fire or a robbery. We are not pretending to be objective. To the contrary, we are preaching for a verdict, and it is even necessary that we use slanted language in our descriptions of the characters in our illustrations so that they will come alive for our readers.

The preacher is chiefly responsible for his congregation's interest or lack thereof. As you learn to use dramatic techniques in your preaching, you will observe a greater interest on the part of your people.

We have a message that is eminently worthy of being heard and received. We must so present that message that it will be interesting and appealing to those who hear us. Some would say our job is not to make the gospel appealing but to make it available. But we are not faced with such an alternative. Rather, we are called to greater effectiveness in delivery so that we can make the gospel appealing as we make it available. Work hard to make the Bible come alive in your stylistic expression. You will discover that your listeners will become much more interested in your sermons.

EVALUATING YOUR STYLE

With this discussion in mind, take some time to look back over the sermon you have composed. Do not be too hard on yourself by supposing that you immediately will begin to fashion sermons that are gems of effective style. Some preachers are unusually gifted in composing sermons, but all of us can improve. As you read and evaluate, pay attention to your way of speaking. Are your sentences too long and involved? Are your words specific and clear? Is there a simplicity and vividness about what you say? Are there some tools you could use at particular points that would enhance your style? An epigram or witticism? Maybe some humor? As you read your sermon or at least go over it in your mind, think about what you are wanting to say, giving careful attention to the qualities of good style.

Obviously, the preacher cannot begin at once to be a master in his use of words. Several avenues are available, however, to help you begin.

STYLISTIC STUDY HABITS

Be a wordsmith. Constantly be enriching your vocabulary. Study the dictionary and thesaurus. The plots will be boring, but you will increase your word power! Listen to effective speakers, both preachers and otherwise, and note the words they use. Increase your own store of picture-building words.

Study local connotations. Take time to learn the local connotations of words in every context in which you preach. Those connotations will affect how the people receive what you say. If the words you use are understood by the listeners in the way you understand them, you will be able to communicate effectively.

Learn from other speakers and writers. On an ongoing basis, spend time studying the style of others. Read the works of good writers and observe their use of words. The works of Charles Dickens and other master authors are especially helpful in learning to use words effectively. Listen to effective preachers. Notice how they use language. Give attention to the kinds of words they use.

Listen to yourself. Listen to your own taped sermons. Check your sentence structure. Listen to the words you use. Always be working to improve the way you say things.

The preacher who would be more effective in sermon style must spend time working on his writing and his speaking.

CHAPTER TEN

PLAYING
THE VOICE

*The voice, strained and fatigued, instinctively sought relief in
a rhythmical rise and fall. . . . They were commonly zealous
and sometimes great men who fell into this fault, and it was
often imitated by those who followed them . . . mistaking the
obvious fault for the hidden power.*

JOHN A. BROADUS

God has prepared a marvelous instrument with which you may convey
His Word to men: the voice. The voice is the quality or tone of sound you
produce. Some people have referred to the voice as the queen of the instruments. This royal instrument has the clarity of the trumpet, the bril-
liance of the violin, and the melody of the oboe. The voice is unsurpassed
in its ability to express with depth and meaning the intended message of
its user. This brilliant instrument is the common property of every person. The words people use every day are colored with the voice's emotional undertones, its energy, and its powers of persuasion. The expression we
discussed in the last chapter ultimately will be given wings to fly by
means of the voice.

Using the vocal instrument to its maximum capabilities in the preaching event involves learning to play it well. Playing your voice begins with
understanding how it works. Then you must master certain skills that enable you to use the voice to its greatest potential. Finally, you constantly
must be working toward voice improvement and voice care. Though the
nature of this chapter should inform your day-to-day activity, here is a
good place to consider the subject in the exposition process.[1]

---

1. For additional help with voice production and care, see Christopher Beatty, *Maximum
   Vocal Performance* (Nashville: Star Song, 1992); Christopher Beatty, *Vocal Workout*
   (Nashville: Star Song, 1992); Morton Cooper, *Winning with Your Voice* (Hollywood, Fl:
   Fell, 1990).

UNDERSTANDING THE VOICE

All of us use our voices daily. Yet, the average person knows little about the vocal mechanism. Such an oversight may be acceptable for persons who are not professional speakers, but it is neglectful for one who uses the voice professionally. Professional speakers—especially preachers—should know something about the nature and function of the vocal mechanism.

MY WAKE-UP CALL
A Personal Testimony

The words hit me like a laser beam. "You will have to be completely silent for the next two weeks. You have a nodule on the anterior third of your right vocal cord. Surgery is the only way to remove it. I'm not sure when you will be back in the pulpit. Perhaps ninety days or longer."

For several years I had experienced some degree of hoarseness. I had never thought much about it. But for several weeks the hoarseness had become rather pronounced and persistent. I could not finish a sermon without getting so hoarse I could hardly speak above a whisper. In the morning in normal conversation I found myself getting hoarse, so I went to a throat specialist.

I was totally unprepared for what he said. The thought of surgery on my vocal cords frightened me. I could hear the voices of several older preachers I knew who had been through throat surgery several times. I did not want my voice to sound that way. Would the surgery be effective? How long would I be out of the pulpit?

The days ahead were emotional and traumatic. I really didn't know what to do. A member in my congregation recommended that I contact Dr. Stephen Olford, who had experienced similar difficulties. Dr. Olford gave me the name of Dr. Friedrich Brodnitz, a throat specialist in New York City. Dr. Brodnitz confirmed that I did have a vocal nodule, but he did not recommend surgery. He said surgery would remove the nodule only for a while. I needed to correct the habits that had produced the nodule. If I didn't start speaking differently, another nodule would form. He recommended that I return home and find a competent speech pathologist.

That is exactly what I did. Dr. Sam Faircloth, a speech pathologist in Mobile, Alabama, helped me determine the abuses that had created the nodule in the first place. When those abuses were corrected the nodule disappeared within a matter of weeks—without surgery! From that day until now I have had no recurrence of the problem.

What seemed the worst thing that ever happened to me actually was one of the greatest blessings to come my way. I am able to preach several times every day without strain. Unless I have a cold or some problem with allergy, I never experience hoarseness. In the course of my recovery from vocal problems, I became much interested in the subject of speech itself. Reading books on speech almost became a hobby for me.

The results of my journey and study make up the material in this chapter. I am genuinely interested in helping my preacher brethren learn to be more effective in the delivery of their sermons. My primary qualification for sharing this information is that I am a preacher. I preach many, many times each week. My life is spent either in the pulpit or preparing for the pulpit. The contents of this chapter have been hammered out in my own ministry. To be sure, I do not perfectly demonstrate what sermon delivery ought to be. I am still in the process of learning.

I did settle one issue, however, during the time I was experiencing my vocal problems. A particular question kept nagging me. If I am preaching in the power of the Holy Spirit, why, then, is the Holy Spirit abusing His own temple? Am I relying on the Spirit or on my own abilities and efforts? I discovered some good news. You can express the deepest feelings of your faith and your ministry with power and fervor without abusing your voice. Understanding certain aspects of sermon delivery will enable you to preach with all the fervor of your soul and still maintain a healthy voice.

THE NATURE OF THE VOCAL MECHANISM

The man whom God has called to preach is assigned to communicate the eternal Word of God in his own words. Those words are produced by a complex vocal mechanism. For this reason the preacher's voice may be considered his God-given tool. A great deal of the effectiveness of his message depends upon the manner in which he handles that mechanism. In addition, knowing more about the voice will assist the preacher in guarding its health.

How much do you know about your vocal mechanism? Do you know the location of the vocal cords? Are your vocal cords suspended vertically or horizontally? Few preachers really know much about the structure and function of the vocal mechanism. Most are taught the basic techniques of speech, but few understand the nature of the mechanism that produces speech. Even fewer know how to employ it effectively or how to care for it adequately.

Some people believe that too much knowledge about the vocal mechanism may upset the balance that is intuitive in the speaking process. That fear is unfounded. Certainly, we must not allow ourselves to become so occupied with the mechanics of delivery that the tool becomes a hindrance rather than a help. However, any person can use a tool more effectively if he understands how the tool is designed. The baseball pitcher can become even more effective when he learns as much as possible about his pitching arm, the baseball, and the factors that make for good delivery. The same truth applies to the preacher and a working knowledge of his voice.

A working knowledge begins with the basic aspects of the vocal mechanism. Probably you can name most of the body parts involved: nose, throat, voice box, vocal cords, windpipe, and lungs. You also have a diaphragm, sinuses, and many muscles related to the throat, voice box, and chest cavities. It is interesting that the organs used for speech are the same organs used for breathing. Some evolutionists theorize that speaking came as an incidental result of the function of breathing. Creationists do not share this view. We understand that the faculty for speech is a divinely designed function that makes possible man's communication with his fellowman. Observing the dual functions of speaking and breathing is a fascinating study.

THE FUNCTION OF THE VOCAL MECHANISM

To understand the function of the vocal mechanism, take an imaginary tour through the vocal organs. Trace the course of air through all those parts of the body that make up the channel of inhaled air: the nose, throat, voice box, windpipe, bronchi, and lungs.

Air enters your body in one of two ways. As you are sitting quietly reading this book, your mouth is probably closed and you are inhaling through your *nose*. The air comes through your nose by means of the nostrils and travels through the nasal cavity to the *throat*. Air may also come into the body through the *mouth*. When we are speaking, we bring air into our bodies through the mouth as well as the nose.

Just a few matters relating to the voice and mouth should be noted. The tongue is a part of the mouth, and it is much larger than you might suppose. Actually, most of your mouth is filled with your tongue. Do not be offended when someone says that your tongue is the biggest thing in your mouth! The air moves gently over your tongue down into the throat. In the back of your mouth cavity you also have *adenoids*. They form a cushion behind your soft palate. On each side of your tongue are *tonsils.* You may or may not still have them. If infected, the tonsils can become greatly swollen and hinder the free use of the voice.

When air leaves your nose or mouth and goes to the throat, it enters the respiratory tract. The air goes from there into the *windpipe,* then passes into the chest by means of pipelines called *bronchi.* You have two bronchi for each *lung.* The air flows through the bronchi into the lobes of the lungs. The lungs fill most of your chest. Room is left for your heart and the esophagus. The chest cavity is actually a cage formed by your breastbone, ribs, and the spinal column. When air is pushed from the lungs through the pressure of the diaphragm, the process is called *exhalation.*

Air leaves the lungs by means of exhalation and passes back through the bronchi and the windpipe until it arrives at the voice box. The proper name for the voice box is the *larynx* (pronounced *lar'ingks*). The larynx is a remarkably complex organ. The method of suspension used in its construction anticipates the use of springs in much of our modern technical design. The larynx consists of several muscles and cartilages.

Our primary interest is in the vocal cords, or *vocal folds.* They are actually folds of muscle tissue suspended horizontally in the larynx. The two vocal folds are attached in front of the voice box to the thyroid cartilage. These folds, like wings, meet at the front of the throat. They always touch each other at that point. In the rear of the voice box the folds are connected to muscles that make it possible for them to be opened and closed. Normal folds have a smooth, glistening surface. They are covered above with folds of mucous membrane called false cords or folds.

Sound is produced when the folds are brought together and air pushes through them. Contraction of the muscles in the vocal folds makes them thicker, shorter, or more tense. This tensing of the vocal folds makes speech possible. When air blows through the vocal folds, the resulting sound is called *phonation.* This sound is carried through the throat into the mouth cavity. At this point the sound is amplified by the cavities of the mouth, nose, and throat. The amplification of sound is *resonation.* The human voice is unique because its resonating cavities can be altered partly. Only the nose is a rigid, unalterable structure. The throat, mouth, tongue, and lips all can be changed by muscular action.[2] This action forms the sound that is produced into words. Thus, the process of speech—"voice or voiceless breath, modified by articulation—has occurred."[3]

2. Friedrich Brodnitz, *Keep Your Voice Healthy* (Springfield, Ill.: Thomas, 1973), 36.
3. Ibid., 45.

MASTERING THE VOICE

Playing the vocal instrument demands that the preacher master his voice. Such mastery involves certain skills necessary for proper use. Learning to relax the body and especially the vocal mechanism is crucial in the high-tension work of pastoral ministry. Proper breathing and articulation also are essential for effective speech. Integrating the various factors of good vocal production such as rate, volume, phrasing, and pause is crucial for maximum use of the voice. Mastering each of these skills will help the preacher's voice to be music to his listeners' ears.

SKILL #1: RELAXING

We live in tension-filled times. Perhaps more people are under pressure than ever before. The advent of our modern conveniences and advantages has brought with it definite liabilities. The average person works more hours than ever before. Battling traffic to and from work increases the tension level. Pressure to succeed and produce in the marketplace has greatly increased the level of stress. Our day is one of heart attacks and high blood pressure. The ulcer has almost become a status symbol.

More and more industries and businesses are recognizing the necessity of proper relaxation on the part of their employees. Overall productivity is increased when organizations assist their personnel in alleviating as much job tension as possible. All across the country much emphasis is being placed upon proper exercise, stress management, and quality leisure time.

Identifying preacher tensions. The preacher does not escape the tensions of the times. The average pastor experiences as many or even more tensions than do his people. If you are going to learn to relax, you must first learn to recognize some of the factors that contribute to your stress. Certain tensions are common to the territory of the preaching ministry.

First, *normal life stresses are a reality for the preacher.* The preacher is not exempt from the normal struggles of life as a member of a complex society. He faces the stress of making a living, the pressure of providing adequately for his family, as well as the constant push to succeed in his occupation by seeing that his church grows.

Second, *kingdom idealism is a daily struggle.* The man of God studies his New Testament and sees clearly what God expects of the church and the individual. On the other hand, the preacher sees his church as it actually is. More than anyone else he is keenly aware of its shortcomings as well as his own. The level of living he observes in his people too often is far below the biblical standard. Thus the preacher encounters the disparity between the ideal and the real, a pressure point that can create tremendous frustration and anxiety.

Third, *similar to kingdom idealism is emotional struggle.* The preaching of the gospel of Jesus Christ is the most vital part of the preacher's life. Deep within are feelings of love, gratitude, and longing for the Lord Jesus and for those who need to know Him. These emotions must be expressed as we preach.

Fourth, *the preacher can abuse his voice.* If he does not understand how to use his voice correctly, abuse can create nagging throat problems. This tension is especially a problem for persons brought up in the South, where a distinction often is made between preaching and just talking. The preacher's verse in that part of the woods is "Cry aloud and spare not." No sincere preacher from the South wants to be a dry, lifeless preacher. Many people believe that if you can speak above a whisper on Monday morning, you must have compromised on Sunday! Preaching in the South is an all-out, heartfelt, top-of-your-voice affair that can place tremendous strain on the throat.[4]

Fifth, *congregational difficulties are a frequent reality.* You may encounter problems with your voice due to a difficult pastorate. Many congregations are pleasant and congenial, but you may find yourself in the midst of a people with unusual spiritual problems. Animosity may exist among the members, or the church staff may be bickering, jealous, and carnal. Every ministry of the church may be in jeopardy. Preaching in this kind of atmosphere can bring tremendous physical tension upon the preacher. Although you may not be aware of it at first, vocal difficulties can arise that stem from the tensions of the pastorate.

Sixth, *poor logistics can put strain on your voice.* The church auditorium may be a speaker's nightmare. Many churches do not allocate enough funds for purchasing or operating good sound systems. In some buildings, getting adequate sound is not even an option with a good sound system. Designed for architectural beauty rather than speaking and hearing ease, some facilities simply are acoustically inadequate. Multiple echo chambers may be present due to things such as horseshoe balconies with massive pillars. Such poor physical facilities increase the difficulty of speaking, thereby increasing the pastor's tension.

---

4. Such cultural characteristics also bring the opposite reaction. Because some preachers are overzealous and too emotional in their delivery, men who do not want to be identified with such fervor tend to go to the other extreme. Any expression of feeling or fervor in pulpit delivery is looked down upon. Their approach is to present the sermon in an inanimate, unemotional, matter-of-fact manner. This extreme is just as detrimental in preaching the Word as the other fault—perhaps more so.

Seventh, *an uptight personality can add subtle tension.* The total personality of the preacher will affect his voice. If you are tense vocally, chances are you are tense in many other ways. Make careful evaluation of the causes of that tension. Take a good look at the circumstances of your life. Honestly face your negative attitudes and unspoken fears. Evaluate your attitude toward the pastorate where you serve. Evaluate your own inner tensions. You may need to reorganize your thinking and develop new methods of coping with your personal and pastoral difficulties. Such self-examination may be the first step in learning to speak in a relaxed manner.

Recognizing tension. A man's tension goes to his job, and undue tension makes it difficult to perform adequately. The accountant battles tension headaches. The baseball pitcher struggles with a sore arm. The pianist with taut fingers cannot play creditably. The artist with tense hands cannot paint as he desires. The preacher is no different. Tension inevitably will force him to grapple with throat problems. When you have undue tension in your life you cannot expect to speak with a clear, positive, pleasant voice.

Many other signs of undue tension may surface in the preacher's life. Excessive tension may be manifest in an uncomfortable nervousness, inadequate breathing habits, a jerky rhythm in speaking, or an unusually fast delivery.[5] The preacher who is speaking with ease and in a relaxed condition will indicate the same in the vitality and quality of his speaking voice. Without relaxation the voice cannot be well coordinated, free in its function, and vibrant in its expression.

Applying muscle tonus. Proper relaxation is the first step in developing a well-coordinated voice. The muscles in your face, tongue, jaw, chin, throat, and neck affect the muscles that control your vocal folds. Unless you accomplish muscular freedom, your speaking will be tension bound.[6] Understand, however, that we do not want total relaxation of all muscles related to speaking. Using the vocal mechanism for speech is an active function of the body. Any action of body muscles is dependent upon some degree of tension. Physiologists call this *muscle tonus.* Every biological function is dependent upon a proper balance between tension and relaxation. The vocal mechanism depends on use of the right muscles and the application of a proper degree of muscle tonus.

Friedrich Brodnitz, an authority on the proper use and care of the voice, maintained that most voice troubles result from exaggerated mus-

5. Dorothy Mulgrave, *Speech* (New York: Barnes & Noble, 1954), 162.
6. David Blair McCloskey, *Your Voice at Its Best* (Plymouth, Mass.: Memorial, 1972), 4.

cle activity. Correcting this problem requires a reduction in the hyperfunction of the muscles that relate to the vocal mechanism.[7] If the muscles of the throat and mouth are too tense, the vocal mechanism will be cramped. The result will be poor speaking quality. The voice will sound strained because it actually is strained. In addition to a poor, unpleasant sound, vocal health problems inevitably will result. The speaker will tend to place the voice in a wrong pitch and to speak louder in order to overcome the lack of sound produced by such a restricted mechanism.

The muscles of the voice box are in two general groups. Some are located inside the larynx. They directly control the vocal folds. They move the larynx and enable it to function. These muscles are called the *intrinsic muscles*. You need not concern yourself about manipulating them, for merely thinking of speaking alters them to their task. They operate without conscious thought.

The second group of muscles is called the *extrinsic muscles*. They are on the outside of the vocal mechanism, around the throat. If the extrinsic muscles are unduly tense, the intrinsic muscles cannot function properly. Our purpose is to relax this outer set of muscles enough to allow the inner muscles to function without being in a cramped position. The goal was summarized rightly by Dwight E. Stevenson and Charles F. Diehl: "Speech . . . is not complete relaxation, but tonus. Tonus is that delicate balance of tension and relaxation—neither too much nor too little—appropriate for what has to be done."[8] Individuals who speak publicly on a regular basis must be aware of visible laryngeal strain in the muscles of the throat area.

Learning to relax. You can eliminate muscle tension before you speak in several ways. The exercises found in Appendix 3 will help you to be relaxed when you preach. Take time to familiarize yourself with them and practice them often.

In addition to these exercises, be sure to dress in such a way that is conducive to relaxation. Select a shirt with a loose collar when you preach. You might call these shirts your preaching collars. Keep in mind that the throat has a tendency to enlarge during the heat of delivery. For this reason, your collar should be as loose as possible.

Read about relaxation. Continue to learn to relax. This practice will facilitate your ability to use every aspect of your vocal mechanism correctly.[9]

You also will discover that other facets of vocal mechanics contribute

7.   Brodnitz, *Keep Your Voice Healthy,* 19

8.   Dwight E. Stevenson and Charles F. Diehl, *Reaching People from the Pulpit* (Gr Rapids: Baker, 1958), 44.

9.   Several good books are available on the subject of relaxation. Edmund Jacobson's *Must Relax* (New York: McGraw-Hill, 1942) is one such volume.

to relaxation. The following discussions, for example, relate the role of good breathing and the place of proper articulation in effective vocal delivery. These two activities are important in maintaining a relaxed throat. Improper breathing and poor articulation greatly increase the tension in one's voice box.

SKILL #2: BREATHING

Breathing is done both unconsciously and consciously, making it a rather unusual bodily function. In the normal course of our daily activities we do not consciously tell our bodies to breathe. During most normal conversation we do not have to instruct our lungs to supply the necessary air. For speaking or preaching, however, breathing must be consciously controlled. The key to a smoothly functioning vocal mechanism is proper breathing.

Understanding proper breathing. When we are not speaking or consciously thinking about breathing, the body provides enough air to do everything we need to do. Whether we are running or climbing, our bodies give us the air we need. As soon as we begin to speak, though, a different kind of breathing must begin. We must see to it that we have sufficient breath to complete our sentences without gulping or losing the closing words. In addition, we must have enough air and control of that air to sustain—and maybe amplify—our voices during the sentence. This air supply must be taken in and expelled without disturbing our flow of speech. We must gradually propel our breath in a relaxed manner, completing each statement in the most effective way possible.

Correct breathing is closely related to speaking with relaxation. Breathing correctly greatly relieves muscle tension in the throat. If a speaker does not have an ample supply of air, he will find himself squeezing for air at the throat. This effort can do great damage to his voice.

Many writers minimize the importance of breathing. For example, Jay Adams said, "Breathing is not a problem at all for most speakers. Shoulder raising habits and exercises in so-called diaphragmatic breathing are useless in improving one's breathing for speech. In the first place, all breathing is diaphragmatic."[10] This approach is somewhat simplistic, however. The large number of preachers who encounter voice difficulties causes one to question Adams's conclusion. Failure to breathe properly creates several problems for the speaker. A sufficient supply of air is essential if the necessary volume is to be achieved. Proper breathing also will permit

---

10. Jay Adams, *Pulpit Speech* (Phillipsburg, N.J.: Presby. & Ref., 1971), 131.

a person to speak at length before crowds without undue fatigue or an aching throat.[11]

Actually there are two kinds of breathing, which are very different from one another. We need to breathe one way for our physical, biological needs and another way for speech. Reviewing the operation of the respiratory system assists in understanding proper breathing for speech.

Respiration provides the power source for speaking. The lungs themselves provide no power of movement but respond to changes that are made in the size of the chest cavity. During inhalation the muscles of the chest lift the ribs upward and outward away from the lungs. During this motion, the diaphragm moves downward from its dome-shaped position. The result of this action is a rush of air from the nose down the windpipe through the bronchi to the lungs. When exhalation occurs, the diaphragm returns to its dome shape. The rib muscles relax themselves, and the rib cage returns downward and inward as air is thrust from the lungs.[12]

Breathing for speaking can be accomplished in two different ways. The diaphragm divides the chest cavity into two main sections, the clavicle area and the abdominal area. The clavicle area is the upper chest. Breathing may be accomplished by pressure from the clavicle area. This process is similar to the breathing of an athlete during competition. The upper chest is expanded in a relatively short and quick period of time. Such breathing places pressure upon the entire throat area. Tension is created in the throat as well as the voice box. Prolonged speaking using clavicular breathing will give one a constricted tone, a weary sounding throat, and a hoarse voice.[13] Vocal difficulties inevitably will result from such breathing.

The best breathing for speaking is abdominal breathing. The earlier writers and voice teachers referred to this as diaphragmatic breathing. Actually that term is somewhat misleading, for all breathing is diaphragmatic. All breathing is not abdominal, however. During expiration, the abdominal muscles should do the work. The slow relaxation of the diaphragm ensures smooth control of expiration, but the conscious control of the abdominal muscles makes this possible. In correct breathing for speaking, we consciously must be aware of the action of our abdominal muscles.

11. William G. Hoffman, *How to Make Better Speeches* (New York: Funk & Wagnalls, 1976), 174.
12. Judson S. Crandell and Gerald M. Phillips, *Speech: A Course in Fundamentals* (Glenview, Ill.: Scott Foresman, 1963), 35.
13. Stevenson and Diehl, *Reaching People*, 42.

You easily can tell if your breathing is clavicular or abdominal. Place your hand upon your upper chest. Inhale and quote John 3:16. If your upper chest expands when you inhale, you are breathing incorrectly. Then place your hand upon your abdomen, inhale, and quote John 3:16. If your abdominal muscles expand, you are breathing correctly. Undue tension in your throat as you exhale also will alert you to improper breathing. If your voice is breathy, weak, or has a harsh quality, you likely are breathing incorrectly.

Be aware that breathing abdominally does not mean that you must always take long, deep breaths. Such deep breathing can cause unnecessary tension in your throat just as much as clavicular breathing. You only need to breathe deeply enough to maintain a sufficient amount of air for good speaking and good support. The amount of air that remains in your lungs after you exhale is residual air. The maximum amount of air you can exhale as you speak is the vital capacity available for speaking. You should breathe only deeply enough to complete your sentence with good support and emphasis.

Practicing proper breathing. If you have been breathing incorrectly, begin immediately to change your method of breathing for speaking. The new method will seem unnatural to you for a while. As you learn to breathe more deeply utilizing the abdominal muscles, you even may experience some dizziness. That dizziness will mean that you have not been utilizing your full lung capacity. Dizziness will disappear after a few days.

You can establish new breathing habits by means of good breathing exercises. The exercises in Appendix 4 are designed to assist you in controlled breathing for speaking and in maintaining an adequate reserve supply of breath. They will train you to get the most economical use of breath as you speak.

Breathing correctly will help you maintain a good, strong vocal mechanism and will support the other vocal delivery skills discussed below. Do not expect to be able to breathe correctly after going over these exercises a few times. Very often good breathing habits must be developed over a long period of time. Practice the drills in Appendix 4 in your study. Practice them while you drive your car. Practice them as you walk on the sidewalk. Use the method of proper breathing when you read aloud from printed material. However and whenever you do it, you will replace poor habits with good habits only by practice. These exercises should be practiced daily until proper breathing for speaking is as natural to you as normal breathing is for living.

One of the best ways to improve breathing habits is to observe good speakers who have adequate vocal power and breath control. Notice the expansion of the lower chest cavity as they inhale. Notice also that the chest cavity decreases gradually and slowly so that a reserve of breath is constantly maintained, providing good support of the vocal tone. Also notice that the well-coordinated speaker seems to have a reserve of breath that enables him to release air when he feels the need for emphasis.

Good posture is necessary to proper breathing. Stand erect as you practice proper breathing. The concentration of energy should be at your belt line rather than your throat. Practice inhaling quickly and unobtrusively.[14] One of the primary purposes in learning to breathe correctly is to enable you to replenish your air supply quickly, without disturbing your flow of words. Learn to take your deepest breaths between sentences. Along the way you might want to take little "teacup" breaths as well.

Learning to breathe correctly may be somewhat frustrating at the beginning, so be sure to practice outside the pulpit. Do not try to change your method of breathing during your sermon next Sunday! You have enough to think about while you preach without being burdened with altering breathing habits. The process will be like learning to change gears in a car. The experience is a jerky, frustrating one. During your sermon is not the best time to learn to breathe correctly. Instead, practice during informal conversation as well as through drill work. As your breathing improves, the process will become as natural as shifting into high gear on the open road.

SKILL #3: ARTICULATING

The process of producing sound for speaking is composed of four facets: breathing, phonating, resonating, and articulating. We have discussed the importance of proper breathing in producing adequate breath support for speaking. Phonation has to do with the actual producing of the sound as the breath passes through the vocal folds. Resonation is concerned with the alteration of the sound by the cavities of the mouth, throat, and nose. Both phonation and resonation are complex physiological functions. Problems in these areas are the concern of a medical specialist.[15]

Articulation, however, is a skill that can and must be mastered by the

---

14. Charlotte I. Lee and Frank Galati, *Oral Interpretation* (Boston: Houghton Mifflin, 1977), 107.

15. Due to the complexities, this book cannot treat adequately all of the factors involved in the two processes. Some preachers very well may have difficulties in either producing or amplifying sound. If you have trouble in these areas, consult a good speech pathologist or throat specialist. For the most part, phonation and resonation cannot consciously be improved through the procedures recommended in this book.

preacher. The preacher who wants to communicate the Word of God effectively will be concerned about this facet. If he fails to articulate his words properly, the ability of the congregation to understand what he is saying will be greatly diminished. One congregation complained about its preacher: "For six days a week he is invisible, and on the seventh he is inaudible." Take pains to ensure that those who listen to you can understand what you are saying. Learning to articulate properly will significantly improve your sermon delivery.

Understanding articulation. Articulation is the process of forming the sounds that characterize connected speech. The air that vibrates in the mouth and nose is modified by the tongue, the lower jaw, the lips, and the hard and soft palates.[16] This process transfers mere sound into speech sounds. Articulation is synonymous with *enunciation,* but should not be confused with pronunciation. Pronunciation has to do with the correctness of the sounds and accents in spoken words. Articulation, on the other hand, has to do with the shaping of those sounds by the lips, teeth, tongue, and hard and soft palates.[17]

Articulation is a key ingredient in achieving maximum relaxation during sermon delivery. Actually, proper breathing and proper articulation work together. As we already have seen, adequate breath support prepares the vocal mechanism to function in a relaxed manner. Likewise, articulating words properly will enable you to speak with a minimum of tension in the extrinsic muscles.

Three basic speech elements are related to articulation: vowels, diphthongs, and consonants. Vowels are sounds formed in the resonating cavities as air flows through the mouth. For our purposes, think primarily in terms of the letters *A, E, I, O, U.* The vowels give color to the sounds of speech. Diphthongs are sounds produced by a combination of two vowel sounds occurring in the same syllable and blending continuously from one to the other without interruption.[18]

The consonants might be regarded as the bones of speech. Whether we say "Good morning!" to the paper carrier or "Good night" to our wife, we cannot communicate by means of vowel sounds alone. Hardly any sounds are expressed without using consonants as well as vowels. Actually, without consonants there would be no speech. The correct articulation of the consonants does more to assist in adequate vocal communication than any other factor.

16. Crandell and Phillips, *Speech,* 35.
17. Lee and Galati, *Oral Interpretation,* 118.
18. John A. Grasham and Glenn G. Gooder, *Improving Your Speech* (New York: Harcourt, Brace & World, 1960), 161.

Consonants are produced in three zones of articulation. The first zone is found between the lower lip and the upper front teeth. Consonants in this group are: *P, B, W, WH, F, V, M.*

The second zone is found between the front teeth, the tip of the tongue, and the hard palate behind the teeth. This group includes: *T, D, TH, R, S, SH, ZH, Y, N.*

The third zone is formed by the back of the tongue and the soft palate. Included in this group are these consonants: *K, G, NG.*[19]

Sometimes consonants are explained in terms of the positions of the articulators as they are produced. Those consonants produced by the action of the lips are called *labials.* The labials also are divided into two groups according to the vocal mechanisms used to produce each one:

The lips alone

W as in wind
WH as in which
M as in meat
P as in pork
B as in bee

The lips and the teeth

F as in father
V as in very

Consonants produced by the tongue primarily are called *linguals.* The linguals are divided into four groups according to the vocal mechanisms used to produce each one:[20]

The body of the tongue and the hard palate

S as in so
Z as in zebra
SH as in show

N as in no
L as in lip
R as in row

The tip of the tongue and the hard palate

T as in tip
D as in do
N as in no
L as in lip
R as in row

The tongue and the teeth

TH as in thick or that

19. Brodnitz, *Keep Your Voice Healthy,* 48.
20. McCloskey, *Your Voice at Its Best,* 46–48.

The tongue and the soft palate

C as in cat
K as in king
G as in get
NG as in sing
Y as in yes

Improving articulation. The preacher can improve his articulation in several ways. You might begin right now. Stop your reading for a moment and say each of the letters in the three consonant groups discussed above. As you say them, notice where each sound is produced. This practice will help you learn to place each consonant in its proper position for good articulation. Notice that the tongue, teeth, lips, and hard and soft palates assume different adjustments in relation to each other as the consonants are produced.

One of the biggest needs in articulation is to develop greater flexibility in the tongue, lips, and jaw. Laziness in any of these areas greatly will hinder proper articulation. Diehl and Stevenson provided several helpful suggestions for eliminating stiffness in the articulators. First, purse your lips and move them in all possible directions. Next, draw the lips back and forth and then purse them. Stick your tongue out as far as you can. Touch your lower lip and upper lip with the tongue. Move the tongue from side to side. Then rotate the tongue tip slowly around your lips from left to right. Rotate the tongue tip from right to left. Touch the tongue tip to the center of the upper lip, the lower lip, then each corner of your mouth. Lift the tongue tip to the hard palate, then slowly relax it until it is flat in the mouth.[21]

Perhaps you have noticed that chewing is a function quite similar to speaking. The same muscles used for speaking are used in chewing. Maybe you have also noticed that you can speak and chew at the same time. Though talking with your mouth full is not considered good etiquette, chewing and speaking at the same time can be helpful in developing flexibility in the articulators.

Try this exercise sometime. Imagine you have your mouth filled with food. Then begin to chew like a savage. As you chew with exaggerated movements of the mouth, tongue, and teeth, slowly begin to add speech. This exercise will do wonders in correcting stiffness in your articulators. The approach was popular among German speech therapists in correcting vocal disorders. Although the method has not gained wide acceptance in

21. Stevenson and Diehl, *Reaching People,* 152.

this country, it can be helpful in relaxing the lips, mouth, and tongue.

A helpful mental exercise for improving articulation in sermon delivery is to imagine you are plucking words off your lips as you might pluck the notes off a guitar string. Voice teachers sometimes refer to this practice as "placing the tone." In the strictest sense, waves of sound cannot be directed or placed. However, psychologically there seems to be some advantage to this approach. To think in terms of the words being plucked from the lips has a tendency to relax the throat muscles. This relaxation enables the vocal mechanism to function with a minimum of constriction.

Additional drills to help you practice articulation can be found in selected books on speech communication and public speaking.[22] Spend some time each day going over a few of these drills. As you practice them, overexaggerate the motions of your articulating organs. Think about what sounds you are forming. Again, do not work on articulation during the delivery of a sermon. You might become so involved in proper articulation that you overarticulate. This extreme can be as detrimental to your delivery as poor articulation. Gradually work on this area of speech production, but do not go to seed over it.

SKILL #4: INTEGRATING

As you have studied the mechanical aspects of delivery, you may have experienced a common apprehension. Perhaps you know a preacher who studied speech with the result that his sermon delivery actually was made worse rather than better.

All of us are anxious to convey the gospel truth with the fervor and excitement deeply embedded in our souls, and vocal training does not have to hinder that result. Rather, attention to the mechanical aspects of delivery can assist the preacher in making his delivery more powerful than ever before. His sermons still can be on fire. As he preaches, the thunder can clap and the lightning can crack. For this end to be realized, though, the vocal variables must be used properly. When the preacher uses the vocal variables rightly, his sermon delivery will be lively and dynamic. Such employment of the vocal variables is called *integration*.

Understanding integration. The vocal aspects of delivery, built on the foundational elements of good breathing and proper articulation, must be integrated correctly if sermon delivery is to be effective. At this point, most delivery problems that plague preachers become apparent. Eight particular variables are especially important and demand keen integration if the message is to have maximum impact. These variables should be

22. See McCloskey, *Your Voice At its Best,* 52–57, and Hoffman, *Better Speeches,* 171.

considered as four couplets based upon the relationship between the members of each pair: rate and pace, volume and stress, phrasing and pause, pitch and inflection. Practical guidance regarding how to integrate these in actual delivery will be discussed in chapter 12.

Rate has to do with the speed with which we speak. Speech rate may be measured by the number of words spoken divided by the minutes that elapse during the speaking. Each person has his or her own rate of speaking. Acceptable rates normally vary between 120 and 160 words per minute. *Pace* is related to rate of speaking and gives the sermon a sense of movement. Some people refer to this movement as fluency.

Volume is the amount of sound you use to say what you say. Volume is essential because, if the preacher cannot be heard, then nothing else matters. *Stress* may be considered the intensity or the force we use—the emphasis on the words that count in what we are saying.[23] Certain ideas in every sentence are primary. Other ideas take a more subordinate place. Failure to distinguish properly between the important and the unimportant causes our speech to lack emphasis and clear meaning.[24]

Pitch has to do with the movement of the voice up and down the scale in different registers with various inflections. Essentially, this quality is the melody of your voice.[25] Proper use of pitch is a vital factor in increasing the attractiveness of sermon delivery.

Inflection is a change of pitch within a syllable or word. By means of inflection the preacher may express a question, convey sarcasm, express conviction, or suggest doubt. Good inflection greatly enhances the understandability and the interest of what the preacher says.

We actually speak our sentences in a series of words organized into units of thought. We group both words and sentences by thoughts. These word groups are called *phrases*. A phrase might be described as a continuous utterance bound by pauses. Phrases aid us in expressing what we want to say, and they aid the listener in understanding what we say. Phrasing is one of the most important tools of the preacher. *Pauses* are the punctuation marks of speech. They are the commas, periods, and exclamation points of our language. King defined pauses as momentary silences in communicating meaning.[26]

Improving integration. Certain exercises will help you improve your integration of the vocal variables in preparation for sermon delivery. One of the most helpful exercises is to read Scripture aloud. The Psalms are ex-

23. Hoffman, *Better Speeches*, 99.
24. Ibid., 191.
25. Haddon W. Robinson, *Biblical Preaching* (Grand Rapids: Baker, 1980), 204.
26. Robert King, *Forms of Public Address* (Indianapolis: Bobbs-Merrill, 1969), 80.

cellent to develop proper breathing, phrasing, pitch change, and rate. Take a short psalm. Study its content. Determine how to phrase it well. Mark where your pauses will be. Determine where you need to change your pitch. Ask yourself where you should speed up or slow down your delivery. The Psalms lend themselves quite well to this kind of drill.

The material in 1 Samuel is excellent for developing proper integration of rate, phrasing, and inflection. Read several of the chapters. Again, be sure each of the vocal variables reflects the meaning of what is being said. Luke is a good portion of Scripture to use in improving pitch, inflection, phrasing, and pause. As you read the gospel narrative, take note of its descriptive dialogue. These kinds of exercises will help you master phrasing and pause, as well as increase your ability to speed up or slow down your rate of speaking.

IMPROVING THE VOICE

The subjects considered thus far have given the basic information needed to point you toward improvement in sermon delivery. Actually, every man called to the ministry should avail himself of every opportunity for special training in the areas of voice and speech. Ideally, all ministerial students should be required to take several courses in voice as part of their preparation for the ministry. If such training is not possible, however, they should make an effort on their own to train the voice God has given them.

Obviously, some preachers are blessed with voices of finer quality than others. Nothing can be done about the size or texture of the vocal folds. Wise is the preacher who does not try to speak in a deeper voice than his optimum pitch allows. Wiser is the preacher who uses the voice God has given him to the fullest level of efficiency. But even if you never become a master of sermon delivery, with hard work you can improve your delivery considerably over a period of years. The following five suggestions are offered to help you improve your voice.

STUDYING VOICE PRODUCTION

Study carefully the basic processes involved in voice production. Reread the previous sections on vocal skills and use them as a starting point for increasing your understanding of the principles of voice production. Learn all you can about your voice, an effort that will help you be a better communicator. A study of the vocal mechanism will help you discover any vocal problems you may have. By making this discovery, you will be able to improve those problems on your own or will realize the need to consult an expert. In most cities there are good throat specialists and speech pathologists.

EVALUATING YOUR VOICE

A personal study of your own voice can be productive. A study of this type is easier for preachers today than it has ever been before. Do whatever you can to have your sermons recorded. Videotape is helpful for evaluating all aspects of delivery, but audiotape is more functional for evaluating voice for several reasons. First, audio alone forces you to focus on the voice. Second, you can do your evaluation in more places, such as in the car as you drive.

Be prepared for a surprise when you first hear yourself speak! You probably will not sound on tape as you sound to yourself while you are preaching. When you listen to yourself on tape, you are hearing how you sound to the ears of others. When you actually are preaching, you are hearing the sound of your voice through the bones and nerves of your mouth and head. You will notice a major difference. Do not let yourself become discouraged. You are probably not as bad as you may sound to yourself. You may not be as good as you sound to yourself, either!

Listen to every sermon you preach. As you listen, pay attention to the various aspects of delivery. Ask yourself, How could I have said that better? Stop the tape and rephrase it aloud. Some preachers find it helpful to have a little chart listing all the vocal variables mentioned earlier. Listen to your sermon, keeping the variables in mind. Rate yourself on each one.

For instance, is your volume too loud or too low? Does your delivery demonstrate good variety in volume? What about your rate? Are you speaking too fast or too slow? Do you vary your rate enough to avoid monotony? Do you stay in the same pitch too long? Is your inflection consistent with what you are saying? What about your phrasing? Are your words grouped together well? Do you utilize pause in order to breathe correctly and to help prepare yourself for what you want to say next? The purpose here is not to evaluate the content of your sermon. Rather, you are concerned about how the content was delivered. Constantly ask yourself, How could I have said this better?

You will be surprised how much this analysis can help to improve your delivery. If you do not listen to yourself constantly, you will tend to lapse into poor vocal habits. The necessity of doing a week-by-week evaluation of your sermon delivery needs to be emphasized in the strongest terms possible. The time spent in the effort will richly repay you in the improvement of your preaching. The importance of all these variables during actual delivery will be underscored in more detail in chapter 12.

STUDYING EFFECTIVE SPEAKERS

Another step in improving your voice is to study the delivery of good public speakers. Warren Wiersbe wrote, "There is both a science and an art to preaching, and you need to learn both. . . . The art of preaching is something you learn from a successful preacher, a role model."[27] He added: "In one sense preaching is not taught—it is caught. Happy is that student who somewhere meets a teacher or preacher who lights a fire in his soul."[28]

Select several preachers you consider to be superior in sermon delivery. Study the delivery of men who are effective communicators. See what they do. Listen to them, not for what they say but for how they say what they say. Learn from them. Be careful not to imitate their styles, but glean from them helpful ideas about how to improve your own delivery.

Some individuals in secular fields also can help you improve your delivery. Many of today's television commentators are well trained in the use of their voices. Some of the great political speakers of the past and present also are worthy examples. Listen to the speeches of Winston Churchill, Martin Luther King Jr., and Ronald Reagan. Learn from them. Great speeches of history are now available on audio- and videocassette, CD-ROM, and over the Internet for careful auditory analysis.

ESTABLISHING A PROGRAM OF SELF-IMPROVEMENT

Establish a regular program of self-improvement. Several books and videotapes on voice improvement offer plans to be followed, but you probably should develop your own plan. Certain ingredients in any program of sermon delivery should be followed. Study the vocal aspects of delivery one by one. Spend some time on the matters of volume and stress. Work for a while on rate and pace. Then spend some time working on phrasing and pause. Later, study the use of pitch and inflection. Work on proper breathing and correct articulation. Try to isolate any problems you may have in these areas. Locate whatever problems may be apparent. Work on one aspect of vocal delivery at a time.

A good way to improve your sermon delivery is to read aloud. By reading aloud you can check yourself on how well you are using the various mechanical aspects of speech. In addition, you can check to see if you are breathing properly, and you can work on your rate of delivery. Do not read only prose. Reading good poetry is sometimes an excellent drill for practice in vocal delivery.

27. Warren W. Wiersbe and David Wiersbe, *Making Sense of the Ministry* (Chicago: Mo 1983), 109.
28. Ibid., 112.

Remember that reading certain sections of Scripture can be helpful. Profit also can be derived from reading printed sermons. The sermons of Charles Spurgeon, R. G. Lee, Chuck Swindoll, and Warren Wiersbe are especially helpful. Try reading some of their sermons aloud. As you read them, practice all the aspects of delivery.

PRACTICING YOUR PLAN

Whatever plan you have, you must put that plan into action. After you plan your program, practice your plan. Then practice it some more.

Again, a word of caution must be noted. Remember that your efforts for improving vocal delivery should be done outside the pulpit. You will make a grave error if you try consciously to implement your growing knowledge of the vocal mechanism as you preach. The results will be disastrous. You will find yourself involved in mental gymnastics. Especially the preacher who preaches without notes has enough mental activity as it is. To carry to the pulpit the added load of thinking about all the aspects of sermon delivery is more than the normal mind can bear. Jay Adams counseled:

> Such thoughts must not be allowed to come to mind during the delivery of the sermon itself. It is self-defeating for a preacher to think about the delivery he is using when preaching. Where proper practice takes place you will soon find new habits begin to bleed over into one's speech.[29]

Do your practicing outside the pulpit. Through reading out loud and the use of the exercises discussed earlier, you will correct poor habits and develop proper habits of speech. Then put these new habits to work in your daily conversations. Through much practice the improvements will carry over into your pulpit delivery.

Sometimes a sympathetic friend can assist you, someone who genuinely is interested in helping you improve your delivery. If your wife is able to work with you in this manner, she may be a great help. But do avoid trouble at the parsonage! If she can help you without difficulty, do not hesitate to let her do so. Whomever you use, make sure that it is someone other than yourself who can point out flaws that you do not notice in your sermon delivery.

Practice until improvement comes. Do not expect to have a brand-new speaking voice overnight. Many very gifted singers remain students of voice throughout their lifetimes. The preacher should look upon im-

29. Adams, *Pulpit Speech,* 40.

proving his sermon delivery as a lifelong enterprise. Vocal improvements do not come easily, just as you do not correct faulty speech patterns in a few sessions. Work on improving your delivery weekly. Practice until good vocal habits become second nature to you.

Do not become obsessed with sermon delivery, however. Despite its importance, delivery is only one aspect of your preaching assignment. To focus unduly on your sermon delivery actually can create problems for you during the preaching of your sermons. Bacon said:

> The quality of the vocal instrument is important because flexibility of the instrument increases the range of things it can encompass. Nevertheless, experience has shown that too narrow a focus on such matters often produces an interpreter more concerned with his instrument than with his music.[30]

The preacher can become so interested in his voice that he fails adequately to convey his message. Your voice is a tool, not an altar.

You only have one voice. God has given it to you. Use that one voice to the fullest extent of its capabilities. Do not be satisfied to allow your voice to be less than it can be by proper training and practice. Make your vocal instrument a help in communicating the Word of God, not a hindrance.

CARING FOR THE VOICE

Delivering a sermon is rigorous physical activity. Some have estimated that one hour of speaking is the same as six hours of manual labor. Virtually the whole body is involved in delivering a sermon. Stevenson and Diehl have said that to speak loudly the single letter *b* one uses at least ninety-five different muscles.[31] The weariness the preacher feels after a long day of speaking on Sunday testifies to the tremendous physical exertion involved.

Today's pastor carries a speaking load much heavier than his predecessors. Rapid growth, limited space, and the high cost of land and new construction are all factors that cause many pastors to preach two and even three times on Sunday morning and another time on Sunday night. More and more churches are having full-fledged midweek preaching services. A growing emphasis on seeker-sensitive services and services with varying worship styles has led many churches to offer services on Friday and Saturday nights as well. Luncheons, special ministry meetings, teaching activities, community groups, and so on fill the average pastor's week

30. Wallace A. Bacon, *The Art of Interpretation* (New York: Holt, Rinehart, & Winston, 1972), 5–6.
31. Stevenson and Diehl, *Reaching People,* 5.

with even more speaking responsibilities. Weekly radio messages often must be prepared. Preaching revival meetings may be on the calendar. All of these events make it important for the preacher to know how to adequately care for his voice.

RECOGNIZING VOCAL DISORDERS

Rigorous weekly speaking schedules cause most pastors to abuse their voices and therefore suffer from a variety of vocal disorders. A sore throat may be the preacher's constant companion. Strain of the voice, allergies, and changes in temperature all militate against the preacher's throat. In addition, he may suffer hoarseness and chronic problems with his throat because of failure to use his voice properly. Many preachers barely can speak above a whisper on Monday morning. This reality is too common to be amusing.

Some vocal disorders are even more serious in nature. The pastor may suffer from chronic laryngitis. There may be varying degrees of hoarseness, huskiness, and throat fatigue on a weekly basis. These disorders can greatly hinder him in fulfilling his various speaking assignments. Bowed vocal folds can become a problem. Instead of remaining straight, the edges of the folds curve because of incorrect muscular function.

A still more serious problem the preacher may develop is the vocal nodule. (The most common voice disorders experienced by preachers are vocal nodules, vocal polyps, and contact ulcers.) Usually, vocal nodules are caused by incorrect use of the voice, although sometimes they are caused by allergies. A nodule is a benign growth on the vocal cords and is much like a corn on the toe. The preacher should see the nodule as an extremely important danger signal.

Vocal nodules are detected in a variety of ways. The preacher's voice begins to sound hoarse and breathy. He experiences uncertainty in pitch. Sometimes a sudden wavering in his voice occurs. His voice becomes hoarse at the very beginning of a sermon. This hoarseness may even appear in normal conversation. Sometimes the nodule will disappear with a few days of voice rest. In more severe cases, some have recommended surgery.

Actually, according to the experts in the field, surgery is not the best answer. The original cause of the nodules must be remedied. Nodules may be removed by surgery, but new ones will appear as soon as speaking is resumed according to the same poor speech patterns. The only adequate way to deal with vocal nodules is a radical correction of all mistakes in the use of the voice.[32] If you have a vocal nodule, immediately consult

32. Brodnitz, *Keep Your Voice Healthy*, 158.

a throat specialist who works in cooperation with a qualified voice therapist. In fact, if you have a persistent voice problem, especially without associated medical problems, see your doctor as soon as possible even if your health care plan does not cover it. Your voice is too valuable to your ministry for you to ignore warning signs.

UNDERSTANDING CAUSES OF VOCAL PROBLEMS

When voice problems appear, they usually are caused by one or more of three bad speaking habits.

Inappropriate force. Too much muscular force or force in the wrong places of vocal production may create problems. Preaching with too much volume over a sustained period of time may cause serious vocal problems. Abrupt onset of forced speech also is abusive to the voice.

Wrong pitch. Some voice disturbances come about because of wrong pitch. During the stress and excitement of sermon delivery, the muscles near the vocal folds may tense unduly. The voice becomes constricted, throaty, and harsh. This activity causes the pitch to go up. Under the influence of such prolonged nervous tension, this constriction focuses on the vocal folds, causing the folds themselves to be extremely tight and to bang together in an abusive manner.

Incorrect breathing. When the breath is not used as an adequate support for speaking, smooth coordination of the vocal mechanism is impossible. Failure to breathe correctly—and thereby maintain a sufficient supply of air during speaking—places too much tension on the muscles of the throat and voice box. The aim of adequate abdominal breathing is to expend a minimum of air for a maximum of vocal effort. When this kind of abdominal breathing does not occur, voice problems may result.

ENSURING GOOD VOCAL HYGIENE

Your voice is a delicate, highly complex instrument. When it is used properly, lives can be touched and blessed. If your voice is not in good condition, you cannot use it to maximum benefit. Take every step necessary to ensure good vocal hygiene. Several suggestions will help you develop such a program.

Be sensitive to weather and climate. On humid days the air we inhale is warm. Enough moisture is in such air to keep our vocal mechanism in good condition. The nice, cool winter days are most dangerous for the voice. Preachers often are involved in traveling from place to place on preaching assignments. In a day's time a preacher may move from one climate into an entirely different one. Such transitions can play havoc with the voice. The body must make tremendous adjustments to the changes in weather and climate. If at all possible when you are traveling, allow for a day of rest before you are to speak. This interlude will give your vocal mechanism time to adjust to the new atmosphere.

Give attention to clothing. Some people feel that dressing heavily helps avoid catching colds. Actually, the opposite frequently occurs. Wear sufficient clothing to keep warm but not so much that you begin to perspire. Avoid tight collars or neckties.

Regulate the temperature in your house. The home is an important factor in your vocal hygiene. Ensure that your home is properly heated. Also, be careful to have proper ventilation. A stuffy, overheated home can cause problems with the voice.

Develop good nutritional habits. Organize your eating around a diet of fresh vegetables, salads, whole grain bread, fruit, and dairy products. Avoid consuming milk or other dairy products just before you preach. These items have a tendency to accumulate mucus in the throat. Sweets also create mucus. The mucous membranes do better with food in which starches are at a minimum. In addition, be careful about the times you eat. Do not eat a heavy meal before you preach. You may ruin a good sermon because you are so full you cannot speak properly.

Drink plenty of water. Since the vocal cords are membranes, they need moisture. Six to eight glasses of water are recommended daily. Water is especially essential when taking decongestants or fighting vocal problems.

Get plenty of rest. Go to bed early the night before you preach. Try staying in the night before so that you can go to bed early and be fresh the next morning. If at all possible, pastors should take their day off on Saturday. A day of relaxation and rest before your main preaching day is highly desirable.

Exercise regularly. A good exercise program can be helpful to your voice. Good muscle tone will be beneficial to the entire process of speaking. A body in good shape will assist you in preaching in a healthier manner.

Give proper attention to ailments. Numerous remedies have been suggested for sore and tired throats. Many doctors question the healing value of throat lozenges. Lozenges that contain eucalyptus may even be a hindrance, since the cool effect of the eucalyptus may create the impression that the throat is better than it is. The only value of throat lozenges for sure is that they stimulate the flow of saliva.

The best remedy for a sore, tired throat is to inhale steam in the shower. Get the water as hot as you can bear. Fill the bathroom with steam. With mouth wide open, breathe in the steam through your mouth and nose. This practice will have a soothing, healing effect on your throat.

The only one truly effective method of treating colds is rest. Rest your body so that it has time to fight the infection attacking your vocal organs. If your throat problem persists, consult a throat specialist. Do your best to avoid speaking when you are experiencing problems with your voice. To be sure, the preacher often has no choice in the matter. When you must preach even though you experience vocal problems, go as easy as you can.

Avoid using your voice excessively before and after you preach. Conserve your vocal strength. Do not feel you have to sing above all the congregation during the song service. Use the song service to warm your vocal mechanism, not to wear it out. After the service, you may do great damage to your voice by talking loudly and laughing lustily. Your voice is already tired. To talk excessively after preaching merely places undue strain upon it. Keep your tones as subdued as possible. Get a good night's sleep. Rest your voice.

Use your voice as often as possible. Many full-time evangelists speak night after night, week after week. Few of them ever experience voice problems except on those occasions when they go without speaking for a few days. Keep in mind that your vocal folds are muscles. Frequently using them will strengthen them. Spurgeon maintained the importance of frequent speaking:

> If ministers would speak oftener, their throats and lungs would be less liable to disease. Of this I am quite sure; it is a matter of personal experience and wide observation, and I am confident that I am not mistaken. Gentlemen, twice a week preaching is very dangerous, but I have found five or six times healthy, and even twelve or fourteen not excessive.[33]

Practice your voice daily. "Nothing has a tendency to tire the voice like the occasional prolonged speaking, alternating with long intervals of rest."[34]

Limit caffeine intake. Preachers generally love their coffee. Although you do not necessarily need to give up drinking coffee, you should limit caffeine consumption during times of excessive use. In addition to coffee, caffeine products include tea, soft drinks, and chocolate. Caffeine dries out the vocal cords, as do citrus products such as lemons, oranges, and grapefruit.

Ensure quality acoustics. If it is within your power to do so, by all means seek to have adequate sound reinforcement in your church building. The building in which you preach can be a problem for your voice. Some men actually have caused great damage to their voices because they were speaking in poorly designed buildings. Too many buildings are de-

33. Charles Haddon Spurgeon, *Lectures to My Students* (London: Marshall, Morgan & Scott, 1954), 121.

signed for architectural beauty rather than for sight and sound. Poor acoustics can be devastating to the preacher's voice.

Use quality sound equipment and personnel. The sound system can help or hurt the voice. Make every effort to have an adequate sound system. Churches today have no excuse for shackling their preachers with poor sound reinforcement. A good microphone can be a tremendous help in keeping the voice from being abused. The sound engineer can make or break the preacher. He can emphasize the lower or higher frequencies of the preacher's voice. He can completely change the way the preacher sounds. If a sound system and its operators are good, the preacher is given support during his speaking. If they are poor, the preacher finds himself battling the microphone. More will be said about sound reinforcement in chapter 12.

Minimize throat clearing. Clearing the throat is almost reflexive when one is experiencing mucus buildup or a tickling sensation. Throat clearing is very abusive to the vocal cords and does not assist in relieving discomfort. Instead, drink water, or suck on a hard candy to increase saliva buildup.

34. Ibid.

CHAPTER ELEVEN

MAKING
THE CONNECTION

*The supreme test of a sermon is
whether or not it communicates.*

F. D. WHITESELL

If the preacher is to be effective in sharing the Word of God with his people, he must have a keen interest in whether or not his message connects with his audience. In other words, he must be interested in communication. He must never allow his sermons to become polished works of sermonic art that cause people to praise him for his gift of sermon preparation. Neither must he allow the sermon to exist only for himself. He must ensure that communication between pulpit and pew is always maintained.

Some homileticians suggest that if a man learns to use his voice correctly, then he will be a good preacher. Such advice is good, but it does not go far enough. Mastery of the mechanical aspects of delivery alone will not make you a good preacher. In fact, too much attention to technique can become a subconscious hindrance in the act of preaching.

The solution is found instead in understanding the mental dynamics that produce our flow of words. The delivery of a sermon is made effective and compelling when the preacher understands the concepts of visualization and vitalization, while at the same time having a clear understanding of how to communicate his message. These tasks all are involved in making sure that the sermon connects with the audience.

VISUALIZING THE SERMON

Good mental perception will free you to speak naturally and effectively. Thus, you can make your sermon come alive by calling up mental images and experiencing the emotions of your message while you are saying the words. In essence, you must see what you say. This process is *mental visualization.*

THE NEED FOR MENTAL VISUALIZATION

When some preachers preach, the people listen with rapt attention and offer an enthusiastic response to what is being said. His words are alive and vibrant. On the other hand, others receive little response. People are moving around. The preacher talks on and on, but his words fall upon disinterested ears. Some seem to be able to convey their message in an understandable and interesting fashion. Others seem to have little or no ability to generate a favorable response from the hearers. What is the difference?

To be sure, some dullness in the preaching experience can be attributed to a basic lack of interest on the part of the listeners. We are living in times where many people seem to have little or no interest in what preachers are saying. For the most part, however, people hunger to know what God says in the Bible. If inattention and lack of interest pervade, the problem usually originates in the pulpit. Jay Adams postulated:

> Why do you think it is that the average modern congregation is so unaffected and undemonstrative? Could it be—at least in part—because contemporary preachers by dull, lifeless, abstract preaching fail to appeal to their senses?[1]

Robert Kirkpatrick concurred, suggesting the following imaginary scene:

> In colonial times in America, an official was appointed in each church, whose duty it was to maintain a keen lookout during the preaching for any member of the congregation who may have fallen asleep. When he discovered such a person, it was his further duty to take in his hand the long stick, one end of which was sharpened to a very fine point. With it he was to walk quietly down the aisle—and prod the preacher![2]

The primary problem is in the preacher's delivery. Many have observed a difference between actors and preachers at this point. Actors speak of fiction as if it were real; too many preachers speak truth as if it were fiction.

1. Jay Adams, *Sense Appeal in the Sermons of Charles Haddon Spurgeon* (Grand Rapids: Baker, 1975), 32.
2. Robert White Kirkpatrick, *The Creative Delivery of Sermons* (Joplin, Mo.: Joplin College, 1944), 1.

Certainly preachers do not want to be dull and uninteresting. The average pastor is a deeply committed man who seriously desires to communicate God's Word in an effective, interesting, and powerful manner. Why does this desire not communicate itself in the delivery of his sermon? The difficulty is to be found in a failure to understand the dynamics of mental visualization.

THE PROCESS OF MENTAL VISUALIZATION

Understanding the mental processes of good speaking can do much to cure the preacher of lifeless preaching. Stevenson and Diehl said:

> To be alive, a sermon must rise out of the real world of objects, events and persons; and it must throb with this world of color and sound. A living sermon goes back to the grass roots of human experience.[3]

Behind the words we speak are mental images. If these images are alive to us mentally, then what we say also will be alive. Our speech will be in living color. This process involves four main elements: perception, sensory images, imagination, and words.

Perception. Perception is the process of taking stimuli from the world around us and attaching meaning to them. We perceive the tangible world through five primary senses. The visual—our ability to see—enables us to view the sky and the clouds. We see the ground and the water. We see the trees and the flowers. Visual stimuli bring all the objects of sight to the brain. The auditory is our ability to hear the countless variety of sounds in our world. We hear the voices of other people. We hear the noise of machinery. We hear laughter and singing, crying and shouting. The olfactory sense brings all the fragrances and odors of our environment to our brain through the sense of smell. We smell the sweet roll being baked in the kitchen. We smell the smoke from the fire. We smell the fragrant perfume worn by our wives. The gustatory sense—our sense of taste—enables us to enjoy the sweetness of honey or the bitterness of a crab apple. We taste the flavor of salt and the yeast of bread. Then, we use our tactile sense to touch the baby's skin and sense its softness. We sense the coarseness of tree bark by a touch.

Sensory images. Sensory images are those messages sent to the brain by means of our perception. All five senses constantly bombard our minds with innumerable stimuli. The continuity with which these images

3. Dwight E. Stevenson and Charles F. Diehl, *Reaching People from the Pulpit* (Grand Rapids: Baker, 1958), 66.

flow and correspond to each other in our thought processes is what earlier psychologists called the "stream of consciousness."[4] For purposes of speech, these sensory perceptions form two kinds of images.

First, *memory images* recall the previous sensory experiences that closely resemble the original perception. The pleasant sights and sounds of an outing in a beautiful country setting with a cool stream, green trees, and melodious birds singing create certain impressions upon our memory. Recalling these images of sound, color, taste, smell, and touch creates vividness and interest in the words we use. They enable us to re-create in our words those things we have seen and experienced.

Second, these memories are formed into *creative images*. Much as the ballet dancer gives creative interpretation of a text through new and imaginative movement, a speaker may take memory images and reconstruct them. Instead of saying, "The stream was a swift one," the speaker may say, "The gurgling stream rushed happily on like a schoolboy bounding from the schoolhouse." These images are new units of mental experience. They build upon past original perceptions but combine and rearrange them into original and unique creations.

Imagination. Imagination is the mental activity that takes these images and handles them creatively. The brain spontaneously and sometimes unconsciously rearranges the original perceptions we have had into creative images. We previously discussed the place of imagination in the incubation part of sermon preparation; the preacher must understand its vital role at the point of delivery.

The role of imagination has long been understood as important to the ability of a preacher to present his sermon in an effective manner. Whitesell said:

> Imagination is one of the most God-like capacities of man. It plays a significant role in all creative pursuits. The poet, the novelist, the dramatist, the musician, the painter, the sculptor, and architect would be sadly handicapped without the use of imagination.[5]

The same thing can be said about the preacher. Every preacher must know how to use his powers of imagination effectively. By imagination he helps his people to see what he is saying.

4. Horace G. Rahskoph, *Basic Speech Improvement* (New York: Harper & Row, 1965), 108.
5. Farris D. Whitesell, *Power in Expository Preaching* (Old Tappan, N.J.: Revell, 1963), 103.

Imagination is a marvelous gift of God. By means of imagination we are able to conceive the invisible and make it visible to those who listen to us preach.

> Without imagination the principles of preaching cannot be utilized in effective practice. It is regarded by many as the most important of all factors which go to make the preacher. Imagination is the imaging function of the mind. It is thinking by seeing, as contrasted with reasoning.[6]

To speak in terms of light, sounds, odors, and tastes adds charm and subtle force to sermon delivery. If by means of words we can re-create experiences we have had that are common to our listeners, our words will be understandable and interesting. The imagination will enable us to do this. Imagination in delivery is the difference between a good and an average preacher.

Unfortunately, imagination can run away with you. The greater danger, however, is that we will smother our imagination. The preacher may so analyze Scripture and so dwell on its contents that he stifles the lively imagery it creates in his mind. Imagination can transform your sermon from being a dull lecture into satisfying spiritual food. Wiersbe said:

> A wise use of the principle of hermeneutics will give you information, but you need to add imagination if your ministry is to be effective. It has well been said that the purpose of a sermon is not to discuss a subject, but to achieve an object; and that requires a certain amount of imagination.[7]

Words. Words are the symbols we use for the objects we perceive. They enable us to place the images we have organized in our minds into forms that can be shared with others. By means of words we are able to create in the minds of listeners the same images that are in our own. The discussion on style in chapter 9 contains detailed information on the use of words in effective expression.

THE RESULT OF MENTAL VISUALIZATION

Seeing what you say and saying what you see creates powerful sense appeal in your words. As you speak, relive the mental images that flow behind your words. Respond so strongly to those images that your words

---

6. John A. Broadus, *On the Preparation and Delivery of Sermons,* 4th ed., rev. Vernon L. Stanfield (1870; revision, New York: Harper & Row, 1979), 220 (page citation is to the revised edition).
7. Wiersbe and Wiersbe, 104.

help your listeners respond to them as well. Adams explained well a mathematical formula for the law of sense appeal: "Sense perception plus synthetic imagination plus realistic description equals sense appeal."[8] By perception we get the materials for our mental images. By imagination we organize and arrange them. By description we use words that convey pictures to the minds of our listeners. The result is sense appeal.

Jonathan Edwards had remarkable powers of visualization. In his famous sermon "Sinners in the Hands of an Angry God," he compared the unsaved to a spider or other loathsome insect suspended over the flames:

> You hang by a slender thread, with the flames of divine wrath flashing about it and ready every moment to singe it and burn it asunder; and you have . . . nothing to lay hold of to save yourself, nothing to keep off the flames of wrath, nothing of your own, nothing that you have done, nothing that you can do, to induce God to spare you one moment.[9]

So vivid were his words, and so filled with sense appeal, that people grasped the pillars and pews of the church to keep from sliding into hell.

George Whitefield also could paint pictures with his words. On one occasion he compared the lost sinner to a helpless blind beggar wandering on the edge of a precipice. He described the blind man stumbling forward, his staff slipping from his hands and falling into the abyss. Unconscious of his danger, the beggar stooped down to recover it. Carried away by Whitefield's picture painting ability, a man in the congregation exclaimed, "Good God, he's over!"[10]

Be sure that behind the words you speak lies an unending stream of mental images that are made vivid and alive by means of the imagination. This will make your sermon delivery much more powerful and interesting.

When we understand and utilize the process of visualization, our sermon delivery is helped in another practical way. To accurately reflect in our words what we see in our minds will enable us to use the mechanical aspects of delivery in a much less mechanical way. As the mind sees clearly each successive idea of the sermon, the voice tends to express itself naturally in such a way that the ideas will be conveyed correctly. Once the preacher has learned to use his vocal mechanism properly, its various aspects become the willing servants of the mental images that call forth

---

8. Adams, *Pulpit Speech,* 44.
9. Warren W. Wiersbe, comp., *Treasury of the World's Great Sermons* (Grand Rapids: Kregel, 1993), 202.
10. Frank S. Mead, "The Story of George Whitefield," *The Sword of the Lord* (January 31, 1992), 3–4.

speech. He will not have to think about volume and rate. He will not have to phrase his words mechanically or consciously pause at certain times. He will not have to think about how he is going to inflect the words he says. All these acts will be dictated by the stream of sensory images in his mind. The result will be a most natural and effective delivery.

VITALIZING THE SERMON

A sermon must not only be born, it must be born again. The average congregation today is much more intelligent than congregations in previous years. People are more demanding of their preachers than before. Visual media make clear to our people the ideas they present. The preacher, therefore, must present his ideas with as much clarity as possible. He must not only think in pictures himself, but he must enable his people to visualize what he is saying as well. This "rebirth" of the message in their minds will enable them to become actively involved in the truths you are conveying. As you visualize what you say, that visualization will vitalize your words as you speak them. This process is *mental vitalization.*

THE NATURE OF MENTAL VITALIZATION

All preachers share a common experience from time to time. During sermon preparation, a pastor discovers truths in God's Word that are profound and significant. These truths burn in his heart. The message is so hot that it threatens to burn the paper upon which it is recorded. He anticipates that the sermon literally will set the people on fire. He can hardly wait until Sunday. He is going to preach a barn burner! The people will be shouting in the aisles. Then Sunday comes. When he preaches, the fire does not burn. The ideas that so excited him during preparation are now dull and lifeless. Ideas that leaped with life are now limp. The content of the sermon is there, but there is no life, no lift, no leap. What went wrong?

Probably the letdown came because the preacher did not understand the mental processes involved in vitalizing his sermon during delivery. Though his message was alive during its preparation, he failed to bring it to life again for his people. Learning some principles of mental vitalization will help you get your sermon from the study to the pulpit without losing its life and dynamic. The sermon must be "born again." Steps must be taken in the preparation time and just prior to delivery to ensure that the sermon comes alive again in the mind and the heart of the preacher.

As with visualization, preaching with mental vitalization relieves you of the necessity of concentrating on how to use your voice. While you are delivering your sermon, you will not have to be overly concerned about the mechanics. You are master of your material instead of its being master over you. The content will dictate to the vocal mechanism how you say what you say. Such delivery will result in a conversational style of speaking, not merely standing in the pulpit and talking in a calm manner but in a manner interesting to the listeners. Your message will be intense, compelling, captivating, and convincing. Such delivery will have a positive effect on your hearers.

THE STEPS TO MENTAL VITALIZATION

Several steps in sermon preparation come to bear upon mental vitalization at the moment of delivery. Consider each one carefully.

Ponder your people. Think about the people to whom you will be preaching. You will recall that Alexander Maclaren placed an empty chair before him as he prepared his sermons. That empty chair represented to him the people who would listen to him preach. It was a constant reminder that his sermon was being prepared for real people.

Although Maclaren's method may not appeal to you or be practical, always be aware that you are preparing the truths of Scripture to be delivered to *real people.* Older people concerned with health and dying will be listening to you. Busy men will be there, taking time from the hectic pace of the daily business world. Young people who are dealing with peer pressure and making crucial decisions in life will be listening to what you say. Keep them in mind.

Appraise your application. Remember the importance of applying the timeless truths of Scripture to the pressing needs of people today. Be constantly asking yourself, So what? What does this subject have to do with my people? Make your illustrations and applications understandable to them.

Familiarize for freedom. Sermon delivery is alive to its finest degree when it is as free from dependence upon notes as possible. More will be said about various approaches to delivery in the next chapter. But at this point in your preparation, give yourself to becoming very familiar with your material regardless of which delivery approach you choose. Such familiarity will heighten the powers of mental vitalization.

To preach in such a way that makes your sermon come to life for your hearers, you must be able to remember in a dynamic way what you have studied. In this sense, Rahskoph's definition of memory is appropriate. He said, "Memory is the process by which past learning becomes effective in the present."[11] The three main phases in this process are learning, retention, and recall.

11. Rahskoph, 202–3.

The first phase of developing meaningful memory for delivery involves *learning* your material. Below are some helpful guidelines:

THE LAWS OF LEARNING

The Law of Frequency—*The more times the material is reviewed, the greater the familiarity at the time of delivery.* Go over your material many times. Frequency of contact with the material will place the basic concepts firmly in your mind.

The Law of Recency—*The shorter the time span between review and delivery, the greater the familiarity at the time of delivery.* For a Sunday morning message, go over your sermon notes on Saturday night and again on Sunday morning.

The Law of Intensity—*The greater the mental energy applied in review, the more vivid the material at the time of delivery.* Your best mental abilities must be focused intensely and with all clarity upon your material.

The second phase in preparation for free delivery is *retention*, or preserving what you have learned during a latent period. Frequently repeating what you have learned will greatly aid retention. Obviously, the preacher does not have time to go over his material in the moments just before he stands to preach. He can review before that point, however, and the number of times he does so will greatly enhance his powers of retention.

The third phase in this kind of preparation for delivery is *recall*. As you thoroughly assimilate the details of the message, you will be able to recall them with clarity and vividness. The idea is not to reconstruct the individual words but the concepts and principles of your sermon that will enable the words to flow smoothly.[12]

Master your material. The preacher should strive to become a master of each sermon he prepares. Several steps listed on the next page can help you firmly grasp your sermon content.

Internalize the information. The sermon must be worked into the mind and heart of the preacher before it is ready for delivery. McFarland said, "What is in the well of your heart will show up in the bucket of your speech."[13] That assertion is another way of saying that good expression depends upon good impression. If the sermon is not alive to the preacher

---

12. Ibid., 202–3.
13. Mc Farland, 49.

as he delivers it, little chance is present of its being real to the congregation. Robinson said, "An audience senses when a preacher reads words from the wall of his mind. Let a preacher agonize with thought and words at his desk, and what he writes will be internalized."[14]

MASTERING YOUR MATERIAL

Step #1   Deepen your understanding of your material so that you thoroughly know what you are saying.

Step #2   Have strong organization for what you want to say.

Step #3   Understand the logical relationships of the ideas in your message—know how the various ideas in your sermon fit together.

Step #4   Rehearse the thought sequences of your sermon one by one; speak them out loud; master the ideas and pictures; depend upon logical rather than verbal memory. You will be surprised at how many actual phrases and word sequences will come back to you when you know thoroughly the logical sequence of your concepts. When you are not trying so hard to remember the words, they will flow much better. Words cluster better around ideas and pictures than they do around attempts at memorization.[15]

Step #5   Distribute your review over several different times; always review the night before you preach and then again shortly before you preach.

Step #6   Overlearn your material. Be so familiar with what you are going to say that it is a part of you.

Although you are not forbidden to use ideas you glean from others, those thoughts must be made a part of your own thinking and feeling. Too many pastors borrow thoughts from others but never digest them by reflection and meditation. As a result, the thoughts are not internalized. The preacher must live the truths of the sermon he is preparing. The sermon must be preached to himself before it is preached to others.

14. Robinson, *Biblical Preaching,* 178.
15. Demaray, 138.

INTERNALIZATION ITINERARY

I have found certain practices helpful in internalizing my sermon material for the moment of delivery. In addition to the notes I prepare for filing purposes, I also prepare preaching notes. Normally these are written out by hand. They are as simple as possible. The key words of the sermon design are included. Certain quotations and essential data in the sermon are also included.

During this specific preparation time, I try to relive each part of the sermon in my imagination. I try to make the thoughts as vivid as possible. I visualize the mental pictures in my message. For more abstract concepts, I try to imagine pictures that will easily convey to me the meaning. For instance, if I am talking in terms of progress, I may think in terms of a train moving along the track, making progress from station to station. If I am discussing liberty, I may picture the Statue of Liberty or a liberated slave. This enables abstract concepts in my sermon to come alive in my imagination.

After I have gone over each part of the sermon, attempting to live it out in my imagination, I speak the sermon to imagined hearers. I check the way I say certain parts. Does it sound right? Will this make the maximum impact upon those who hear it? Then, in my imagination, I become several of my prospective hearers. I try to imagine how they would respond to this particular sermon. This procedure enables me to make the sermon real in my own soul.

THE MODES OF MENTAL VITALIZATION

Two particular modes are involved in vitalized preaching—the *intellectual* and the *emotional*. The intellectual mode is the language of the mind. This mode is expressed by the words we use. If done well, the specific words used in sermon delivery will convey adequate intellectual content so that the listeners will be able to understand what the preacher is saying. The emotional mode, on the other hand, is the language of the feelings. The emotional mode is expressed by the way the words are said, muscle tension, and the overall mood created in delivery. The emotional mode does not refer to emotional preaching but rather to the overall emotional communication that comes from within the deepest feelings of the preacher himself.

Stevenson and Diehl observed two levels of emotion expressed in the delivery of a sermon. *Pathos*, which already has been discussed, refers to the preacher's attitude toward himself and others. Pathos is the deepest level of the preacher's emotions. On the other hand, *melism* has to do with his immediate feelings about the particular sermon he is to deliver.[16] All of us are more interested in some subjects than others. Our attitude toward the sermon will be communicated as we preach. If you are alive to your sermon, your sermon will be alive to you.

When the intellectual mode and the emotional mode cooperate with one another, your message is delivered with a great deal of effectiveness. When the emotional mode contradicts the intellectual mode, be aware that the emotional message is more readily accepted by the listeners.[17] The preacher may have the right message, but the way he handles his message may cause his listeners to reject it.

This tension is why some preachers are able to preach on stern, negative subjects and still receive a favorable response from the listeners. Others may preach on positive subjects, yet create negative response. If the preacher conveys through the emotional mode a sense of empathy with the people, the listeners are much more likely to respond favorably. He may say nearly anything he wants to say if the people are convinced he loves them, is interested in them, and wants to help them.

Search your inmost heart about your deepest attitudes. Ask yourself these questions: How do I feel toward this message? What do I feel toward myself? What are my feelings toward the audience? If the answers to these questions are not good, do some heart searching before you deliver your message.[18]

The night before you preach and earlier the same day you preach, take some time to look again at the sermon as a whole. What is your overall purpose? What do you want to accomplish? These considerations must be clearly in mind as you look to the time of sermon delivery.

Another helpful procedure is to pray the message to the Lord. On your knees in His presence, go over each part of your sermon. Can you ask the Lord's approval on what you are going to say? Is the sermon pleasing to Him? This practice is a helpful step as you prepare to preach with heartfelt emotion.

16. Stevenson and Diehl, 77.
17. Al Fasol, "A Guide to Improving Your Preaching Delivery" (Southwestern Baptist Theological Seminary, Ft. Worth, Texas, mimeographed), 8.
18. Stevenson and Diehl, 74.

THE GOAL OF MENTAL VITALIZATION

The sermon will be alive as you deliver it if you have a definite desire to share its contents with your people. A sermon must never become a soliloquy. Too often ministers deliver a sermon as if it were merely a work of art. Because they have focused so much on the sermon, they have forgotten that the sermon was prepared to be delivered to a congregation. When a man preaches this way, his attention is turned away from the people. He has poor eye contact and is unaware of the reaction of his listeners. As a result, he is unable to adjust his delivery to the changing responses of the congregation. You can avoid such a disaster and increase your desire to share your sermon with others in several ways:

DEEPENING YOUR DESIRE

Remember your calling. Go back to the time when the call of God first came upon your soul with force and freshness. All of the emotions and high aspirations that filled your being at that time must be made to live in your soul again. You must place yourself where the people sit. Be aware of all the different ages represented in your congregation. Become aware of the problems, the burdens, the heartaches, the hopes and aspirations of your people.

Keep your heart warm and receptive. If you are spiritually vital, your sermons will also be vital. Maintain a daily devotional life. Through reading the Bible and daily contact with God in prayer, you will keep yourself in a position to be God's effective spokesman to men.

See each idea as you present it. The ideas of your message must actually come alive in your mind. You must see all you possibly can by means of your imagination. Imagination has previously been described as the ingredient that makes the difference between a good preacher and a poor preacher. Allow your imagination to work freely on the pictures your sermon content provides to your mind.

Create intellectual and emotional stimuli. Give your hearers as many intellectual and emotional stimuli as you can to make your sermon alive to them. They will be able by means of their imaginations to see, hear, touch, taste, and smell what you are talking about. Perhaps you are describing the Cross. As the scene comes alive in your own mind, based on your preparation and the exercise of your emotion, express what you see. Do not let mental laziness cause you to think of how you saw the Cross in your preparation time. See the scenes of Calvary during the actual moments of delivery. If you can re-create these images in the minds of your listeners as you preach, they will be stirred and moved by what you say.

Watch the reactions of your people. Look at your listeners while you deliver your sermon. Their reaction will let you know whether or not they are with you and understand what you say. See individuals as you speak.

Provide adequate emotional support. Be sure to use a proper amount of emotional support for the things you say. By means of word color, gesture, and bodily tension you can support the intellectual content of your sermon. These practices will enable your message to be more than an intellectual presentation of a series of ideas. Through this method of sermon delivery you actually "flesh out" the truths of your sermon.

Nurture a sincere desire to communicate God's truth to your people. If this desire is present, you will use as many ways as you can to convey your message. The doctor who wants his patient to quit smoking will draw upon all his knowledge of the dangers of smoking, will use every potential danger smoking may create, will paint every dark picture he can paint to warn the patient against smoking. The same thing is true of the pastor who earnestly desires to convey the great truths of the Bible to his people.

COMMUNICATING THE SERMON

Some men preach for years without understanding the psychological dynamics of the preaching event or speaking situation. Yet, to a large degree, the whole matter of effective speaking is essentially psychological. Much training for public speaking today seems to miss that point altogether, especially in the area of sermon delivery. Emphasis is placed upon the arrangement of ideas, sentence structure, enunciation and diction, gestures, and so on. And all these matters are important. But the preacher may be aware of them—even use them effectively—and still be a failure in the pulpit. For this reason many preachers are wooden and unconvincing in their delivery. A basic understanding of communication theory, the motivational cycle, and the electricity between pulpit and pew can assist the preacher in avoiding such drabness.

COMMUNICATION THEORY

Communication theory explains how the process of communication takes place. Four factors are involved in the communicative process as they apply to preaching:

Source— the person who desires to communicate with others

Message—the content which the source desires to communicate

Channel—the words used to transport the message; also called the medium

Receiver—the object of the communication, who must decode or interpret the message given

These four factors obviously apply to sermon delivery. The preacher is the source. He stands before a congregation, called of God to preach and gifted and empowered to do so. He takes the message from the Bible, places it in his words, and conveys it to the waiting congregation via the medium of spoken words. The persons in the congregation receive the words delivered by the preacher and then decode them in categories that are understandable to them.

Listeners respond both internally and overtly. In the average congregation, the overt reactions may not be as apparent, but they still are happening. The listeners may smile, laugh, wriggle, or yawn. These little clues let the preacher know whether or not he is being understood. These clues also let him know if his message is being received favorably or unfavorably. At this point he is not merely a transmitter but also a receiver. Similarly, the listeners are not merely receivers but are transmitters as well. You might think of a preacher, then, as a kind of "transceiver." As he delivers his sermon, he is at the same time responding to the feedback from his audience.

A final ingredient must be added to the preaching situation. Because a congregation consists of more than one listener, audience interstimulation and response occur. People laugh louder in a group because of the laughter of others. The mere presence of others directs the behavior of the individual.

Much more is involved in being an effective speaker than one might assume. The preacher will be helped if he takes the attitude that he and his listeners are participating in the preaching situation as a group. His attitude cannot be "they, the audience, and I, the speaker." Rather, his attitude must be "you and I." A minister must help his hearers sense that they are as much a part of the communicative process as is he. The idea is to create the feeling that "we are all thinking this through together." The more the preacher makes his listeners aware of their participation in what he is saying, the better he will communicate.[19]

19. Milton Dickens, *Speech: Dynamic Communication* (New York: Harcourt Brace Jovanovich, 1954), 11–16.

THE COMMUNICATIONS REVOLUTION

Our generation continues to witness a communications revolution. The field of cybernetics—the study of the mechanisms of human and electronic communication—highlights the dramatic changes taking place as a result of the development of an almost infinite variety of technical electronic equipment.[20] Preachers who want to be heard must give careful attention to what is being done in modern communications. The secular world is serious about communication. Preachers can be no less serious. Those of us who stand before congregations week after week must be sure that we connect.

MASS MEDIA MENACES

John Stott noted five negative tendencies of television viewing that also can be applied to other mediums of mass communication.[21]

Physical laziness. Every conceivable entertainment is to be found within the comfort of one's den. Even worship services are available. Why should people bother to get in a car, battle traffic, and sit in a crowded building to hear a sermon? Without question, television worship services provide an opportunity for the sick and elderly to hear the gospel. In some parts of the country where there is no clear-cut Bible witness, television makes it possible for people to hear the truth. On the other hand, worship by television does not provide fellowship, corporate worship and witness, or other scripturally mandated elements regarding the gathering of God's people.

Intellectual laziness. With the increase in the number of channels available to the average viewer, programs with good intellectual content are more accessible than ever before. People have a tendency, however, to watch television merely as a relaxer and entertainer. This motivation, then, leads them to view instead of analyze what they see and hear.

Emotional insensitivity. People generally are shocked and concerned upon first viewing the horrors of war, the miseries of poverty, and the brutality of murder. When these are viewed over a long period of time, however, the emotions become jaded. The human personality can endure only a certain amount of pain and tragedy. The time comes when the individual is left with little or no feeling.

20. Stott, 64.
21. Ibid., 70–73.

Psychological confusion. Much of the viewing matter on television deals with artificial, contrived subject matter. The families portrayed are not real. Their experiences may seem lifelike, but the viewer is aware that the events depicted on the screen are not actually happening. People who are exposed constantly to unreality will likely have difficulty in relating positively to truth as it is revealed in Scriptures. Furthermore, the same people usually find it difficult to move from the world of fantasy to the real world, thus failing to make the proper distinctions between the two states.

Moral disorder. Sexual promiscuity and physical violence frequently are portrayed in television drama as normal behavior. The impression is given that "everybody does it." The additional impression is given that death is not real, and anyone who dies will be resurrected for the sequel, the next season, or a different show. Godlessness and immorality are popular. Faith in God and old-fashioned moral standards are castigated. This negative aspect of television is especially damaging to children, who generally spend about 30 percent more viewing time each week than adults.

In one sense, modern communication has brought a variety of competitors for the pastor. Of course, preaching always has had its competition. As the twentieth century dawned, the dramatist, the newspaper writer, the author, and the playwright all competed for the ear of the people. At the daybreak of the twenty-first century, the communications revolution has added other significant competitors.

In addition to the aforementioned rivals, the contemporary preacher is up against a new breed of competitors: (1) television, video, and the movie industry; (2) advancements in the personal computer such as CD-ROM, e-mail, and the Internet; and (3) interactive mediums such as virtual reality and holograms. By means of the most sophisticated technology, rival voices call the preacher's people to listen and to heed their appeals. Foolish is the preacher who fails to be aware of his competition.

Modern communications mediums bring numerous benefits. People are more knowledgeable about a wider variety of events and experiences than previous generations. By means of public and network television they can attend great events. By means of cable television they can view films, plays, and political functions that otherwise would not be broadcast. Via video, people have access not only to a variety of entertainment but also to a host of educational resources. Computers and other interactive devices heighten the qualitative value of both entertainment and education.

No technological advance has had greater impact on our society than television. The influence of the TV writer and producer cannot be overestimated. People are bombarded by the voices of the evening newscasters, the luring wit of advertisers, and the insistent appeals of contemporary musicians. None of us would doubt that television is a major factor in our lives. In 1979, the TV was on six hours and fourteen minutes a day in the average American home, two hours per day more than the average in 1969."[22] The amount of viewing time has dropped to four hours per day in recent years, but television viewing trends continue to be shocking. The average American youth spends 1,500 hours per year in front of a TV, compared to 900 hours in the classroom. In addition, six million videos are rented daily in America and another three million are checked out of public libraries. We may never know all the ramifications of such extended TV viewing.[23]

This wide exposure to ideas and events, along with the enhanced quality of modern communication, undoubtedly has an effect upon the preacher's assignment. It is more difficult for people to listen attentively to sermons. As a result, the pastor has a harder time gaining and holding the attention of his people. Newscasters are attractive and fluent. The advantages of TelePrompTers, on-the-spot reporters, and guest speakers are not feasible for the preacher. People listen to polished presentations on television, videotape, and audiotape. Then they come to church to listen to their pastor, who in turn faces a more selective audience than did previous generations of preachers. Cable and satellite television, with their proliferation of choices, heighten the prospects of more entertaining and more professional presentation. Furthermore, the sermons of well-known and especially gifted preachers are broadcast into the homes of church members every week, making it even more difficult for the average local pastor to "measure up."

Preachers must come to grips with the fact that their congregations have been brainwashed by television and other technological advancements. We must not assume that they are anxious to hear what we have to say. We cannot be satisfied with average or below average sermon presentations. If we do not get with the modern communications program, people will turn us off in a heartbeat. A generation accustomed to the swift-moving images and infinite choices of satellite and cable television,

22. Paul Lee Tan, *Signs of the Times* (Rockville, Md.: Assurance, 1980), 1439.
23. EnviroWeb. Enviroissues. System. Media. "Interesting Facts About TV," July 24, 1997. Online. Available from CWIX@http://www.enviroweb.org/enviroissues/system /media/tv_fact.html.

as well as the lifelikeness of video technology, will not tolerate a boring, lifeless, drab presentation of the gospel. Modern communications challenges us to preach the gospel in the most attractive manner possible. Some practical suggestions for enhancing your presentation will be offered in the next chapter.

THE MOTIVATIONAL CYCLE

Study in communications theory will help the preacher understand how his listeners are motivated. Experts in the field of speech communication often talk about the motivational cycle. Five factors are involved in this cycle:

Attention. The average congregation will be attentive for only four minutes at a time. The minister, therefore, must use many different devices to revive attention. Several of these devices will be discussed in detail in the next chapter.

Need. Early in his message, the preacher must establish some need his sermon can meet. This need must be universal, related to all people, and timeless. The preacher will do well to study the psychology of the human personality. The basic needs of men have not changed.

Satisfaction. The preacher must show in his sermon how that need can be met. He can do this by applying the truths of the gospel to the contemporary needs of men.

Visualization. At this point, the preacher brings his audience in for the first time. He has their attention. He has brought before them some particular need. He shows them how the need can be met. Now he enables the people to visualize how this need can be met in their own lives.

Action. Here the minister shows the people what the sermon calls them to do. This course of action should be kept constantly before them throughout the message. Actually, the preacher begins his invitation in his introduction. Very early in the sermon, he establishes the fact that they will be called upon to take a certain course of action.

THE SPEAKING SITUATION

Ultimately, the preacher delivers his sermon for the glory of God. Practically, however, he delivers his message for the sake of an audience. His purpose is to reach those who listen to him. Some men seem to have no awareness that anybody is listening while they preach. They are so filled with their subject that they seem to have forgotten its object. When the preacher is focused upon his subject matter, the bond of communication between himself and the congregation is broken. Remember that the subject matter is not the only vital aspect of the preaching situation. The audience is equally as important. In fact, you have been preparing your message all along with a specific audience in mind.

One task of the preacher in sermon delivery is to manage the speaking situation. Therefore, you must learn to do audience-centered preaching rather than subject-centered preaching.[24] In essence, you must engage the audience in the preaching event by grabbing and holding their attention. Though gaining attention is largely dependent upon your content, content alone will not hold attention. If you concentrate on the audience during delivery and carefully adjust to their responses, you can manage the listening situation to a large degree and keep your audience involved. You can condense, expand, or vary your message as you proceed.

Keeping attention is one of the most important aspects of the preacher-audience relationship. The crucial question that must be answered in the relationship is, Who's doing the work? Attention takes work, and, if it is going to be maintained, someone has to do the work—either the speaker or the listener.

The reality of the public speaking event is that the listener will not do the work for very long! Since the average attention span is approximately only four minutes—a span that will vary from audience to audience and even from individual to individual—the preacher must be thinking constantly about how to engage his audience and maintain their interest. He wants the people to hear what he has to say and then to respond to the truths. If his audience is not attentive, his goals in speaking to them cannot be achieved.

The preacher faces several hindrances to maintaining audience attention. Using abstract words that are difficult to understand will tax the attention of an audience. In chapter 9, with regard to stylistic expression, we noted that words having few syllables are easier for most people to understand. Hackneyed ideas and phrases also tend to lower the attention level. People soon tire of hearing the same things over and over again. The pedantic preacher who is too detailed will bore his audience. Such a preacher's ideas seem to stand still. There is no forward movement. The pastor whose personality is colorless, whose voice is monotonous, and whose bodily actions are rigid will have a difficult time maintaining interest. The good preacher will take the initiative of doing the work, not only to catch attention but also to maintain it by using a variety of techniques that are kept in flux during delivery.

24. Kirkpatrick, 14.

The Electric Spark

Something exciting takes place between a man and his audience when genuine preaching occurs. He gathers his material in the study. He sets it on fire in the pulpit. When a man speaks who has been saved and called to preach, whose soul is on fire with truth, who speaks to other men face to face and eye to eye, a kind of electricity flashes between him and his people. A beautiful teamwork occurs. Preacher and listeners lift each other up, higher and higher, until they are borne as on chariots of fire to another world. In such a dynamic situation there is power to move men, to change character and destiny. No other medium possesses such power.[25]

The electricity that flows between the preacher and his people is the distinguishing mark of many of the great Bible expositors. Although their content was superior and their voices appealing, much of their effectiveness was due to that personal electricity that flowed between them and their congregations. This spark between preacher and people must be present if preaching is to accomplish its intended end.

Because of this dynamic, a sermon is not to be regarded as something that exists upon paper. Nor is a sermon a series of facts presented in an appealing or interesting manner. Neither was preaching ever intended to be a monologue delivered for its own sake. Preaching is a two-way street.

The brethren who are African-American have much to teach the rest of us about genuine heartfelt worship. Their worship services are unashamedly emotional and expressive. True audience participation occurs. The worshipers actually talk back to the preacher. He knows how to pace himself accordingly. He leads in two-way communication. The response of the congregation provides the preacher with inspiration and stimulation. He soars to the heights as he delivers his sermon.

The sermon will be effective when the preacher delivers it to the heart. He must not preach over his people's heads in flowery oratory or beneath their feet with trite expressions. He must go to their hearts with scriptural, personal application. To be effective, we must not merely preach *before* the people; we must preach *to* them. As we look at our people one by one, our whole demeanor and expression must indicate to them that we have a message from God for their personal benefit.

If no two-way communication occurs, preaching has no point. A poor woman left the service of a prestigious church in Scotland. A famous and scholarly preacher had preached. Someone asked if she had enjoyed the sermon. Her response was affirmative. She also was asked, "Were you able to follow him?" She replied, "Far be it from me to presume to understand

25. Henderson, 95.

such a great man as that!"[26] The story is somewhat humorous, but mostly it is sad. If we fail to connect with our listeners, we fail.

Every preacher will be much more effective if he will learn to preach to his audience not en masse but one by one. Be aware of your hearers and observe their response to the message while you are preaching. This awareness is heightened by your love for your people. Richard Cecil, an Anglican preacher in London, said, "To love to preach is one thing, to love those to whom we preach is quite another."[27]

26. Quoted in Lloyd-Jones, 122.
27. Quoted in Lloyd-Jones, 92.

CHAPTER TWELVE

PREACHING THE WORD

And I, brethren, when I came to you, did not come with
excellence of speech or of wisdom declaring to you the
testimony of God. . . . My speech and my preaching were
not with persuasive words of human wisdom, but in
demonstration of the Spirit and of power, that your faith
should not be in the wisdom of men but in the power of God.

PAUL THE APOSTLE

Exposition is not complete until the sermon is preached. The preaching event culminates in the actual presentation of the exposition. The time finally has come in the process for you to deliver the sermon.

Preachers have debated variously the value of learning techniques of sermon delivery. Some believe that giving attention to delivery is a fruitless endeavor because such a study ignores the role of the Holy Spirit in preaching. We do not study effective delivery techniques to *displace* or even *complement* the work of the Spirit, however, but instead that we might not *hinder* it. Such an understanding demands that expositors give attention to various aspects of sermon delivery.

HOLDING THE EAR

The preacher must be intentional about his delivery if he is going to hold the attention—the ear—of his audience. The principle underlying such intentionality is variation. Put very simply, variation maintains attention. As discussed in chapter 10, variation is accomplished when certain vocal variables are integrated properly. The following counsel regarding the exercise of these variables is not intended to be a "quick fix" for all the sermon delivery problems you may experience. These guidelines are offered simply to help you coordinate these variables properly so that you can preach in an appealing, attractive, and compelling manner. Giving attention to these variables—adjusted appropriately throughout the message—will help you do the work of maintaining your listeners' attention.

OVERCOMING THE MONOTONY MONSTER

Proper use of the vocal variables will go a long way toward solving the problem of monotony in delivery. Probably nothing is more devastating to effective sermon delivery as monotony. People are put to sleep when there is a constant recurrence of any of the vocal variables. Sometimes preachers develop certain speech habits that make them very difficult to follow. These habits are called ministerial whines or tunes. Normally these whines or tunes involve a combination of pitch, rate, inflection, and volume patterns.

The ministerial whine is sometimes developed by the preacher in an attempt to add authority and importance to what he says. The preacher's voice sounds as if he has a steeple in his throat. Actually, he accomplishes the opposite of his intention. People are repulsed by such monotonous, pious-sounding speech.

All of us have had the experience of listening to a speaker with an affected sound. The preacher needs to speak as a real man to real men. He must rigorously eliminate from his delivery any inkling of or tendency toward ministerial whine. The availability of tape recording makes it inexcusable for a preacher to be monotonous in his delivery. Constant monitoring of his sermon delivery will help catch any recurring speech patterns that cause his delivery to be dead, uninteresting, or offensive.

Take away variety in volume, pitch, inflection, or phrasing, and what remains in the speech lacks luster and sparkle. Spurgeon said, "A preacher can commit ministerial suicide by harping on one string, when the Lord has given him an instrument of many strings to play upon."[1] In any case, the audience will not do the work of listening very long. You must do it for them. The way you do the work of listening for your listeners is to vary your use of the vocal qualities.

Be unpredictable. Learn to use combinations in the vocal variables. Vary the rate of your speech, slowing down or speeding up at different parts of your message. Pause frequently. Use different inflections for your words. Produce variety by various degrees of loudness. Alter your pitch. A combination of all these techniques will contribute greatly to vocal variety. Your delivery will be much easier to follow. The people will not have to force themselves to listen. They will not be able to keep themselves from listening.

---

1. Charles Haddon Spurgeon, *Lectures to My Students* (London: Marshall, Morgan & Scott, 1954), 111.

RATE

No hard-and-fast rules dictate the rate of delivery. Acceptability is determined when the listeners are able to grasp what the speaker says. Communication is hindered when the speaker speaks too fast or too slow.

The tendency of young preachers is to talk too fast. Indeed, a sermon should be delivered with excitement and vigor. But, in his enthusiasm, the young preacher may speak too fast to be understood clearly. Rapid delivery does communicate a sense of excitement, but any sound—no matter how exciting it may be at the beginning—will lose attention if it is continued without variation. Niagara Falls is hardly noticed by the people who live nearby.[2] If you speak too rapidly, you will not be understood, and you may leave your listeners out of breath.

Preachers talk too fast for other reasons also. Many speak rapidly because they are quick thinkers and fluent. Do not radically change your rate if rapidity is natural to you. You might develop an artificial style that communicates something other than your personality. Instead, make an effort to slow down just a bit, and use other devices of speech to keep the rate from becoming difficult to follow. A wonderful help in regulating a rapid delivery is pause, which will be discussed later.

Rapid speech rate suggests nervousness and lack of ease. Remember that every second does not have to be filled with sound. Spurgeon warned:

> Excessively rapid speaking, tearing and raving into utter rant, is quite inexcusable; it is not, and never can be powerful, except with idiots, for it turns what should be an army of words into a mob, and most effectually drowns the sense in floods of sound. It is an infliction not to be endured twice, to hear a brother who mistakes perspiration for inspiration, tear along like a wild horse with a hornet in its ear until he has no more wind, and must need to pause to pump his lungs full again; a repetition of this indecency several times in a sermon, is not uncommon, but is most painful. Pause soon enough to prevent that cough, which rather creates pity for the breathless orator than sympathy with the subject in hand.[3]

To move on at a frantic pace may convey to the listeners a sense of personal insecurity and uncertainty about your message.

The opposite tendency is to speak too slowly, a trait common to old-

2. William G. Hoffman, *How to Make Better Speeches* (New York: Funk & Wagnalls, 1976), 196.
3. Spurgeon, *Lectures,* 115.

316 ♦ POWER IN THE PULPIT

er preachers. As a person matures, the mind has a tendency to slow down. Thoughts normally do not come as rapidly as they once did. Also, the older preacher may not have the physical vigor he once had. All of us have had the experience of listening to some dear brother who spoke so slowly that we found it difficult to stay with him. Our minds were constantly going off on little mental excursions. Avoid speaking so slowly that your listeners constantly have to work at listening to you.

Thus, the rate of your delivery becomes your helper when you use it with variety. The rate should never be constant. To speak too fast or too slow all the time is deadly to effective delivery. Be constantly changing your rate according to the following determinants:

RATE REGULATION

Emphasis. Less important content may be spoken more quickly. The more important statements of your sermon may be slowed down for emphasis.

Building size. The size of the building in which you speak will have much to do with your rate. A smaller room will allow you to speak a bit faster. The larger the room, the greater the reverberation. In these situations you must be more deliberate as you preach.

Mood. The intellectual and emotional content of what you are saying also should guide you in the rate you use. Grief and contempt are slow. Joy and enthusiasm are faster.[4]

PACE

Your rate should never be allowed to become constant. A sense of flow should characterize the entire message. Good delivery has a sense of pace. The sermon marches with a sense of movement.

Though change in pace is needed throughout, hesitation should be avoided as the rate is suited to the desired meanings of particular words. The thoughts and emotions conveyed should themselves alter pacing appropriately as you proceed through the message. Your sermon must never sound as if you have memorized it or as if you are reading it. It should demonstrate the same flexibility in rate and pace as in your everyday

4. Grand Fairbanks, *Voice and Articulation Drillbook* (New York: Harper & Row, 1940), 112.

speech. Changing pace is intended to keep your audience rested, refreshed, and anxious to go on with you.

Pace may be changed in any number of ways. You may make a quick change in speech content. You may tell a story, a joke, or make a pointed remark. Just be sure your story or other element is related to the last thing you said before you shifted. You may direct a remark to some well-known individual in the audience. This technique never fails to arouse a lethargic audience—especially the dear brother or sister you address! Change of pace also may be achieved by lowering the voice in volume, pitch, or both. Pause, cough, tell a funny story, slap on the podium, raise your voice, whisper—but do something. W. A. Criswell once stopped in the middle of a sermon to give three cheers for the Baylor football team! He certainly had the attention of the people again.

VOLUME

If the preacher speaks with too much volume, he sounds unnatural and oppressive.[5] Again, Spurgeon warned:

> Two or three earnest men now present are tearing themselves to pieces by needless bawling; their poor lungs are irritated and their larynx inflamed by boisterous shouting, from which they seem unable to refrain. . . . Be a little economical with that enormous volume of sound. In fact, too much noise stuns the ear, creates reverberations and echoes, and effectually injures the power of your sermons.[6]

Regrettably, preachers have a tendency to go to extremes in the use of volume. The preacher is either so soft he cannot be heard or so loud the ears of the people are overwhelmed.

Variety, once again, is the key. Volume should be governed by content. A change in volume indicates the importance of what is being said. Volume may be a great help in giving proper emphasis to important ideas you hope to convey. Sometimes you should open all the stops. If you are loud all the time, however, then nothing you say will receive appropriate emphasis.

At other times, a whisper can be even more effective than a loud exclamation. Vary your degrees of loudness. Try going from a whisper to a roar and from a roar to a whisper.[7] Again, allow the content of your ser-

---

5. Hoffman, *Better Speeches*, 99.
6. Spurgeon, *Lectures*, 116.
7. Milton Dickens, *Speech: Dynamic Communication* (New York: Harcourt Brace Jovanovich, 1954), 186.

mon to dictate the appropriate volume used. Do not make the mistake of thinking that mere loudness is evidence of preaching in the power of the Holy Spirit. To be sure, there are times when the Holy Spirit will utilize the full capacity of your vocal strength. Do not forget, however, that sometimes the Lord speaks in a still, small voice.

STRESS

The use of proper stress can be just as effective as volume in conveying what we want to say. We stress a word by making it stand out in a phrase. We may do this by means of higher pitch, longer duration of tone, or increased volume. Choose the words that are to receive prominence in what you say and focus your attention on them. Give stress to the thought-bearing words in your sentences.[8]

Nouns, verbs, adjectives, and adverbs usually carry most of the meaning and, therefore, need high intensity. On the other hand, conjunctions, articles, prepositions, and pronouns usually have lower intensity.[9] As you listen to normal conversation, notice the words people emphasize. Notice how effective communicators stress certain key words.

Coupling volume and stress will enable you to be much more effective in your sermon delivery. Project your voice according to the size of the room in which you speak. Generally, you will need enough volume to reach every person in the room. Be constantly aware of your audience. By means of your voice reach out to your people with every sentence. Do not think, however, in terms of throwing your voice at your listeners. Rather, speak as if you were hitting baseballs—high flies to your audience instead of low grounders. Hit them up and over to the people. Give the sense that you know what you are doing. Convey the awareness that volume and stress are your servants.

Keep in mind that variety is again the key. Vary your volume. Give appropriate stress to the most important words in your sentences and phrases. Deemphasize nonessential words. Use volume and stress together to increase the "listenability" of your sermon. Sometimes use stress instead of volume for emphasis. Give a word a higher pitch with increased volume. Then speak a word on a lower pitch with less volume. But always subjugate volume and stress to the ideas you seek to convey.

PITCH

In order to use speech variation effectively, the preacher needs to

8. Robert King, *Forms of Public Address* (Indianapolis: Bobbs-Merrill, 1969), 80.
9. Fairbanks, *Voices and Articulation,* 122.

know the difference between habitual pitch and optimum pitch. Habitual pitch is the level on the scale at which you most often speak. Optimum pitch is the level at which your voice functions best. These two levels may or may not be the same.[10] Each human voice has an appropriate pitch. This pitch changes naturally during the maturing of the voice. Once puberty has been passed, however, one particular pitch is best for your voice.

You easily may find your optimum pitch. Using a piano, sing down to the lowest note you can sing comfortably. Go up the scale five piano keys. This pitch usually will be the one you should use most of the time. Check tapes of your sermons to see if you are speaking, for the most part, at your optimum level. Young preachers, especially, have a tendency to develop a habitual pitch different from their optimum pitch. They want to sound mature and impressive, so they push their voices into the lower registers. This habit puts an unhealthy strain upon the vocal folds and creates an unnatural sound. Each preacher must be willing to accept the voice God has given him. That voice then must be trained and developed to its fullest extent.

The pastor will be wise to utilize as wide a variety in pitch as possible. A good preacher distributes his voice over a range of approximately two octaves. Do not be content to stay within a restricted range.

Spurgeon described the importance of using the full range of your vocal instrument: "Brethren, in the name of everything that is sacred, ring the whole chime in your steeple, and do not dun your people with the ding-dong of one poor cracked bell."[11] Regarding the need for variety in pitch, he further appealed:

> I have often in this room compared the voice to a drum. If the drummer should always strike in one place on the head of his drum, the skin would soon wear into a hole; but how much longer it would have lasted him if he had varied his thumping and had used the entire surface of the drum-head! So it is with a man's voice. If he uses always the same tone, he will wear a hole in that part of the throat which is most exercised in producing that monotony.[12]

Fully utilize all the notes the Lord has given you in your vocal instrument.

The older preachers used to give this kind of advice about pitch:

10. Anna Lloyd Neal, *A Syllabus for Fundamentals of Speech* (Greenville, S.C.: Bob Jones Univ., 1977), 36.
11. Spurgeon, *Lectures*, 111.
12. Ibid., 119.

"Start low, go slow; rise higher, strike fire." This counsel was their way of saying that it is normally good to start in the lower pitch levels, enabling you to rise in pitch as you warm to the sermon. To start in the very highest pitch leaves you nowhere to go later on in the message. Do not be afraid to drop into the lower range at certain key points. Those ranges can be very effective. If you throw force into them, they will be heard along with your higher notes.

INFLECTION

The direction of inflection points to what you are trying to say. For instance, a rising inflection indicates that the mind is looking forward. Rising inflections suggest question, doubt, uncertainty, or incompleteness. Consider these statements: "Is this your book?" "Are you going to town?" When book and town are said with rising inflection, question and uncertainty are conveyed.

Downward inflections generally are used to indicate that a thought is being completed. An inflection that falls toward the end gives the impression of certainty, emphasis, and strong affirmation. For example: "This is your pen." A circumflex inflection indicates irony, innuendo, sarcasm, cynicism, or skepticism. Consider these statements: "Well, look who's here!" "Who do you think you are?"[13] A flat inflection indicates disappointment or disgust. Consider: "I can't go." "It is all over."

INFLECTION CORRECTION

Mark Twain was known as a profane man. His language was often very shocking. His wife, Olivia, tried desperately to break him of the habit of swearing. Getting ready for dinner on an occasion, he frantically was working with the collar button of his dress shirt. The button slipped through his fingers and rolled under the dresser out of sight. From his lips came some of his most spectacular speech. Olivia was disgusted and angry. She decided to teach him a lesson to shame him. Word for word she repeated what Mark had said, then defiantly waited for his reply. Mark looked at her silently for a time, then said, "Livy, you got the words right, but the tune's all wrong."[14] Inflection plays an important role in carrying the meaning of what you say!

---

13. John Eisenson, *Voice and Diction* (New York: Macmillan, 1974), 100.
14. Quoted in Hoffman, *Better Speeches,* 200.

The length of inflection is also important in conveying meaning. The most important word in a sentence usually is given the longer inflection. Length of inflection often will indicate the degree of importance of what is said. Intensity and excitement also are indicated.

Abruptness of inflection is also significant. A gradual change in inflection indicates calmness, repose, contemplation, and command. On the other hand, an abrupt change in inflection indicates excitement, intensity, and vigor.

Proper inflection of words may best be achieved through clear thinking about what you are going to say. Your sermon should have enough mental pictures to create expressive inflection in your words.

Phrasing

Proper phrasing has been described as just a simple matter of starting where you should and stopping where you should![15] Most of us who speak frequently do not find phrasing to be that easy. Much thought and effort must be given to properly arranging the words into good thought units. Some phrases may be spoken quickly with little force. Other phrases are more significant. They must be spoken more slowly, with emphasis.

Effective speech must have distinction in its phrasing. The preacher whose sermons change lives will employ not only accuracy but also power in his use of phrasing. Group words together. Give proper emphasis to the main words in your phrases. Avoid not only the one-tone voice but also the one-tone mind. The one-tone approach makes all matters in your phrase of equal value—there is no emphasis, no hurrying over unimportant details, no slowing up at more significant phrases. This approach simply is characterized by a steady drone. Avoid also the string-of-beads tendency. In this approach, one fact is strung along after another with no observable relationship between them. Keep your audience aware of the important facts in each phrase as you speak.[16]

Good phrasing and breathing are related. The preacher must learn to breathe before and after complete thought units. Breathing must be coordinated with phrases so that the thought unit will not be interrupted as he stops for breath. If the preacher interrupts the thought unit, he likely will hinder good understanding of what he is trying to say.

Pause

Rudyard Kipling said, "By your silence you shall speak."[17] Pauses can

---

15. King, *Public Address*, 80.
16. H. A. Overstreet, *Influencing Human Behavior* (New York: Norton, 1925), 83–84.
17. Quoted in Haddon W. Robinson, *Biblical Preaching* (Grand Rapids: Baker, 1980), 206.

be meaningful in the delivery of a sermon. Every good preacher knows the value of a pause placed at just the right point. Pauses serve a multitude of purposes:

PAUSE FOR A PURPOSE

1. Pauses permit variety in the voice.
2. Pauses help the preacher keep his speaking rate from becoming too fast.
3. Pauses enable the preacher to regulate his pace so that his sermon delivery is convincingly like that of conversation.
4. Pauses enable the preacher to keep his pitch level from rising to a nervous squeak.
5. Pauses may indicate a change of topic.
6. Pauses encourage better stress and inflection on significant words and phrases.[18]
7. Pauses are excellent ways to emphasize punch lines.[19]
8. Pauses allow the listeners to comprehend the preacher's preceding statement(s).

Actually, pauses are not merely times of silence and should not be confused with hesitation. Hesitation is empty silence—the silence of frozen forgetting. Pause is eloquent and meaning-conveying silence.[20]

Pauses help the preacher physically. They allow him opportunity to replenish his supply of breath. They assist him mentally. When he pauses, he looks ahead to his next thought. Pauses assist the preacher psychologically as well. During pauses, he may look at the listeners, gauging whether or not they understand what he is saying. A pause may be used effectively before an important word, calling attention to it. A pause may heighten the dramatic effect of what one is saying. The preacher must be careful, though, to see that his pauses are not all of the same length. Without adequate, well-timed pauses, his sermon will sound rattled off.

Pauses also are one of the most useful tools in securing or regaining attention. Spurgeon said:

---

18. Hoffman, *Better Speeches,* 100.
19. Mary Forrest and Margot A. Olson, *Exploring Speech Communication* (St. Paul: West, 1981), 97.
20. Ibid., 196.

Pull up short every now and then, and the passengers on your coach will wake up. The miller goes to sleep while the millwheels revolve, but if by some means or other the grinding ceases, the good man starts and cries, What now? On a sultry summer's day, if nothing will keep off the drowsy feeling, be very short, sing more than usual, or call on a brother or two to pray. Make a point of interjecting arousing parentheses of quietude. Speech is silver, but silence is golden when hearers are inattentive. Keep on, on, on, on, with the commonplace matter and monotonous tone, and you are rocking the cradle, and deeper slumbers will result; give the cradle a jerk, and the sleep will flee.[21]

Spurgeon spoke rightly of the natural, practical effect of pause in recapturing the attention of the wandering mind.

Pauses also serve the people. Whereas for the preacher a pause primarily looks forward, for the people the pause primarily looks backward. A pause gives them opportunity to think about what the speaker has just said, to feel, and to respond mentally and emotionally to the content of his words. The people are given a brief mental digestion time. In a sense, pauses also allow the people to look forward. A well-timed pause may create in the congregation a sense of anticipation and interest in what the preacher is going to say next.

Pauses should be used properly. Avoid the tendency to fill the silence with interjections or speech tics such as *er* and *uh*. Robinson called these "word whiskers."[22] For a preacher, such filler words may be "Praise the Lord," "Amen," or "Glory to God." Although nothing is wrong with using any of these expressions, the capricious use of such terms simply to fill in your pauses will rob them of their spiritual meaning and impact. Instead, you will convey a sense of nervousness.

Do not be afraid to use pause. The tool can do much for your sermon delivery. Do not be afraid of silence. Silence can be one of the most meaningful times of the sermon.

SPEAKING WITH THE BODY

When you preach to your congregation, you convey your message in two ways. You speak by means of words—verbal communication. You also speak by means of body language—nonverbal communication. These two means of communicating must complement and support one another. If they conflict, the nonverbal message is more likely to be believed than the verbal.

21. Spurgeon, *Lectures,* 138.
22. Robinson, *Biblical Preaching,* 206.

Communication experts have given nonverbal communication increased attention in recent years. Research has shown that nonverbal signs and symbols are much more significant than we previously imagined. Studies reveal that 7 percent of the impact of a speaker's message comes through his words, 38 percent springs from his voice, but an overwhelming 55 percent comes from facial expressions.[23]

Effective delivery must include conscious and appropriate use of nonverbal communication. The preacher will soon discover that he still is communicating even when he is not speaking. Feelings are communicated nonverbally. If the preacher's body is not responsive to what he says, he is not likely to be heard. Therefore, the body is an active participant in effective sermon delivery.

ESTABLISHING PULPIT PRESENCE

The term *kinesics* has to do with the interaction between what the voice is saying and what the body is saying. Normally the relationship is called body language. The preacher's use of body language largely will dictate what is sometimes referred to as *pulpit presence*. A preacher's pulpit presence is extremely important in preaching. Eye contact, gestures, facial expressions, posture, and mobility all determine the quality of your pulpit presence and give your listeners clues as to what you really feel about God, yourself, and them.

Eye Contact

Eye contact is an extremely important psychological aspect of the preacher-audience dynamic and must be understood if the preacher is to communicate effectively. Look at your audience, and your delivery will be much more effective. Cicero said, "Everything depends on the countenance, while the countenance itself is entirely dominated by the eye."[24]

Many congregations sense that their pastor is not really looking at them. He seems to be looking only toward them. That perception is extremely detrimental. The impression is given that the speaker is distant, aloof, or uninterested. Avoiding the listeners' eyes sends a message of extreme discomfort or lack of interest. The preacher's credibility is reduced. Look into the eyes of the various members of the congregation. Any part of your audience constantly ignored will feel less and less involved in the preaching event. Stott said, "Look at your people face to face and eyeball to eyeball. Always talk to people. Never merely spray the building with

---

23. Ibid., 193.
24. Cicero, *De Oratore* (London: William Heinemann, 1942), III, 59, 221.

words."[25] The use of good eye contact may be the most effective means of nonverbal communication.

Looking at the people will also enable the preacher to pick up the response of his congregation. He can tell if they understand what he is saying and can adjust his message accordingly. If they do not seem to understand, he can repeat, simplify, or illustrate. If they are not interested, he can use a variety of means to stir their interest. He may adapt his style and manner to their response. The preacher must constantly be searching for signs of the hearers' reactions to his message and modify his delivery accordingly. By their facial expressions, blandness, or frowns he may determine what they are thinking.

Do not hesitate to isolate certain people in the congregation to serve as barometers. A few people will have unusually expressive faces. You can easily read their reactions at a glance. Should their eyes not meet yours for a period of time, chances are the attention of your entire audience is straying. Take this signal to change pace before your crowd becomes noticeably restless.

Looking selected individuals in the eye benefits every person sitting in that section. You do not have to look at each person in the section. The fact that you are looking at one gives the entire section a feeling you are looking at them. Also, this technique creates a sense of expectancy. If you look at one person in the section, you may look at others. Be careful to include every section of your building in your eye contact. Simple eye contact also suggests an interest in people. This perception might be called eye touching. Eye touching says you value another person's independence, knowledge, and friendship.[26]

In certain circumstances you will want to look away from your audience. You may be describing a falling building, and therefore you look upward as a gesture to convey the effect of height. Maybe you are telling a story and wish to dramatize someone who was downcast or discouraged. You naturally would look down in this situation. On these occasions, regain eye contact as soon as possible.

Gestures

Some thoughts are better expressed by gestures rather than words or facial expressions. Fingers on closed lips are sometimes more effective than saying, "Be quiet!" Outstretched arms mean more to a little child than merely saying, "Come here." Pointing to the door often more effectively says, "Leave the room," than any language or look could express.

25. John R. W. Stott, *Between Two Worlds* (Grand Rapids: Eerdmans, 1982), 252.
26. Perry W. Buffington, "Psychology of Eyes," *Sky* 13, no. 2 (February 1984): 92–96.

A JESTER ON GESTURES

Spurgeon had an interesting as well as humorous discussion of the problems of gestures.[27]

He talked first about the *stiff gesture:*

> Men who exhibit this horror appear to have no bend in their bodies and to be rigid about the joints. The arms and legs are moved as if they were upon iron hinges and were made of exceedingly hard metal. A wooden anatomical doll, such as artists use, might well represent their limbs so straight and stiff, but it would fail to show the jerks with which those limbs are thrown up and down.

Next he mentioned the regular *mechanical gesture* as one used by men who seem not to be living beings possessed of will and intellect. They appear to be mere automatons formed to go through prescribed movements at precise intervals.

Finally, he talked about the *ill-timed gesture.* In this example he referred to the preacher whose hands do not keep time with his lips. He said:

> The good brother is a little behind hand in his action, and therefore the whole operation is out of order. You cannot at first make the man out at all; he appears to chop and thump without rhyme or reason, but at last you perceive that his present action is quite appropriate to what he said a few seconds before.

Naturally employed, a gesture is any movement that helps express or emphasize an idea or emotional response. In some ways, gestures embrace the entire field of kinesics. Included are clearly discernible bodily movements and all subtle changes of posture and muscle tone. This discussion, however, will treat facial expressions, posture, and mobility separately. Gestures, here, primarily refer to movements of the hands and arms.

Gestures are an expression of the preacher's use of his whole body as he preaches. This holistic action is twofold. First, *overt* action involves body movements that are clearly observable. This action is manifested in the conspicuous play of the muscles and major members of the body. Sec-

27. Spurgeon, *Fundamentals of Speech Lectures,* 289–95.

ond, there is *covert* action, the action that involves subtle muscle tensions and relaxations.[28]

Some people think of gestures only in terms of overt actions. This understanding is limited in that the various parts of the body do not function separately. Rather, they involve a follow-through that is affected by and affects the whole body's degree of muscle tension. As the preacher learns to use his body in preaching, his muscles learn to respond without apparent prompting or effort. The whole body is brought into play to some extent in all gestures, for gestures are themselves preceded by subtle or more obvious muscle tensions.

Facial Expressions

The countenance of the preacher is vital in good pulpit communication. Earlier we discussed the importance of eye contact. The eyes are the most eloquent part of the body. They have such expressive power that they control to some extent the expression of the whole countenance. By them we search and discover. By them we project cheer, fear, or anticipation. Who has not been enchanted by the dancing eyes of a little child or depressed by the empty stare of the terminally ill?

Physiologists have estimated that the facial musculature is such that more than 20,000 different facial expressions are possible.[29] Television has called attention to the importance of facial expressions.

An audience looks at the preacher as much as it listens to him. You must be ready, therefore, to communicate facially as well as vocally. A fleeting glance may speak volumes. A curl of your lip or a twitch of your nostrils can instantly convey your feelings to the audience. Body communication that is consistent with the words we say can be extremely effective. This observation is true especially of the face. If our facial expressions are consistent with our message, the people will understand we are sincere. Nonverbal expressions such as frowns, excitement, concern, smiles, or happiness help the listener sense that we are truly involved in what we are saying.

Posture

The way you stand in the pulpit communicates to your listeners. Although the preacher should position himself to be comfortable during delivery, he should be more concerned about communicating eagerness and self-confidence.[30] You may feel more comfortable slouching over the pulpit, but your message will be more effectual if people perceive you to be interested in your subject and confident in your presentation of it.

28. Neal, 46.
29. Loren Reid, *Speaking Well* (New York: McGraw-Hill, 1977), 243.
30. Al Fasol, *A Complete Guide to Sermon Delivery* (Nashville: Broadman & Holman, 1996), 79.

The way you position your feet is important. Find a position that enables you to shift the body smoothly from front to back and from side to side. Regarding the communicative ability of such movement, Fasol commented,

> You may move one foot forward and then put most of the body weight on that foot. This causes a slight leaning toward the congregation and communicates a sense of urgency. Conversely, putting most of your weight on the back foot communicates a sense of rejection or withdrawal.[31]

Like other body movements, however, make sure that your posture and its changes are in keeping with your content.

As you change posture to support your message, be careful not to shift your weight from one foot to another in a regular, rhythmic fashion. Such movement creates a swaying motion and is extremely distracting to an audience. Swaying usually results from nervous energy. The preacher normally can correct the action by placing one foot slightly in front of the other and putting most of his weight on the forward foot as noted above.[32]

Mobility

Movement around the platform during preaching can be either distracting or beneficial, depending upon how the preacher uses it. Like other aspects of body language, the relationship of mobility to content determines whether it will be positive or negative.

To be sure, mobility during the preaching event largely is a matter of individual personality. Some preachers are more animated and energetic than others. These men must be careful not to allow their energy to dominate the message to the point of distraction. Preachers who are more reserved have a tendency to remain behind the pulpit or in one place during the entire sermon. Though nothing is wrong with a stationary delivery, these men should be cognizant of the communicative advantage of some mobility. A visual generation accustomed to action via television and theater are more likely to follow a preacher who does not stay in just one place.

Mobility during delivery also should be intentional and deliberate. Like posture, a slow, rhythmic movement gives a lethargic "stroll in the park" impression and can lull the audience to sleep. If and when you move, move aggressively and with purpose. Pause between movements and make an assertion. Then move to another place and say something else. Be careful, however, not to be moving constantly throughout the ser-

31. Ibid., 79–80.
32. Ibid., 80.

mon. Your audience can grow tired following you around. In addition, if you leave your Bible on the pulpit, such constant traveling can detract from your desired emphasis on the text. Make sure that significant blocks of time are spent in stationary positions, especially in front of your Bible. This practice will give your audience time to relax, concentrate, and digest bits of information while maintaining a focus on the Bible.

ENHANCING BODY MOVEMENTS

The essence of effective body language can be summarized by several qualities. Seek to incorporate each one when you speak with your body.

Natural. One of the worst things a preacher can do is to create an atmosphere of artificiality by means of gestures that obviously are practiced and forced. The gestures of some speakers are so preplanned that they actually take away from the message rather than add to it. Body language is true only when it is spontaneous and actually unconscious.

The various aspects of body language—eye contact, facial expression, gestures, and mobility—are in much the same position as the variables in our vocal mechanism. When we see the words we are saying and feel the emotions that flow from our words, correct bodily actions will naturally occur without our giving them conscious attention.

Make your body the servant of your thoughts and feelings. Let its movements arise naturally from what you are saying. If you are talking about a church steeple, the mental pictures behind your words should affect your movements as well. When you see a steeple, you might naturally find yourself wanting to raise your hands and lift your eyes as if to point to the steeple. When you talk about the world, do not only see the world but form the world with your hands and arms. In other words, let your gestures be consistent with the meaning of what you say. A preacher should not be, to misuse Shakespeare, "full of sound and fury, signifying nothing."[33]

Well timed. Issuing forth from naturalness, effective body language is well timed. Any gesture used in a message should accompany or precede the key word or phrase it describes. If the timing is poor, the gesture calls attention to itself instead of undergirding the thought it was intended to serve.

A sermon is delivered effectively when every action of the body so definitely adds to the effectiveness of the ideas it expresses that the listeners are not consciously aware of the bodily movements at all. One Sunday

---

33. Quoted in King, *Public Address,* 2. The expression is from *Macbeth,* act 5, sc. 5., lines 27–28.

morning, a sincere, earnest country preacher was preaching on his favorite subject, the story of David and Goliath. Rather dramatically he recounted how little David whirled the sling around his head and sent the smooth stone unerringly to Goliath's forehead. As the preacher came to the climax of his sermon, his voice rose high with excitement: "You see, folks, the whole point is it wasn't just that little rock that kilt that big bloke—it was the way that kid throwed it!"[34] Effective sermon delivery is not merely speaking a sermon to your people. Be aware of how you "throw" it.

Appropriate. Suit the action to the word and the word to the action. In a sense, the preacher gives two speeches at the same time: that which his listeners hear and that which they see. To be most effective, the minister will mold the two speeches to form one communicative process.

Bodily movements used inappropriately can negate what is being said. For example, take care not to *point* to the audience when you are saying, "Come to Jesus!" You would not want to place your hand on your chest when using the second person pronoun in a sentence. Neither would you shake your clenched fist when describing the peace of God. Like inappropriate use of volume and rate, certain body movements can communicate the opposite of what we actually are saying.

Varied. Body language should be original and varied. Just as sameness in vocal expression will tend toward boredom, so too will repetition of any movement. The body is capable of an amazing number of movements. Use a wide variety of them as you preach. The preacher who stands before his listeners stiff and rigid creates extreme discomfort in his audience and raises questions about his confidence and sincerity. On the other hand, the preacher who appears alive to his message will communicate more effectively with his listeners. Effective body communication lends action to one's message.

Demosthenes was a great public speaker. He said there are only three fundamentals of good speaking: action, action, and action. He was not merely equating action with emotion, nor was he talking about flamboyant gestures. He simply was saying that the message had a force, or enlivening power, about it.[35] The same observation can be made of good preaching when it is served by a variety of bodily movements.

IMPROVING BODY LANGUAGE

Spend some time preparing for sermon delivery by giving attention to

---

34. Quoted in Kenneth McFarland, *Eloquence in Public Speaking* (Englewood Cliffs, N.J.: Prentice-Hall, 1961), 152.
35. R. C. Forman, *Public Speaking Made Easy* (Grand Rapids: Baker, 1967), 61.

its nonverbal aspects. Just as you would work on the different aspects of effective vocal delivery, give some attention to effective body communication. Be aware of the responses your body makes as you think and speak your words in normal conversation. Notice how your eyes and the muscles in your face and body respond to what you are saying, even without prompting or effort. Pay attention, as well, to what you do with your hands. All of your day-to-day body movements come naturally as a result of what you are saying. Allow the same to be true during the delivery of a sermon.

Generally, specific aspects of body language should not be practiced. In earlier years, speakers were trained in elocution and expression with extensive study given to aspects such as gestures. Today, such training is considered unnecessary at best and harmful to good communication at worst. What the preacher does need to know is that body language is a definite part of preaching and should result naturally from an intelligent response to the content of his sermon. Natural impulse should be the foundation of all body language. If a movement of the hand or any other expression does not assist in communicating the sermon, that movement is not a gesture but merely a distracting and annoying movement that calls attention to itself.

Although trying to practice specific gestures usually is fruitless, giving attention to body language in general outside the pulpit may help you use it more naturally and effectively when you are preaching. Some preachers respond bodily to their material with greater ease than do others. If you have difficulty in using your body, practicing while reading aloud might help you. Large, exaggerated movements in practice will have a tendency to set your body free.

Read a sermon aloud. Move freely about the room. Periodically pause in front of a mirror and continue speaking. Respond consciously with pronounced movements to the content of what you are reading. Such overt response will have a tendency to train your muscles to respond to what you say in the pulpit. As you practice, talk with your hands. Use any movements that help you communicate the content of what you are reading.

A distinction should be made between practicing body language to be forced into one's preaching and working on the elimination of detrimental movements. Remember, our task in delivery is to work toward not being a hindrance to the supernatural work of the Holy Spirit through God's Word. Practicing in the above manner can help you catch any habitual bodily movements that are likely to distract your audience and actually hinder communication. We all have a tendency to develop repetitious movements—raising and lowering a hand, tilting the head—that direct attention to ourselves and keep the audience from fully concentrating on the sermon.

In addition to the above routine, review some of your sermons on videotape or get selected individuals to critique your delivery. As you detect distracting and annoying movements, conscientiously work toward eliminating them.

BENEFITS OF BODY SPEECH

Effective, expressive body language is beneficial in several ways. First, it assists verbal communication. We can better explain and picture what we are saying by helping our audiences see birds soar, walls topple, and arrows fly. Second, good bodily movement is a positive factor in holding attention. Motion pictures and television have geared our people to fast-moving, rapid-paced action. The preacher who stands lifelessly and listlessly in the pulpit almost guarantees that his audience will be disinterested. Third, good body language during our message will make our audience sense that they are truly a part of the sermon. As we react expressively to the subject matter, they will react. If we frown as we describe taking a dose of NyQuil, they will frown as well. They will be empathic to what we have to say. Get your audience to react as you do to the various ideas of your sermon. They will become involved creatively in your sermon.

Good sermon delivery involves not only speaking the message with your voice but saying it with your body as well. Shakespeare said, "There was speech in their dumbness, language in their very gesture."[36] Let your body speak for you.

AUGMENTING THE MESSAGE

The realities of the communications revolution discussed in the last chapter can be quite depressing for the expositor. Rather than feeling defeated, however, the pastor should be encouraged greatly for several reasons.

First, as a preacher of the gospel you have a miracle of communication at your disposal. You do not have to communicate the Word of God merely using your own skills as a communicator. The indwelling Holy Spirit is able to take the sermon you preach and apply it with power and effectiveness to your listeners.

Second, modern communications has placed at your disposal wonderful tools to assist you. Some resources have evolved from technological

---

36. Quoted in Hoffman, *Better Speeches*, 102. The statement is from *The Winter's Tale*, act 5, sc. 2, line 12.

advances. Other tools have been around for a while but have increased in relevance due to the nature of contemporary listening audiences. Imagine what the apostle Paul would have done with some of these tools. Preacher, get up to speed on some of the following communications augmentations—and go for it![37]

SOUND REINFORCEMENT

Modern technology makes it possible for the preacher to have better sound reinforcement than any previous generation. Superior sound systems for church auditoriums are now available. That technology, however, often is not used.

Modern churchgoers also attend the great entertainment centers of our nation at which they hear superior sound. Then they go to church and try to listen to a preacher who labors before a microphone preserved from the 1930s. Speakers that appear to have been used in a 1950s movie theater bring the poor sound to their ears. The fact that some preachers are never able to communicate should not shock anyone. More than one pastor has lost his congregation because they literally could not hear him. Today, no excuse is available for churches to have inferior sound reinforcement.

Learn how to use sound effectively. Become acquainted thoroughly with the techniques required in speaking before a microphone. Use the microphone as a tool. Have monitor speakers that pour the sound back on you, giving you a sense of "presence" as you speak. If you can hear yourself, you will relax and be able to say what you want to say in the most effective and forceful manner.

Decisions need to be made about how you will use your sound system. You must decide whether to use a wireless microphone or pulpit microphone, depending upon your style of delivery. The negative factor in a pulpit microphone is that it restricts the preacher's ability to move very much. The positive factor is that it enables him to "milk" the mike, moving in when he wants to be softer and more intimate and then moving back when he wants to use more volume.

Get acquainted with the sound engineer. Again, the man who operates your sound system actually can make or break you as a speaker. Learn to work closely with him. He can help you be a better communicator.

VISUAL AIDS

Through the years, object lessons have been relegated almost exclu-

---

37. See Harold Freeman, *Variety in Biblical Preaching* (1987; reprint, Ft. Worth: Scripta, 1987, 1994), for additional help in many of the areas discussed in this section.

sively to children's sermons. Many pastors frequently use some kind of visual prop to communicate spiritual truth to younger listeners. The fact of the matter, however, is that visual aids enhance communication to listeners of every age, from preschoolers to senior adults. These visible assistants can and should be used to augment biblical exposition whenever helpful and appropriate. In addition to the traditional object lessons of yesterday, many new forms of visual augmentation are available. Computer-generated presentations, video, and drama, as well as traditional object lessons, all can be used to heighten the impact of a sermon.

Caution and discretion must be employed, however, when using visual aids. They should be used, not overused and abused. Some pastors unwittingly use visual aids as a substitute for preaching. Instead of delivering biblical exposition, they simply deliver a presentation that is a series of comments sandwiched between slides or introducing and concluding a drama. Such an approach not only falls short of the nature of preaching, but it is also boring. Think about how you feel when a friend invites you over to watch slides from his recent vacation.

Visual aids are like drugs—you can become overly dependent upon them. The sermon is the oral projection of the truth of the biblical text served by the preacher's personality, experiences, and ideas. The sermon is not a mechanical projection. "No inanimate screen can match a flesh-and-blood presentation."[38] The same assertion can be made regarding other nonhuman objects. The preacher is not a technician, simply introducing slides or other visual aids. Consequently, he must use visuals as a prop, not a crutch.

Two reasons often are cited for filling up contemporary sermons with visual aids. First, an old Chinese adage says "a picture is worth a thousand words." Second, phenomenal things can be done today with graphic arts and other visual augmentations. At the heart of the matter, however, is some preachers' love for toys. Access to state-of-the-art visual enhancements can easily lead to overuse instead of effective use. Humes rightly observed that Americans have a "naive faith in anything mechanical. They are suckers for any new gadget or contraption that they think will do their work for them."[39] The preacher can become dependent on visual aids, thus escaping the stark challenge of preparing adequately or simply facing an audience. Though one picture may be worth a thousand words, another Chinese maxim must be embraced: "The tongue can paint what the eye can't see."

38. James C. Humes, *The Sir Winston Method: The Five Secrets of Speaking the Language of Leadership* (New York: William Morrow, 1991), 130.
39. Ibid., 131.

SLIDING YOUR SERMON

James Humes offered an easy acronym that sums up the dos and don'ts of using slides in a speech.[40] The same counsel can be applied to the use of computer-generated presentations, overhead projections, and other visual aids:

Slogan — Make the caption under each slide a slogan, a punch phrase, or a one-sentence line. Don't write an epistle. If you are putting your outline on a screen, just display the major divisions and maybe selected key points.

Large — Put the print in large caps and use a font that is clearly readable from all points in the room.

Illustration — Keep the illustration—or slide—simple and uncluttered.

Directional — Don't use any kind of directional stick or laser pointer. They're too distracting.

Erase — Erase one picture before you move to the next one. Otherwise, it detracts from your talk. If you have a series of slides, place black ones in between.

Speech — Don't read your sermon from the slide captions. Your audience can read. You are delivering a sermon, not a series of introductions to slides.

Visual aids actually are illustrations. For this reason, the expositor should follow the same counsel in using them that was offered in the discussion of illustrations back in chapter 7. Following those guidelines and keeping the above concerns in mind, seek every appropriate opportunity to augment your sermons with visual aids. They can be used effectively to explain abstract ideas, argue controversial subjects, apply relevant information, or illustrate cloudy concepts. At the same time, visual aids always offer a refreshing change of pace from the bread-and-butter of oral speech.

Numerous software programs for developing computer-generated

40. Ibid., 133.

presentations are available at relatively inexpensive prices. The problem comes with the cost of projectors, screens, proper lighting, and other equipment to use the programs effectively. If you are able to access this kind of equipment and your congregation is open to its use, presentations can be used to display the main divisions or assertions of your sermon, show illustrations or other kinds of art, or simply display the biblical text you are referencing. Boldfaced type, italics, underline, or other highlighting features can be used to call attention to selected material. In addition, slides can be used to guide listeners through an interactive fill-in-the-blank listening guide provided in the worship bulletin or order of service.

The possibilities regarding the use of computer-generated presentations are endless, but several words of counsel are in order. If possible, let someone with expertise develop your slides so that they will be of good quality and so that you do not spend precious study time on technical matters. And allow trained personnel to control slide transitions so that you can be free to concentrate on your message. Do not detract from your preaching ministry because of technical concerns.

Video clips and drama are especially helpful for making connections with the contemporary world and establishing the relevancy of biblical truth. Though great discretion should be used in the choice of clips, a video segment from a familiar movie or television program can go far in helping the audience identify with certain concepts. A clip from a documentary or a recent newscast might serve to bring the text into the contemporary world. Dramas depicting real-life scenarios can be used to introduce or summarize a message, as well as to illustrate or apply some point *within* the sermon. Again, make sure skits are high quality so as not to affect the sermon adversely. Also, video segments and dramas should not be left to the listeners' interpretation. Make sure you always establish a clear connection with your point so that the wrong message is not communicated.

Object lessons are wonderful ways to explain and illustrate biblical truth, as well as to drive a memory stake into the listeners' minds. Use simple items that are familiar to the audience. They can be used to introduce a message or to serve a particular assertion during the sermon. As noted in chapter 7, for example, simply removing a mismatched coat and putting on a matching one may be used to explain Paul's concept of taking off the old man and putting on the new in Ephesians 4:22–24. Such a visual illustration is one that listeners will revisit time after time in the coming week as they stand before mirrors to make sure their clothing is appropriate. A Nike tennis shoe, along with comments on the slogan *Just Do It,* could establish a connection with the Greek word *nika*

PREACHING THE WORD ♦ 337

in Revelation 5:5, which describes the prevailing work of Christ. Jesus did what no one else was worthy to do—take the scroll and open its seals. He *just did it!* A particular object lesson also may be used as a running illustration throughout the sermon. An actual yoke, for example, is tremendously helpful in helping people to understand and apply Jesus' invitation to get in the yoke with Him (Matt. 11:28–30).[41]

In summary, use visuals to reinforce your sermon, not to replace it. Use computer-generated presentations, video clips, dramas, object lessons, and other visuals as appetizers or desserts but not as entire meals. No prop should deflect attention from the preacher or detract from the message. Used correctly, visual aids as well as the personality of the preacher elevate the audience's understanding of the truth of the message. These two components are crucial to real preaching.

INNOVATIVE FORMATS

Certain nontraditional sermon formats provide additional ways to augment sermons. Innovation takes the preacher and the audience outside the normal expectations of the preaching event. Such an experience can be a powerful way to deliver a message that will have long-lasting impact.

Innovation, by nature, implies difference. For something to be innovative, it must be compared to a norm. Consequently, the effectiveness of innovation is only as good as the norm with which it is contrasted. The innovative sermon format is like the drop shot in tennis. The drop shot becomes effective only as the player consistently plays his or her opponent against the baseline. Then, without warning, the ball is merely lobbed just over the net to the surprise of the opponent. The innovative sermon format is only as good as the normal week-by-week delivery of solid biblical exposition. Then and only then will the periodic innovative delivery score many points with its surprise. Like the drop shot, innovation that is used every time will lose its effectiveness.

In addition to visually augmented sermons discussed above, two particular creative formats can serve the preacher well from time to time. The *interactive sermon,* or dialogical message, involves the audience in the preaching event in some physical way. Every sermon should engage the *minds* of the listeners in mental conversation, but the truly interactive sermon usually calls for listeners to respond orally or physically to certain segments of the message. Such interaction may include a question-and-

---

41. See Jim Shaddix, "The Yoke's on You!" *Preaching* 13 (May–June 1998), 33–34.

answer time at some point, the prompting of an oral response to a key issue, or a responsive reading related to the given Scripture text. Pre- and post-sermon feedback groups also can enhance listener involvement. Depending upon the size and nature of the congregation, breaking the audience into small discussion groups or asking them to make some physical gesture of response may be other ways to involve listeners. Simply filling out a listening guide also allows the listeners to interact with the preacher.

When employing interactive augmentation, be careful about two things. First, remember that you are the preacher called to deliver God's message. Do not allow your efforts at audience participation to displace the exposition of Scripture. God's Word is the message that will change people's lives. Audience opinion, reflection, and "sharing" will not. Second, audience response almost always should be controlled by the preacher. Although permitting people to dialogue spontaneously with your sermon might have an occasional place, such activity is dangerous and easily can steer the message off course. Dialogue is better employed when the preacher prompts and guides the responses of the people.

The *segmented sermon* is another innovative way to deliver your message. This innovative approach involves dividing the oral presentation of the sermon into segments, each of which is presented alternately with other mediums of communication or elements of worship. These other components are interspersed at strategic points between selected parts of the message. Freeman observed that "the end result is that the minister does not speak long at any one time, but the total preaching time may equal or exceed that of the normal sermon."[42] Advantages of this technique include accommodation to the limited attention span of modern listeners and the production of a more cohesive worship service.

Many other components might be used in a segmented sermon, including some of the elements discussed above. Scripture readings and responsive readings, various forms of music (congregational, choral, solo, or instrumental), drama, and video clips all can be peppered at key places through the message with powerful impact. A segmented sermon using the Lord's Supper and an actual baptism, for example, is a highly moving way to preach on the death and resurrection of Christ. The expositor may use a variety of components to augment a particular message, or he may use one component that contains different content with each presentation. One sermon might use music, drama, and a responsive reading all at different points in the message. Another sermon might simply use several different video clips strategically placed in the message.

42. Freeman, *Variety in Biblical Preaching*, 174.

PLATFORM DECORUM

The matter of platform decorum is important in augmenting the sermon. Many church traditions have depended on pulpit furniture and certain art forms to serve as symbols of doctrine, church history, and other major elements of the Christian faith. Such matters always must be taken into consideration when determining the degree and type of platform decorum.

Several general suggestions may be offered regarding platform decorum in preaching. (1) Make sure each piece of furniture and decoration serve a purpose. Avoid using elements simply because they always have been used, especially if they are a hindrance to preaching or other aspects of worship. (2) Make sure that platform decorum is attractive and up-to-date. Cluttered and crowded platforms have a tendency to stifle worship participation. Openness seems to encourage freedom and interaction. Dated furniture is an obvious downer. While your decorum always must be appropriate for Christian worship, no reason exists for it to be reflective of several centuries—or even decades—removed. Neither should it be reflective of a den or living room. An overrelaxed atmosphere can impact the worship event adversely. (3) Make sure your platform decorum is functional. Choose styles of furniture and decoration that serve their respective purposes *most effectively*. Issues such as the presence or absence of carpet, the size of the pulpit, and the use of banisters all need to be determined according to how well they enhance the worship experience.

Many believe that our interactive culture today suggests the need to use no pulpit at all. They contend that the pulpit, or even a small lectern, creates a barrier between the preacher and his audience. Though these discussions probably are overrated, the call for more interaction with the listeners needs to be heeded. Former President Richard Nixon was a master at such an approach to public speaking. He called this technique "the man in the arena" format—using no notes, lectern, table, or chair. At the same time, he never spoke off the top of his head. Hours of preparation went into his speeches, including writing them out word for word and committing them to memory.[43]

At the same time, be aware that the presence of a pulpit in the preaching event serves a purpose that is not relevant to political speech-making or other kinds of public speaking. For centuries the pulpit has highlighted the centrality of preaching in the church's worship experience. The physical presence of the "sacred desk" makes a bold statement that the ac-

---

43. Humes, *The Sir Winston Method*, 167.

tivity that takes place in conjunction with it is of utmost importance in the people's encounter with God. For this reason, the use of a pulpit is encouraged strongly.

Should you choose to eliminate the pulpit from your platform decorum, be sure you prepare thoroughly. Do not allow your attempt at interaction with the audience to lead to rambling and shallowness. Furthermore, always carry your open Bible as you stand before the people. Visibly highlight your frequent references to the Scriptures. Never view your Bible as a prop that hinders interaction with the audience. Remember, you want them primarily to interact with the Word of God, not with you as the messenger.

Be aware that the absence of a pulpit or lectern also magnifies poor body language. Poor posture, the absence of hand gestures, and immobility all become more evident. If you preach without a pulpit, give special attention to the matters of kinesics mentioned earlier so that your presentation is natural and appealing. The absence of a pulpit can work against you if you are not careful.

One final word should be noted regarding platform decorum: *This issue is not a hill worth dying on.* If adding, removing, or altering furniture or decoration will create dissension in the congregation, do not make it a major item on your agenda. The pastor always should employ great wisdom, discernment, and other leadership skills when addressing this subject. Be patient and buy the right to make needed changes. The gospel can be proclaimed powerfully even when platform decorum is not ideal.

DELIVERING WITHOUT NOTES

One of the biggest complaints people make about their pastor is that he uses a manuscript or notes. Constantly looking down at his paper hinders the effectiveness of his delivery. Certainly, some men can use a manuscript or sermon notes quite well. They have developed techniques that enable them to rely upon some form of written sermon help without making it noticeable. Most preachers, however, never develop such an ability. Consequently, the best way to deliver expository sermons is to use no notes at all. This approach is called *free delivery.*

Many of the great preachers in the Christian faith have used the free delivery method. Alexander Maclaren prepared for each sermon very carefully. Actually, he prepared more carefully than if he were planning to read the message or speak it from memory. Then he allowed the words to well up from his heart at the moment of delivery. G. Campbell Morgan, that "Prince of Expositors," also used this method. Morgan believed that a manuscript or notes would interfere with the eye contact characteristic of animated conversation.[44]

Understanding Free Delivery

Free delivery is characterized by the preparation of a full or partial manuscript, complete familiarity with the written material by identity instead of memory, and delivery of the sermon without the use of the notes.[45] Highlighting the rhetorical benefit, Brown, Clinard, and Northcutt said the approach

> has every advantage of other delivery options without their inherent disadvantages. Like the manuscript and memory methods, it affords the most careful preparation, but it does not limit audience rapport or pulpit freedom. Like the extemporaneous method, it demands creative thought during delivery and affords maximum rhetorical excellence, while at the same time demanding more rigorous preparation.[46]

In essence, free delivery is the best of all worlds in the presentation of the exposition.

Numerous other advantages also characterize free delivery. Great freshness in expression is more likely with this approach. When the actual expression is reserved for the moment of delivery, the preacher may have in his full control all the variable factors in a good speaking situation. Regarding this connection Broadus said:

> If, full of his theme and impressed with its importance, he [the preacher] presently secures the interested and sympathizing attention of even a few good listeners, and the fire of his eyes comes reflected back from theirs, till electric flashes pass to and fro between them and his very soul glows and flames—he cannot fail sometimes to strike out thoughts more splendid and more precious than ever visit his mind in solitary musing.[47]

Free delivery is a powerful medium of spontaneous expression.

Furthermore, free delivery allows the preacher to observe with greater awareness how his message is being received. As he continues through the sermon, he may change the ways of expression as well as the manner of his delivery, according to the response of the audience. In this manner the ser-

---

44. Andrew Blackwood, *Expository Preaching for Today* (Grand Rapids: Baker, 1943), 157.
45. Ralph L. Lewis, *Persuasive Preaching Today* (Ann Arbor, Mich.: LithoCrafters, 1979), 245.
46. Brown, Clinard, and Northcutt, 191.
47. John A. Broadus, *On the Preparation and Delivery of Sermons*, 4th ed., Vernon L. Stanfield (1870; revision, New York: Harper & Row, 1979), 327.

mon may be preached fully utilizing the voice, the eye, the body, and every factor of speaking just as they are intended to be used. Speaking freely also helps the preacher develop freedom and spontaneity of expression. He will learn to voice new thoughts that come to him as he delivers his sermon.

Free delivery helps develop what Jay Adams called *full fluency,* or the ability to choose words that are right orally and psychologically at high speed and arrange them in clear and effective speech.[48] Adams also mentioned the *jelling factor* that comes into play in free delivery. As the preacher preaches, careful preparation and previous extensive thought come together.[49]

Free delivery can have some disadvantages, however. If the preacher is not careful, he may find himself using the same words, phrases, and terminology over and over. He also may face the danger of rambling. Furthermore, preachers who speak freely especially well may tend to abuse the ability. When the preacher relies too heavily upon his gifts in free speaking, he may tend to relax his study habits. When this laziness sets in, free delivery becomes extemporaneous or impromptu delivery instead, which generally makes for bad preaching. Done poorly, free delivery can bring discredit to the expository method of sermon preparation.

THE DELIVERY DILEMMA

Each individual preacher has to determine which approach to delivery best fits his own personality. At the same time, all preachers should be open to mastering the approach or approaches that communicate the Word of God in the most effective way. Basically, sermons can be delivered in four ways. Below, these methods are presented according to varying degrees of preparation and written form.

Manuscript. In this method the sermon has been written out in full, and the preacher reads the manuscript word for word. The great advantage of this approach is that you can give careful attention to the choice of your words and the beauty of the language. Also, it all but eliminates any anxiety about the possibility of forgetting your sermon. A sermon that is read, however, most often will sound read. Rare is the preacher who can read so well that the message seems to be coming from his heart as well as from his head. Reading a manuscript tends to lose the sense of live, personal communication, while breeding a strong likelihood of monotony.

---

48. Jay Adams, *Pulpit Speech* (Phillipsburg, N.J.: Presby. & Ref., 1971), 116.
49. Ibid., 114.

Memory. This approach calls for writing out a manuscript in full or at least in detail, committing it to memory, then delivering it without any reference to manuscript or notes. Again, a memorized sermon usually sounds as if it has been memorized. You always run the danger of lapses in memory as well. To attempt to deliver an entire sermon depending only upon one's powers of memory is a feat most preachers would hesitate to attempt.

Free. This method also assumes careful and thorough preparation in the study. A full or partial manuscript usually will be written. The actual vocalization of the sermon, however, is left to the moment of delivery. While preaching, the preacher uses no written notes other than maybe brief notations in his Bible or a skeletal outline on a small sheet of paper. The logical flow of ideas clearly is established. The sequence of ideas is the same as the prepared written material, but the choice of the particular words may vary at the time of delivery.

Extemporaneous. Also called impromptu speech, this approach involves the preacher's speaking "off the cuff" or "from the top of his head." No prior preparation is made. He stands and says what comes to his mind at the moment of delivery. The occasions when such a method would be used are rare. This method is completely contrary to the expositional process discussed in this book. Outside of few exceptions, effective expository sermons cannot be delivered this way. From time to time the preacher may suddenly be called upon to deliver a message. In those times, however, he certainly will draw upon previous preparation.

DELIVERING THE SERMON FREELY

Free delivery is best done by means of a composite approach that utilizes the advantages of several different kinds of sermon delivery. Such a method employs all the advantages of the written sermon without reaping the disadvantage of trying to read a manuscript in the pulpit. The approach involves careful preparation, yet retains the dynamics of free delivery. The principles of mental vitalization discussed in the last chapter will inform this process. This basic pattern can be summarized in four words:

Organization. If you have followed the process of exposition to this point, your sermon should be carefully prepared and well organized. The sermon should have minimal main divisions that are clear, concise, and simple. If your sermon is organized properly, you are well on the way to note-free delivery. Check one last time to ensure that your message is well organized.

Memorization. After your sermon is organized properly, a certain amount of memorization is necessary. At the very least, your main divisions must be memorized. If you have drawn them from the Scripture passage itself, mere reference to the passage will help you to recall them. Certain key phrases may need to be memorized.

Perhaps a better word than memorize would be *familiarize*, for if you memorize these phrases or key expressions too intently, your eyes may be lackluster and focus inward as you try to remember them during preaching.[50] Try reading your notes aloud a number of times. Think about what you are saying as you vocalize each expression. Then put the notes aside and try to re-create the basic sections of your message. Overlearn your material. Depend on *logical* memory rather than verbal memory.

Saturation. Once you have memorized—or familiarized—key portions, immerse yourself in your message. Get yourself into the sermon and get the sermon into you. Let the sermon become a part of your very being. Stamp the essentials of your message upon your consciousness so deeply that you will not fail to recall them. As the time approaches for the delivery of the sermon, review it again and again. On the night before you preach, go over it before going to bed. If you make this exercise the last thing you do, it will help put the subconscious mind to work on the message.

Presentation. When the time comes to preach, rely upon the Lord to help you. Prayer has been a vital part of your preparation all along the way. Now you are ready to share with the people what God has revealed to you from His Word and what has been indelibly stamped upon your mind and heart. If you forget something, do not panic. Times will come when you leave out something that you thought to be very important. If the impression of what you wanted to say was so weak that you could not remember, however, it may have been just as well that the material was left out of the sermon. In a positive vein, often thoughts you had *not* intended to include will come during the delivery of the message. This occurrence will become a very exciting part of your preaching ministry. Simply prepare as if it all depends upon you, then stand to preach as if it all depends upon the Lord.

USING NOTES WITHOUT BEING NOTICED

Expounding the Word without the use of any notes is encouraged strongly. If, however, after working hard at a totally free delivery, you discover that you are much more comfortable using a full manuscript or detailed notes, learn to use them well. Your goal should be to handle your notes in such a way that your listeners do not realize you are using them.

50. Dorothy Sarnoff, *Speech Can Change Your Life* (New York: Dell, 1970), 203.

Even Koller, while titling his work *Expository Preaching Without Notes,* contended that such an approach did not suggest necessarily the absence of *any* form of notes in the pulpit.[51]

The key to developing such an art, then, is twofold. (1) Never say anything while your eyes are looking down. (2) Use good body language to offset your dependence upon notes. Speakers who try to read from prepared notes in a natural style normally fail for two major reasons: their pacing sounds unnatural, or unconversational, and they lose eye contact with the audience. If you can avoid looking at your notes while communicating their content, you will be able to simulate the pace and look of conversational delivery.[52]

Simulating the pace of conversational delivery can be attained by following a simple procedure practiced by great speech makers such as Winston Churchill, Franklin Roosevelt, and Ronald Reagan. Humes called the technique the "snapshot/snatch plan" for reading a speech.[53] Each of these speakers would look down at one or two lines of his manuscript, snapshot—or snatch—the words by memorizing them, and then look toward the audience to conversationalize the expressions.

The technique is easily adapted to preaching, especially when using a full manuscript in the pulpit. Practice with your sermon manuscript. Place the document on a makeshift pulpit. Glance down and memorize a couple of phrases or sentences. Then bring your head back up and, while looking at a fixed object across the room, conversationalize aloud what you just memorized. The procedure can be summarized as follows:

SERMON SNAPSHOTS

Step #1 Look down and snapshot a phrase or two.

Step #2 Look up and pause.

Step #3 Deliver the words conversationally and pause.

Step #4 Look down and take another snapshot.

Step #5 Look up and pause.

Step #6 Deliver the words conversationally.

51. Charles W. Koller, *Expository Preaching Without Notes* (Grand Rapids: Baker, 1962), 88–89.
52. Humes, *The Sir Winston Method,* 158–60.
53. Ibid., 160.

Notice the inclusion of the *pause* in the summary procedure. As you develop this technique, do not be afraid of pause, for it is the most powerful component of the whole process. In fact, the pause actually enables you to read your sermon while keeping your eyes fixed on the audience. Additionally, the pause allows your listeners to digest your words. When you stop and think about it, pauses are what make speech sound conversational. Conversation is not nonstop—it is peppered with pauses. If you will pause, especially after you bring your head back up, your listeners will think that you simply are glancing at notes instead of actually reading from a manuscript.[54]

When you prepare your manuscript for use in the pulpit, make it reader-friendly. Type or write it triple-spaced in bulleted lines with built-in pauses. Use a larger font if you desire. Indent every new sentence like a paragraph. Your pulpit copy should not resemble an article. If it does, it will sound like an article. In an article, words are laid out one after another, broken not by phrase or thought but by the right margin. Such a layout is not conversational. Print your sermon like prose, and it will sound prosaic. Instead, format it as you want to say it, including the pauses. "Lay it out like verse."[55]

You may be thinking that an entire sermon formatted in this way will take up many pages, especially if it is printed on half sheets. You are right. The number of pages will not matter, however, if you handle them right during delivery. Do not turn over each page as you finish preaching from it. Such a practice is distracting and tells the audience you are reading the lines instead of speaking from notes. Put your notes on the right side of the pulpit. Your Bible either can be held in your right hand or placed at the center of the pulpit just above your notes. As you finish each page slide it with your left hand to the left side of the pulpit (you can put them back in the right order after the sermon). Format your manuscript in such a way that you plan for the page breaks while you are either looking at the audience or reading from the biblical text. This practice will go a long way toward making your message more conversational.

PROCLAIMING FROM THE HEART

To be sure, spiritual fervor must flow through a man from outset to conclusion in the preaching event. In chapter 2, we noted that such fervor is manifested toward the beginning of the process in the anointing of God on the preacher's life. At the moment of delivery, this fervor surfaces in the

---

54. Ibid., 161–62.
55. Ibid., 165–56.

passion of the preacher for both the message and the listeners. Although these two ingredients each have distinctive qualities, they undoubtedly are bound together in an inseparable relationship when it comes to proclaiming God's Word. When one is present, the other is surely close by. When one is absent, the other is unlikely to be manifested either. Thankfully, both ingredients are available to the preacher who desires to preach with power. The final word about exposition, regardless of whether or not you augment your message creatively or preach without notes, must be given to the need for passion—heart—in the preaching event.

THE NATURE OF HEART PREACHING

Passionate preaching flows from the heart. To a large degree the modern pulpit is devoid of passion. Few seem to have the element of heart in their preaching styles. We need a return to heart preaching. Perhaps some would use other terminology. Perhaps you would prefer the term *sincere*. Or maybe you like the word *earnest*. Whatever you choose to call it, we desperately need it! When the preacher's heart is on fire, his speech comes as a volcanic flow. To be genuinely effective, preaching must be eloquence on fire. The preacher must preach from his heart as well as from his head. He must combine proper exposition with heartfelt exhortation.

Heart preaching issues forth from a broken heart. Modern preaching has become too dry-eyed. There needs to be a return to genuine, heartfelt weeping in the pulpit. Joel admonished, "Let the priests, who minister to the Lord, weep between the porch and the altar" (Joel 2:17). Many preachers have lost their capacity to weep. They have become so professional, academic, and intellectual that they do not seem to feel what they say. There even seems to be an aversion to any expression of emotion in the pulpit. This affliction is not limited to liberal preachers. Many conservatives suffer from the same malady. Many of us are much too casual and matter-of-fact in our preaching. This kind of preaching will not move modern men. Samuel May said to Lloyd Garrison, "Oh, my friend, do try to be more cool; why, you are all on fire." Garrison replied, "I have need to be on fire, for I have mountains of ice about me to melt."

Sermons actually are born in the heart. Though the preacher gets his sermon from the Bible, he must bring it to life in his heart. Though he may prepare his message on paper, he must deliver it from his heart. A distinction must be made between the preparation of a sermon and the act of delivering the sermon. A man went to hear George Whitefield preach and asked if he might print his sermons. Whitefield replied, "Well, I have no inherent objection, if you like, but you will never be able to put on the printed page the lightning and the thunder."[56]

Only heart preaching will stir others to action. A sermon is not a sermon if there is no heartbeat. The preacher must not communicate merely the contents of a message; he must also communicate his own heartbeat. In addition, he must stir the heartbeat of his hearers so that they will act upon the truths he presents to them. Only heart preaching will move the hearts of people. Congregations must not only be mentally stimulated by the sermon; they must be emotionally stabbed by it as well.

Undoubtedly, the role of the congregation in the preaching dynamic must be considered. The listeners must cooperate if the preacher is to preach with heart. Someone once said that the average congregation places its preacher in a refrigerator and then expects him to sweat. A cold, lifeless, indifferent congregation can greatly hinder the preacher who genuinely wants to communicate the message from his heart. But the preacher cannot let lack of response in the pew hinder him. Who knows? A weekly diet of heart preaching may thaw out many a cold heart in the congregation. So many congregations have not heard heartfelt preaching in so long that they actually do not know how to respond to it.

Perhaps the reason for the recoil against heart preaching is the extreme to which some preachers have gone. Many have preached with an insincerity that is obnoxious, if not embarrassing. The preacher who sheds crocodile tears and purposely stirs up his congregation to accomplish his own end is not a heart preacher. Such preaching is basic insincerity covered with a pretense of emotion. This kind of insincerity, however, should not cause us to abandon genuine earnestness and sincerity in our preaching.

THE LEGACY OF HEART PREACHING

A casual survey of the preachers in the Bible indicates that they preached not only from their heads but also from their hearts. Jesus was a heart preacher. He became so moved that He wept over those to whom He ministered. As He viewed Jerusalem, He wept. When He spoke to the disciples on the Emmaus road, there was such earnestness and fervor about His words that they declared: "Did not our heart burn within us while He talked with us on the road, and while He opened the Scriptures to us?" (Luke 24:32). Their hearts burned because His did.

Paul was a heart preacher. One of the early church Fathers said he wished he could have seen three things: Solomon's temple in its glory;

---

56. Quoted in D. Martyn Lloyd-Jones, *Preaching and Preachers* (Grand Rapids: Zondervan, 1971), 58.

Rome in its prosperity; and Paul preaching. Listen to him express the deep conviction of his heart: "I tell the truth in Christ, I am not lying, my conscience also bearing me witness in the Holy Spirit, that . . . I could wish that I myself were accursed from Christ for my brethren, my countrymen according to the flesh" (Rom. 9:1–3). Those are not the words of cool logic. They are words from the furnace of the soul.

Many great preachers of the past preached with heart. John Knox, who prayed, "Give me Scotland or I die," was such a man. When he was old, he had to be helped to the pulpit. But as he prayed for the lost of Scotland, strength was given to him, and he almost shook the pulpit apart because of his burden for lost men. Hugh Latimer was a preacher of the English Reformation. Someone said of him: "He spoke from the heart and his words went to the heart."[57] Pulpiteers in recent history such as George W. Truett and Robert G. Lee continue to move listeners through their taped messages. In addition to their spellbinding eloquence, these men demonstrated remarkable earnestness in their preaching. They could move audiences like leaves in a strong summer wind. W. A. Criswell, beloved pastor-emeritus of First Baptist Church, Dallas, is still a heart preacher even in his nineties. Johnny Hunt, at the First Baptist Church in Woodstock, Georgia; James Merritt at the First Baptist Church in Snellville, Georgia; Rick Ousley at the Church at Brook Hills in Birmingham; and Fred Luter at Franklin Avenue Baptist Church in New Orleans are among a host of contemporary preachers who expound the Word fervently and passionately. Many a young preacher has been shaped by such men who know how to preach with heart.

This note of sincerity and depth of feeling has characterized the great preachers throughout the history of the Christian church. These men are the preachers who have moved their listeners, stirred their souls, and moved them to tears. They did not do this merely by telling emotional stories. What they were saying came from their hearts. All of them were not necessarily the most scholarly men who ever preached. Their preparation and delivery may not always have measured up to the standards presented in this book. Nevertheless, there was something about them that gripped their audiences and moved them as they listened.

THE MARKS OF HEART PREACHING

Like anointing, heart preaching is almost undefinable and, therefore, elusive. The best we can do is to look for common denominators that

---

57. Hugh Latimer, *Selected Sermons and Letters of Dr. Hugh Latimer* (n.p.: R.T.S, n.d.), 10, as quoted in Stott, *Between Two Worlds,* 26.

seem to be present in the lives of those who preach with such passion. The following marks are almost always present in heart preachers and serve as noble goals toward which we all may strive.

A sure calling. The preacher's call must be definite. You must know that God has placed the burden of the Word of the Lord upon you. As you carry this burden, God will cause your heart to break for those people to whom you preach. He will heighten your desire to see them saved and then transformed into the image of Christ. The shepherding ministry is not one with many accolades, great financial gain, or exciting worldly recognition. Sometimes your calling will be all you have to get you through. The preacher who doubts his calling and wavers in his service to the Lord will find himself indifferent to a lost world and a weak church.

An intimate walk with God. As you solidify your call from God, maintain the sense of reality of that call by a strong devotional life. Although this necessity has been mentioned in several other places in this book, its importance cannot be overestimated. As you spend time alone with God in Bible study and prayer, you will cultivate the reality of God in your life. Scientists may lose God in the laboratory, but you must take care not to lose God in the study. Do not allow the sacred truths you handle weekly to become unfelt truths. Let your sermons take possession of your heart on your knees before the Lord. Let their substance become real in your own experience. Preach your sermons to yourself first, in the presence of the Lord. Then, when you stand to preach, your message will not come merely from your notes or from your mind but from the depths of your heart and from God's Spirit.

A love for people. Though you must never fear men, you must desperately love them. Stott said:

> It has to be admitted that some preachers enjoy thundering forth God's judgements. They find a morbid satisfaction in seeing their audience writhe under the lash of their whip. . . . Sometimes preachers use the pulpit to preach Good Chidings rather than Good Tidings.[58]

Ask God to give you a love for the people before whom you stand to preach. One of the best ways to learn to love people is to be a personal soul winner. Going into the homes of lost people on a weekly basis and presenting the gospel will help you keep a warm, loving heart. You cannot expect to mount the pulpit on Sunday with passion if you have not been about His first business personally during the week.

58. Stott, *Between Two Worlds,* 212.

Another way to learn to love people is to pray for the people to whom you preach. You may recall E. M. Bounds's expression noted in chapter 2:

> The preacher who has never learned in the school of Christ the high and divine act of intercession for his people will never learn the art of preaching, though homiletics be poured into him by the ton, and though he be the most gifted genius in sermon-making and sermon-delivery.[59]

If people know you love them and are genuinely concerned for their souls, you may say most anything you want to say.

Conviction about the great truths of the Bible. To be unmoved by the great truths of the Bible indicates that one has never really understood them. Who can be unmoved by the truth that God loves us though we have desperately sinned against Him? Who can remain untouched by the truth that Jesus Christ loved us so much He was willing to suffer at Calvary an infinite burden of sin in a finite period of time? Can we talk about the lostness of men and not be stirred in our hearts? Can we look into hell with no emotion? It is unthinkable that the preacher who believes and preaches these truths should be dull, boring, or apathetic. If you have been gripped by these truths, you cannot help but stir those who hear you speak. Do not be like the boring preacher mentioned by Lloyd-Jones: "The good man was talking about fire as if he were sitting on an iceberg."[60] The Bible is not a museum piece to be held up indifferently before people. Rather, the Bible is God's living Word to living men. Proper comprehension and appreciation of Bible truths will enable you to preach with heart.

Personal heartbreak. Throughout the Scriptures we find examples of God's bringing blessing out of brokenness. The broken flask produced a fragrant odor (see Mark 14:3). Jesus broke the loaves of bread and blessed them (see Mark 8:6). Many great preachers have experienced a personal Gethsemane before becoming heart preachers. George W. Truett experienced the heartbreak of accidently killing a close friend in a hunting accident.[61] Through personal agony and heartbreak, God made him a heart preacher. G. Campbell Morgan heard a gifted young preacher and commented to his wife that the young man was a very good preacher. His wife responded, "Yes, and he will be a better preacher when he has suffered

---

59. E. M. Bounds, *Power Through Prayer* (N.d.; reprint, Grand Rapids: Baker, 1991) (page citation is to the reprint edition).

60. Lloyd-Jones, *Preaching and Preachers,* 88.

61. Powhatan W. James, *George W. Truett: A Biography* (Nashville: Broadman, 1939), 85–86.

some." When your heart is broken, you learn how to preach to others who have broken hearts. If you have known significant heartbreak in your own life, allow that experience to keep your heart pliable. If not, ask God to do whatever He needs to do to give you a soft heart. As John Newton said, preaching should break hard hearts and heal broken hearts.[62] Those purposes are accomplished most effectively when you have been through your own valley.

THE CALL FOR HEART PREACHING

We live in an emotion-centered generation. People listen to music that assaults their emotions. Television, videos, computer games, virtual reality, and other forms of entertainment are designed to create innumerable thrills and chills. These same thrillseekers are passing churches in droves on their way to other places to have their emotional needs met. Though preaching should never be thought of as a form of entertainment, the questions must be asked: Why should the preacher not present the genuine sources of emotional satisfaction? Why should the preacher present the ultimate answers to the problems confronting people today in an unemotional, lackadaisical manner?

In real preaching, the pastor delivers his soul. Country preachers have been known to say at the conclusion of their sermons: "Beloved, I have delivered my soul to you this morning." This confession is very true in the matter of preaching. The preacher not only delivers his sermon; he also delivers himself. By means of his voice, his gestures, his intellect, and his heart, the preacher lays before the throne of God and the hearts of the people his very life. Thus, sermon delivery is not so much the art of delivering a sermon as it is delivering the preacher. The genuinely effective preacher is one who puts everything he has into his sermon. When he speaks, his sincerity and enthusiasm generate sparks. That kind of effectiveness cannot be imitated, for sincerity and earnestness are impossible to manufacture. They come from deep within the heart and spirit of a preacher.

Heart preaching is the secret of eloquence. William Jennings Bryan defined eloquence as "the speech of one who knows what he is talking about and means what he says. It is thought on fire."[63] God must create this eloquence in the heart of a man. As He does, this eloquence born in the heart will move men to action. Our purpose is not merely to present a Bible message for information. We preach in order to bring men to decision. Our purpose is to change behavior for the better, to bring men to obedience to God, and to lead them to accept the challenge of a Christ-

62. Stott, *Between Two Worlds*, 314.
63. Quoted in McFarland, *Public Speaking*, 17.

centered life. Heart preaching works to this end.

When Cicero spoke to the people, it was said, "How well Cicero speaks." But when Demosthenes spoke, the people said, "Let us march against Carthage."[64] Preacher, for the kingdom's sake, preach with heart!

64. Ibid., 29.

CONCLUSION

The dawn of the twenty-first century is an exciting time to be a preacher. Almost daily, new and thrilling concepts emerge in the field of sermon preparation and delivery. Today's preacher has in his hands tools and techniques that will enable him to preach the Word of God more effectively than ever before.

In one sense, preaching is a science. Much of this book approaches preaching from this dimension. Good books written by homileticians can improve one's techniques of preparation and delivery. Learning these techniques will help the man of God channel the fire burning in his soul into more effective means of reaching people with God's eternal Word.

In another sense, however, preaching is an art. Though much can be learned from the homiletics professors, more can be learned from the effective preacher. Much learning comes from listening to those who know how to preach. The man who is preaching becomes the best mentor. Preaching not only must be taught—it must be caught. Students of preaching need to get acquainted with good preachers, talk with them about preaching, and learn from them the methods that have made them effective.

The best way to learn to preach, however, is to preach. If, in fact, preaching largely is an art, then you must practice, practice, and then practice some more. However, merely preaching week by week is not sufficient. The carpenter weekly plies his trade, but if he does not develop and sharpen his carpentry skills, he may repeat the same mistakes weekly. Likewise, the preacher must engage in *meaningful* practice. He must carefully observe his strengths and his weaknesses. He must develop and improve his preaching skills.

Reading (or even heeding) the counsel of this book will not be a wonder drug for your preaching. You may master the basic contents, yet you will never get to the point where you will not need additional study and improvement. You will have days when you struggle in the study and in the pulpit. You will move with the difficulty of the snail. On other days, you will soar like an eagle. The words will flow, the ingredients of effective exposition will come together in a powerful combination, and you will preach the stars down. If this book can make the latter experience occur more often, its aim will have been realized.

Hopefully, these discussions will get you started toward a lifetime of study in the area of sermon preparation and delivery. Many areas of the preaching dynamic—some of which have been addressed in this work and some of which have not—need additional research and study by other homileticians and practitioners. Keep abreast of the latest information in the field. Listen to good speakers and preachers and learn from them. Benefit from their strengths and avoid their mistakes.

Also listen to yourself. See that every sermon you preach is taped. Listen to each one carefully. Correct your mistakes during practice sessions. Learn from them. Ask yourself, Why was this not effective? Ask, How could I have said that better?

One word of caution: Do not allow the mechanics of sermon preparation and delivery to become an obsession to you. You can become so concerned about the details that you bind yourself and make it difficult to preach. An unlearned preacher once summed up his approach to preaching this way: "First, I reads myself full. Next, I thinks myself clear. Next, I prays myself hot, and then I lets go." Your goal should be for the nuts and bolts offered here to become second nature to you so that good preparation and delivery become natural.

Finally, preach Jesus, and you always will have an audience. Bernard said, "Yesterday, I preached myself, and the scholars came up and praised me. Today, I preached Christ, and the sinners came up and thanked me." Make a full surrender of yourself to preach Jesus and His wonderful Word. Then, as you stand to preach, God will bless you wonderfully as you "lift up your voice."

Preparing effective expository sermons can be a most frustrating work. Our hearts are overwhelmed weekly with a sense of inadequacy. Who among us can do justice to our responsibility to preach what God says in His Word? But God has chosen in the past, and still chooses today, to use weak and inadequate human vessels to communicate His living Word. May He bless us as we give ourselves weekly to sermon preparation and delivery, so that we will indeed be "workmen not ashamed."

STRUCTURAL
DIAGRAMS

JEREMIAH 17:5–10

5 Thus says the Lord:
"Cursed *is* the man
           who trusts in man
           [And]
           makes flesh his strength,
           Whose heart departs from the Lord.

6   For he shall be like a shrub in the desert,
           [And]
           shall not see when good comes,
           [But]
           shall inhabit the parched places in the wilderness,
                In a salt land *which is* not inhabited.

7   "Blessed is the man
           who trusts in the Lord,
           [And]
           whose hope is the Lord.

8   For he shall be like a tree planted by the waters,
                Which spreads out its
                roots by the river,
                [And]
                will not fear when heat
                comes;
                [But]
                its leaf will be green,
                [And]
                will not be anxious in
                the year of drought,
                [Nor]
                will cease from yielding
                fruit.

9 "The heart is   deceitful above all *things,*
                  [And]
                  desperately wicked;
  Who can know it?
10 I, the Lord,   search the heart,
                  I test the mind,

                              Even to give every man   according to
                                                       his ways,
                                                       According to
                                                       the fruit of
                                                       his doings."

MARK 4:35–41

35 *On the same day, when evening had come,*   **Life Situation**
He said to them, "Let us cross over to the other side."
36 *Now when they had left the multitude, they took*
Him along in the boat as He was. And other little
boats were also with Him.
37 *And a great windstorm arose, and the waves beat*
into the boat, so that it was already filling.

38 *But He was in the stern, asleep on a pillow. And*   **Conflict/Climax**
they awoke Him and said to Him, "Teacher, do You
not care that we are perishing?"

39 *Then He arose and rebuked the wind, and said to*   **Resolution**
the sea, "Peace, be still!" And the wind ceased and
there was a great calm.

40 *But He said to them, "Why are you so fearful?*   **Application**
How is it that you have no faith?"
41 *And they feared exceedingly, and said to one*
another, "Who can this be, that even the wind
and the sea obey Him!"

HEBREWS 4:12

[For]
The word of God is   **living**
                       [and]
                       powerful
                       [and]
                       sharper than any two-edged sword
                       piercing even to the division of   soul
                                                               [and]
                                                               spirit,
                                                               [and]
                                                               of joints
                                                               [and]
                                                               marrow,

                       [and] is a
                       discerner of the   thoughts
                                                [and]
                                                intents
                                                    of the heart.

SERMON SUMMARY SHEET

Text: _____

Primary Audience: _____

Central Idea of the Text: _____
_____
_____

Proposition: _____
_____
_____

Purpose: _____
_____
_____

Method of Development: _____

Design: _____
_____
_____
_____
_____
_____
_____
_____

Title: _____

RELAXATION EXERCISES

RELAXATION EXERCISES

Home exercises. Begin your preparation for speaking before you leave home. In a private room (an observer might think you're crazy), begin by lying down flat on your back on a bed or on the floor. Completely stretch out your arms and your legs. Tense your whole body. Hold the tension until you feel your muscles begin to quiver. Then, with a sigh, release the tension. Allow every part of your body to slump in exhaustion.

Next, tense the muscles of your legs until they quiver. Release the tension. Now, tense your arms until they quiver. Release them. Tense your facial and throat muscles. Release them. Tense the muscles of your abdomen, chest, shoulders, and neck. Release them.

At this point, glance around the room to be sure no one is present! Begin to talk softly to your body. Begin with your feet. As you gradually move your feet at the ankles, tell your feet to relax. Repeat the process with your legs, bending them at the knees and hips. Move to your arms. Turn your wrists, move your elbows and your shoulders, talking to them all the while in soothing tones. Then, gradually move your head from side to side. With a big sigh tell your body to take it easy. Be careful not to go back to sleep and be late for the preaching service!

Mobile exercises. As you drive to where you are going to preach, use the time to prepare your voice. Try going over the notes on the musical scale with a soft *ah* sound to warm up your voice. You might use this time to do some of the breathing and articulating drills that will be discussed later. By the time you arrive at your preaching point, your voice should be warmed up and ready to go.

Pre-preaching exercises. If possible, find a quiet place to spend a few uninterrupted moments before you preach. Sit in a comfortable position and try to eliminate any disturbing thoughts that might increase your tension. Do the following exercises in an unhurried, unpressured manner. When you get ready to go into the pulpit, you should be as tension-free as you need to be for effective speaking.

1. Starting at the hairline and working down to your lower neck, massage very gently all the muscles of your face and throat. You will be able to feel with your fingers any tension in these muscles. As you stroke these muscles downward, let your face become as limp as possible. Move your fingers over your eyes, closing them in the process. Let your jaw hang limp. When your jaw drops, allow your tongue to come over your lower lip as much as you can. Do not force the process, but let it happen naturally.

2. Relax the swallowing muscles next. Using the fingers of both hands, press gently on each side of your throat, beginning at the jaw and moving to the Adam's apple. Massage these muscles very gently. Swallow, and feel how much more relaxed these muscles are than before. This process will greatly reduce tension in your throat.

3. Take your chin in hand and move it up and down, right and left. This activity will decrease any resistance in your jaw. The jaw muscles tend to stiffen when there is too much tension. Work your jaw muscles until they are as relaxed as possible. Take your time.

4. Take your voice box between your thumb and fingers on one hand and move it from side to side until it is free of tension.

5. Make sure the muscles of your neck are relaxed. Allow your head to nod up and down and roll from side to side.[1]

6. Yawn several times. This activity will relax all the muscles of the face and throat.

---

1. David Blair McClosky, *Your Voice at Its Best* (Plymouth, Mass: Memorial, 1972), 6–8.

BREATHING
EXERCISES

Use a series of simple exercises to develop your breath as you speak:

1. Inhale easily as though you are about to speak. Hold the inhaled breath silently for a moment. Imagine you are speaking a simple word or phrase. Release the breath and let the air flow out gradually without forcing it.

2. Repeat the previous exercise, and gradually increase the length of time you can hold in the air without excessive tension or strain. Release the breath.

3. Repeat the exercise again, and speak a single word or phrase. Be aware of the outer movement of the abdomen during inhalation. Also be aware of the inward movement of the abdomen as you exhale during the speaking of the word or phrase.

4. Inhale a sufficient supply of air. Then exhale, using a single word or vowel such as *ah, oh, e, u*. Maintain the tone as long as your breath will allow. Stop before you lose an awareness of a reserve supply of breath in your lungs.

5. Repeat the exercise. This time speak a series of numbers such as *one, two, three, four, five,* in sequence. Continue counting as long as you can maintain a comfortable flow of breath. See how high you can count on one breath without releasing all your reserve air. This approach is merely for the purpose of exercise. In preaching, you should never try to speak as much as possible on one breath.

6. Use the following exercises, suggested by a speech pathologist, to increase your capacity for adequate breath for speaking. Learn to read

each of them in one breath. Inhale a sufficient supply of air. Then, maintaining smooth expiration, read each sentence.

THE HOUSE THAT JACK BUILT

This is the house that Jack built.//

This is the malt that lay in the house that Jack built.//

This is the rat that ate the malt that lay in the house that Jack built. //

This is the cat that caught the rat that ate the malt that lay in the house that Jack built.//

This is the dog that worried the cat that caught the rat that ate the malt that lay in the house that Jack built.// (10 seconds)

This is the cow with the crumpled horn that tossed the dog that worried the cat that caught the rat that ate the malt that lay in the house that Jack built.// (12 seconds)

This is the maiden all forlorn that milked the cow with the crumpled horn that tossed the dog that worried the cat that caught the rat that ate the malt that lay in the house that Jack built.// (15 seconds)

This is the man all tattered and torn who kissed the maiden all forlorn that milked the cow with the crumpled horn that tossed the dog that worried the cat that caught the rat that ate the malt that lay in the house that Jack built.// (17 seconds)

This is the priest all shaven and shorn that married the man all tattered and torn who kissed the maiden all forlorn that milked the cow with the crumpled horn that tossed the dog that worried the cat that caught the rat that ate the malt that lay in the house that Jack built.// (20 seconds)

SELECTED BIBLIOGRAPHY

Achtemeier, Elizabeth. *Creative Preaching: Finding the Words*. Nashville: Abingdon, 1980.

Adams, Jay. *Pulpit Speech*. Phillipsburg, N.J.: Presby. & Ref., 1971.

_____. *Sense Appeal in the Sermons of Charles Haddon Spurgeon*. Grand Rapids: Baker, 1975.

Autrey, C. E. *Basic Evangelism*. Grand Rapids: Zondervan, 1959.

Bacon, Wallace A. *The Art of Interpretation*. New York: Holt, Rinehart & Winston, 1972.

Barna, George. *Today's Pastor*. Ventura, Calif: Regal, 1993.

Baumann, J. Daniel. *An Introduction to Contemporary Preaching*. Grand Rapids: Baker, 1972.

Beatty, Christopher. *Maximum Vocal Performance*. Nashville: Star Song, 1992.

_____. *Vocal Workout*. Nashville: Star Song, 1992.

Bell, Ralph. *Giving a Successful Invitation: Preaching for a Verdict*. Minneapolis: North American Conference of Itinerant Evangelists, 1994. Cassette S202A.

Blackwood, Andrew. *Expository Preaching for Today*. Grand Rapids: Baker, 1943.

_____. *Preaching from the Bible*. New York: Abingdon, 1941.

_____. *The Preparation of Sermons*. Nashville: Abingdon, 1948.

Bounds, E. M. *Power Through Prayer*. London: Marshall, Morgan & Scott, n.d. Reprint, Grand Rapids: Baker, 1991.

Braga, James. *How to Prepare Bible Messages*. Portland: Multnomah, 1981.

Broadus, John A. *On the Preparation and Delivery of Sermons*. 4th ed. Revised by Vernon L. Stanfield. N.p.: John A. Broadus, 1870. Revision. New York: Harper & Row, 1979.

Brodnitz, Friedrich. *Keep Your Voice Healthy*. Springfield, Ill.: Thomas, 1973.

Brooks, Phillips. *Lectures on Preaching*. New York: E. P. Dalton. Reprint, Grand Rapids: Baker, 1969.

Brown, H. C. *A Quest for Reformation in Preaching*. Nashville: Broadman, 1968.

Bryson, Harold T., and James C. Taylor. *Building Sermons to Meet People's Needs*. Nashville: Broadman, 1980.

Buffington, Perry W. "Psychology of Eyes." *Sky 13,* no. 2 (February 1984).

Bullinger, E. W. *Figures of Speech Used in the Bible: Explained and Illustrated*. London: Eyre & Spottiswoode, 1898. Reprint, Grand Rapids: Baker, 1968.

Busch, Eberhard. *Karl Barth: His Life from Letters and Autobiographical Texts*. Philadelphia: Fortress, 1976.

Buttrick, David. *Homiletic*. Philadelphia: Fortress, 1987.

Buttrick, George Arthur, ed. *The Interpreter's Dictionary of the Bible*." Vol. 4. Nashville: Abingdon, 1962.

Chappell, Clovis G. *Anointed to Preach*. New York: Abingdon-Cokesbury, 1951.

Cicero, *De Oratore*. London: William Heinemann, 1942. III.

Cooper, Morton. *Winning with Your Voice*. Hollywood, Fl: Fell, 1990.

Corley, Bruce, Steve Lemke, and Grant Lovejoy. *Biblical Hermeneutics: A Comprehensive Introduction to Interpreting Scripture*. Nashville: Broadman & Holman, 1996.

Cox, James. *A Guide to Biblical Preaching*. Nashville: Abingdon, 1976.

Crandell, Judson S., and Gerald M. Phillips. *Speech: A Course in Fundamentals*. Glenview, Ill.: Scott Foresman, 1963.

Criswell, W. A. *The Holy Spirit in Today's World*. Grand Rapids: Zondervan, 1966.

_____. *W. A. Criswell's Sermon Preparation in His Study*. Dallas: The Criswell Foundation, 1997. Videotape.

Dargan, Edwin Charles. *A History of Preaching*. Vol. 2. New York: George H. Doran, 1905.

Davis, Benjamin, and Edward C. Mitchell. *Student's Hebrew Lexicon*. Grand Rapids: Zondervan, 1960.

Davis, H. Grady. *Design for Preaching*. Philadelphia: Fortress, 1958.

Demaray, Donald E. *An Introduction to Homiletics*. Grand Rapids: Baker, 1974.

Dickens, Milton. *Speech: Dynamic Communication*. New York: Harcourt Brace Jovanovich, 1954.

Dodd, C. H. *The Apostolic Preaching and Its Developments*. New York: Harper & Row, 1964.

Douglas, J. D., ed. *The Calling of an Evangelist*. Minneapolis: World Wide Publications, 1987.

Duduit, Michael, ed. *Handbook of Contemporary Preaching*. Nashville: Broadman, 1992.

Eden, Martyn, and David F. Wells, eds. *The Gospel in the Modern World*. London: InterVarsity, 1991.

Eisenson, John. *Voice and Diction*. New York: Macmillan, 1974.

EnviroWeb. Enviroissues. System. Media. "Interesting Facts About TV." July 24, 1997. Online. Available from CWIX@http://www.enviroweb.org/enviroissues/system/media/tv_facts.html.

Evans, William. *How to Prepare Sermons*. Chicago: Moody, 1964.

Fairbanks, Grand. *Voice and Articulation Drillbook*. New York: Harper & Row, 1940.

Fasol, Al. *A Complete Guide to Sermon Delivery*. Nashville: Broadman & Holman, 1996.

————. "A Guide to Improving Your Preaching Delivery." Ft. Worth, Tex.: Southwestern Baptist Theological Seminary. Mimeographed.

————. *Essentials for Biblical Preaching*. Grand Rapids: Baker, 1989.

Fee, Gordon D. *New Testament Exegesis: A Handbook for Students and Pastors*. Philadelphia: Westminster, 1983.

Fee, Gordon D., and Douglas Stuart. *How to Read the Bible for All Its Worth*. Grand Rapids: Zondervan, 1982.

Fish, Roy. *Giving a Good Invitation*. Nashville: Broadman, 1974.

————. *How to Give an Evangelistic Invitation*. Dallas: Baptist General Convention of Texas, 1991. Videocassette.

Flesch, Rudolf. *The Art of Plain Talk*. New York: Harper, 1946.

Forman, R. C. *Public Speaking Made Easy*. Grand Rapids: Baker, 1967.

Forrest, Mary, and Margot A. Olson. *Exploring Speech Communication*. St. Paul: West, 1981.

Freeman, Harold. *Variety in Biblical Preaching.* Ft. Worth, Tex.: Scripta, 1987. Reprint, 1994.

Gaebelein, Frank E. *The Meaning of Inspiration.* Chicago: InterVarsity, 1950.

The Gallup Organization. Gallup Poll Archives. "Religious Faith Is Widespread but Many Skip Church." December 17, 1998. Online. Available from CWIX@http://198.175.140.8/poll_archives/1997/970329.htm.

Graham, Billy. *Just As I Am: The Autobiography of Billy Graham.* New York: Zondervan, 1997.

Grasham, John A., and Glenn G. Gooder. *Improving Your Speech.* New York: Harcourt, Brace & World, 1960.

Greidanus, Sidney. *The Modern Preacher and the Ancient Text.* Grand Rapids: Eerdmans, 1988.

Griffin, Emory A. *The Mind Changers.* Wheaton, Ill.: Tyndale, 1976.

Hall, E. Eugene, and James L. Heflin. *Proclaim the Word!* Nashville: Broadman, 1985.

Hamblin, Robert L. "Evangelistic Preaching in Today's World." *Proclaim* 23 (January/February/March 1995).

Hamilton, Donald L. *Homiletical Handbook.* Nashville: Broadman, 1992.

Henderson, George. *Lectures to Young Preachers.* Edinburgh: B. McCall Barbour, 1961.

_____. *The Wonderful Word.* Edinburgh: B. McCall Barbour, n.d.

Hiebert, D. Edmond. *An Introduction to the New Testament, vols. 1–3.* Chicago: Moody, 1975.

Hoffman, William G. *How to Make Better Speeches.* New York: Funk & Wagnalls, 1976.

Horne, Chevis F. *Dynamic Preaching.* Nashville: Broadman, 1983.

Hughes, Kent. "The Foundation of Our Vision" in *Vision 2000.* Publication of College Church in Wheaton, Ill. January 9, 1994.

Hull, Bill. *Right Thinking.* Colorado Springs: NavPress, 1985.

Humes, James C. *The Sir Winston Method: The Five Secrets of Speaking the Language of Leadership.* New York: William Morrow, 1991.

Huss, John E. *Robert G. Lee.* New York: Macmillan, 1948.

Hybels, Bill, Stuart Briscoe, and Haddon Robinson. *Mastering Contempo-*

rary Preaching. Portland: Multnomah, 1989.

Jacobson, Edmund. *You Must Relax*. New York: McGraw-Hill, 1942.

Jefferson, Charles. *The Minister as Shepherd*. Hong Kong: Living Books for All, 1980.

Jensen, Irving L. *Enjoy Your Bible*. Chicago: Moody, 1969.

Jones, Winston E. *Preaching and the Dramatic Arts*. New York: Macmillan, 1948.

Jowett, J. H. *The Preacher: His Life and Work*. New York: Harper, 1912.

Kaiser, Walter C., Jr. "The Crisis in Expository Preaching Today." *Preaching* 11. September/October 1995.

_____. *Toward an Exegetical Theology*. Grand Rapids: Baker, 1981.

Kelley, Charles S., Jr. *How Did They Do It? The Story of Southern Baptist Evangelism*. New Orleans: Insight, 1993.

King, Robert. *Forms of Public Address*. Indianapolis: Bobbs-Merrill, 1969.

Kirkpatrick, Robert White. *The Creative Delivery of Sermons*. Joplin, Mo.: Joplin College, 1944.

Knox, John. *The Integrity of Preaching*. Nashville: Abingdon, 1957.

Koller, Charles W. *Expository Preaching Without Notes*. Grand Rapids: Baker, 1962.

Kooienga, William H. *Elements of Style for Preaching*. Grand Rapids: Zondervan, 1989.

Lang, David. "Taming Bible Study Software." *Computing Today*. March/April 1998: 22–24.

Larsen, David L. *The Anatomy of Preaching*. Grand Rapids: Baker, 1989.

_____. *The Evangelism Mandate: Recovering the Centrality of Gospel Preaching*. Wheaton, Ill.: Crossway, 1992.

Latimer, Hugh. *Selected Sermons and Letters of Dr. Hugh Latimer*. N.p.: R.T.S, n.d.

Lee, Charlotte I., and Frank Galati. *Oral Interpretation*. Boston: Houghton Mifflin, 1977.

Lenski, R. C. H. *The Sermon: Its Homiletical Construction*. Reprint. Grand Rapids: Baker, 1968.

Lewis, Ralph L. *Persuasive Preaching Today*. Ann Arbor, Mich.: Litho-Crafters, 1979.

Lloyd-Jones, D. Martyn. *Preaching and Preachers*. Grand Rapids: Zondervan, 1971.

Logan, Samuel T., Jr., ed. *The Preacher and Preaching*. Grand Rapids: Baker, 1986.

Lowry, Eugene L. *The Sermon: Dancing the Edge of Mystery*. Nashville: Abingdon, 1997.

MacArthur, John, Jr. *Rediscovering Expository Preaching*. Edited by Richard L. Mayhue. Dallas: Word, 1992.

MacArthur, John, Jr., ed. *Rediscovering Pastoral Ministry*. Dallas: Word, 1995.

MacGregor, W. M. *The Making of a Preacher*. Philadelphia: Westminster, 1946.

Magoon, E. L. *The Modern Whitefield*. New York: Sheldon, Blakeman, 1856.

May, Rollo. *The Courage to Create*. New York: Bantam, 1975.

McCarter, P. Kyle, Jr. *Textual Criticism: Recovering the Text of the Hebrew Bible*. Philadelphia: Fortress, 1986.

McCloskey, David Blair. *Your Voice at Its Best*. Plymouth, Mass.: Memorial, 1972.

McCroskey, James C. *An Introduction to Rhetorical Communication*. 3d ed. Englewood Cliffs, N.J.: Prentice-Hall, 1978.

McDill, Wayne. *The 12 Essential Skills for Great Preaching*. Nashville: Broadman & Holman, 1994.

McDowell, Josh. "Syllabus on Communication and Persuasion." Josh McDowell, 1983. Mimeographed.

McFarland, Kenneth. *Eloquence in Public Speaking*. Englewood Cliffs, N.J.: Prentice-Hall, 1961.

McKenzie, E. C. *Mac's Great Book of Quips and Quotes*. Grand Rapids: Baker, 1980.

Mead, Frank S. "The Story of George Whitefield." *The Sword of the Lord* (January 31, 1992): 3–4.

Merriam Webster's Collegiate Dictionary (1994).

Metzger, Bruce M. *The Text of the New Testament: Its Transmission, Corruption, and Restoration*. 3d. ed. New York: Oxford University, 1992.

Meyer, F. B. *Expository Preaching*. Grand Rapids: Baker, 1974.

Morgan, G. Campbell. *Preaching*. New York: Revell, 1937.

Morgan, Jill. *A Man of the Word*. Grand Rapids: Baker, 1972.

Moulton, Richard G. *A Short Introduction to the Literature of the Bible*. Boston: D.C. Heath, 1901.

Mulgrave, Dorothy. *Speech*. New York: Barnes & Noble, 1954.

Neal, Anna Lloyd. *A Syllabus for Fundamentals of Speech*. Greenville, S.C.: Bob Jones Univ., 1977.

Olford, David L., comp. *A Passion for Preaching*. Nashville: Nelson, 1989.

Olford, Stephen F., and David L. Olford. *Anointed Expository Preaching*. Nashville: Broadman & Holman, 1998.

Overstreet, H. A. *Influencing Human Behavior*. New York: Norton, 1925.

Pache, René. *The Inspiration and Authority of Scripture*. Chicago: Moody, 1969.

Packer, James I. *Fundamentalism and the Word of God*. Grand Rapids: Eerdmans, 1958.

Perry, Lloyd M. *A Manual for Biblical Preaching*. Grand Rapids: Baker, 1981.

Phillips, John. *One Hundred Sermon Outlines from the New Testament*. Chicago: Moody, 1979.

Powhatan, James W. *George W. Truett: A Biography*. Nashville: Broadman, 1939.

Prochnow, Herbert V. *Speaker's Handbook of Epigrams and Witticisms*. Grand Rapids: Baker, 1955.

Rahskoph, Horace G. *Basic Speech Improvement*. New York: Harper & Row, 1965.

Ray, Jefferson D. *Expository Preaching*. Grand Rapids: Zondervan, 1940.

The Reader's Digest Great Encyclopedic Dictionary (1966).

Reid, Loren. *Speaking Well*. New York: McGraw-Hill, 1977.

Reid, Robert, Jeffrey Bullock, and David Fleer, "Preaching as the Creation of an Experience: the Not-So-Rational Revolution of the New Homiletic." *The Journal of Communication and Religion* 18, no. 1. March 1995.

Robinson, Haddon W. *Biblical Preaching*. Grand Rapids: Baker, 1980.

_____. "The Heresy of Application." *Leadership* (Fall 1997): 20–27.

Roth, Robert. *Story and Reality*. Grand Rapids: Eerdmans, 1973.

Rueter, Alvin C. "Issues Shaping Effective Proclamation." *Emphasis* 14 (February 1985).

Rummage, Stephen N. "Toward Contemporary Apologetic Preaching: An Analysis of the Argumentative Methodologies of Richard Whately, William Bennett, and Josh McDowell." Ph.D. diss., New Orleans Baptist Theological Seminary, 1998.

Ryrie, Charles C. *Basic Theology*. Wheaton: Victor, 1986.

Samoff, Dorothy. *Speech Can Change Your Life*. New York: Dell, 1970.

Shaddix, Jim. "The Yoke's on You!" *Preaching* 13 (May-June 1998): 33–34.

Shannon, Harper. *Trumpets in the Morning*. Nashville: Broadman, 1969.

Soper, Donald O. *The Advocacy of the Gospel*. New York: Abingdon, 1961.

Spurgeon, C. H. *An All-Round Ministry*. Carlisle, Pa: Banner of Truth, 1960.

_____. *Commenting and Commentaries*. Edinburgh: Banner of Truth, 1969.

_____. *Lectures to My Students*. London: Marshall, Morgan & Scott, 1954.

Stevenson, Dwight E., and Charles F. Diehl. *Reaching People from the Pulpit*. Grand Rapids: Baker, 1958.

Stott, John R. W. *Between Two Worlds*. Grand Rapids: Eerdmans, 1982.

Stowell, Joseph M. *Shepherding the Church into the 21st Century*. Wheaton: Victor, 1994.

Streett, R. Alan. *The Effective Invitation*. Old Tappan, N.J.: Revell, 1984.

Sweazey, George E. *Preaching the Good News*. Englewood Cliffs, N.J.: Prentice-Hall, 1976.

Tan, Paul Lee. *Signs of the Times*. Rockville, Md: Assurance, 1980.

Terry, Milton S. *Biblical Hermeneutics: A Treatise on the Interpretation of the Old and New Testaments*. New York: Phillips & Hunt, 1890. Reprint, Grand Rapids: Zondervan, 1964.

Thayer, Joseph Henry. *Greek-English Lexicon*. Grand Rapids: Zondervan, 1963.

Turnbull, Ralph G., ed. *Baker's Dictionary of Practical Theology*. Grand Rapids: Baker, 1967.

Unger, Merrill F. *Principles of Expository Preaching*. Grand Rapids: Zondervan, 1955.

White, James Emery. *Opening the Front Door: Worship and Church Growth*. Nashville: Convention, 1992.

White, Jerald R., Jr. *Fellowship with God*. Denham Springs, La: Barnabas, 1995.

Whitesell, Farris D. *65 Ways to Give Evangelistic Invitations*. Grand Rapids: Kregel, 1984.

_____. *Power in Expository Preaching*. Old Tappan, N.J.: Revell, 1963.

Wiersbe, Warren. *Walking with the Giants*. Grand Rapids: Baker, 1976.

_____. "Your Preaching Is Unique." *Leadership* 2 (Summer 1981).

Wiersbe, Warren W., comp. *Treasury of the World's Great Sermons*. Grand Rapids: Kregel, 1993.

Wiersbe, Warren W., and David Wiersbe. *Making Sense of the Ministry*. Chicago: Moody, 1983.

INDEX OF SCRIPTURE

INDEX OF SUBJECTS

Moody Press, a ministry of Moody Bible Institute,
is designed for education, evangelization, and edification.
If we may assist you in knowing more about Christ
and the Christian life, please write us without obligation:
Moody Press, c/o MLM, Chicago, Illinois 60610.